CHARLOTTE GRAY

THE PROMISE OF
CANADA

150 YEARS—PEOPLE AND IDEAS
THAT HAVE SHAPED OUR COUNTRY

PHYLLIS BRUCE EDITIONS

SIMON & SCHUSTER CANADA

New York   London   Toronto   Sydney   New Delhi

Simon & Schuster Canada
A Division of Simon & Schuster, Inc.
166 King Street East, Suite 300
Toronto, Ontario M5A 1J3

This Simon & Schuster Canada edition October 2016

SIMON & SCHUSTER CANADA and colophon are registered trademarks of Simon & Schuster, Inc.

For information about special discounts for bulk purchases, please contact Simon & Schuster Special Sales at 1-800-268-3216 or CustomerService@simonandschuster.ca.

Manufactured in the United States of America

1   3   5   7   9   10   8   6   4   2

Library and Archives Canada Cataloguing in Publication

Gray, Charlotte, author
The promise of Canada : 150 years—people and ideas that have shaped our country / Charlotte Gray.
ISBN 978-1-4767-8467-0 (hardback)
1. Canada—History. 2. Canada—Civilization. 3. Canada—Social life and customs. I. Title.
FC51.G72 2016 971 C2016-901487-8

ISBN 978-1-4767-8467-0
ISBN 978-1-4767-8469-4 (ebook)

*For Pat and Jimmy Altham, and Nick and Ann Gray, in England,
and Jean and John McCaw who arrived here first*

CONTENTS

A Note on the Illustrations:
The Look of Canada

Successive generations of Canadians have evolved their own versions of what it means to be Canadian, as I describe in these pages, but most of these visions were expressed in words.

Images are different. For Canadian artists, there were difficult challenges—I touch on some of them when I introduce Emily Carr. For the first century after Confederation, the Canadian imagination was cramped by poverty and visual illiteracy. How could European-trained artists capture panoramas that contained no man-made features? How could commercial artists work with such a limited choice of symbols when they wanted to promote national pride in their audience?

Only Indigenous artists were confident in the deeply rooted traditions of their different cultures, and produced extraordinary artifacts that spoke to the land they knew so well. But their work was not respected by newcomers, and it was valued only as trophies or museum specimens.

This has changed.

Within the text of this book, there are dozens of black and white images that relate directly to the stories I tell. But the colour inserts give a parallel commentary on the evolution of the Canadian imagination. My selections are entirely subjective, just as were my choices of whom to highlight in the main text. The colour illustrations are works that speak to me directly. Other people would have made very different choices.

For the first insert, I chose artworks that reflect artists' response to past and present, ideas and ideals. Since 1867, Canadian artists have been melding the aesthetic traditions of this northern land with approaches and techniques from every part of the globe. Most of my choices are representational (like the majority of canvases hanging on the walls of established art galleries), but gathering them has been an exciting voyage of discovery. Some of the best sources for exploring the Canadian art world are the ebooks produced by the Art Canada Institute: http://www.aci-iac.ca.

Posters fill the second colour insert. Most of the early examples are vivid attempts to "brand" Canada (although their creators would not have recognised such Madison Avenue jargon). Later examples intensify the propaganda element, by reflecting the budding postwar pride in country. By the end of the twentieth century, poster art was often protest art, illustrating values that, hoped their sponsors, their viewers might share.

There is no single image that captures our country, just as there is no single narrative in our multi-layered history. Every vision, every story is part of the promise of Canada.

Preface: How We Got Here from There

When I immigrated to Canada from Britain, I was stunned to discover the wobbly sense of national identity here. I had arrived in 1979, a year when panic about the future had erupted and there was anxious debate about "whither Canada?". The separatist Parti Québécois was about to hold a referendum on the province's future relationship with the Rest of Canada (or ROC, as we learned to call it). I recall the passion on both sides of the debate: the fierce speeches by Prime Minister Pierre Elliott Trudeau about how it was possible to be a Quebecer and a Canadian; the poignancy of Premier René Lévesque, facing the defeat of his dream of a sovereign Quebec, as he said to his weeping supporters, "À la prochaine."

Back then, I was confused. I began to wonder if the whole was less than the sum of its parts. My stereotype of Canadians was of sensible, mild-mannered North Americans who still had the same head of state as the people that I had left behind me. In common with most outsiders, when I thought about this country at all, my mind reeled across a colourful kaleidoscope of static images: blue lakes, glistening mountain ranges, green forests, and police in scarlet tunics. The potential of Canada seemed limitless, given its vast geography, its ability to absorb strangers, its resource wealth. How could this stoic, sprawling federation be in danger of collapse? Yet I discovered in my new homeland an almost palpable sense of the country's fragility.

When I asked my new compatriots what being "a Canadian" meant, their replies were often a stuttering medley of generalizations about what it did *not* mean (Canadian meant not being American, or British, or like residents of other former colonies such as Australia). Often the focus appeared to be on the stresses of the past rather than the potential for the future. I began to understand a remark by one of the few Canadian authors I had heard of, Robertson Davies: "This is not a country you love, it is a country you worry about."

Since then, as I gradually morphed into a Canadian, there have been regular spasms of national insecurity, prompted by such events as a trade deal with the United States, anguished constitutional negotiations, a second Quebec referendum. Each crisis prompts the same concerns about whether there is enough glue to keep the country together. What do Canadians from coast to coast have in common?

During close to four decades here, I've acquired a bookshelf of titles such as *The Search for Identity, On Being Canadian, What Is a Canadian?, The Canadians, The Unfinished Canadian,* and *Nationalism without Walls: The Unbearable Lightness of Being Canadian.* I've found some hilarious definitions of Canadian identity in them, such as Peter C. Newman's quip "This is the only country on earth whose citizens dream of being Clark Kent instead of Superman." But over the years I've come to wonder if these books take us in the wrong direction. While presenting insightful analysis alongside self-deprecating witticisms, they feed the insecurity that prompted the question in the first place and encourage an impulse to put others (usually Americans) down in order to build Canadians up. The authors occasionally imply that there might be a clear-cut definition of Canada, which we could discover if we just got over our loser mentality and tried a bit harder.

But this country defies definition. There is no master narrative for Canadian history: there are too many stories to package into a tidy, tightly scripted identity. Yet Canada exerts a sense of endless promise because over the years it has successfully managed so many competing pressures: parallel identities, layers of allegiance, deep-rooted hostilities, overlapping loyalties. This country has reimagined and embellished its self-image in every generation since the proclamation of the British North America Act in 1867, which means that each of those books has had a limited shelf life.

Now I am adding another book to the shelf. I come at the question not as a political scientist, historian, or journalist, but as a biographer who believes that the ideas and actions of individuals can shape larger social changes, and those changes, in turn, mould national identity. As the sesquicentennial anniversary of the creation of the Dominion of Canada loomed, I decided to write about a handful of individuals who helped shape the way we think about ourselves. Their stories reflect the evolution of Canada over the past 150 years, and the potential for this process to continue into the future.

The conventional milestones in the history of post-Confederation Canada—the building of the Canadian Pacific Railway, fierce battles in two world wars, the Great Depression, political highs and lows—are background to what I've written here. And I have made the deliberate choice not to focus on any of Canada's twenty-three prime ministers: the best of them already have excellent biographers. I've also passed over business titans, generals, and (the riskiest decision in a puck-crazed country!) hockey players. I know there are regions I have not covered. Instead, I've chosen to tell the story of Canada through portraits of people whose contributions speak to me as a Canadian. Some of them are well-known; others are almost forgotten today. In some cases, their impact was immediate; in others, it took decades for their contribution to be recognized.

Individual lives can be a petri dish for seeing what is going on in the larger society. These particular individuals—all products of their culture and times—helped shape not just the character of the Canada we live in today but also the way we think about ourselves and our future. One way or another, their reflections on being Canadian have become embedded in our collective subconscious. Their lives take a reader deep into the experience of the past. What was it like to exist in eras so different from our own? By bringing some long-dead figures back to life and by approaching from new angles a handful of living Canadians, I am reminded that people didn't always think the way we do these days.

Modern ideas shouldn't be retrofitted onto the past. There have been remarkable changes as the baton of narrative perspective has been passed from one generation to the next. Our visual perspective on Canada has evolved too: as I selected the images in these pages, I have had fun tracing the evolution of the way we see our country.

My choices include three idea-driven political leaders, an artist, a writer, an Oji-Cree elder, a lawyer. Other writers would undoubtedly approach our history from a different point of view and put together a very different list. But that's one of the remarkable aspects of Canada today, isn't it? Our country owes its success not to some imagined tribal singularity but to the fact that, although its thirty-five million citizens do not look, speak, or pray alike, we have learned to share this land and for the most part live in neighbourly sympathy. As we embark on the next 150 years, it helps to recall Canada's extraordinary resilience during constant turbulent change, and to recognize subconscious as well as conscious change. The historian Desmond Morton once observed that Canadians "have spent too much time remembering conflicts, crises, and failures. They forgot the great, quiet continuity of life in a vast and generous land."

⁊~₊

Canada's history stretches way, way back: there have been people living in the northern half of North America for millennia, surviving and thriving and building communities. And there have been people calling themselves Canadians (or, more accurately, Canadiens and Canadiennes) since the French settled New France in the seventeenth century and adopted the Algonquin word "Canada" for the region that is now Quebec.

But when we talk of "Canada" today, we are usually referring to the country created in 1867 by the British North America Act. The act embodied a deal that had emerged three years earlier after twenty-three polite men in top hats met in Prince Edward Island. The Charlottetown meeting—a week of chat and compromise—led to Confederation, the founding event of the "Dominion of Canada."

Canada slipped quietly into the world. The cliché about the mild-mannered Canadian is rooted in the Dominion's birth. The 1864 Charlottetown Conference seemed little more than a sketchy real estate deal: the highlight of the conference was a ball at Prince Edward Island's Government House. Confederation was a defensive strategy then, not an epic dream of nationhood. A bunch of impoverished, underpopulated, raw-boned, and rough-mannered British colonies came together not for a group hug but because their leaders foresaw unpleasant alternatives. British politicians wanted to shrug off their North American colonies while American politicians gazed north with naked greed.

When the British North America Act was finally passed in 1867, Canadians had their constitution only because, 3,300 kilometres away, the British Parliament and monarch had approved it. The deal nearly crumbled before the ink was dry. Only four of today's ten provinces belonged to the newly created federation (and one of those four immediately tried to walk away from it). International borders in the Far North and the West remained fluid. The act virtually ignored the country's Indigenous inhabitants. The project proceeded so slowly that it took thirty-eight years after Confederation for the other six mainland provinces to join—and Newfoundland (later called Newfoundland and Labrador) waited another half century. Today, Indigenous peoples are still challenging governments and their fellow citizens to recognize their rights.

To most immigrants, Canada's origins seem spectacularly tame. Elsewhere, civil war and carnage usually accompanied the birth of new countries or regimes. I was raised on the blood-spattered history of Britain and gulped down stories of murdered queens and military victories. French schoolchildren absorb the lessons of the guillotine in the construction of "la gloire de la République." Youngsters in China hear about the brutally demanding Long March while Japanese students hear stories of fierce shoguns and kamikaze pilots. The history of the United States recalls corpses on the Gettysburg battlefield alongside the bold promise of the Declaration of Independence.

Such chest-thumping rhetoric and bloody birth pangs cement a sense of national purpose. But in the new Dominion of 1867, the only national institution to unite the scattered colonies was the distant government. There would be no coast-to-coast adoption of a "Canadian identity" for decades. Not even a new flag until a century later. Founded on a political compact, Canadian nationhood inched forward. Yet the deal stuck: Canada remains united and the Canadian sensibility has grown sturdier, even as the population has become more diverse. Nonetheless, the idea that the country might fall apart remains one of our few binding national myths.

〜

Defining the Canadian identity is a race without a finish line, because as the country evolves, so does our collective sense of self. Perhaps only a poet can capture the momentum: a poet like Shane Koyczan, the spoken-word artist who rocked the audience at the opening ceremony of the 2010 Vancouver Olympics with his poem "We Are More." You can still catch the whole performance on YouTube, as the bearded, Yellowknife-born poet appeared on the Vancouver stage, surrounded by thousands of people from all over the world.

"Define Canada," he began, in a voice that was both conversational and mesmerizing. In simple language, he listed some of our country's clichés. Hockey, fishing lines, good manners, maple syrup, tree planting, whale-watching . . .

> *But we are more*
> *than genteel or civilized*
> *we are an idea in the process*
> *of being realized*
> *we are young*
> *we are cultures strung together*
> *then woven into a tapestry*
> *and the design*
> *is what makes us more*
> *than the sum total of our history . . .*

By the time Koyczan reached the final line, the Vancouver crowd was roaring in ecstasy. He had drawn his listeners into a shared sense of national well-being that Canadians rarely feel, let alone express. He had reminded us that this is still a land of promise. I was shocked and moved by the collective enthusiasm—an enthusiasm that the Fathers of Confederation could never have imagined, as they looked around the table in Charlottetown.

The pace of change during the intervening years has been startling. In 1867 this country was dirt poor and scrambling to survive. Yet its potential, as many of those Fathers of Confederation recognized, was immense. Now, 150 years later, Canadians live in one of the most prosperous and peaceable countries in the world. As we approach Canada's sesquicentennial birthday, here are some of the people whose ideas, over time, have helped this country achieve some of the promise it continues to offer.

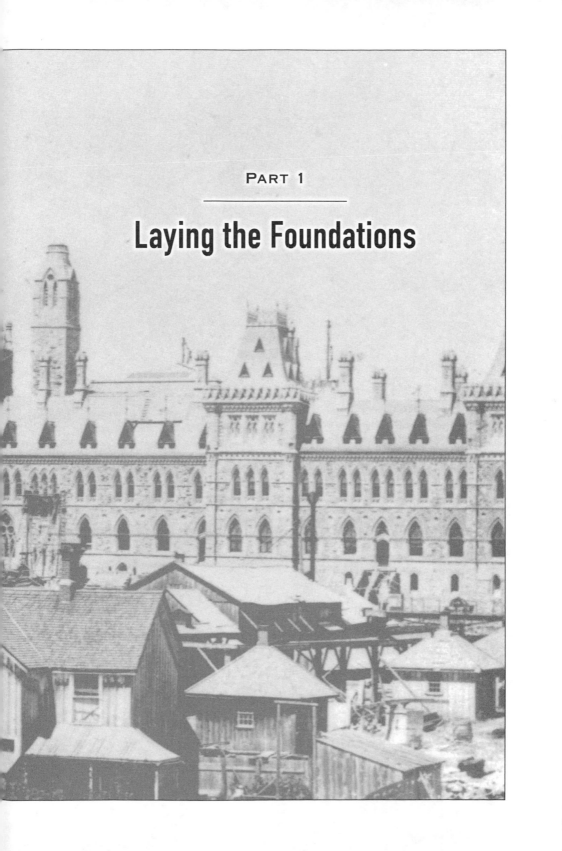

PART 1

Laying the Foundations

CHAPTER 1

A Tapestry of Peoples

*George-Étienne Cartier and
the Idea of Federalism*

In our own Federation we will have Catholic and Protestant, English, French, Irish and Scotch, and each by his efforts and his success will increase the prosperity and glory of the new Confederacy. . . . I view the diversity of races in British North America in this way: we are of different races, not for the purpose of warring against each other, but in order to compete and emulate for the general good.

—George-Étienne Cartier, Confederation Debates (1865)

Everyone acknowledges that Canadian Confederation has been a great success, and those who had the greatest doubts about the venture are now ready to confess that the plan was a wise one.

—*Globe* (Dominion Day, 1877)

L et's start with one of the most famous images in Canadian history: the photograph taken in September 1864 of the Fathers of Confederation on the steps of the lieutenant-governor's mansion in Charlottetown, Prince Edward Island.

If I didn't know what this old-fashioned picture recorded, I'd give it barely a glance. Our public institutions are full of similar compositions—a bunch of men standing in front of a sturdy classical building. They could be school trustees or railway engineers. It is an excruciatingly exclusive image: a blur of white-haired, bearded patriarchy, with not a woman, non-white person, or Indigenous Canadian in sight. That was official Canada 150 years ago.

But I do know that this particular photo records a momentous event. Those men had just invented a new country called the Dominion of Canada. There were still plenty of details to work out, and it would be another thirty months before the British North America Act would be signed on the other side of the Atlantic. Yet these twenty-three sombrely clad lawyers, farmers, and merchants, from five British colonies, had listened carefully to each other and reached consensus. No wonder they decided it called for a commemorative picture. Today, there would be lights, video cameras, and reporters on the spot. Back then, in the cozy little island capital, there was one local photographer with a cumbersome camera that laboriously captured images on glass plates.

When I look more closely, I see interesting dynamics in this image. Most of those posed on the porch—provincial premiers, cabinet members, opposition leaders—radiate the self-assurance of powerful men. However, at least a third of them are looking not at the camera but at the figure who is dead centre in the group: John A. Macdonald, who had just used his extraordinary negotiating skills to broker an agreement. The man who would now become the first prime minister of post-Confederation Canada draws all attention to himself as he sprawls on the steps in the nonchalant pose of a matinee idol. Very clever, John A.

However, my eye is also caught by another figure, standing to Macdonald's right and sporting a stylish tailcoat, a well-groomed shock of white hair, and an air of private triumph. This is George-Étienne Cartier. "As bold as a lion" is how Macdonald himself described his elegant French-Canadian colleague. Macdonald even admitted, "But for him Confederation could not have been carried."[1] Without question, John A. Macdonald had the original vision that a country like Canada could exist. But it was the brains and quiet persistence of George-Étienne Cartier that turned the vision into reality.

George-Étienne Cartier, a shrewd Montreal lawyer, is the man we have to thank for making Canada a federation. Unlike the "Mother Country," as his contemporaries called Great Britain, the Dominion of Canada would not be a unitary state with one central government. Instead, the new Dominion would be designed with two levels of government: a federal government in Ottawa, to handle matters that affected the whole federation

Astute and elegant, George-Étienne Cartier ensured that French-Canadian interests would be protected within the new Dominion.

(relations with Westminster, interprovincial railways, and trade), and a more local government in each province that joined up. Unlike British counties, French *départements*, or even American states in the late nineteenth century, Canadian provinces would have an extraordinary degree of control over their own affairs. By pushing such a federal system, Cartier ensured that Quebec would join the Dominion. French-speaking Canadians living in the new province of Quebec were reassured that they would run everything that was essential to the survival of their culture. His major challenge was to find the right partner to help him achieve his goal. He found such a partner in Macdonald, the charismatic lawyer from Kingston, Ontario. At Charlottetown, Cartier's idea was the most crucial component of Macdonald's vision.

One hundred and fifty years later, the federal system that Cartier envisaged is the basic building block of Canada's uniqueness. It is Cartier that we can thank for developing the government structure that in our country's early years allowed two very different groups of immigrants—the French who had started settling the St. Lawrence Valley three centuries earlier, and successive waves of British who had scattered elsewhere, particularly after the mid-eighteenth century—to live alongside each other. That same federal structure has helped Canada absorb endless new stresses: dramatic expansion across the continent, a troubled relationship with Indigenous peoples, demands from regions that felt ignored, shifting economic patterns, surges of immigrants from every corner of the globe.

In any discussion of what has shaped the character of our country—not just the structure of Canadian government, but the pluralism and tolerance for difference that are still hallmarks of Canada—Cartier's contribution forms the bedrock. That is why I decided that his vision for Canada should kick off my exploration of this country's enduring potential.

Over the course of the past century and a half, Cartier's reputation has been overshadowed by that of John A. Macdonald, "the man who made us," according to Macdonald's biographer Richard Gwyn. When Cartier is remembered at all, it is as Macdonald's sidekick. In my hometown, Ottawa, we have the Macdonald-Cartier International Airport and the Macdonald-Cartier Bridge. In George-Étienne Cartier's own province of Quebec, nationalists have tried to eradicate him from collective memory. But if he shaped Canada, what shaped George-Étienne Cartier? Who was this enigmatic figure in the Confederation photograph, who started his adult life as a rebel and ended it as a British baronet with a valet, a country estate, and a coat of arms?

~

Quebec's Richelieu River is modest compared with the great rivers flowing through the Canadian landscape, such as the St. Lawrence, the Fraser, and the Mackenzie. The Richelieu, rarely more than half a kilometre wide and not particularly deep or fast-flowing, reminds me of a European waterway, with oaks and weeping willows along its banks and plenty of evidence of human habitation. These days, heavy traffic flows in and out of nearby Montreal along autoroutes, leaving the river to pleasure boats and fishing enthusiasts. From the water, I glimpse the silver steeples of churches and houses with the steeply sloping roofs that characterize Quebec rural architecture. Behind them stretch fields planted with corn and soybeans.

George-Étienne Cartier was born on the fertile banks of this river on September 6, 1814, in the village of Saint-Antoine-sur-Richelieu. Today, a bronze bust of him stands here on a granite plinth, surrounded by red impatiens flowers; the inscription reads, "Cartier: Son Village Natale, La Patrie Reconnaissante." The bust features mutton chop whiskers and a truculent expression—every inch a senior statesman. But when he was growing up here, the community knew him first as a rambunctious little boy, and then as a young man with attitude. Only his family's status protected him from several cuffs on the ear.

George-Étienne was the seventh of eight children of a grain merchant, who claimed (on scant evidence) that he was a descendant of *the* Jacques Cartier, the great French navigator who in 1534 became the first European to map the Gulf of St. Lawrence. George-Étienne's family was probably not quite so venerable, but it undoubtedly had deep roots in North American soil: his great-grandfather, Jacques Cartier I, left Europe for Quebec City, New France's most important city, in 1735. The Cartiers built up a lucrative grain business, then moved it closer to the rapidly expanding commercial city of Montreal. Their life in the bucolic Richelieu Valley was comfortable and privileged. Compared with most of their Saint-Antoine neighbours—farmers and tradespeople—the Cartiers were important and worldly. They lived like country squires in a large stone house, and when guests arrived, the brandy flowed and the tables groaned. Youngsters raised in such comfortable circumstances acquire a sense of entitlement.

But George-Étienne would also have been aware of the battle-scarred history of his region. Originating in Lake Champlain and flowing north into the St. Lawrence River, the Richelieu River had been an important trade route for centuries. Before Europeans arrived, Haudenosaunee (Iroquois), Wyandot (Huron), and Algonquin peoples regularly paddled along its length. Because the river teemed with bass, sturgeon, and pike, they named it Masoliantekw, which means "water where there is plenty of food" in the local Abenaki tongue. Once French and English traders showed their

Known as the House of the Seven Chimneys, the Cartier mansion was a landmark for boatmen on the nearby Richelieu River and had its own private wharf.

faces, it also brimmed with conflict. The river's strategic position between New France and New England meant that it was frequently the site of murderous clashes between French and Haudenosaunee, and French and English. The scuffles subsided only after the 1759 defeat by the British of the Canadiens (as inhabitants of New France were known) on the Plains of Abraham.

When George-Étienne and his brothers paddled upriver, they saw the ruins of several forts, both French and English, scattered among the willow trees and prosperous farming communities. However, they rarely caught sight of the region's Indigenous inhabitants. Depleted by disease and hunger, most had retreated west. Local Mohawks kept to themselves in their communities at Kanesatake, on the Ottawa River, and Kahnawake, on the south shore of the St. Lawrence opposite Montreal.

For the small boy, the solid stone house in Saint-Antoine-sur-Richelieu and his extensive network of uncles and cousins were his whole world. There were plenty of diversions for a wealthy family like the Cartiers— dances and balls in each other's mansions, contacts with fellow merchants in Boston and New England. However, Lower Canada (as Quebec was then known) was a small enclave in a larger backwater far from any power centres. In the year of his birth, the combined population (not including Indigenous people) of all the British colonies on the North American mainland was only about five hundred thousand, of whom perhaps three hundred thousand were French-speaking. Unlike the Cartiers, most colonists spent their days tilling the land, logging the forests, fishing the rivers and oceans, or shipping furs, grain, and logs; Montreal, which was now the largest city in British North America, had only twenty thousand residents. Compared with the booming republic to the south, with eight million citizens and big ambitions, British North America was poor, backward, and isolated. Only Halifax in Nova Scotia, with its British military base, and Quebec City, with its wealthy Roman Catholic seminaries and cathedral-basilica, offered any competition to cities like Boston or Philadelphia.

Nevertheless, Lower Canada was rich in tradition: as well as a larger population, it boasted more history and culture, and a higher birth rate, than any of the other impoverished British colonies—Nova Scotia, Prince Edward Island, New Brunswick, Newfoundland, and Upper Canada (today's Ontario). George-Étienne's father, Jacques Cartier III, filled his son with pride in his people. Although he named the son born in 1814 George after the reigning British monarch, King George III (on the birth certificate, the name is spelled in the French style, Georges), he loved to belt out voyageur paddle songs and point to the sturdy survival of Lower Canada's *habitants*. And there was no shortage of village elders who reminisced about the old days, when their region was part of New France, owing allegiance to Paris and enjoying wine exported from French ports such as Le Havre and La Rochelle.

To a small boy, the rhythms of Canadien rural life must have seemed timeless. However, dramatic changes lay just over the horizon. Imperial power brokers in Westminster were losing interest in British North America. In their view, the North American colony was important only as a source of masts for the Royal Navy and as a dumping ground for demobilized soldiers and destitute Irish peasants. As the costs of maintaining troops and separate colonial governments in each colony rose, enthusiasm for these distant, frozen lands fell.

When he was ten years old, Cartier's life changed abruptly: he was shipped off to the care of the most powerful institution in Lower Canada, the Roman Catholic Church. He was too young to recognize it at the time, but his political indoctrination had begun.

George-Étienne and his brother Damien were enrolled at the Collège de Montréal, run by the Sulpician Fathers, the dominant religious order in Quebec after the Jesuits were expelled in 1762. The college was the preeminent seat of learning for French-speaking boys in Lower Canada. Although it has changed dramatically since George-Étienne entered its doors, it is still considered one of the best high schools in Montreal. The two Cartier youngsters would spend the next six years within the college's forbidding stone walls and tightly disciplined routines. Their teachers, all born and trained in France, gave them a superb classical education in language, science, religion, and music. The college bridged the two solitudes of Quebec society, since it catered to the sons of the English-speaking as well as French-speaking merchant class. As a result, Cartier emerged from his years there with a strong sense of linguistic duality as well as a sturdy old boys' network. He also absorbed a firm commitment to the idea of "survivance de la race": the Canadiens must fight to protect their language, their culture, and their church. They must resist any attempt to drown them in a sea of Protestant English. That lesson became the lodestar of George-Étienne's approach to public life. It would, in turn, shape the country that we live in today.

After graduating from the college, what next? For the fifth son of a good Canadien family, there was only one course: the law. In 1831, just before his seventeenth birthday, Cartier began studying for the bar in Montreal with Édouard-Étienne Rodier; he would be called to the bar four years later. Rodier was another Collège de Montréal graduate who was already a member of the Legislative Assembly in Quebec City, the capital of Lower Canada. Cartier also found a niche within the influential network of college alumni who hung out in the taverns and coffee shops around Montreal's Place Jacques-Cartier. This band of well-educated, French-speaking Quebecers chafed at the power of the Château Clique, a group of unelected and predominantly English-speaking politicians in Quebec City. The clique's patronage machine excluded them from government jobs. As one of the young firebrands told an English visitor, "I can show you a hundred young men of family, with cultivated and honourable minds, absolutely running to seed for want of occupation."[2]

If I had time-travelled back to one of those smoky taverns, would I have picked George-Étienne Cartier as the man to watch? Was he obviously a leader who would influence the emergence of British North America as it cut most of its ties with Westminster? No. At age twenty he was unimpressive. About five feet six inches tall and oddly shaped, with an enormous head and short limbs, he was awkward, belligerent, and prone to interrupting others. Everybody acknowledged that he was clever and likely to go places; a fastidious dresser (in later life he favoured striped pants and a silk hat), he kept his thick dark hair neatly cut and brushed straight back from his wide brow. But he had a tiresome manner and a screechy voice. Others in the room had more gravitas.

However, George-Étienne Cartier's fundamental commitment to his fellow Canadiens was already established, and Confederation was still a long way down the road. He would spend the next few years deciding how best to protect the interests of French-speaking Canadians. He would learn to curb his tongue and his tendency to annoy people.

The stirrings of nationalism in Lower Canada were as intoxicating to French-speaking romantics in Cartier's day as they would be to Quebecers in the second half of the twentieth century. George-Étienne Cartier was soon branded a radical because he was active in the Patriote movement. The fiery Patriotes demanded that the emerging French-speaking elite should replace the autocratic Château Clique. At this stage, young Cartier's most notable contribution to the noisy Patriote meetings in Montreal taverns was the chest-thumping patriotic songs he composed, with titles like "O Canada, Mon Pays, Mes Amours" and "Avant Tout Je Suis Canadien." The name "Canada," at this point in our history, referred only to present-day Quebec.

Resentment against unelected British officials exploded in both Upper and Lower Canada in the autumn of 1837. In Lower Canada, several hundred ardent Patriotes organized themselves into a paramilitary force they called Fils de la Liberté, which came to blows with British troops in the Richelieu Valley, Cartier's home turf. In Upper Canada, the red-haired, reckless William Lyon Mackenzie led a march of rebels down Yonge Street. Both uprisings were summarily defeated.

George-Étienne Cartier had participated in several of the Richelieu Valley clashes. Learning that a price had been put on his head, he went into hiding near Saint-Antoine. Six of his fellow Patriotes were hanged; others were exiled to Bermuda or Australia. Soon there were rumours that Cartier was dead, and an obituary in a Quebec City paper mourned the loss of "a young man endowed in the highest degree with qualities of heart and mind and before whom a brilliant career opened."[3] In fact, he had fled to Vermont to avoid capture by British troops.

And that was the end of our pugnacious young lawyer's fling with revolutionary fervour. Whether it was the shock of being officially declared a traitor, fears for his future in the law, or the dawning awareness that an American-style revolution was not going to happen, the reason for his change of direction is unclear. But Cartier now adopted a different course. However, to the exasperation of British authorities, he loved to brag about his days "as a rebel."

Cartier quietly reappeared in Montreal in the summer of 1838. From now on, the clever young lawyer focused on two goals. The first was to achieve non-violent change that would give Lower Canada a degree of self-government. The second was to become a successful corporate lawyer.

The obstacles to the first goal multiplied immediately after the 1837 uprising. On the advice of Lord Durham, a British grandee sent across the Atlantic to quell colonial unrest, the Westminster government reorganized the political map. It merged the provinces of Upper Canada and Lower Canada into one colony with a single legislative assembly serving both English- and French-speaking Canadians. The intent was clearly to assimilate the French.

Cartier and his fellow Patriotes had to find a way for their region to survive as an autonomous, French-speaking nation within North America. Some of the rebels floated the notion of union with the United States. But there was already a chilling example of what had happened to a French-speaking society in the great Republic. By the 1840s, the former French colony of Louisiana had lost most of its unique francophone culture. In 1870, Cartier would express a strong opinion on American attitudes: "Individually, the Americans are good neighbours, but as a nation, there are no individuals who are less liberal towards other peoples, except the Chinese."[4]

For the next few years, Cartier kept his head down and concentrated on his second goal: getting rich. He had his grandfather's savvy mercantile instincts; he could see that if Montreal was going to remain the most important city in British North America, it needed to become a hub in the rapidly spreading network of railways. So he acquired property and promoted railways. As early as 1845, he invested in the railroad that would link Montreal to the ice-free harbour of Portland, Maine, to ensure that western produce would be routed through Montreal rather than an American hub. When the railroad was bought out by the Grand Trunk Railway, he became the GTR's solicitor. His stocky figure might be seen swaggering around rail-yards in Point St. Charles to inspect newly laid tracks and freight cars loaded with grain.

At the same time, he made it his business to become tight with English-speaking entrepreneurs like Alexander Galt and J. J. C. Abbott, and he was welcomed at their social events such as the Saint James's Club ball. (However, I don't think he went overboard with eagerness to merge into the Scots elite: there is no evidence that he sported a kilt at the fancy St. Andrew's Ball.) Hugh Allan, the Scots shipping magnate and banker, began to use the services of this hard-nosed young French lawyer as a fixer, a lobbyist—the francophone lawyer with influence in both church and government circles. But Cartier also kept close ties with the Roman Catholic Church: he was the Sulpicians' lawyer too.

Despite his growing respectability, Cartier remained in constant communication with his former Patriote comrades, especially Louis-Hippolyte LaFontaine, another Patriote turned moderate reformer. LaFontaine had struck up a powerful alliance with the Upper Canadian reformer Robert Baldwin; Cartier became "his propagandist and arm-twister."[5] In 1848, thirty-four-year-old Cartier yielded to pressure from his former comrades and took the plunge into politics. He ran for the Legislative Assembly of the united Province of Canada in a by-election in the Richelieu Valley riding of Verchères, which included his hometown of Saint-Antoine. He took his seat under the banner of the Liberal-Reformers—a Lower Canada coalition that despite its name was in fact conservative and was known as *les bleus*. The *bleus* would demonstrate that Lower Canada (now officially called Canada East) could enjoy the benefits of commerce, education, and agricultural reform without threatening the pillars of French-Canadian society: the Roman Catholic Church, the Montreal business community, and the *habitants'* almost spiritual connection with the land.

Even the most impulsive firebrands simmer down with time, especially if they find other ways to reach their goals. Over the next few years, the honourable member for Verchères became an agile player in a complicated bilingual political arena. He travelled regularly to Toronto and Kingston and mingled comfortably with English Canadians who never set foot in Montreal. He was impatient, full of himself, and short on charisma, but people listened to him because he had a string of successes to his name. Thanks to his efforts, the educational and judicial systems of Canada East were strengthened, and all its residents, whatever language they spoke, were subject to the French Civil Code. Soon Cartier was acknowledged as a leader of Canada East's *bleus.*

At the same time, Cartier pursued his business interests. He manoeuvred himself into the chair of the legislature's all-important Railway Committee while continuing to act on behalf of railway companies. (Before the adage "No conflict, no interest" was coined, he was a skilled practitioner.) And he learned to hold his tongue when necessary. The leading Upper Canadian Reform politician George Brown, publisher of the Toronto *Globe,* repeatedly mouthed off against Roman Catholic Canadiens, and he allowed his newspaper to rant, "Rome is blindness. Rome is intolerance. Rome is despotism."[6] Cartier did not react in public.

Most important, Cartier struck up a partnership that would become, in the words of his biographer Alastair Sweeny, "the most significant relationship in Canadian history."[7] In 1855, he had joined a Conservative cabinet that also included John A. Macdonald, the Scots-born Tory lawyer from Kingston, who was English Canada's craftiest politician. Each man swiftly recognized a kindred spirit; together, they could help each other achieve not only personal ambitions but also an incredibly bold long-term dream: a viable state in the northern half of the continent.

Such a dream seemed ridiculous to many of their contemporaries. Canada was divided between French and English, Catholics and Protestants, Maritimers and central Canadians (the continent's Indigenous inhabitants

The partnership of John A. Macdonald and George-Étienne Cartier proved sufficiently sturdy to overcome language, religious, and legal tensions.

did not even feature in the debate). How could this strange agglomeration of peoples ever be fashioned into a nation? Yet Cartier and Macdonald pursued the dream because, for different reasons, neither of them liked the alternatives.

What a pair they were: the wild-haired, charming Scots pragmatist, always ready with a quip or a compliment, and the dapper, abrasive French Canadian who worked fourteen hours a day and was a bit of an autocrat. They had much in common: they were both tough-minded operators who preferred men's company to women's, who often drank to excess (although Cartier rarely went on binges), and who enjoyed each other's sense of humour. And they were both consummate politicians, with complementary skills. In the Legislative Assembly, Cartier would labour until after midnight to assemble the facts and claims required to push an argument, then hammer it home in his grating, high-pitched voice. A critic described his speeches as "horrible, incomprehensible, untranslatable and unrepeatable."[8] One lasted for fourteen hours: seven hours in English, followed by seven hours in French. Macdonald would rely on Cartier's careful preparations, but then he would take over and prove himself the ultimate people manager, cajoling colleagues with compelling reasons or quiet bribes.

Macdonald needed Cartier because of the votes he controlled in the assembly: he was the most important politician from the largest demographic group (Macdonald referred to the Canadien members as his "sheet anchor"). Cartier needed Macdonald because he was one of the rare English-speaking Canadians who appreciated, as Sweeny points out, "the justice as well as the political advantages to be found in Cartier's demands for the French Canadians."

The Cartier-Macdonald alliance was consummated when the two became joint premiers in 1857. But even their sturdy partnership could not save the uncomfortable amalgam of the future Ontario and Quebec from a roller coaster of legislative crises: six different ministries were upended in the six years leading up to 1864. How could the British colony achieve the social stability and economic expansion it desperately needed?

Schemes of federation for the British colonies had been floating around for years. The United States had adopted a federal system of government more than half a century earlier, but this example didn't inspire confidence since the country had lately been locked in a brutal civil war. For the previous three years, battlefields had been littered with thousands of bloody corpses as the southern Confederacy fought the Union (composed of northern states) over the degree of autonomy it should be allowed, particularly in its treatment of slaves.

Nevertheless, Cartier realized a federation might achieve his own long-held goal: to protect the interests of French Canadians. The need for a bold step was growing urgent: with thousands of immigrants from the British Isles, particularly Ireland, moving into unsettled British land, Canadiens were being outnumbered by Upper Canada's swelling population. Macdonald began as a total skeptic about such a federal system of government but then took a closer look at it when he, in turn, realized that a federation might be the solution to his own challenge: to prevent British North America from becoming an outpost of the United States.

However, such a dramatic political reorganization could take place only if the colonial secretary in faraway London approved. So Cartier travelled across the Atlantic in 1858 to make the proposal. The colonial secretary brushed off the notion, saying that he needed evidence that the smaller Atlantic colonies wanted such a system. But Cartier loved the trip: the sophistication of the capital's tailors, doctors, libraries, and social life appealed to his tastes. He announced with gusto, during an audience with Queen Victoria, that a Lower Canadian was "an Englishman who speaks French."[9]

Although Canadien chauvinists might interpret this as cringing deference, for Cartier himself it was a bold statement that French Canadians were entitled to all the same rights as Englishmen.[10] It also reflected his innate conservatism. In his view, a monarchy was far preferable to the republicanism that characterized Paris. Back home, Cartier impressed Upper Canadians with his unabashed anglophilia: he was a passionate monarchist who named his third daughter Reine-Victoria and believed that the Conquest in 1763 had saved Lower Canada "from the misery and shame of the French Revolution." (Then and now, these statements are anathema to Quebec nationalists.)

The year 1864 was crucial, for Cartier and for the future country of Canada. By June of that year, politicians from all sides—even the intemperate George Brown—had had enough of constitutional deadlock. A ministry that called itself the Great Coalition was formed. It was a remarkable compromise since it included Macdonald, Cartier, and Brown. Better still, the three leaders undertook to "bring in a measure during the next session for the purpose of removing existing difficulties by introducing the federative principle into Canada." Moreover, the leaders were thinking big. They made a bold commitment that went beyond the borders of their own colonies. They were prepared to explore "such provisions as will permit the Maritime provinces and the North-West Territories [the area that would eventually become Manitoba and northern Ontario] to be incorporated into the same system of government."[11]

Federation was a gamble. George Brown crowed to his wife that "French Canadianism would be entirely extinguished." Cartier's opponents in his own province regarded the "federative principle" with deep suspicion and derided him as a spokesman for railway interests and the dupe of Upper Canadians who would "throw him aside like a worn-out towel."[12] Cartier's confidence remained undented. He waved aside others' concerns, and when a colleague reproached him for acting alone, he shrugged: "That is quite correct, I do not consult anybody in making up my mind."

His alliance with Macdonald promised a solution to the problem he had wrestled with since the 1837 Patriote rebellion: how to guarantee the preservation of French language and culture within British North America. He anticipated that Montreal, with its booming industrial sector and powerful English-speaking population, would become the centre of the new country. He ignored his critics and marshalled all-important support from the future Quebec for this bold new idea. He knew that the Canadiens could make a federal system work to their advantage if they stuck together.

+~+

So far, I've explored the influences that shaped George-Étienne Cartier's political career. But there is another side to this man that I'm determined to bring in here, not least because it shows how clever he was at juggling different interests. It is also an irresistible piece of historical gossip, of which there is too little in Canadian history (not because we don't do scandal, but because Canadian historians—unlike those elsewhere—often regard it as unimportant).

Cartier had a complicated private life. Two years before he entered politics, he made a strategic marriage. His bride was a pretty eighteen-year-old named Hortense Fabre, who was the daughter of a successful Montreal publisher, printer, and bookseller. Fabre *père* had been a fellow rebel in 1837 but now held the powerful position of mayor of Montreal. The wedding at the Sulpician Church of Notre-Dame was a notable social event, and the Quebec newspapers reported that the couple had left for a three-week honeymoon in New York and Washington. The Cartiers would have three daughters: Josephine, Hortense, and Reine-Victoria (who died as an infant).

Perhaps the marriage was doomed from the start. Hortense was deeply religious, rather prim, and utterly bourgeois. By now her husband, fourteen years her senior, was a self-assured and wealthy man who liked to throw his weight around. For all his public discretion, in private he often picked fights. (He once fought a duel.) His wife's pursed lips and angry reproaches drove him into the boisterous company of his male friends. Soon Cartier was spending all his evenings working late or going to his club, rather than returning to his silent, stuffy mansion on Montreal's Notre-Dame Street. Much more fun to entertain his friends at raucous parties! "Mr. Cartier sang or croaked after dinner," harrumphed an unfriendly dinner companion, "and made every one he could find stand up, hold hands, and sing a chorus. The wretched servants brought in tea, and he pushed them away till after his song was over. He pushed one on his arm lightly, and I saw the servant rubbing his arm much annoyed, and looking like a dog with a trodden-on tail."[13] In his later years, in his Ottawa house on Metcalfe Street, he threw the best stag parties, which were enjoyed by John A.'s son Hugh John Macdonald.[14]

Yet George-Étienne Cartier liked women: he once admitted to the governor general's sister that he adored "les activités de la coeur." Women liked his flirtatious manner, and at official balls, he was a popular dance partner. In the early 1860s he embarked on a love affair with Luce Cuvillier, the daughter of a Montreal businessman whom Cartier had met through politics. Soon Cartier's colleagues were uncomfortably aware that the *bleu* leader had a mistress—and this was no lighthearted fling.

Today, the Cartier-Cuvillier relationship would be catnip to the paparazzi. Luce Cuvillier had real shock value. Eleven years older than Madame Cartier, Cuvillier was educated, unconventional, and far more sophisticated than her lover's wife. Widely read, she particularly admired the French writer George Sand (the pen name of Aurore Dupin). In imitation of Sand, she smoked cheroots and wore trousers in the privacy of her country home. Cartier and his mistress flaunted their liaison: they travelled around together in complete disregard of the Victorian proprieties. Journalists often reported that Monsieur Cartier's wife had not accompanied him to this or that event, but that Mademoiselle Cuvillier was among the other guests.[15]

Yet the affair never grew from a topic of gossip to a public scandal.

Luce Cuvillier was a spirited, intelligent woman with little time for bourgeois convention.

Newspapers of the day got more excited by partisan invective than by personal peccadilloes. For nineteenth-century Canadians, let alone Roman Catholic Montrealers, divorce was impossible, sanctioned by neither church nor state. But George-Étienne Cartier's double life reflects more than the straitjacket of contemporary mores and religion. It shows how he could juggle competing interests—a skill, subsequent prime ministers would discover, that was crucial to success within Canadian politics. (Think of William Lyon Mackenzie King's artful compromise on an explosive issue such as conscription in the Second World War.) Just as Cartier combined devotion to francophone interests with loyalty to the British monarchy, so he balanced convention and inclination.

✦

Events moved with stunning rapidity after June 1864, once George-Étienne Cartier, John A. Macdonald, and George Brown had formed their Great Coalition and committed themselves to exploring the idea of federalism.

A remarkable aspect of this story is that the Fathers of Confederation had few models to follow. The only countries that had established two-level systems, with one central government plus several regional ones, were Switzerland and the United States. British North Americans had watched the American Civil War sap British North America's fragile economy and spawn fears of American expansionism.

In London, the colonial secretary had declared that he was sympathetic to the idea of regional consolidation in Britain's American colonies—as long as any scheme had the consent of all concerned. (By now, the British government was impatient to withdraw its expensive red-coated battalions from Canada. The *Times* sniffed, "Our colonies are rather too fond of us, and embrace us, if anything, too closely."[16]) Then the Great Coalition leaders heard that the four Maritime provinces were planning a conference to discuss Maritime union. They decided to crash the party, and they sat down in the cabinet offices in Quebec City to draft proposals for a federal constitution.

On Monday, August twenty-ninth, in the warmth of a summer's evening, George-Étienne Cartier made a formal farewell to his wife and daughters and joined Macdonald, Brown, Galt, Hector Langevin, and William McDougall on board the *Queen Victoria*, a Canadian government steamer. As the ship weighed anchor and proceeded downstream, the gaggle of politicians watched the silver steeples, curved roofs, and well-tilled land of the Île d'Orléans slip by. By dawn on Thursday, the *Queen Victoria* had traversed the Gulf of St. Lawrence, and the red ochre bluffs of Prince Edward Island were in sight. The following day, in the island's legislative building, George-Étienne Cartier rose to present the case for a federal union.

Cartier's arguments overwhelmed his deficiencies as a speaker. He explained to Maritimers that he supported the federal system because it split the united Province of Canada into two, returning its two original components, Upper and Lower Canada, to their pre-1841 state. This meant that French Canadians could preserve their nationality because they would have their own provincial legislature. The canny Maritimers listened carefully and realized that this system would suit them fine, because each of the other British North American colonies would also get its own legislature, under the federal umbrella. Maritimers had made it plain that they would resist any attempt to absorb their small colonies into a unified Canadian state; in fact, they weren't even prepared to join together into a Maritime union. (To this day, the idea is unacceptable.) But Cartier's proposal was a solution that would work for them too, because it would preserve their provincial autonomy.

There were a few more hours of discussion, and deals to be made about financial arrangements for railways and tariffs. But by Friday afternoon the thirty-three delegates were enjoying a champagne lunch on the *Queen Victoria*, now nicknamed "the Confederate Cruiser." And in no time at all, Cartier broke into his song: "O Canada, Mon Pays, Mes Amours."[17]

The details would be hammered out in Quebec City a month later. Macdonald, the skilful manager of discussion, took the lead here, allegedly drafting fifty of the seventy-two resolutions that would become clauses in the British North America Act. George Brown, an impulsive fountain of ideas, kept interrupting, then retreating. Cartier stayed silent, knowing that he controlled enough votes to ensure that his agenda was never derailed.[18] Macdonald was keen on establishing a strong central government and giving very limited powers to the provinces. However, Cartier would not let his colleague dilute federal principles or the status of the French language. He successfully ensured provisions guaranteeing the official use of French in Parliament, the federal courts, and the courts and legislature of Quebec, as well as the continuance of Quebec's Civil Code.[19] He also ensured important constitutional guarantees to Quebec's English-speaking minority for schooling and political representation.

In 1867, the British North America Act sailed through the Westminster Parliament, and the Canadian Confederation became a legal entity.

In London, Cartier crowed with delight. "We have founded a great empire which will extend from the Atlantic to the Pacific Ocean; we intend that all that immense territory will be well governed and governed not merely as a selfish principle as applied to us, but in order to add to the power and to the prosperity of the Mother country."

But there was a further challenge for the wily Montreal lawyer. He had to sell the deal to his fellow French-speaking Canadians in what would soon be called Quebec. He had to persuade them that Confederation was the key to the preservation of their unique identity, not the first step in its gradual dissolution. How did he succeed? A crucial element was support for the new Dominion from Quebec's Roman Catholic Church. But Cartier also developed a subtle argument. In a speech in Montreal he made no mention of the "Mother Country," and he quietly introduced a concept that at the time, in any of the European nation-states (let alone the United States), would be considered bizarre if not revolutionary. He distinguished between political and cultural nationality, arguing that "the establishment of a federal government will strengthen the culture that is dear to us. A federal government is the only system in which the survival of French Canada will be secure."[20]

On July 1, 1867, French- and English-speaking Canadians celebrated the birth of the Canadian Confederation with bonfires and parties. But were they celebrating the same thing? In the new province of Ontario, George Brown's *Globe* told its English-speaking and largely Protestant readers, "With the first dawn of this gladsome midsummer morn, we hail the birthday of a new nationality." Meanwhile, in Quebec, the editor of *La Minerve*, a strong supporter of Cartier's, declared that Confederation had achieved autonomy for Lower Canada's French-speaking residents. On July 1, *La Minerve* observed, "In giving ourselves a complete government we affirm our existence as a separate nationality."

What an incredible juggling act! Cartier had achieved his goal and ensured that the new country of Canada was a political unit in which different peoples could cohabit and protect their own culture. In time, this would become a template for federalism beyond Canadian borders—a political system in which political and ethnic nationalisms could coexist without necessarily overlapping. Other British colonies, such as Australia and South Africa, drew lessons from the Canadian experience as they moved towards independence.

Cartier cared only about the language, laws, political institutions, and culture of French-speaking Canadians in Lower Canada: French-speaking

Canadians elsewhere in the new Dominion would not enjoy the same protections. But in the Confederation Debates, Cartier explicitly spoke of "a political nationality" in a speech that has an astonishingly modern ring of inclusivity, even if the groups mentioned don't seem particularly diverse today. He argued that the "idea of unity of races was utopian—it was impossible. Distinctions of this kind would always appear. . . . In our own federation we should have Catholic and Protestant, French, English, Irish and Scotch, and each by his efforts and his success would increase the prosperity and glory of the new confederacy."[21] The concept of Canadians sharing a political nationality but not necessarily a culture was now "part of Canada's DNA," as Macdonald's biographer Gwyn put it.[22]

〜

The newborn Dominion of Canada had teething problems. Before those whiskered patriarchs had even left Charlottetown, Newfoundland had walked away from the whole idea of Confederation. Prince Edward Island refused to sign the deal. New Brunswick nearly went AWOL before the vote at Westminster. Nova Scotia tried to secure the repeal of the union after it had taken place. As the journalist Blair Fraser wrote a hundred years later, "The fight for Canadian independence was never directed against the British. It was always a running fight among Canadians."[23]

But in the end, Confederation stuck . . . and grew. In retrospect, it seems solid from the start. Yet for all the biblical magnificence of its name, the new Dominion of Canada would be unrecognizable to twenty-first-century Canadians.

First, it occupied only a third of present-day Canada: it reached from the Atlantic Ocean to just beyond the Great Lakes. Newfoundland had opted to remain an independent British colony. Most of the vast area between the border of Ontario and the Pacific Ocean, home to thousands of peoples from various Indigenous groups, was an uncharted wilderness that belonged to the Hudson's Bay Company, which made the HBC about the largest landowner in the world. Beyond the HBC's string of fur forts across its territory, and perched on the edge of the Pacific Ocean, was the British colony of British Columbia, which wasn't even invited to send representatives to Charlottetown. The only way to reach the distant British colony was to travel, by rail and wagon, through the United States.

Next, the new Dominion had only a tenth the population of our country today: the combined population of Quebec, Ontario, Nova Scotia, New Brunswick, and Prince Edward Island was three and a half million. Most people were dirt poor. Ottawa, the federal capital, already had its splendid Gothic Parliament Buildings, but they looked wildly out of place. They towered above a boisterous and smelly lumber town of 20,000 inhabitants who complained incessantly about the bitter winter cold and the suffocating summer humidity. The rest of the Dominion's cities—Halifax, Saint John, Quebec City, Montreal, Kingston, and Toronto—had poor drainage, few amenities, and only a handful of buildings of any style. Even the largest (Montreal, with 115,000 residents) was swept regularly by smallpox and typhoid epidemics. The only type of facility of which there was a surfeit was taverns—lined with spittoons and serving rotgut liquor and home-brewed beer.

Most of us cannot imagine a world with no automobiles, telephones, electric devices—let alone airplanes, computers, Internet. So by our standards, the Canada of 1867 was a stark, silent, and lonely country. The wail of steam engines was starting to be heard in more populated areas in Canada, and entrepreneurs were eagerly stringing the first telegraph wires between buildings, but travel and long-distance communication were difficult. Most of the Dominion's residents preferred to stay put rather than travel by wagon or carriage over primitive, unlit roads (unpaved in the countryside, cobblestoned in cities) to other provinces. Canadians remained strangers to each other.

Who were their neighbours in this vast new land? Over a hundred thousand of the residents of the northern half of North America were invisible to the Canadians enumerated in the 1861 census. As immigrants continued to arrive and settle in populated areas or push westward into the prairies, Indigenous peoples including Anishinaabe, Haudenosaunee, and dozens of other groups found themselves squeezed to the margins, while northerners like Inuit and Innu were ignored altogether. The Fathers of Confederation had made no provision for them, except to identify "Indians" as a subject of federal, not provincial, jurisdiction. Only the Royal Proclamation of 1763 afforded them some protection, in its declaration that Indians should not "be molested or disturbed" on their historic hunting grounds.

Those Canadians enumerated in the census—immigrants themselves, or descendants of European immigrants to North America over the previous three centuries—lived narrow, hardscrabble, and often illiterate lives. Four out of five of them were settled on isolated farms and in villages, usually in dirt-floored one-room shacks. The men spent long days planting, harvesting, fishing, or working in the lumber industry; the women worked equally long hours, raising and feeding families and looking after hens, pigs, and vegetable gardens. Winter was a time of hibernation: flour mills and lumber mills shut down when the freeze-up started. Prosperous farmers might enjoy visiting each other, sleigh bells jangling as they sped over smooth ice roads to feasts of carefully preserved pork, fruits, and vegetables. For the less successful, winter could be a killing time. In January 1872, the Montreal *Gazette* reported two children frozen to death in a wretched slum one bitterly cold night.[24] Religion was central to most people's lives, and churches (Roman Catholic or Protestant) were usually the focus of community activities.

Nevertheless, the new Dominion was on the cusp of change. Soon education would be made compulsory in most provinces, and public health programs would reduce the incidence of diseases like typhoid, smallpox, and diphtheria. Rapid industrialization would fuel the growth of cities and incomes (though the economy grew in fits and starts, and a major depression hit North America in the 1880s and 1890s). But there would be no sense of shared identity until the following century: British North Americans clung to their self-images as Islanders, Nova Scotians, New Brunswickers, Canadiens, or Upper Canadians. In 1867 the Maritime provinces were separated from Quebec and Ontario by forested wilderness: there were no road or direct rail links. Only the St. Lawrence River gave a direct connection; when most of that mighty waterway was frozen during the winter months, Maritimers could reach central Canada only by travelling through Maine. Since most residents of the eastern seaboard boasted deeper roots in North America than Ontarians, they regarded English speakers in central Canada with chilly skepticism. Meanwhile, Newfoundland turned its back on the new Dominion and continued as a self-governing British colony, with its own House of Assembly. In 1907 it proudly acquired new powers as the Dominion of Newfoundland and claimed equal status with the Dominion of Canada.

The term "Dominion" had a lovely biblical ring, but it was still a wobbly idea. In 1867 the Dominion of Canada was not an independent country: Britain remained "the Motherland." Canada had no say in its foreign affairs; they would remain in British hands until the 1931 Statute of Westminster. The Dominion was united by neither language nor ethnic homogeneity: it was cobbled together out of English-speaking and French-speaking peoples, with hundreds of Indigenous groups living on its fringes. And it had a large and hungry neighbour waiting for Confederation to fall apart. "When the experiment of the 'Dominion' shall have failed, as fail it must," stated the *New York Times* soon after the British North America Act had been proclaimed, "a process of peaceful absorption will give Canada her proper place in the Great North American republic."[25]

The truth was that the central government was almost irrelevant to most people's lives. Citizens expected little from the new federal government in Ottawa: municipalities provided most policing; provincial governments administered most laws; people looked to churches and service clubs for charity. There was only one national symbol in the Dominion, and that was a symbol that resided elsewhere. In parlours across Canada, you would likely find a picture of Queen Victoria—dumpy, unsmiling, but a crucial part of Canadian federalism. Loyalty to the distant monarchy was a defining difference between Canadians and Americans.

What could knit together this sprawling transcontinental country? After John A. Macdonald's skilful leadership through constitutional negotiations in Charlottetown, Quebec City, and London, he was the Crown's inevitable choice to form the new nation's first government. Macdonald's closest ally, George-Étienne Cartier, became Canada's first minister of militia and defence. However, Cartier held on to the chairmanship of the all-powerful Railway Committee. Since his earliest years as a Montreal lawyer, Cartier had understood that economic growth was possible only if markets were linked together by railways; now he set to work to build the railways that would glue the whole Dominion together. He had remained in London after the British North America Act received royal assent in order to arrange financing for the Intercolonial Railway.

Cartier was back in Canada for the first celebration of the new Dominion on July 1, 1867. But he was in a foul mood. Governor General Lord Monck had announced that the new prime minister would receive a knighthood, becoming Knight Commander of the Bath, while Cartier along with five others would be awarded the lesser honour of Companion of the Bath. Cartier bluntly declined to accept, on the grounds that it was an insult to French Canadians. Sir John A., as Macdonald was now universally known, needed Cartier's support too much to shrug this off as a temporary outburst. Within months, thanks to Macdonald's intervention, Cartier leapfrogged over his colleague in rank: he was created a baronet. This gave him the title "Sir," which could be handed down to any male heirs. (Not much comfort to the father of daughters only, but Cartier was far too much of a Victorian conservative to question archaic British rituals.)

By now Sir George-Étienne Cartier was the smartly tailored, silver-haired figure of the iconic Charlottetown Conference photograph: he had been in elected politics for more than two decades, and like anyone who has been so powerful for so long, his success outshone his arrogance. The prime minister depended on him heavily: Cartier often replaced Macdonald as prime minister when the latter was either on official business elsewhere, on an alcoholic binge, or sick. Sir Stafford Northcote, governor of the Hudson's Bay Company, noted in 1870, during a prolonged Macdonald absence due to gallstones, that Cartier "was behaving remarkably well at the present crisis, taking the whole responsibility of negotiations upon himself, but refusing to supplant Macdonald.... Other ministers had asked

Cartier to take the Premiership, but . . . he had refused to do so, and had kept the Cabinet together."[26]

When he was awarded his baronetcy, Cartier had chosen as his motto "Franc et sans dol" ("frankness without deceit"), and that is how he struck others. Observing the bluff French Canadian at dinner one night, Northcote admired his manner. "He has the happy quality of being always thoroughly well satisfied with himself, and this makes him very good humoured with other people. But he is much more than good humoured. He has the great merit of being thoroughly honourable and loyal. Everyone says that once he has given his word, he is quite sure to keep it if he can." (Northcote also noted, "The misfortune is that being very sanguine he sometimes makes promises which he cannot perform.") Lady Macdonald, usually a harsh critic of her husband's colleagues, echoed this assessment: she called Cartier "the fairest of men. He always seems to me full of life and pleasant chattiness but extremely egotistical." But she also recognized that, unlike her husband, he was not a popular favourite; despite his being respected for his moral strength, "qualities which please are wanting."[27]

✦

With the British North America Act firmly secured, the Montreal lawyer threw himself into the nation-building project with a vigour at least as forceful as his boss's. Like Macdonald, Cartier recognized that if Canada was to survive, it had to stretch beyond its present boundaries, to cross the prairies and the Rocky Mountains until it occupied an unbroken line from Atlantic to Pacific. And the former rebel also knew that only the survival of the fledgling nation would guarantee the sure survival of the French-Canadian people; otherwise, both French and English Canadians would tumble into the North American melting pot.

Control of the West was the first challenge, particularly in the face of American expansionism. With the end of the Civil War in 1865, politicians in Washington looked north with barely concealed greed. The admission of Nebraska as the thirty-seventh state in the Union in 1867 was immediately followed by the American purchase of Alaska from the Russians. This put the squeeze on the vast lands in the North and West of North America—more than a quarter of the continent—that had been granted to the Hudson's Bay Company two centuries earlier.

Which Canadian politician hurried over to London in October 1868 to negotiate the acquisition of these lands from the HBC? George-Étienne Cartier. Everybody wanted the deal to happen, so Cartier held his bulldog instincts in check as he met the new colonial secretary, Lord Granville, whose suave manner had earned him the dangerous nickname "Pussy." The Hudson's Bay Company handed over its territory in return for the handsome sum of £300,000 and about one-twentieth of the land. Canada now stretched to the foothills of the Rockies, and Cartier had not yet finished. He returned in triumph to Canada and presented the deal he had made to Parliament with the words "The British North America Act will soon apply to a chain of provinces extending from the Atlantic to the Pacific. I hope we shall no longer hear of annexation."

The only problem was that nobody had consulted the inhabitants of this vast acquisition. The Canadian government made a clumsy attempt to occupy the new western territories and quickly ran up against armed resistance from the French-speaking Métis of Red River, offspring of European voyageurs and Indigenous people. Their leader was twenty-four-year-old Louis Riel, a tall, curly-haired, charismatic man. Like Cartier, Riel had been educated by the Sulpician Fathers in Montreal, and he hero-worshipped the leader of the Quebec *bleus*. There is no evidence that Cartier and this intense young warrior ever met. Nevertheless, Cartier certainly sympathized with Riel's complaints on behalf of the Métis people: that their territory was being overrun by English-speaking Upper Canadians, that their farms were being surveyed and broken up for the new settlers, that their rights and Catholic religion were not being respected.

Thanks to Cartier's intervention, a settlement was negotiated that created the new territory of Manitoba, in which the Métis were guaranteed land, the rights of both English and French were recognized, and a political and administrative system analogous to that of Quebec was put in place. The settlement allowed Cartier to tick off two of his concerns: it secured a

Louis Riel, educated, like Cartier, by the Sulpician Fathers in Montreal, fought to protect Métis rights and land.

Canadian presence on the Red River, and it offered a congenial new area of settlement for Quebecers. But it left one dangerous, dangling thread: the fate of Louis Riel himself.

During the Riel-led uprising of 1869–70, an obstreperous surveyor from Ontario named Thomas Scott had been involved in clashes between Métis and Canadian militia. Scott was captured by the Métis, and after a travesty of a trial, Louis Riel authorized his execution. Protestant Ontario rose up in rage against the Métis leader, demanding his arrest for murder. Cartier knew that such an arrest, followed by a trial, had the potential to inflame a vicious English-French, Protestant-Catholic battle, and he quietly arranged for the tempestuous young leader to go into exile. Memories of his own rebellious youth must have resonated with the silver-haired statesman. For the rest of his life, he pressed the British government to grant an amnesty to Riel, as he himself had been unofficially pardoned after the 1837 Patriote rebellion.

There was still one more leap to be taken in the Canadian march westward: the giant step over the Rocky Mountains. Here again, Cartier was the man who made it happen.

In June 1870 a delegation from New Westminster, capital of the tiny colony of British Columbia, came to Ottawa for a meeting in the Privy Council chambers. There they found Sir George-Étienne Cartier, "in his shirtsleeves, hard at work"; he gave them a warm welcome and pressed glasses of sherry on the three delegates.[28] The delegation told the acting prime minister that the three-year-old federal government was welcome to extend its control right across the continent. However, there were conditions. Ottawa must assume the colony's crippling debt of over $1 million, undertake a public works program, build a carriage road, and begin construction of a transcontinental railway.

This was quite a package of demands. But to the delegates' amazement, they got all they asked for and more: Cartier urged them to ask for a railway to be begun in two years and completed in ten. The British Columbians were astonished by Ottawa's pledge to lay the 4,345-kilometre line in so short a time. Macdonald, recuperating from ill health in faraway Prince Edward Island, might have given a similar welcome to the delegation, but it was Cartier, with his deep commitment to the country's steel spine, who made the extravagant offer.

On July 20, 1871, British Columbia formally entered Confederation as its sixth province. Macdonald and Cartier had solidified their dream: a Canada that stretched from coast to coast. "Before very long," Cartier prophesied, "the English traveller who lands at Halifax will be able within five or six days to cover half a continent inhabited by British subjects."[29] To head off anger in Ontario at the cost of this deal, the government announced that the railway would be built not by government but by a private company to which it would give subsidies and land grants. In the spring of 1872, Cartier introduced a bill into the House of Commons to authorize the building of the Canadian Pacific Railway with the exultant cry "All aboard for the West."

The British Columbia deal was Cartier's finest hour. From then on, his luck began to run out. Ill health and tangled railway politics would sap both his energies and his reputation.

Cartier had relied on Sir Hugh Allan, the flamboyant and ruthless shipping magnate who was an old friend from his days as a successful Montreal lawyer, to organize and head the Canadian Pacific Railway Company. Allan could expect to make millions of dollars from the CPR contract, but he was also expected to show his gratitude. During the 1872 elections it emerged that, in expectation of receiving the CPR contract, Allan had funnelled large sums into Conservative Party funds. Cartier had been the conduit: he himself had received $85,000. For the first time in his life, he suffered the humiliation of defeat in his Montreal East constituency. Within weeks he sailed for England (ironically, on one of Sir Hugh Allan's steamers) to get treatment for a chronic kidney condition that had been bothering him for some months.

Cartier left Sir John A. to deal with the outrage that the patronage deals and slippery electoral financing triggered. The uproar caused Sir John A.'s

Between 1881 and 1884, about 15,000 Chinese labourers were brought to Canada to work on the Canadian Pacific Railway. They were paid half the regular wages—and given the most dangerous jobs—but the railway was finished on time.

defeat at the polls and kept him out of power for five years. But in the end, Cartier would shoulder much of the blame for the Pacific Scandal, allowing Macdonald to emerge tarnished but vigorous. In 1878 the Kingston lawyer was back in office, ready to continue the weighty task of making the Dominion of Canada a national as well as a constitutional reality.

⁓

As a biographer, I am always sad to say goodbye to my subjects. I try not to be an advocate so much as a mediator between their times and ours, but I have found it hard not to morph into George-Étienne Cartier's champion. He himself watched his role in the creation myth of Canada being belittled when he was not awarded a knighthood at Confederation. Over the years, Cartier's significance has faded while Macdonald's importance has been hammered into the boilerplate of Canadian history.

Why has this happened? Confederation launched Macdonald's remarkable career as prime minister, an office he would hold for nineteen of the next twenty-four years. But Cartier, his indispensable partner in the Confederation project, was by his side for only six years after the 1867 celebrations. Cartier's single-minded zeal for a federal system has been progressively forgotten. There are two thorough biographies of him in English, by Alastair Sweeny and Brian Young, but both were written more than thirty years ago and have been unable to halt the slow fade. And Quebec's francophones are ambivalent about Cartier's achievements. His unabashed devotion to the monarchy, the British Empire, and London doesn't sit well with modern Quebecers. Even defenders within his own province are apologetic. "When we judge him," wrote J.-C. Bonenfant in the *Dictionary of Canadian Biography*, "we must place him in his time and avoid condemning him in the light of the events that have taken place in the last 100 years, and that he could not reasonably have foreseen."[30]

Moreover, I have to admit that John A. Macdonald was the more attractive personality, and his charisma resonates down the years. Without Macdonald's exceptional negotiating skills, plus that easy charm, the path to Confederation would have been rockier. Unlike his co-premier, Cartier lacked that quality that was as important in politics 150 years ago as it is today: likeability. Macdonald sheathed his ruthlessness; Cartier was brutally tough. He held many views that are anathema today: he opposed frequent elections, the secret ballot, and universal suffrage, and he would have been appalled at proposals to give the vote to either women or Indigenous Canadians.

Yet within his own lifetime, Cartier's significance was acknowledged by his peers. At a Montreal banquet in November 1866, Cartier's colleague Thomas D'Arcy McGee gave an effusive toast to him. The Irish-born poet and politician, who was one of the first to embrace the notion of a Canadian nationalism and who had played a crucial role during the Confederation debates, observed that "one of the main obstacles to [Confederation] has arisen from the conflict, real or imagined, between racial interests, religions and languages, existing in Canada today." McGee then went on to say, "And this conflict could not have been avoided except by the utmost firmness, and a great deal of mutual liberality, and by a large amount of impartiality in the administration of the country, and it is above all to the Hon. Mr. Cartier that we are indebted for the happy consequences of this enlightened and far-seeing administration."[31]

Eight months after Cartier sailed for England, he was dead of Bright's disease. When Macdonald received the news by telegram on May 20, 1873, he wept. Then he entered a crowded House of Commons and took his seat next to Cartier's empty desk. As the House fell silent, Macdonald wearily rose to his feet. "Mr. Speaker, I have a painful duty to fulfill to this House. I have received a telegram . . . which I will read to the House. 'Sir George Cartier had a relapse last Tuesday and he died peacefully at six o'clock this morning. His body will be sent by Quebec steamer on the 29th.'"

The prime minister paused for a few seconds, then said, "I feel myself quite unable to say more at this moment." Sobbing uncontrollably, he placed his right arm on Cartier's desk and buried his head on his left arm, while his whole body shook with grief.[32]

Macdonald was never able to find another Canadien partner with whom he could work in such equilibrium and mutual trust, and Canada was the poorer for it. Cartier left many what-ifs behind him. If he had remained in charge of railway policy, would there have been more control over the proliferation of small, money-losing lines that sapped shaky local economies? If he had been alive in 1885, would he have saved Louis Riel from the gallows and prevented the profound alienation of French Canadians from the Conservative Party? If he had been at Macdonald's side throughout the 1870s and 1880s, would his fellow Quebecers have felt more confident that their voices counted within the federal government?

Hard to know. But George-Étienne Cartier confirmed Quebec's role at the heart of Confederation and guaranteed the survival of its laws, language, and customs. "Je me souviens" on Quebec licence plates has many implications, but without Cartier there might have been nothing to remember. And for succeeding generations, Cartier's vision of Canada as a country whose citizens share a secular identity that transcends but does not crush religious and ethnic identities would have an even more powerful impact. It has become a key element within the pluralist Canada of today.

CHAPTER 2

Mountie Mythology

Samuel Benfield Steele's Iron Fist in a Velvet Glove

It would do . . . you good to see what a different lot of people the Canadians of both languages and the British from the Old Country are from the rest of the foreigners, more intelligent and polite. . . . [Please tell your uncle to] assure [Prime Minister] Sir Wilfrid Laurier that if the honour of the country depends on our behaviour in the Yukon it is perfectly safe.

—Samuel Steele, letter to Marie Steele, Yukon (1898)

Sam Steele was a reformer, getting the NWMP to move beyond the cavalry traditions of days gone by and to adopt practices more suitable for the Canadian West.

—Preston Manning, *Think Big: My Adventures in Life and Democracy* (2002)

George-Étienne Cartier's legacy of federalism might be the political bedrock of Canada, but the geological bedrock of the new Dominion was impervious to the hoopla surrounding Confederation. It was all very well to design a fancy new system of government for a new country, but who was going to enforce the laws passed by its Parliament?

When I look at a map of Canada in 1877, one decade after the Dominion's birth, my first impression is that it is a coherent whole—a great sweep of British Empire pink stretching from sea to sea, with a clear horizontal line marking the border with the United States. But on the ground, residents of this new country would never have seen it this way. The five provinces in Maritime and central Canada, crowded together in the East, are pimpled with small towns, and a larger dot on each represents a capital city. Inhabitants of those towns, and of the lumber camps, farms, and villages scattered between them, would rarely travel more than fifty kilometres from their place of birth during their lifetimes. Waterways were the principal thoroughfares; roads were few and often impassable. Yet those provinces, along with the tiny square of Manitoba and the untracked forests of British Columbia, occupied less than a third of the country. The land from Lake Superior to the Rockies is a vast blur, veined with rivers. In some regions even the exact line of the United States–Canada border was up for grabs.

Lakes, mountains, plains, waterfalls, forests, tundra, rocky coastlines, islands—the geographic features of this territory had been roughly sketched, during the previous three centuries, by fur traders. Most of it comprised Rupert's Land, which had belonged to the Hudson's Bay Company and had just been sold to Canada. It was called "the Great Lone Land" by officers who traversed it, and "home" by the Métis, Inuit, and nomadic buffalo-hunting First Nations who peopled it. The total population of the Dominion—a land mass half the size of Europe—was somewhere close to 5 million, including 3.5 million non-Indigenous people.[1] For almost all of them, Ottawa, with all its nation-building rhetoric, was a long way away.

But that was going to change. It would change because American trad-ers (with covert backing from American authorities) were pushing north, happy to build fortified posts with Wild West names like Slide-Out and Whoop-Up, and to supply cheap whisky to the Indigenous peoples. And it would change because Sir John A. Macdonald and Sir George-Étienne Cartier were determined to give the country a steel spine, a railroad that linked the prosperous East with the distant West. The Canadian Pacific Railway would bring a surge of newcomers west—first, the gangs of la-bourers required to clear track and lay four thousand kilometres of rails, and after that, the thousands of immigrants lured from the East and from Europe to farm the prairies.

Prime Minister Macdonald knew that, to avoid the mayhem that had characterized the American West, he had to expel the traders and get in front of the expected rush of settlers. His solution? A paramilitary force of mounted police, trained and equipped for plains warfare but with civil re-sponsibilities. A force that would establish friendly relations with Indige-nous peoples and maintain peace as settlers arrived.

The North West Mounted Police (renamed the Royal Canadian Mounted Police in 1920) would be the first distinctly Canadian institution. And within three decades of Confederation, the horsemen in their scarlet tunics symbolized Canada both within and outside the country. Starting with Queen Victoria's 1897 Diamond Jubilee celebrations, they regularly represented the Dominion at royal coronations, weddings, and funerals in London parades. The Mounties' Musical Ride was a headliner at events throughout North America and Britain.

When I was twelve, the Musical Ride appeared at the Bakewell Agricul-tural Show, near my childhood home in Derbyshire. I remember our ex-citement as each Mountie, ramrod straight in the saddle, steered his glossy black horse through the intricate performance. For me, and for many Brit-ish children through most of the twentieth century, the Mounties were an essential part of Canada's image. It struck me only later that no other coun-try uses agents of law and order as promotional tools or has a police officer as a central figure in its mythology. But for a country that (unlike its neighbour to the south) has often put community safety before individual rights, it seems to fit.

✛

How did a mounted police force, along with beavers and maple leaves, become one of Canada's first national symbols?

Sir John A. Macdonald can claim most of the credit. It was his inspired idea to create a paramilitary force that looked absolutely nothing like the gunslinging sheriffs of the American Wild West. The U.S. federal government had left it to the settlers to establish justice on the frontier, and the results had not been pretty. Clashes between gold miners, land-hungry settlers, and the A'aninin (Gros Ventre), Sioux, Tsêhéstáno (Cheyenne), Apsáalooke (Crow), and Siksika (Blackfoot) peoples in the territories of Dakota and Montana had been notoriously brutal, as Indigenous peoples saw both the buffalo herds and their land base shrink. Indian wars had cost the American government millions of dollars: thousands of Indians had been massacred, along with hundreds of troops and settlers.

Macdonald knew that Canada could not afford a large army to keep the peace in the Northwest, and he also wanted to demonstrate that settlement in the Canadian West was going to be different from the rough-and-ready justice of the American frontier. The first clause of the British North America Act promised "Peace, Order and good Government." Although that phrase was legal boilerplate inserted into British colonial constitutions from New Zealand to Sierra Leone,[2] it captured what Macdonald hoped to achieve with the North West Mounted Police. He wanted a force that would be "a civil, not a military body, with as little gold lace, fuss, and rough and ready—particularly ready—enforcement of law and justice." Most important, it would be in place *before* the arrival of CPR work gangs and settlers.

Known as "Old Tomorrow" for his endless delays, Macdonald dragged his feet for a while. But then American whisky traders slaughtered twenty Assiniboine in the Cypress Hills in 1873, in what was clearly Canadian territory. Parliament in Ottawa quickly approved a force focused on "the preservation of peace, the prevention of crime." Modelled on the Royal Irish Constabulary, it was to consist of three hundred men; all had to be fit, of good character and horsemanship, and able to read and write in English or French. Members of the force would carry guns and wear scarlet tunics—a significant statement in itself. Recruitment began immediately. By year's end, 150 men had set up their headquarters in Manitoba. The American writer Wallace Stegner once observed that the NWMP uniform transformed the border into "a color line; blue below, red above, blue for treachery and unkept promises, red for protection and the straight tongue."[3]

That was just the first taste of the mystique that soon adhered to Canada's peace officers. However, there is another reason why the Mounties were mythologized as brave young men overcoming hardships to build a great nation: spin! From the outset, the force's bosses understood the benefits of good publicity. Moreover, one of the first recruits to the new militia was a man ripe for mythmaking: Sam Steele. Although Steele was never appointed commissioner of the NWMP, he became a legend thanks to pulp fiction and movies. In the rapidly changing landscape of English-speaking Canada in the late nineteenth century, Canadians hungered for an orderly story of decency and civility that reflected well on their new country—and incidentally made American settlers look bad. Sam Steele fit the bill because he radiated broad-shouldered manliness and respect for hierarchy. It was an image that he himself assiduously promoted in his memoir *Forty Years in Canada*, published in 1940.

Steele is a compelling figure, although this macho Victorian is not a natural hero for the twenty-first century. Nevertheless, he was a fair-minded, hard-working man with a romantic gloss. The history of the NWMP is larger than the biography of Samuel Benfield Steele, but with his hunky pioneer origins he was typical of its early recruits. His father, Elmes Yelverton Steele, had been an officer in the British navy during the Napoleonic Wars; he came to Canada in 1832 to take up the free land grant to which decommissioned officers were eligible. Elmes Steele settled in Upper Canada's Simcoe County, a few kilometres west of Orillia. There, on the edge of the Canadian Shield, he laboriously cut a road through the bush, cleared the land, and built a house for the family he had brought from England. The area was remote, but it gradually filled up; many of the new neighbours were British navy and army veterans like Elmes Steele. I can imagine them all gathered around a fireplace on winter evenings, swapping war stories from their days in uniform back home. Elmes Steele emerged as a community leader: he donated land and paid for the construction of an Anglican church near his farm, was appointed a magistrate in 1833, and became colonel of the local militia. When the Rebellion of 1837 broke out in Upper Canada, Elmes and one of his sons turned out with the militia to suppress the uprising.

All these events occurred long before Sam's birth, which was probably in 1848. (The date is obscured by Sam's eagerness to lop a few years off his age. He wasn't short of male vanity.) By then, Elmes had served a term in the legislature, after being elected as "the Backwoodsman's Friend." Despite his rush to defend the Upper Canadian government in 1837, Elmes evidently had strong democratic instincts. However, politics soon lost its appeal, and he returned to farming. His first wife died, leaving him a widower with six children; when he was sixty-six, he married Ann MacIan Macdonald, aged nineteen. Sam was the oldest child in Elmes's second family; five more Steeles were born after him. When Sam was eleven, his mother died and he was sent off alone to live with his half-brother John, forty years his senior and now his father surrogate. Within a few years Elmes Steele had died too, aged eighty-five. Given that few immigrants during these years saw their fiftieth birthdays, this was a truly ripe old age.

Sam Steele's sense of duty developed early. He always felt responsible for his own siblings; throughout his life he kept in close touch with them, lent them money, and found them jobs. According to his biographer Rod Macleod, this "was one of the forces behind his drive to succeed." But his prospects were limited: he was a boy from the backwoods with the minimum of schooling and no influential contacts.

One choice was clear from an early age. Sam had a taste for the kind of adventures that the British novelist G. A. Henty would describe in books like *In Times of Peril: A Tale of India* and *By Sheer Pluck: A Tale of the Ashanti*

War. Sam Steele may never have read a Henty novel, but he would certainly have recognized the courageous, Christian, and chivalrous young heroes who stride through Henty's historical fiction: such stock characters were idealized within the British Empire's military and naval families. Sam always knew that he didn't want to be an Ontario farmer, scratching a living out of the rock-strewn fields of the Canadian Shield. A life in uniform was an obvious alternative.

However, Britain was now withdrawing its troops from Canada, and Canada had only a half-hearted force called the Sedentary Militia, which existed largely on paper. This was Sam's only chance. In the hope of qualifying for it, he enrolled in a three-month course of infantry instruction from a British regular when he was sixteen. His opportunity finally came in 1870, after trouble erupted at the Red River Settlement.

The Red River Rebellion had been sparked by the transfer of the huge Hudson's Bay Company landholdings, which included most of the northwestern quarter of the continent, to the new Dominion. Métis farmers and hunters, under their leader Louis Riel, feared they would lose control over their land and culture. They set up their own provincial government at Fort Garry to negotiate the settlement's relationship with a federal capital thousands of kilometres away. Riel and his supporters (mostly Roman Catholic and French-speaking) achieved their objective: Ottawa gave official recognition to a new, postage-stamp-sized province called Manitoba. But there had been an appalling cost to this achievement: the execution of Thomas Scott—the offensive English-speaking settler from Ontario who had opposed Riel—had inflamed passions in Ontario, especially among Protestant Conservatives, who demanded that Riel be tried for murder. Tempers flared.

Ottawa put out a call for volunteers from militia units to march west with the King's Royal Rifle Corps, a British unit under the command of Colonel Garnet Wolseley, a much-decorated Anglo-Irish officer with a reputation for fierce efficiency. Sam Steele's hand shot up. He was finally in uniform, as a private in the First (Ontario) Battalion of Rifles.

The Wolseley expedition was intended by Ottawa as a show of strength.

Sam Steele was eager for adventure; a life in uniform was preferable to the backbreaking work of a pioneer farmer on the Canadian Shield.

It would assert Ottawa's authority and Canadian sovereignty in the West, and squash any ideas among expansionist Minnesotans about moving onto the rich farmland around the Red and Assiniboine Rivers. But it was an ambitious and daunting proposition. How were the twelve hundred men, with tonnes of heavy supplies, to reach Manitoba? The Canadian Pacific Railway was still just a dream. All that existed was a long-abandoned fur trade loop.

Sam Steele was the kind of exuberant youngster who relished extreme challenges; today, he would be hiking up mountains and running rapids with a GoPro camera strapped to his forehead. The eight-hundred-kilometre route from the Lakehead to Red River led across boggy lakes, down foaming rivers, and through brush, forest, and swamp. While other men, appalled at the hardships, dropped their packs and fled across the American border, Sam didn't flinch. At each portage, he easily shouldered a barrel of pork or an arms chest, each of which weighed ninety-one kilograms, plus a tent weighing thirty-four kilograms, through clouds of mosquitoes and blackflies.[4] He enjoyed watching his muscles harden and his chest expand: all his life, he took pride in his stamina. (He padded his jacket in official photos, to enhance the impression of six-pack vigour.) He also got the grunt's-eye-view of army life that would prove invaluable. "I was better off without chevrons," he recalled, "and learned how to appreciate the trials of other men to an extent that I should never have been able to do had I been promoted."

The Wolseley expedition was magnificent—but, in the end, slightly ridiculous. By the time the soldiers reached Fort Garry, in August 1870, Riel had withdrawn and the Métis had left on their annual buffalo hunt. Most American settlers had returned south. Within a few weeks, Colonel Wolseley and his British regulars marched back east, then sailed home—the final stage in the British military withdrawal from Canada. They left behind fewer than a hundred ill-clad Canadian troops, shivering in an uncomfortable, chilly barracks at Fort Garry.

Some of the men had already decided to settle in Manitoba; others, including Steele, conscientiously carried out their duties while waiting impatiently for Ottawa to establish a professional Canadian army. But still Sir John A. shied away from spending money on soldiers while railway construction was draining his treasury. Steele decided that Manitoba was a dead end and made his way back to Ontario. Macdonald's government took a modest step forward by creating a handful of military training schools, manned by professionals, to train a volunteer militia. Steele signed up at a new artillery school at Kingston and was soon an instructor himself. But peacetime soldiering involved too much paperwork and not enough adventure.

Finally, in 1873, the prime minister announced a new police force for the Northwest. Steele's career frustrations were finally resolved. He was a perfect fit for the force's requirements, as specified in the North West Mounted Police Act: "of sound constitution, active and able-bodied, able to ride, of good character, able to read and write either the English or French language, and between the ages of 18 and 40 years." Major James Walsh, one of the force's new officers, appointed him a staff constable (the equivalent of a sergeant major in military terms) in "A" Division, a unit of fifty men. Aged twenty-five, he was the fortieth recruit to the force, the third to be sworn in,[5] and among the first 150 men who left Toronto in the fall of 1873, heading west before freeze-up in order to establish the force's own headquarters at Fort Garry.

Steele was better prepared than most of the recruits who marched alongside him, brawny young men desperate to escape from boring desk jobs or subsistence farms in Ontario and Quebec. He spoke a little French; he had more military training; he had already made the gruelling journey west; he had some inkling of the vast wilderness the new force was intended to police. During his service at Red River he had learned how to handle hot-tempered military rookies, and he had shown an unusual respect for the culture of the Métis peoples and others. Most important, there was nothing else he wanted to do.

＋〜＋

"Drill, drill, drill," a newly fledged Mountie wrote home from Manitoba in the winter of 1874. "Foot drill, rifle practice, guard mount, horseback, all fatigues. Breaking in my new mount isn't my idea of fun. Especially with Steele drilling. The man has no feelings. He drills four rides a day."[6]

If the North West Mounted Police was going to have credibility, it needed decent horses and horsemanship; Steele's first job was to ensure it had both. At the newly constructed headquarters at Lower Fort Garry, he was in charge of breaking the half-wild prairie broncos the force had purchased, training them, and instructing the riders, throughout the long, bitter winter. (When the temperature fell below minus thirty-eight degrees Celsius, training was cancelled for the benefit of horses, not men.) "The men were repeatedly thrown with great violence to the frozen ground," Steele wrote in his autobiography, "but no-one lost his nerve, they always 'had it with them.'"[7] NWMP records tell a different story. As Steele's biographer Rod Macleod points out, "By the spring, even with replacements from the local militia, there were only 120 men left from the original 150."[8]

The legend of Sam Steele, the toughest man in the troop, was starting to spread. He acquired the nickname "Smoothbore Sam," reflecting his artillery background, his hardness, and his bellowing parade-ground style.[9]

The federal government's plan was that the new police force, its numbers swelled by a second contingent from central Canada, would ride westward toward the Rocky Mountains, establishing a series of posts in the unsettled lands as they went. The destination was Fort Whoop-Up, the notorious whisky post at the junction of the Belly and Oldman Rivers (the site of Lethbridge in present-day Alberta). Politicians bragged that they were going to "tame the West," although for the Siksika (Blackfoot) and other peoples who had lived on the prairies for centuries, the West was a congenial homeland that the influx of Europeans was rapidly destroying. In June 1874, twenty-six-year-old Steele led the Lower Fort Garry contingent to a rendezvous just north of the North Dakota border to meet the second contingent of 201 men, 16 officers, and 244 horses. There the force established its first full camp.

There was a surprise addition to the contingent from Toronto—all part of the spin: twenty-one-year-old Henri Julien, an illustrator and reporter with the Montreal-based *Canadian Illustrated News*, "Canada's Leading Picture Periodical." The force's first commissioner, Colonel George Arthur French, gave Julien a horse and full kit, so he could send home sketches and descriptions of the brilliant exploits that the force would undoubtedly perform.

The expedition did not start brilliantly: a severe thunderstorm created chaos in the camp on the very first night. As sheet lightning lit up the sky and tents collapsed in the driving rain, terrified horses stampeded out of the corral, injuring guards and destroying wagons as they galloped south. Julien's first sketches to appear in the *Canadian Illustrated News* showed rearing horses and men running in all directions. It was an inauspicious start to what would come to be termed, with macho bravado, "the Great March West."

The truth about the Great March from today's Winnipeg to Lethbridge is that it was ill-equipped and badly organized. Over the next weeks, Colonel French's troops picked their dusty way through the burnt-up desert strewn with buffalo bones in baking temperatures, travelling at a far slower pace than their officers had anticipated. The column, straggling over four kilometres, included polished brass guns, ammunition wagons, field kitchens, laden ox-drawn wagons, cattle, mowing machines, plows, and anything else required for both battling lawbreakers and building forts. The travellers faced prairie fires, quicksands, supply and water shortages, a plague of locusts, and virulent mosquitoes that invaded, in the words of Julien, "your eyes, your nose, your ears.... If you open your mouth to curse at them, they troop in. They insinuate themselves under your clothes, down your shirt collar, up your shirt sleeve cuffs, between the buttons of your shirt bosom.... They send a dog howling off in pain. They tease horses to desperation."

By late July, so many men, horses, and cattle were sick that Colonel French decided to split the column. Sam Steele, hungry for adventure, discovered that he would miss the action at Fort Whoop-Up: he had to escort the weakest animals and sickest men to Edmonton. "We were a disconsolate lot when we saw the force depart on their long trek," he recorded forty years later.[10] It was small comfort that, after the gruelling journey north to Edmonton, Sam's commanding officer, Inspector Jarvis, reported, "Sergeant Major Steele has been undeviating in his efforts to assist me, and he has also done the manual labour of at least two men."[11]

When the main column reached Fort Whoop-Up, Colonel French discovered that the traders had already fled. He directed his attention to building new police posts, first Fort Macleod, originally on an island in the Oldman River, then Fort Walsh and Fort Calgary.

Farther north in Edmonton, Steele dutifully followed orders while aching to get back in the spotlight. His chance came a couple of years later when he was put in charge of the escort and logistical support for a major treaty signing: Treaty 6, between the federal government and more than fifty nations (predominantly Plains and Wood Cree). The treaty covered a huge territory from today's Manitoba-Saskatchewan border to the Rockies. Steele ensured that this important occasion had appropriate gravitas: he even rustled up a brass band for the ceremonies.

Over the next two decades, the NWMP established itself as far more than a simple police force in the West: it filled civil, military, and legal functions. It suppressed the whisky trade, enforced agreements with First Nations, supervised the mail service, dealt with wildcat strikes by railway workers, administered the law among the settlers, and, most important, kept the peace. In the late 1870s Steele's immediate boss, Major Walsh, protected Sitting Bull and his Sioux people when they fled north across the border from the U.S. Army, and he eventually persuaded them to return south. In 1885 the NWMP helped quell the Northwest Rebellion led by Louis Riel, during which twelve officers were killed and eleven wounded during the Battle of Duck Lake. (Five Métis were also killed, and several wounded including Louis Riel's right-hand man, Gabriel Dumont.) By 1885 a thousand Mounties were serving in the prairies and the foothills of the Rockies, with the Union Jack flying over their log forts.

The story of the North West Mounted Police's first decade was pockmarked with problems, as historians have pointed out. The Mounties weren't quite the well-groomed, muscular keeners that their publicity machine has always suggested. In his triumphant dispatches home from the Great March, the reporter Henri Julien did not mention poor training, desertions, shortages of supplies, breaches of discipline, pay problems, and heavy drinking within the force. Not everything that the Mounties bestowed on prairie nations was benevolent: they brought venereal infections and viral diseases.[12] According to a medical board examination held in 1874 at Fort Garry, "two men recruited in the previous year were blind in the right eye, five suffered from acute heart disease ... one from tuberculosis ... and one from a fracture of the upper part of a leg—all of which conditions existed previous to enlistment."

Nevertheless, the force did an incredible job of keeping the peace. While the army or vigilante squads ruled by the gun on the American front, the NWMP ensured that the law was applied equally to all, Indigenous person or settler, in the Canadian West. Police officers hauled before the courts as many non-Indigenous persons accused of crimes against Indigenous people as Indigenous persons accused of crimes against non-

Indigenous people. (South of the border, all-white juries routinely refused to find settlers guilty, however blatant their lawbreaking.) The force ensured that there were no massacres of First Nations as there had been in the United States, and that the land treaties were observed. When the Siksika chief Isapo-Muxika (Crowfoot) signed Treaty 7 in 1877, he did so because, in his words, "the Mounted Police protected us as the feathers of the bird protect it from the frosts of winter."

↜↝

During these years, Sam Steele's reputation grew alongside the force's. He steadily climbed the ranks, and by 1883 he was a senior officer. The same year, he dealt with a threatened strike by CPR labourers, then averted conflict on the Ontario-Manitoba border. His specialty was an iron fist in a velvet glove: calm and tough. According to his biographer Macleod, Steele "emerged as one of the chief trouble shooters of the Mounted Police; a man who could act coolly and decisively in an emergency."

All the milestones of western history, as defined by old-fashioned Canadian historians, featured an appearance by Sam Steele. In the 1885 Northwest Rebellion, Steele led a mixed group of mounted police and local militia, nicknamed "Steele's Scouts," in pursuit of the Cree chief Mistahimaskwa (Big Bear). Although Steele was not present at the crucial Battle of Batoche, a magnificent sketch of him appeared on the front page of the *Canadian Pictorial and Illustrated War News*, which was eastern Canada's main source of information about the rebellion. Within months, he was on the fringes of another famous image: the ceremonial driving of the Canadian Pacific Railway's Last Spike at Craigellachie, British Columbia, which connected the sections of track laid from the West with those laid from the East across the Rockies. Superintendent Sam Steele had been chosen to represent the NWMP, and he climbed aboard the first transcontinental train ever to run in Canada. It steamed through Eagle Pass, picking up speed as it went, roaring up and down hills, plunging through tunnels. Steele was in the crowded last car, which whipped around the sharp curves. Even this joyride enhanced his reputation: he was one of only three VIPs who didn't throw up.[13]

Whisky traders, settlers, and the disappearance of the buffalo destroyed Indigenous peoples' traditional way of life in the Northwest. The NWMP strove to protect them.

His next assignment was in British Columbia, where he confirmed his reputation as an adroit negotiator by settling a bitter dispute between a local British-born landowner and the Ktunaxa people around the Kootenay River. He also built a particularly sturdy NWMP post, which was immediately named Fort Steele; today it is a popular tourist attraction. By now Superintendent Steele was one of the force's most respected veterans, and he was given command of one of the force's largest posts in the West: Fort Macleod, south of Calgary. Southern Alberta was still fairly wild. A notice in a local hotel read, "When guests find themselves or their luggage thrown over the fence, they may consider that they have received notice to quit."[14] Smoothbore Sam soon had the place running with what he himself described as "monotonous regularity."[15]

Steele, aged forty, was ready to settle down, but men far outnumbered women among the Mounties and settlers in the West. However, at Fort Macleod, he met Marie Elizabeth Lotbinière Harwood, a twenty-nine-year-old Quebecer who was the niece of a colleague and the daughter of a Conservative MP from Quebec. For many men of Sam's WASP background, the idea of marrying a French-speaking Roman Catholic would have been dangerously unconventional. Sam Steele ignored religious and ethnic taboos and married Marie in January 1890 at the Harwood family home outside Montreal.

The best part of this story is that the newlyweds went to New York City for their honeymoon. There the fire department greeted Steele like a conquering hero, with a parade of sixty engines. Mountie mythology was germinating: reporters from western newspapers like the *Fort Benton Record* (Montana) had spread the news of the NWMP's success at managing the Sioux and controlling the whisky trade. A Mountie stereotype was starting to emerge that supposedly said something about the Canadian identity. And for Americans, Sam Steele *was* that stereotype.

✦

How do we define our national identity? A standard Canadian response is to say what we are not: we hide behind other national stereotypes, as in "less brash than Americans," "less class-conscious than the English," "less clannish than the Chinese," "not as fussy as the French." Dig deeper and ask about uniquely Canadian qualities, and it is impossible to find a one-size-fits-all answer. Many Canadians discover their national identity only when they are travelling abroad, and a random mention of Tim Hortons, the Habs, Alice Munro, or Arcade Fire prompts a jab of homesickness. If there are any shared national characteristics, we prefer to acknowledge them in self-deprecating jokes. "How do you get fifty Canadians out of a swimming pool on a hot day? Politely ask them to leave." "What is the difference between a Canadian and a canoe? A canoe tips."

Nationalism is a relatively recent phenomenon. In Europe until about three hundred years ago, people felt loyalty to their families, their religions, their regions, or perhaps a particular leader, but not to their nations. That began to change only with the political convulsions of the American and French Revolutions, when revolutionary leaders invented the idea of a national spirit. It gathered momentum in the nineteenth century, when Europe's map was being redrawn and states got larger and larger. An appeal to "nationalism" proved a powerful social and political motivator as first Italy and then Germany were unified, and the various ethnic groups jammed together within the Ottoman and Austro-Hungarian Empires began to agitate for autonomy.

The whole idea of a "national identity," then, is a deliberate invention. As one of the great scholars of national identity, the late Benedict Anderson, pointed out, governments and leaders construct "imagined communities" by adopting anthems, flags, myths, and other symbols. Anderson argues that a nation is always a socially constructed community, imagined by the people who perceive themselves as part of that group. "It is imagined because the members of even the smallest nation will never know most of their fellow-members, meet them, or even hear of them, yet in the minds of each lives the image of their communion."[16] That "imagined community" is a source of enormous strength to its members.

I grew up in Britain in the 1950s and 1960s, and I absorbed a sturdy sense of my British identity. But Britain has changed dramatically since then and the glue has thinned. Today it has a less homogeneous population, and the United Kingdom is a lot less united. In 2014 a referendum on whether Scotland should become an independent country was only narrowly defeated. Yet there remains a clear sense of "Britishness": the English, Scottish, Irish, or Welsh identity is nested under the Union Jack umbrella. It is a type of muscular nationalism rarely encountered in Canada—particularly today, when one in five of our fellow citizens was, like me, born outside the country. For all the gradual fragmentation of Britain, its inhabitants take pride in their shared sense of humour and taste for soccer and sausages.

Canada, as a relatively new country, has struggled to construct its "imagined community." Even though Macdonald and Cartier were piecing the new Dominion of Canada together at the exact same time as countries like Italy, Germany, and the United States were inventing unique national identities, the two founding fathers probably never discussed the idea. George-Étienne Cartier's idea of political rather than ethnic nationality worked against the whole notion. How could you build emotional ties between people who had only their citizenship in common, rather than their religion, language, or country of birth? Given the nature of Canada's origins and history, post-1867 leaders didn't have much to work with when they mused about a pan-Canadian national identity. There were no national heroes, no anthem, songs, or sports. In the run-up to Confederation, there had been no bloody struggle in which to root a founding mythology.

In fact, the new country could not have been less culturally cohesive. Scots-born John A. Macdonald repeated several times his boast: "A British subject I was born—a British subject I will die." (This wasn't just Scots pride: he was also making the point that he would keep the infant Dominion out of the grasp of the United States.) In the 1890s a New Brunswick logger, a Montreal housekeeper, an Ontario train driver, and a prairie farmer had almost nothing in common beyond the fact that they all lived in the new Dominion. Such nationalism as existed was fragile, artificial, and deeply racist. It didn't include Indigenous people or the thousands of Chinese labourers who had helped build the railway. Outside French Canada, it reflected the prejudices and values of class-conscious white Anglo-Saxon Protestants in Ontario. The deep divide between Roman Catholics and Protestants was exacerbated by separate schooling, and Irish immigrants were regarded with disdain.

However, Dominion citizens would soon hear about an institution that not only was unique to their country but also promoted values they liked to imagine were typically Canadian: stern rectitude and deference to authority. Outsiders recognized the North West Mounted Police's achievements and romanticized Sam Steele's barrel-chested authority for some time before most of Steele's fellow countrymen paid much attention to the "Riders of the Plains." The Canadian habit of discovering talent only after it has been recognized elsewhere is a perennial theme in our history.

✢

By the early 1890s, the NWMP had fulfilled its original mandate to establish law and order in the West, but it was the target of frequent attacks, in particular from the Liberal Party in Ottawa. The Liberals objected not only to its expense but also to the very existence of a centrally controlled police force. They had heard the rumours of heavy drinking, desertions, and breaches of discipline, and wanted to know why local militias in the West couldn't enforce the law, as they did in eastern Canada. One particularly obstreperous Ontario MP argued, "The Indians would be perfectly quiet if they were not constantly harassed by an army of Mounted Policemen. . . . I say it is a standing shame and a disgrace upon the civilization of this country that we have to keep 1000 men to preserve the peace in this Christian country, in this noonday of the nineteenth century."[17] Under this pressure, the governing Conservatives reluctantly shrank the force.

That Ontario blusterer was kidding himself: a volunteer militia would never have worked out west. The population in the newly settled regions was so transient that when a couple of towns tried to set up militia units in the 1880s, the units evaporated within a year because most volunteers moved away.[18] The need for a permanent, paid police force with comprehensive powers and wide jurisdiction was dramatically illustrated at the end of the 1890s, during the Klondike Gold Rush. When an American miner found gold on a tributary of the Yukon River in the Dominion's remote northern wilderness, he set off a stampede that would bring a hundred thousand gold seekers from all over the world into an area virtually untouched by Canadian law. Thanks to the NWMP, the epicentre of the frenzy—Dawson City—never degenerated into a violent, corrupt mining camp such as American gold rushes had spawned. This gold rush would be the making of the Mounties—and of Samuel Benfield Steele.

Steele had spent the early 1890s in charge of Fort Macleod, enjoying family life (he and Marie had two daughters and a son during these years) and polishing his image as Smallbore Sam. Mindful of his own experiences in the ranks, he improved pay, food, and accommodation, but he also drank too much (his boss advised him to be more discreet) and according to Robert Stewart, author of the admiring biography *Sam Steele: Lion of the Frontier*, he drilled the men morning, noon, and night. One veteran would recall, "Some men will stand almost anything, but there were twenty-four who couldn't or wouldn't stand old Sam and his methods—for that number deserted in one month."[19]

However, Steele's subordinates knew that this fierce disciplinarian never asked more of them than he asked of himself, and that he was brutally straightforward (unlike several of his fellow officers). He threatened the principal of a residential school on the Blood Reserve that if the man continued to lock the students in at night, Steele would charge him with manslaughter if any child died in a fire.[20] Today his threat seems negligible: now that we know the horrendous cruelties perpetrated in those residential schools, we wish he had closed the school down. But the past is a different country. And Steele's inflexible principles, which got him labelled as "difficult," were probably why he was not promoted beyond the rank of superintendent for several years.

Was Steele destined to spend the rest of his career as a heavy-drinking martinet on the parade ground? It certainly seemed that way—until a telegram arrived on January 29, 1898, ordering him to report for duty in the Yukon, twenty-five hundred kilometres away. He and Superintendent Bowen Perry were to organize the immediate construction of border posts at the highest points of the White and Chilkoot Passes, the gateways into the Yukon. Once spring arrived, thousands of gold seekers would surge north over the St. Elias Mountains, through these passes, and into the headwaters of the Yukon River, en route to the Klondike.

Samuel Benfield Steele responded to this challenge with the speed of a dog chasing a squirrel. Within seventeen days, he had made the journey up the coast to Skagway, an American town at the foot of the White Pass. He pronounced it "about the roughest place in the world" and got to work.

Steele and Perry faced two problems. The first was physical: the mountain passes were characterized by blizzards, avalanches, lack of supplies, lawlessness, and temperatures as low as minus fifty degrees Celsius. The second was territorial: the Americans claimed that the border was fifty kilometres inland, beyond these treacherous passes.

It is hard to avoid *Boy's Own Annual* gusto when retelling the story of Steele in the Yukon. He and Perry were undaunted by constant snowstorms and the challenge of hauling all supplies, including the firewood, eleven kilometres up the mountain. They successfully raised the Union Jack flag at the highest point of each pass and supervised the construction of proper guard posts. Since possession is nine points of the law, those mountain outposts secured the disputed territory for Canada despite American objections. By the time the first surge of stampeders approached the guard posts, the Mounties were ready to check their kit and charge duty as high as 25 percent on all items, including their underwear, not purchased in Canada. Since four out of five of the gold seekers were Americans, the mountains echoed with cries of outrage. According to Stewart, "The protests met with that implacable courtesy for which the Mounted Police was famous."[21]

Particularly important was the NWMP's insistence that every prospector must carry a year's provisions with him. Given that there was nowhere to purchase items on the long journey to Dawson and constant shortages in the mining town itself, this was not just prudent: it was paternalistic— and very Canadian.

Next, Steele moved across the mountains and down to Bennett Lake, where stampeders eagerly awaited ice-out on the Yukon River so they could sail downriver to the gold fields. Tents and huts stretched along the shores of the lake as far as he could see; the valley rang with the noise of hammers and whipsaws as the travellers cobbled together boats for the voyage. Bars, cafés, hotels, churches, bakeries, and gambling dens had all sprung up in this town of ten thousand speculators, many of whom had no clue how to survive in the North.

Steele spent the next two months creating order out of the chaos. He banished thieves and crooks back across the mountains, and he and his men distributed food, blankets, money, and clothes to those in distress. They advised on boat construction, settled disputes, and informed the next of kin, thousands of kilometres away, when some poor soul died of typhoid, scurvy, pneumonia, or just plain exhaustion.

By now, the new Liberal government in Ottawa, headed by Sir Wilfrid Laurier, had realized that anarchy threatened Dawson City. The mining camp was sited on a mud flat at the junction of the Klondike River and the mighty Yukon that had been a seasonal fishing ground for a handful of Hän Hwëch'in people until 1896. Now hundreds of gold diggers (miners and camp followers) were living there, and several thousand more were en route. Unless the Canadian government could police the remote settlement, it would not only risk people's lives and lose control of this resource town: it would also forfeit all the royalties it could claim on Canadian gold. The minister in charge of the Yukon, Clifford Sifton, increased the size of the force in the North and gave it a separate command structure. Within months, Superintendent Steele was in charge of a force that constituted a third of the entire NWMP.

The situation was made for a man with an iron fist, with or without a velvet glove. "Nothing could have suited Steele better," comments Macleod.[22] "Not only could he run the police as he saw fit, but the isolation of the Yukon allowed him to make up laws and regulations as necessary." Steele personified the "Peace, Order and good Government" promise of the British North America Act.

On May 29, the ice on the Yukon River finally broke up, and the flotilla of homemade canoes, skiffs, paddlewheelers, scows, and Chinese junks took to the water. Steele never forgot "the wonderful exodus of boats. . . . I went up the hill behind the office to see the start, and at one time counted 800 boats under sail in the [twenty-kilometre length] of Lake Bennett." But it was an incredibly dangerous journey, with foaming rapids where the water was squeezed between sheer black cliffs. By the time the NWMP contingent arrived at Miles Canyon, one of the most terrifying parts of the voyage, 150 boats had already been smashed and five people drowned in a single day. The death toll would have been even higher if the Mounties already stationed there had not dragged several people out of the churning waters.

Superintendent Steele was horrified when he reached Miles Canyon. Standing on the cliffs at the top of the canyon and deploying his best parade-ground bellow, he summoned everybody to listen to him. Then he laid down the law, although he had no legal authority to do so. He announced that no boat would be allowed to shoot the rapids until the

Mounties were satisfied that it was not overloaded and that the skipper was competent. If a skipper were judged incompetent, the Mounties would insist that he take a qualified pilot with him. No women or children would be allowed in a boat: they could all walk along the riverbank to the bottom of the Whitehorse Rapids eight kilometres away. The penalty for non-compliance was a hundred dollars. Thanks to Steele's rules, in subsequent weeks not a single life was lost as seven thousand boats ran the rapids.

Steele proved equally forceful when he took over the policing of Dawson City a few months later. Dawson was squalid, chaotic, and crowded with about fifteen thousand residents; another twenty-five thousand people were working the creeks. Steele squelched through "deposits of every imaginable kind of filth" on his patrols and risked typhoid because there were no drains and only three public toilets. (One universal aspect of the past that is rarely mentioned is that most places and people smelled foul.) Saloons, bars, brothels, and gambling houses operated day and night, and there was an army of pimps, prostitutes, gamblers, and thieves—"desperate characters," as he described them. Steele had only thirteen Mounties with him in this "San Francisco of the North," but he was undeterred. "[We] have our hands full and there will [be] a general clean-up of the Augean stable which in this case can be swept properly. The state of affairs is bad and could not possibly be worse but those who have the task of restoring credit to our country will spare none who have displaced it."[23]

He immediately expanded the jail, stepped up law enforcement, and put prisoners to work collecting refuse, washing dishes, shovelling snow, and cutting wood for the barracks' stoves. He insisted that all commercial establishments must close every Sunday: the only sound to be heard on Front Street on the Lord's Day was the Salvation Army band. He ordered that no firearms should be taken into Front Street's bars and saloons—an extraordinary step given the town's Wild West atmosphere, but an interesting preview of the widening gulf between Canadian and American views of gun control. He also asked for help from the Yukon Field Force, a Canadian army battalion 250 kilometres away. Seventy soldiers sailed down the Yukon River to support the NWMP detachment.

Each dawn, Dawson residents could watch the burly figure of "Colonel Steele," as he was always known, doing the rounds of government offices and city limits. Every day, lawbreakers dragged before his judicial hearings would watch him stroke his walrus moustache before he curtly delivered sentence: usually several days' work on the NWMP woodpile. By the end of the year, he reported to Ottawa, "in proportion to the population, crime is not very prevalent, and in fact the crime sheets of the Yukon Territory would compare favourably with those of any part of the British Empire."

Steele described his life in Dawson City in diaries and in long missives to his wife, Marie, whom he had left behind in Fort Macleod. Today, those papers are preserved in the University of Alberta's Bruce Peel Special Collections. The writing is often indecipherable. Many of the letters were soaked by rain or melting snow while Dawson's bags of outgoing mail were transported by dogsled over the mountains. But those that survive reveal a man at the top of his game: working like a dog and revelling in his unbridled authority. "Liquor has not passed my lips since I have been in the Yukon nor will it do so," he bragged to his wife. "I have no desire for it."[24] Steele had total confidence in his mission: "I know a lot of the hucksters in this country will hate the N.W.M. Police but . . . we have right on our side and our motto, Maintiens le Droit, will prevail."[25] NWMP officers were not only the sole source of authority; they were also trusted. Dawsonites "consider us encyclopedias of knowledge and come to us for everything."

The only sorrow in the superintendent's life was Marie Steele's absence, and his affectionate letters give us a rare insight into the emotions of a Victorian patriarch raised to suppress his feelings. Underneath that stuffed shirt beat the heart of a man who wanted the kind of family stability he himself had not enjoyed as a child. "My own sweet wife," he wrote. "How I long to clasp you in my arms, my own love, how I miss you. You are in my mind day after day."[26] In the letters, we can also glimpse his swelling sense of national pride. He asked Marie to tell her uncle, a federal politician, to "assure Sir Wilfrid Laurier that if the honour of the country depends on our behaviour in the Yukon it is perfectly safe."[27]

Steele loved the North but hated being separated from his wife, Marie, and their three children.

Sam Steele spent less than two years in the Yukon, but those months made him the most famous Mountie on the continent. Most of those who experienced his harsh regime were Americans; instead of chafing under Steele's iron fist, they were grateful to him for protecting their interests in Dawson's hurly-burly atmosphere.

Steele himself was well aware of his growing reputation, as scrapbooks in the Steele Papers attest. The books, probably compiled by Marie Steele, are stuffed with magazine and newspaper articles that breathlessly describe NWMP heroism. Many are from Canadian publications, but the most effusive are American. Some described the whole force, such as a *McClure's Magazine* piece entitled "Soldier Police of the Northwest" that ran in the summer of 1899. "How could a force of 750 men guard half a continent, peopled by warlike Indians, so well that a white man may walk from one end of it to the other, unarmed and alone, with greater security than he could pass from Castle Garden to Harlem in New York City?" asked the author, W. A. Fraser.[28] Others put Steele at centre stage and eulogized his dictatorial style, which, had it been displayed on their own frontier, would have enraged speculators and cowboys.

Chicago's *Sunday Chronicle* of May 14, 1899, described him as "a whole army unto himself. He was born to rule in a country where he must become a dictator for he . . . is far away from assistance, from advice and from supplies." New York's *Success Magazine* ran a long profile of Steele two months later: "Since his arrival in the gold district he has been practically king of the Klondike; his word has been law; and his rulings final and beyond appeal. Nine-tenths of the population are glad that it is so. The lawless tenth cowers and glowers, but dare not while Steele and his splendid police rule the Yukon."

An early biographer, Christopher Reed, compared him to a benevolent rajah. "His large presence, his big gruff voice, his dominant personality, his sense of honour, fair play and justice, and a little twinkle in his eye, showing his sense of humour, made him 'It' with a large capital I."[29]

Sam Steele and the Klondike Gold Rush were only a small part of the NWMP story. Between 1890 and 1940, novelists would produce well over 150 Mountie books.[30] Authors like the Canadian Ralph Connor (pen name of the Reverend Charles Gordon) and the American James Oliver Curwood spun stirring yarns in which manly heroes in scarlet tunics used their common sense and compassion to do the "right" thing. Fictional Mounties exuded fairness, perseverance, and self-control as they brought peace, order, and good government to the wilderness—just like Superintendent Steele in the Yukon. Steele's name became synonymous with frontier justice and pluck. In 1906 Frank Baum, the American author who created the *Wizard of Oz* series, even borrowed Steele's name for a rousing story entitled *Sam Steele's Adventures on Land and Sea*.[31]

In 1912 Sir Wilfrid Laurier wrote to Ralph Connor to thank him for the gift of *Corporal Cameron of the Northwest Mounted Police*. The former prime minister recognized the power of the Canadian stereotype that Connor was promoting and said that he found his books "particularly attractive . . . because they will preserve a special phase of our national history, and customs which are rapidly passing away."

The Mountie legend got another boost as the movie industry took off. NWMP officers would appear as central characters in over 250 feature films, including *Riders of the Plains* (1910), *Nomads of the North* (1920), and *Rose Marie* (1936). As Pierre Berton observed, "The movie Mountie was almost invariably brave, noble, honourable, courteous, kind, and trustworthy—all the standard Boy Scout qualities to go with the hat."[32]

In today's terms, the Mounties had become an important part of Canada's brand, and the NWMP itself was busy helping to build it. In the early twentieth century, the British author Arthur Lincoln Haydon (editor of *The Empire Annual for Boys*) would spend several weeks as a guest of the Mounties' top brass, before going on to publish *The Riders of the Plains: Adventures and Romance with the North-West Mounted Police* in 1910. Haydon didn't stint on Hentyesque hyperbole as he described this "fine force, which has maintained the best tradition of the British race in doing its work silently, unostentatiously, and efficiently. . . . How this splendid and unique Force has justified its existence in carrying out its remarkable duties must ever remain one of the Romances of our Empire."[33] Haydon had had significant help in reaching this conclusion. In his preface he gave particular thanks to "Major-General Sir George A. French, KCMG," who had "courteously [revised] the chapters dealing with the history of the corps." The Mounties' first commissioner had proven himself a master spin doctor.

Sam Steele's reputation also benefited from a judicious cleanup. Mentions of his heavy drinking and bully behaviour on the parade ground were carefully buried. In 1927 an American writer named T. Morris Longstreth published a book entitled *The Silent Force: Scenes from the Life of the Mounted Police of Canada*.[34] Longstreth never met Steele, but he interviewed many older NWMP veterans who had served with him. Longstreth's book was never less than admiring of Steele: even Sam's drinking, as recalled by his colleagues, was described as heroic. "Steele's ability to drink was the height of regimental envy; a quart bottle was the measure of his nightcap; yet, however inapposite an ideal such a figure might present on the Sabbath-school platform, to the men in the ranks the sight was more instructive, more inspiring, than even texts from Moses or Isaiah." Yet this passage was eliminated from the second printing of *The Silent Force.*[35] Sam's son, Harwood Steele, was outraged at the suggestion that his father was ever less than sober, and he threatened a lawsuit. He also lined up an impressive collection of distinguished former mounted policemen who were prepared to swear that his father was not a drinker, although some of the statements were quite carefully phrased.[36]

We can tut-tut today about such manipulation of facts (and authors). But there is no question that the NWMP played a crucial role in establishing the Canadian rule of law on the prairies. It also laid the foundation for Canada's image as a well-governed country drenched in peace and order.

꧁

The Mountie saga did not end completely happily for either Samuel Benfield Steele or the force itself. In September 1899, Steele was shocked to receive a telegram from Ottawa summoning him home. He was being transferred, reputedly for resisting pressure from the Liberal government to give plum jobs to political cronies. Dawson residents were so aghast that the local newspaper petitioned the federal government to cancel the transfer. The petition failed. Virtually the whole town turned out to cheer Steele as he boarded a steamer, and the miners presented him with a bag of gold dust. It was obvious that Steele would never achieve his ultimate ambition, commissioner of the NWMP, and he never wore the scarlet tunic again.

However, other opportunities came his way. In 1900 he donned khaki and took command of Strathcona's Horse, a cavalry unit privately raised by the Canadian Pacific Railway tycoon Lord Strathcona to fight in the Second Boer War in South Africa. He officially retired from the NWMP in 1903 but continued to be known throughout Canada as "Steele of the Mounties." He commanded a division of the South African Constabulary for several years, then returned to Canada in 1907 as a senior officer in the Canadian military. Although he was sixty-eight when the First World War broke out in 1914, he lobbied to see action in France. He spent most of the war running a training camp for Canadian soldiers at Shorncliffe, in southern England; in 1917, he was forced into retirement. A knighthood helped soften the blow, but Steele himself felt unappreciated by the country of his birth.

A few weeks after the armistice was signed on November 11, 1918, Sir Sam Steele died in England, probably of complications caused by diabetes.[37] There were two funerals. First, his coffin was accompanied through London by a long military parade led by Royal North West Mounted Police officers (the "Royal" had been added in 1904) who were awaiting transport back to Canada. Then the coffin was shipped across the Atlantic because Steele had asked to be buried in Winnipeg.

And here is one of the great ironies of our history. By the time Steele's coffin arrived in Manitoba in 1919, the Winnipeg General Strike was in full swing. Outraged by massive unemployment and inflation, thirty thousand workers (many of them veterans) were demanding better wages and working conditions and the right to collective bargaining. The city had ground to a halt and there were riots on Main Street. Unsympathetic newspaper editors, politicians, and employers raged that the strikers were "alien scum"—or worse, Bolsheviks—and the federal government ordered them back to work. The young Tommy Douglas watched the Royal North West Mounted Police enforce the order.

But then there was a pause in the conflict. A hush fell over the city as the largest funeral procession ever seen in western Canada passed along Portage Avenue: silent strikers watched a riderless black horse, with shiny black boots in the stirrups, clip-clop past them. Next came the hearse bearing the body of Major-General Sir Samuel Steele, KCMG, on its way to St. John's Cemetery.

The pause was brief; two days later, the Mounties broke up a peaceful protest march. Tempers erupted and two of the Mounties were pulled off their horses; others then drew their guns and fired volleys into the crowd. Twenty-nine strikers were wounded and one man killed, while the Mounties cleared the streets with clubs and baseball bats.

The way that the force handled the Winnipeg strike put the Mounties in a different, more sinister light. Instead of continuing the inspirational story of men like Sam Steele building a law-abiding nation, the police force started to be seen as an instrument of coercion, siding with elites against ordinary Canadians, crushing working-class organizations, and discriminating against women, gay people, and minorities. This version of RCMP history has particular resonance in Quebec, where the former RCMP Security Service engaged in illegal activities in the 1970s, including burning a barn and stealing documents from the separatist Parti Québécois. As the historian Michael Dawson observes, "These two 'Stories of the RCMP'— both woven from factual evidence—offer very different versions of the Force's past."[38]

At the same time, Sam Steele's fame faded. A group of his friends had commissioned a death mask as a first step toward securing a statue, but the monument never materialized. After four years of slaughter in the trenches, Canadians had no time for walrus moustaches, spit 'n' polish, and Victorian values. The death mask lies in the vaults of Calgary's Glenbow Museum. In the words of Rod Macleod, "He was like one of those organisms so perfectly adapted to their environment that a change in external conditions results in extinction." Steele's reputation suffered the same fate as *Tyrannosaurus rex*.

But the image of Mountie incorruptibility and the sense of fair play lingered on in the popular Canadian imagination. It was revived in the 1990s television series *Due South* (broadcast in forty-seven countries by the summer of 1995), in which a handsome, square-jawed, polite Mountie upheld the values of peace, order, and good government. It was rekindled in the outrage that erupted in 1995 when the Walt Disney Corporation bought the rights to RCMP memorabilia, which some Canadians regarded as a sellout of Canadian values to an American corporation. The image incorporates more than a whiff of moral superiority and anti-American smugness, but it is firmly rooted. The RCMP's reputation may have suffered at various times in the past 150 years, but its achievements are part of the texture of our history and identity.

Today, the force remains the most important police force in Canada, enforcing federal laws throughout the country. Drug trafficking, commercial and organized crime, counterfeiting, border integrity, counterterrorism, security for VIPs . . . In addition to these federal responsibilities, the force also provides front-line policing in eight of the provinces, all three territories, more than 190 municipalities, and 184 Indigenous communities.

Outsiders have always regarded Mounties as preeminent symbols of Canada. After my first sighting of red serge, as a child at an English agricultural fair, I would catch sight of RCMP units riding down Pall Mall on BBC newscasts of ceremonial occasions in London. There would be a commentary (often from Richard Dimbleby) that included the information that the Royal Canadian Mounted Police had supplied the Queen with her glossy black horse.

Then, in 1982, I became a Canadian citizen—and met a real live Mountie at my citizenship ceremony. Black boots gleaming, face impassive, he might have been Samuel Benfield Steele asserting the rule of Canadian law in the Yukon. Instead, he stood smartly to attention as the citizenship judge administered the oath of citizenship and welcomed thirty of us to our new country. English was not the first language of most of my fellow newcomers, but we all recognized the Mountie thanks to calendars, travel brochures, and citizenship booklets. Even when life is less orderly, government is less admired, and police are regarded with suspicion, this member of Canada's unique national institution reinforced for the newly fledged citizens the idealized Canadian brand.

CHAPTER 3

Looking Inward, Looking Outward

Emily Carr and Canada's Vast Canvas

There is something bigger than fact: the underlying spirit, all it stands for, the mood, the vastness, the wildness ... the eternal big spaceness of it. Oh the West! I'm of it and I love it.

— Emily Carr, journal entry (1927)

We may not believe in totems, but we believe in our country; and if we approach our work as the Indian did with his singleness of purpose and determination to strive for the big thing that means Canada herself, and not hamper ourselves by wondering if our things will sell, or if they will please the public or bring us popularity or fame, but busy ourselves by trying to get near to the heart of things, however crude our work may be, it is liable to be more sincere and genuine.

— Emily Carr, *Modern and Indian Art* (1929)

The work of Emily Carr and the circumstances in which it was achieved are unique in Canada.

— Lawren Harris, "The Paintings and Drawings of Emily Carr" (1945)

George-Étienne Cartier and Sam Steele are classic Canadian heroes: nation builders with robust egos. Thanks to men like them, by the end of the nineteenth century, Canadians had a sturdy political system, a unique law enforcement institution, and a dawning awareness of nationhood.

Everything was going well in the young Dominion: railways snaked across the map, linking scattered settlements as a decades-long depression ended. Liberal leader Wilfrid Laurier, who became prime minister in 1896, was a silver-tongued promoter of harmony who managed to smooth over friction between Quebec and the other provinces. The financial capital of the country, Montreal, hummed with money deals. In the rapidly expanding city of Toronto, sharp-elbowed entrepreneurs built factories, department stores, and insurance companies.

No wonder outsiders began to see this large chunk of North America as united, prosperous, and optimistic. No wonder thousands of immigrants—more than 2.5 million between 1903 and 1913—arrived by ship at Halifax, Quebec City, and Montreal, eager to board Canadian Pacific Railway cars and head west.

But would today's Canadians recognize it, let alone want to live here? Yes and no. Then as now, this country represented a new world for immigrants seeking a life free from the poverty, class structures, and religious persecution many had left behind. Nevertheless, work in sweatshops, in factories, and on prairie farms was backbreaking, and if you fell ill or had an accident, you could turn only to family and neighbours because employers or the state would offer no help.

Women who worked outside the home were mostly domestic servants, and no women had the right to vote. Even the fashions were constricting and offensive: corsets, hobble skirts, and hats trimmed with feathers from endangered bird species. And Canada was the Gobi Desert of culture, with artists and collectors looking to the United States or Europe for their models. Aesthetically, this was still a colony. Poets borrowed the rhythms of Tennyson or Swinburne; painters made Canadian maples look like British oak trees. Ambitious writers, creators, and performers fled to New York City or London.

At Confederation, the new country had only six museums, and thirty years later there were few art galleries (the Art Association of Montreal's Art Gallery was a fine exception), no publishing industry, and only a handful of outlets for creative writing. Today we recognize that there were some rich cultural traditions: the music and songs of rural Quebec; the extraordinary artistic skills of Indigenous peoples, particularly in the North and West; the fiddlers and dancers of Cape Breton and Nova Scotia. But this wasn't the kind of creativity valued by tastemakers in Montreal and Toronto. In small-town Ontario, most people's idea of a culture seems to have been community evenings for hymn singing, charades, and amateur skits.[1]

Yet people who were the polar opposite of Cartier and Steele were doing as much as they were to shape the way we see our country and ourselves. One such pioneer was Emily Carr.

As a woman, a westerner, and an artist, Carr had none of the advantages that Cartier and Steele enjoyed, and she painted for years in obscurity before being recognized as a genius.[2] Nevertheless, she presented Canadians with a new and original way to look at and think about not just British Columbia but also the whole country—and she persevered despite the dispiriting sexism of her day.

Of all the artists who made the wilderness a powerful element in the Canadian identity, I view Carr as the most important: she acknowledged that the landscape was peopled and alive before Europeans arrived, not vast and empty as most settlers liked to pretend. She was the first to try to capture the spirit of Canada in a modernist style. Her formidable canvases of skies, forests, and First Nations carvings are not macho records of discovery and conquest, but haunting and occasionally erotic paintings of mystery. Her perceptions and images have slowly seeped into the national memory bank. She is our Georgia O'Keeffe.

Too often, women have been written out of our standard histories because the work of nation building was such a masculine business. Only men could be elected to Parliament, where George-Étienne Cartier spent his career. Only men could join the North West Mounted Police and serve alongside Samuel Benfield Steele. Until recently, there was little space in public life for women. But in the privacy of homes, churches, temples, and studios, women have always been busy expressing their creativity and strengthening the bonds of community. Usually, nobody noticed. However, one woman who did have a wider impact, and who added a unique layer to our sense of this country's potential, was Emily Carr.

～

If you want to feel entirely marginal, try being the youngest daughter of deeply conventional English immigrants on the outer fringes of the British Empire. Emily Carr was born on Vancouver Island, British Columbia, the fifth daughter and second youngest of nine children in 1871—the year that British Columbia entered Confederation, changing its status from British colony to Canadian province. The odds were stacked against Carr becoming a major artist. She had to fight her own insecurities as well as the philistinism of her society, with its careless disregard for the questions her paintings asked.

Emily's father, Richard Carr, appears in biographies of his daughter as a prosperous merchant. However, he sounds a bit of a rascal: he was involved in the Klondike Gold Rush (fertile ground for a scam artist) and, according to the documentary maker Michael Ostroff, may have been a bootlegger.[3] But by the time he settled in Victoria in 1863, he oozed respectability. As Carr would write at the end of her life, "He thought everything English was much better than anything Canadian. . . . He saw that nearly all the people in Victoria were English and smiled at how they tried to be more English than the English themselves, just to prove to themselves and the world how loyal they were being to the Old Land."[4]

Carr grew up in a society dominated by British settlers, customs, and pretensions. Although a quarter of Victoria's eight thousand residents were of Chinese origin, most were hidden away in Chinatown; in the homes that

Emily visited, pictures of Queen Victoria hung in the parlours and tea was served in Wedgwood china. The city boasted a surfeit of churches (her father attended the stern First Presbyterian Church; her gentle mother, Emily, worshipped in Christ Church Episcopal) but no art school, city public library, theatre, or concert hall. During Carr's childhood, Victoria grew and evolved, but Confederation, and the new Canadian Pacific Railway link to central Canada, did little to dilute the relentless Britishness of the province's stuffy new capital. Nor did it lose its aggrieved sense of geographic isolation.

Westerners' grudge against the East, which was based on more than complaints about CPR freight rates and Ottawa's indifference, is easy to understand. But there is a larger issue here. The conventional way of exploring our past usually begins with the question "When does history begin?" Maps and texts in school histories start with the arrival on the East Coast of Europeans—Vikings, French explorers, Portuguese and Spanish fishers, English and Scottish fur traders, Irish refugees.

However, there is an equally valid question: "*Where* does history begin?" And westerners like to point out that one answer is "On the West Coast, millennia earlier." One of the first groups of humans to appear in North America was the Clovis people, who arrived via a land bridge from Siberia to Alaska and present-day Yukon about fifteen thousand years ago, then made their way down the continent from north to south. By the time Europeans arrived and started grabbing land and naming colonies, several hundred thousand people were already occupying territory from sea to sea. Without the help of these Indigenous inhabitants, many European newcomers would not have survived the harsh climate and brutal topography.

But a Eurocentric approach to Canadian history has never allowed a longer time frame or a 180-degree reorientation. No matter that human habitation began on the Pacific coast, or that West Coast peoples like the Haida, Kwakwaka'wakw, Nisga'a, and Tlingit had languages, economies, and ways of life that had endured for generations before the British Empire claimed their land for British emigrants. Until recently, the province and its Indigenous cultures have been peripheral to the way we tell our story. For

early-twentieth-century decision makers in Ottawa, Montreal, and Toronto, British Columbia was too far away and underpopulated to merit
much attention. (Many of its twenty-first-century residents grumble that
little has changed.)

So from its early days, British Columbia resented its sense of irrele-
vance. And that frustration finds an echo in Emily Carr's simmering rage
about being snubbed. Carr was the product of her upbringing on the continent's Pacific rim in more ways than one.

When did Emily Carr decide to become an artist, and why was that
West Coast frustration so important? That is not clear from either *The Book
of Small* and *Growing Pains*, the two memoirs written half a century after
the childhood they describe, or the several biographies of her. Nobody in
her family painted, and Victoria's idea of "art" was timid watercolours.
What is clear is that Carr was a determined, volatile little girl who had a
strong visual sense and a huge curiosity about the natural world. A square-
chinned, obstinate tomboy who preferred animals and flowers to people,
she got into fights with her sisters and "mussed up" her pinafores. In her
memoirs, she made much of her early resistance to authority, insisting that
she did not excel in school: she decorated her math textbooks with pigs
labelled "arithmetic" and donkeys labelled "Emily Carr." In fact, she did
perfectly well in school.[5]

Emily Carr was fascinated by aspects of Victoria that most of its residents tried their best to ignore. Through the back fence of the Carr property she could reach Beacon Hill Park, with its ponds, virgin stands of
arbutus and fir trees, and abundant birdlife. And beyond that was the thrill-
ing menace of untracked forest. "The silence of our Western forests was so
profound that our ears could scarcely comprehend it. . . . The birds who
lived there were birds of prey—eagles, hawks, owls. Had a song bird loosed
his throat the others would have pounced. . . . Gulls there had always been;
they began with the sea and had always cried over it. The vast sky spaces
above, hungry for noise, steadily lapped up their cries. The forest was different—she brooded over silence and secrecy."[6]

Carr could look across Victoria Harbour and see the Songhees, members of the Coast Salish people, who regularly came door to door, selling fish, berries, and handwoven baskets. On May 24 each year, Victoria's two disparate communities presented a bizarre contrast at the regatta celebrating the Queen's birthday. While the city's professional elite, dapper in boaters and white ducks, strolled along the wooden sidewalks or participated in sailing contests, members of First Nations from as far away as Haida Gwaii came to compete in canoe races. A highlight was the race between Indigenous women, paddling with fierce intensity under the Gorge Bridge. Imagine the impact this display of female athleticism had on a tomboy forced to wear starched pinafores!

But starched pinafores were the only world Carr knew, and her resentment began to build. In the accounts she wrote of her childhood at the end of her life, she poured scorn on Victoria's citizens who clung to their English origins and on British-born schoolmarms who regarded colonial manners as "crude, almost wicked." "Politeness-education ladies had migrated to Canada, often in the hope of picking up bread and butter and possibly a husband, though they pretended all the while that they had come out on a very special mission—to teach the young of English-born gentlemen how not to become Canadian, to believe that all niceness and goodness came from ancestors and could have nothing to do with the wonderful new land."[7] Carr's biographer Paula Blanchard argues that her fury with such women was crucial to her adult self. It had "a strong negative shaping influence on her personality, accounting for much of her permanently embattled stance." But that fury was also a constructive force, "urging her to question everything around her, to break free and discover her own creativity."[8]

Carr's mother was always sickly; she died of tuberculosis when Carr was only fourteen. Carr describes her father as a rigid autocrat who would not allow her to have a dog and who made his daughters recite sermons and read the Bible together ("begat chapters and all") every Sunday. But Richard Carr recognized his youngest daughter's special talent. When Emily, aged eight, drew an impressive charcoal portrait of her father's dog, Richard arranged drawing lessons for her plus a supply of paints and brushes.

Emily Carr had a difficult relationship with her father. Once the plump, curly-haired little girl started school, she often met him when he was walking home from his store in the evening—much to the relief of the rest of the family because young Emily could jolly him out of black moods. But it wasn't in Emily's nature to be a family peacemaker. As soon as she realized that she was "being used as a soother for Father's tantrums, like a bone to a dog," she started to question his authority and his right to impose his will on everybody. Her waywardness, she decided later, infuriated him. "He turned and was harder on me than on any of the others. His soul was so bitter that he was even sometimes cruel to me."

Richard Carr died only a few years later. His eldest daughter, thirty-year-old Edith, was left to raise her four younger sisters and brother. Emily's relationship with Dede, as she was known, was thorny: an intense and angry adolescent, Carr felt trapped by her family. "Outsiders saw our life all smoothed on top by a good deal of mid-Victorian kissing and a palaver of family devotion, the hypocrisy galled me. I was the disturbing element of the family. The others were prim, orthodox, religious. . . . I would not sham, pretending that we were a nest of doves, knowing well that in our home bitterness and resentment writhed."[9]

What rage! Yet that fierce anger and contempt for "sham" was perhaps one source of her creative genius. Her biographer Blanchard points out that throughout her life, Carr exaggerated the indifference, slights, and setbacks she had faced because a sense of alienation nourished her unique creativity. "Nothing is so deadening to an artist as to be trivialized and women artists have often been patronized to death," observes Blanchard. Emily Carr was raised in a culture that discouraged both anger and artistic vitality in women. "If she was difficult, as she certainly was," writes Blanchard, "at least we can applaud her for not allowing Victoria to make her into an anonymous pleasant lady."[10]

Emily Carr never completed her teacher's certificate, but she kept up her art lessons. She received no encouragement from Dede, who squelched any idea that her youngest sister might study painting in London, England, with a friend. But Emily pestered their guardian, a lawyer called James Lawson, until he finally agreed that she could attend the California School of Design, down the coast in San Francisco. By 1890, she had decided she was serious about art, and she had escaped Victoria's stifling conformity.

+~+

The artistic challenge for Emily Carr was to find her vision and capture it on canvas. How could she learn to channel and depict her passionate re-sponse to the world around her?

Carr would spend a little over three years at San Francisco's California School of Design, housed in a squalid building on Pine Street over the old public market. Founded in 1874, the school was well attended but conser-vative. Nineteen-year-old Carr benefited from instruction in portraiture and drawing, learned that she had a good colour sense, and enjoyed the weekly outdoor sketching sessions. By now, she was an attractive woman with large grey eyes, thick brown hair, and a wide smile, but she was inse-cure—too shy to attend the life drawing classes, with their nude models, and too timid to explore San Francisco. According to the art historian Doris Shadbolt, "Nothing . . . happened at the California school to give her a vision of what art might be for her—nothing at least that showed in her work." But she clung to her ambitions.

The return home in late 1893 was hard. Victoria hadn't changed. Carr was back in the role of mouthy baby sister; she found her sisters' activities (Bible study, good works, church attendance) suffocating. She determined to pursue her art studies elsewhere, this time in Europe, and she raised the money to go to England by giving art lessons to neighbourhood children.

However, Carr had an eye-opening experience before she left Victo-ria—her first serious exposure to British Columbia's "other" culture. Along with her sister Lizzie, she went to visit their friend May Armstrong, who taught at the Presbyterian mission at Ucluelet, a remote Nuu-chah-nulth community on Barkley Sound, halfway up the west coast of Vancouver Is-land and reachable only by water. The Nuu-chah-nulth (then known as the Nootka) hunted whales and seals from open canoes, and they lived in flat-fronted community houses made of thick, hand-hewn cedar planks. Carr was oblivious to the poverty, dirt, and smells that offended her sister, and fascinated by the hammocks hanging from the ceiling, the cedar mats and baskets, the Nuu-chah-nulth people themselves, and their respect for their surroundings. Soon she was busy with her brushes, sketching both stark exteriors and dim, smoky interiors of the houses. The villagers warmed to this polite young woman, who introduced herself with smiles and gestures. Carr was delighted when her hosts gave her the name Klee Wyck: "the laughing one."

The watercolours that Emily Carr brought home from this trip were unremarkable. But the choice of subjects held a hint of the future. She sensed the Nuu-chah-nulth people's bond with the natural world: their belief that they were part of a larger pattern of change and continuity overlapped her own spiritual connection to wild, rugged nature. She was still a nicely raised Victorian lady, but the private Emily was starting to churn.

A few weeks later, Emily Carr arrived in London and enrolled at the Westminster School of Art. The delights of the imperial capital that other visiting Canadians drooled over—the glittering window displays of department stores, the top-hatted equestrians in Hyde Park's Rotten Row—had no attraction for Carr, and the imposing museums and galleries intimidated the young art student. More to the point, the city's art scene was untouched by the modernism that held Paris artists in thrall. Since Carr had never been exposed to modern art, she probably didn't realize that her teachers were numbingly pedestrian—but she knew something was missing.

Carr finally overcame her prudery and took life classes, along with lessons in design, anatomy, and clay modelling. But she abhorred the rat-infested warren of Westminster streets behind the school and "the breath of the monstrous factories, the grime and smut and smell of them."[11] At every opportunity she fled to the countryside, where her most fruitful art education took place. She enrolled in courses in the Cornish seaside village of St. Ives, then an artists' colony, and later in Bushey, Hertfordshire, where "everything was yellow-green and pearly with young spring. Larks hurried up to Heaven as if late for choir practice."[12]

At Bushey, Carr finally found a sympathetic teacher who encouraged her to do what she most enjoyed: work in the woods by herself. John Whiteley, a conservative landscape painter, taught her to see light, shadow, and movement in trees: "The coming and going of foliage is more than just flat pattern." His advice to observe nature and Carr's own recognition that her artistic instincts were most inspired by nature were probably the most useful art lessons that Carr absorbed in England. But the tame English countryside was not her landscape.

Otherwise, Carr's five years in England were unhappy, reinforcing all her insecurity. She felt despised by some of her fellow students as a "colonial." She suffered bouts of ill health including a breakdown, apparently triggered by exhaustion, emotional stress, and insecurity, that required a miserable eighteen-month convalescence in a Suffolk sanatorium. Her favourite sister, Alice, visited and stared at Emily's paintings in a silence that the latter interpreted as indifference. Recalling the event years later, thin-skinned Carr wrote: "It was then that I made myself into an envelope into which I could thrust my work deep, lick the flap, and seal it from everybody."[13]

Something else had happened in England too, although it is hard to find exact details as Carr destroyed most of her personal papers. There was apparently a suitor who followed her from Victoria to London, an eligible young man who later became a wealthy and successful businessman. To the shock of Carr's family and acquaintances, she turned him down. Why? Here biographer's bias takes over. One biographer, Maria Tippett, has argued that Carr's sex life was irrevocably strangled by her father's clumsy attempt to explain human sexuality to her: the "brutal telling," Carr called it in a letter late in life. Tippett goes so far as to suggest Richard Carr might have behaved inappropriately to his daughter.[14] Others have suggested that perhaps Carr was a lesbian.

Along with Paula Blanchard, I prefer a different explanation: I think Carr realized that if she became somebody's wife, she would have to give up any hope of a serious painting life. Many leading female modernists during these years, like Frida Kahlo and Georgia O'Keeffe, chose to fulfill their dreams by turning their backs on conventional lives in favour of unconventional partnerships or the despised "spinsterhood." It was a brave choice for Carr, who was still a young woman fighting for an education, let alone recognition of her talent. But she was a realist, who could see that marriage would frustrate all her hopes. I think that she chose to suppress her sexuality, until it erupted in a handful of her later paintings.

Nevertheless, it must have been a tough decision, particularly as London had not worked out for her. By October 1904 she was back in Victoria, convinced that she had wasted her time, money, and talent in England.

Despite Emily Carr's single-minded pursuit of an artistic career, her creativity seemed to be stunted. Yet alongside new technical skills was a dawning awareness, conscious or unconscious, that she must root her art in her own environment. A hint of this recognition comes in a profile of her that appeared in a Victoria magazine in February 1905. The reporter, Arnold Watson, interviewed Carr, now thirty-four, in her teaching studio on Fort Street as she brewed tea on the wood stove. Afterwards they walked over to the barn behind the Carr family home, where Carr kept a menagerie of squirrels, chipmunks, and canaries. Carr made it plain that she did not enjoy interviews, and her mumbled answers were understatements. Watson asked if she was glad to be home. She said she was, because England was too pretty and orderly. "One misses the mountains and woods."[15]

But Victoria still did not offer her much. Although technology was transforming society, it was slow to arrive at Victoria's shores. Elsewhere in the Dominion, horse-drawn carriages gave way to automobiles, Toronto finally established a public art gallery, and the prairies were becoming the breadbasket of the empire. But Victoria insisted on its "Olde England" quaintness, despite its growth and the splendid new Parliament Buildings and Empress Hotel. There were no kindred artistic spirits for Emily Carr, let alone art patrons. She decided to move across the Strait of Georgia to Vancouver, a larger and more vibrant city, where she was offered a teaching job.

Carr taught in Vancouver for several years. She was hopeless with adult pupils: she regarded the women by whom she had originally been hired as "a cluster of society women [who met to] drink tea and jabber art jargon." (They probably made her feel scruffy and inadequate.) However, her classes for children were soon oversubscribed. "Children loved her imaginative approach to teaching," writes Blanchard. "She would begin with very young ones by asking them to illustrate nursery rhymes, encouraging freedom and fantasy rather than skill."[16] She frequently took her classes to the wharves, the back lanes, or beautiful, forested Stanley Park for outdoor sketching classes. Her young students enjoyed her encouragement and her menagerie (there were always animals around Carr), which included a sheepdog named Billie, a cockatoo named Sally, a green Panama parrot named Jane, and two white rats, Peter and Peggy. Large audiences attended her end-of-year shows. "Miss Carr gave a most successful exhibition of her students' work in her studio on Granville Street," reported the *Province* on March 30, 1907.

None of this was doing much to advance Carr's own painting, although she soldiered on with portraits, still lifes, and landscapes. Her favourite subject appears to have been the towering cedars of Stanley Park, where the "appalling solemnity, majesty and silence was the Holiest thing I ever felt." But she was exasperated by her inability to move beyond the conventionally picturesque or to capture the forest as she felt it. Her paintings were similar to those of other semi-professional artists in Vancouver at the time, who exhibited regularly. Carr's work often merited special mention. In 1909 the *Province* art critic noted: "An artist of strong personality, which finds expression in vigorous work is Miss M. E. Carr, the quality of whose work improves steadily." But within the art community, Carr remained a loner—insecure, hypersensitive to snubs from male peers, yet deeply competitive.

The most important event in these years, as far as Carr's art was concerned, was the trip that she and her sister Alice made in 1907 to Alaska. (Carr wrote and illustrated a witty journal of this trip, which was discovered in a Montreal basement in 2013 after being lost for years.) The two women took a steamer up the Pacific coast to Sitka, Alaska. Originally a Tlingit village, Sitka had then been a Russian trading post and was now an American naval station. As a tourist attraction, its main street featured a contrived "Totem-Pole Walk," consisting of carved poles moved from else-

Carr's journal of her 1907 trip to Alaska reveals her humour and gift for caricature.

where and doused in bright paint. Carr discovered more carvings, weathered and authentic, behind the town when she stumbled into the Sitka village. There the drowsy silence and the smells of woodsmoke, rotting fish, and human waste reminded her of the 1899 Ucluelet trip that had been such an eye-opener.

As the Carr sisters sailed south, Emily brooded over what she had seen. Finally, she had a purpose that she knew would fire her imagination. "The Indian people and their art touched me deeply. . . . By the time I reached home my mind was made up. I was going to picture totem poles in their own village settings, as complete a collection of them as I could."[17] There was another motive too: she hoped to sell these reproductions of Indigenous art to the new provincial museum in Victoria. She might at last make some money. But nobody at the museum took her art seriously.

In the next two years, Carr travelled to several Kwakwaka'wakw settlements on Vancouver Island and the southern mainland, and inland along the Fraser River. Accompanied by her dog Billie and undeterred by mosquitoes and torrential rain, she spent her days in open-air sketching in pen or watercolour, and her nights in mission houses, tents, cabins, Kwakwa-ka'wakw homes, and utility sheds. Back in her Vancouver studio, she expanded the images into large oil paintings that the *Province*'s art critic praised for their "strength and genuineness."[18] Over the next six years, Carr would complete two hundred paintings documenting the villages, carvings, and peoples of the First Nations of Canada's Northwest Coast. However, few of these canvases sold. Vancouverites preferred portraits of the royal family and tidy European landscapes, preferably with cows.

Meanwhile, the dramatic simplicity of Sitka and Kwakwaka'wakw carving made Carr aware of the limitations of her own careful brush strokes and fussy detail. She knew that the most innovative art of the day, and therefore the most interesting teaching, was in Paris. Artists from the United States and central Canada had been travelling there since the 1880s, and she herself must have seen reproductions of post-impressionist painters like Van Gogh and Gauguin. She found the "new art" confusing. "I heard it ridiculed, praised, liked, hated. Something in it stirred me but I could not at first make head or tail of what it was all about. I saw at once that it made recent conservative painting look flavourless, little, unconvincing."[19]

It was a big step for Emily Carr to go to Paris. She didn't speak French and knew no one there. Her years in London had scarred her: she was not a woman who embraced change or liked being too far from home for long. What would Parisians think of this dowdy, middle-aged, reticent woman? But she hungered for inspiration and recognized the suffocating provincialism of her life in British Columbia. On June 10, 1910, the *Province* announced to its readers: "Miss Carr intends to leave in a few weeks for a year's stay in Paris, where she will pursue her studies in art."

In France, in the words of the art historian Doris Shadbolt, Carr would finally shake off "old-world shackles and [join] the ranks of modern painters."[20] Exposure to post-impressionism would enable her to abandon Victorian concepts of art and the remnants of her genteel education, and express what she found unique in her own environment. The process of integrating modernist techniques with her own deeply Canadian imaginative vision would begin.

✦

Paris would lead to Carr's epiphany—but it would prove a shock.

In the early years of the twentieth century, modernism had overtaken every artistic endeavour in Paris: music, ballet, literature, and the visual arts. The shift in aesthetic values was as dramatic as the shift to digital technologies has been in our own day. For visual artists, the emergence of photography had caused an existential crisis. Why paint anything when a camera could capture images more easily and accurately? Artists had been compelled to find something within painting that justified its existence. Painting could no longer be about visual likeness: it had to express something about the visual world that went beyond a photographic recording. Younger artists in France had already cast aside the techniques and examples of figurative art that were drilled into Emily Carr in San Francisco and England. They were surfing through successive waves of innovation: impressionism, pointillism, post-impressionism, abstraction—all attempts to show us how we see, rather than what we see.

Products of this new experimentation initially intimidated Carr. She was no more adventurous in Paris than she had been in San Francisco or London: she did not spend hours in the Louvre or seek out bohemian companions with whom she might discuss Picasso's cubist paintings or Matisse's fauve canvases. I doubt that she ever even entered a Montmartre bar, let alone tasted a pastis. But she knew she was searching for something.

Carr's only entrée into the art world was a letter of introduction to an English artist named Henry Phelan Gibb. The tall, thin, and well-connected Gibb was much celebrated in his own day: he was part of Gertrude Stein's circle and a friend of Cézanne. Although his reputation has faded since then, he would prove an enormous help to Emily Carr. During her first visit to his studio on Boulevard Raspail, she was thrilled and shocked by the vivid colours, bulging bodies, and abstract forms in his paintings. "There was rich, delicious juiciness in his colour, interplay between warm and cool tones. . . . He intensified vividness by the use of complementary color. . . . [His] landscapes and still lifes delighted me—brilliant, luscious, clean." Still a prim Victorian, she enthused about everything but the sex: "Against the distortions of his nudes I felt revolt."[21] These canvases sparked Carr's reassessment of all her assumptions about perspective, scale, and colour.

On Gibb's advice, Carr enrolled at the Académie Colarossi. But working conditions were unpleasant there, instruction was in French, and Carr was the oldest student and only woman in her classes. All her old insecurities surfaced. After three months in Paris she became stressed and "nearly demented with headaches. . . . I began to feel myself going, going as I had in London." She spent three months in hospital, then fled the capital. The remaining weeks of her French adventure would be spent in villages.

This time, Carr did not let physical or psychological problems shackle her progress as they had in England. She knew she had found her teacher. Phelan Gibb was now giving a landscape class in Crécy-en-Brie, a little canal town close to Paris; she joined him there. One day, she watched with awe how he sketched the scene in front of them. "It was not a copy of the woods & fields it was a realization of them. The colours were not matched. They were mixed with air. You went through space to meet reality." She now understood the modernist approach to painting—the "expressive possibilities of paint itself," in Shadbolt's words.[22] Concern for detail was replaced by bold brush strokes and direct patches of colour on the canvas. She was no longer transmitting information: she was simplifying form, using figures as compositional units, and playing with tone and hue, light and shadow. She finally began to feel that what she had in her head and what she put on canvas were starting to mesh.

What a thrill for Carr to see the way forward. Her work, in both oil and watercolour, became steadily more spontaneous, original, and vigorous. When she returned to Paris in the fall of 1911, she discovered that two of her paintings had been accepted for the Salon d'Automne, the large, juried show held each year in the capital's Grand Palais. The show included hundreds of works, and critics focused on canvases by Matisse, Bonnard, Léger, Rouault, and Vlaminck. Nevertheless, Carr's inclusion was an important milestone: she had shaken off the constraints of nineteenth-century art and been accepted as a practitioner of modernism. She returned to Canada eager to apply her new style in the New World. But for Emily Carr, nothing was ever that easy.

＋∽＋

One of my favourite gifts for foreign visitors is a set of four mugs, featuring twisted pine trees, tangled forests, scarlet fall foliage, and rugged rocks, purchased at the gift shop in Ottawa's National Gallery of Canada. The images are taken from paintings by Tom Thomson, prototype of the Canadian backwoodsman artist and forerunner of Canada's most famous artist collective, the Group of Seven. Who can name the group's seven members? Few of us manage more than three—and we often include Thomson, who died before the Group was established. (In case you need a quick primer, they were A. Y. Jackson, Lawren Harris, Frederick Varley, Arthur Lismer, J. E. H. MacDonald, Frank Johnston, and Franklin Carmichael.) But we all know the canvases painted by Thomson and the Group—exuberant celebrations of the Canadian landscape, invariably described as "iconic." The critic Robert Fulford called their work "our national wallpaper," although their most popular paintings depict only Ontario.

The story of Thomson and the Group of Seven is an interesting counterpoint to the story of Emily Carr. When, aged forty, she returned from France in 1911, eager to realize the potential of her vision, most members of the future Group of Seven were still in their twenties and had barely begun their own careers, let alone developed their collective identity. But in addition to their talent, they had advantages of gender and geography. They had the chutzpah to decide that their country needed a uniquely Canadian artistic movement—and they were going to be it.

How did the Group of Seven form? Let's start with Tom Thomson, the moody, dark-haired son of a Scottish immigrant who was born in 1877, grew up on an Ontario farm, and died too young to be a member of the group he helped inspire. A hunter and fisherman from a young age, Thomson drifted around the continent, working as a graphic designer, before

Some members of Canada's most famous artistic school, the Group of Seven (pictured here in 1920), enjoyed a camaraderie and fame that eluded Carr.

ending up in Toronto in 1907. There, at a commercial design firm called Grip Limited, he met a lively group of fellow designers, including at various times Franklin Carmichael from Orillia, Frank Johnston from Toronto, and the immigrants Arthur Lismer and Fred Varley. (I have a particular affection for the latter two artists because they grew up in the grubby English industrial city of Sheffield, my hometown too.) Thomson's first boss at Grip was a good-tempered, dishevelled supervisor called James E. H. MacDonald. MacDonald was already a serious painter who in 1911 had a solo show of landscape oils at Toronto's Arts and Letters Club.

At the Arts and Letters Club, then an exclusively male institution, MacDonald's paintings were seen by his fellow member Lawren Harris, a scion of Ontario's manufacturing elite. Harris's grandfather Alanson had successfully manufactured agricultural implements, then merged his company with his rival Hart Massey's firm in 1891, forming Canada's largest corporation, Massey-Harris. Sales of threshers and reapers yielded a huge fortune for the Harris family, enabling Alanson's descendant Lawren, an aspiring artist, to study art in Berlin. There he was exposed to new currents in European art, both exuberant canvases by French post-impressionists and darker images by Scandinavian artists like the Norwegian Edvard Munch. (He would see more of Munch, plus work by Gustaf Fjaestad from Sweden, at a show of Scandinavian art in Buffalo that he and J. E. H. Mac-Donald visited in 1913.) As Emily Carr had done in Paris, Harris learned how modernists had abandoned the Old Masters' attempts to recreate detailed, three-dimensional scenes and instead were experimenting with flat planes, bright colours, and manipulation of materials. Back in Toronto, Harris perceived in MacDonald's landscapes what he described years later as "intimations of something new in painting in Canada, an indefinable spirit which seemed to express the country more clearly than any painting I had yet seen."[23] Harris began to muse about developing a style that represented "Canada painted in her own spirit."

At first, Harris confined his efforts to paintings of smokestacks and industry, similar to those being painted in Germany. But in 1912, Harris and MacDonald set off together on a sketching trip that would prove momentous. They headed north by train, into logging country. The drawings and paintings produced during and after this trip were not particularly innovative, but the idea of Canada's "wilderness" as an appropriate subject for Canadian artists took hold. The facts that logging country is *not* wilderness, and that other artists including Paul Kane, William Hind, and Frances Anne Hopkins had got there before them, did not dampen the fervour of Harris in particular. Nor did the fact that European artists were moving away from landscape and engaging in fierce debates around figuration and abstraction. Harris saw landscape, particularly uninhabited terrain, as the subject that could be quintessentially Canadian.

The boys had fun. "We lived in a continuous blaze of enthusiasm," Lawren Harris wrote later. "We were at times very serious and concerned, at other times, hilarious and carefree. Above all, we loved this country, and loved exploring and painting it."[24]

The outdoorsman Tom Thomson was also canoeing regularly through Algonquin Park and northern Ontario, to paint and fish. He took Jackson, Varley, and Lismer along with him and introduced them to the region's Jack pines and starry night skies. Thomson picked up from Grip colleagues who had trained abroad tips about the application of paint to canvas and the manipulation of light. In return, he infected them with his passion for the magnificent countryside within a short train ride of Toronto. The following year he painted A Northern Lake for the Ontario Society of Artists' annual show, where it hung alongside landscapes by Harris, MacDonald, and a fiery young Montreal painter named Alexander Young Jackson. The Toronto Daily Star reviewer admired the forcefulness of works by these younger artists, noting their "virile work, fearless brushing, strange, crude colour."[25]

The group was coming together, and members started giving each other the support Carr had never experienced. Lawren Harris fired up his fellow painters with enthusiasm for a distinctly Canadian school of art, and he built a studio in Toronto's Rosedale ravine to provide working spaces for friends including Thomson, Jackson, and Carmichael.

Best of all, a Star reviewer jeered at a small show of A. Y. Jackson's work and suggested that Toronto's innovative young painters "believe in Explosions, Outbursts and Acute Congestions of Pigments."[26] The reviewer, whose regular beat was politics, not art, facetiously referred to Jackson's paintings as "Hot Mush." Instead of suffering Carr-like chagrin or dismissing the derision as ill-informed splutter, the artists leaped at this opportunity for public outrage. Positioning themselves as rebels, fighting to establish a real "Canadian" art, they "swaddled their art in the flag of the Dominion," in the art historian Ross Howard's words.[27] They were building a new mythology for a new country. At the time, nobody asked why the Group of Seven ignored the old mythology of the original inhabitants, now displaced.

The First World War interrupted the group's evolution. Jackson and Varley became official war artists. Tom Thomson's death by drowning in Algonquin Park in 1917, just as he was reaching his artistic peak, shocked the entire Toronto artistic community. But in May 1920, the loose fraternity of Harris and friends reunited for their first exhibition at the Art Gallery of Toronto under the name they had chosen for themselves: the Group of Seven.

In Ottawa, Eric Brown, the National Gallery's first director, heard about the show from his friend Arthur Lismer. Brown was a tweedy, monocled

Englishman who had arrived in Canada in 1910 and surprised everybody by becoming an eager outdoorsman. Under his direction the gallery had already acquired works by several Canadian artists, including Harris and Thomson. Lismer wrote Brown that the artists' intention was to demonstrate in the Group of Seven show "the 'spirit' of painting in Canada."[28] Brown warmly applauded the initiative, purchased three of the canvases for the National Gallery, and helped to organize a smaller touring show in the United States.

Members of the Group were less homogeneous than they seem from today's perspective. Johnston left Toronto for Winnipeg soon after the 1920 show; several others travelled beyond Ontario's borders and went in different stylistic directions. Varley turned to portraiture while Harris became an abstract painter. But they remained loyal to the patriotic goal of affirming Canada's uniqueness through depictions of its rugged landscape—a landscape dramatically different from the well-tilled fields of Europe. Yet their best-known paintings convey no evidence of an Indigenous presence and little trace of the urbanization and industrialization that were profoundly reshaping Canada.

By 1930, the Group of Seven was acknowledged as the "National School." Like it or not, as the painter Harold Town would later put it, we had "something identified as Canadian art, a cohesive lump in our national gut—seemingly rough painters who said to hell with trends and gave us an assessable, simple beginning, a fire for some, dying embers for others. We could love them or hate them, but we had a starting line."[29] The Group had successfully replaced the style and standards of European Old Masters with a quasi-modernist approach to the grandeur and immensity of the North. But it wasn't the artists' undoubted talent alone that underlay their success: curators, collectors, and art lovers embraced them because of their nationalistic agenda. As the historian Daniel Francis puts it, "The Group claimed to be creating not just art but a new national consciousness. . . . In this respect, the Group perfectly matched the spirit of their times."[30]

᠇᠊᠊᠊᠊

While the Group of Seven was exploding onto the art scene in central Canada, Emily Carr was going nowhere. Nobody on the West Coast noticed her "fearless brushing" or her "strange, crude colours," let alone raved about "virile work."

Carr had returned to Vancouver from France eager to continue recording Indigenous cultures. In 1912, the year after her return, she travelled to Haida Gwaii and the Skeena River, documenting the art of the Haida, Gitxsan, and Tsimshian. Many of the villages she visited were almost deserted—on Haida Gwaii several were abandoned—because a smallpox epidemic in the 1860s had laid waste the population. Few poles had been carved once newly arrived Christian missionaries began to preach that the carvings were barbaric. Many First Nations practices, such as the great feasts or potlatches, had been declared illegal. At least twenty-five residential schools had already been established in the province, so Carr rarely saw children in the communities. There is no evidence that she knew much about the cruel government policies, but she saw their impact and assumed (along with most people in her generation of settlers) that the Indigenous inhabitants were vanishing peoples—like ancient Greeks.

Carr's trip was arduous. She was always an outsider in the villages, staying with missionaries or camping out in deserted houses, and now much more interested in artistic technique than in ethnography. Back in Vancouver, she developed her sketches of villages, carved poles, and the exteriors and interiors of houses into canvases, trying to apply the ways of seeing she had acquired in France. Then she organized a public showing of about two hundred paintings, including these paintings along with avant-garde canvases from France, with their brilliant use of colour, completed during the previous fourteen years.

The show included some of her best-known works, including *The Welcome Man, Tanoo,* and *Alert Bay.* She prepared a talk about her own experiences and what she knew of the culture she had painted, trying to explain her self-appointed mission: "I glory in our wonderful west and I hope to leave behind me some of the relics of its first primitive greatness. These things should be to us Canadians what the ancient Britons' relics are to the English.

Only a few more years and they will be gone forever into silent nothingness and I would gather my collection together before they are forever past."[31]

Words such as "relics," "primitive," and "silent nothingness" sound horribly insensitive and ill-informed to modern ears, expressing the convenient assumption within Canada's settler society that Indigenous peoples were close to disappearance. Yet Carr was a woman of her period, and the conventional wisdom about the vanishing First Nations must have seemed even more convincing to her after her travels through depopulated villages, with their abandoned carvings. For all her conventional upbringing, Carr did show a great respect for Indigenous traditions and culture, especially when compared with the brutal and ugly racism of government policy and popular culture that depicted Indigenous peoples as less than human.

Sadly for Carr, her contemporaries weren't so keen; they still didn't want "relics" hanging on their nicely painted walls. The 1913 exhibition was neither the critical nor the commercial success for which she had hoped. Carr immediately decided that Vancouver had rejected her. She packed up her apartment and took the ferry back to her family in Victoria, although she recognized that the city was an "impossible field for work."[32] She was the most advanced modernist artist in Canada, but nobody in her province could appreciate it.

For the next fifteen years, she faced grinding poverty as she scraped a living from a bizarre range of activities. Much of her time was spent running a three-apartment building that she had built; she also bred dogs, hens, and rabbits for sale. She incorporated First Nations designs into rugs and pottery that she made and sold, but as Shadbolt put it, art "had ceased to be the primary drive of her life."[33] Now middle-aged, dressed in shapeless clothes, with her wiry greying hair scraped untidily into a bun, she trudged along the beach with her pack of dogs or trundled a child's pram filled with groceries or supplies through the neighbourhood of James Bay. Her menagerie kept expanding: dogs, birds, chipmunks, a white rat, and from about 1923 an incorrigibly mischievous capuchin monkey called Woo. A small cluster of human friends knew her as warm and funny, but with strangers she could be shy, abrupt, or just plain hostile.

Victoria's social elite enjoyed the British stuffiness of the city's Empress Hotel.

Carr would write later that she felt only "a dead lump . . . in my heart where my work had been."[34] When she did allow the public to see any of her work, she was stung by reviewers' reactions, which ranged from uncertainty to rejection. While Group of Seven painters were being boyish, charming, optimistic, and sharp-elbowed, she earned a reputation for bad-tempered eccentricity. For fifteen years, her painting skills atrophied. In fifteen years, a person can lose a second language and forget most of what they learned in school. In this wretched period, Carr deliberately turned her face away from the drawing and painting skills she had acquired in France and from her completely original vision of how she wanted to engage her country.

The good news for Carr was that the young country was slowly generating an elite that was looking for a truly Canadian vision, to distinguish this country from both Great Britain and the United States. Institutions with an obligation to reflect the whole country appeared. In Ottawa in 1926, Eric Brown of the National Gallery, along with the prominent eth-

Carr's reputation for eccentricity expanded alongside her menagerie of pets.

nologist Marius Barbeau, began to plan an exhibition to be titled *Canadian West Coast Art, Native and Modern*. Barbeau had already seen Carr's works, during trips to British Columbia. He urged Brown to include some Carr canvases, along with work by painters from central Canada (Edwin Holgate, A. Y. Jackson, Pegi Nicol) who had made brief trips to West Coast settlements. In the end, Carr dominated the "Modern" selections in the 1927 show, with twenty-six oil paintings as well as rugs and pottery.

Carr took the train east, to Ontario, thanks to a ticket provided by Brown. There she met the Group of Seven; Harris, Lismer, Jackson, and MacDonald all invited her to their Toronto studios. The warmth of their welcome and their obvious admiration for her work ("You are one of us," Harris told her) were the trigger she needed to rejuvenate her painting career once more.

She was particularly struck by Lawren Harris's work. In his studio, she sat silent in front of his austere, smoothly modelled *Above Lake Superior*, "getting a glimpse . . . into the soul of Canada, away from the prettiness of England and the modernity of France, down into the vast, lovely soul of

Canada, plumbing her depths, climbing her heights, floating in her spaces."[35] On her third visit there, she broke through her shyness and had the kind of discussion with him on techniques and aesthetic values for which she had always hungered. She returned to Victoria determined to be bolder in her documentation of First Nations carving and more concerned with putting herself into her painting. She was ready, as she put it, to go off on a "tangent tear." Doris Shadbolt notes, "Never again would the sense of isolation be crippling nor would she suffer the loss of spirit that had retarded her art for nearly fifteen years."[36]

Lawren Harris had reactivated Carr's drive. Another artist teacher, the American Mark Tobey from Seattle, helped her to achieve the bolder, more authoritative style of her mature years. A cocky, red-haired firebrand nineteen years younger than Carr, Tobey was free with his advice to her to "pep up" her canvases with brighter colours, more light and shade, and greater attention to shape and volume.

Emily Carr adopted what she needed from these teachers to consolidate her own intensely held vision. As she abandoned faithful realism and began to experiment, some of her work shows the influence of cubism (of which Tobey was an admirer) and futurism. She continued to make trips north to sketch in First Nations villages, but from 1928 onward her paintings focused not on the literal characteristics of carvings and scenes but on their expressive power within the dense forests or expansive skies of their settings. She tried to depict in her art the spiritual force that she had always found in nature and that she now understood was embodied in Indigenous carvings. Theatrical grandeur suffuses paintings like *Indian Church* (1929) and *Big Raven* (1931). In the words of Doris Shadbolt, "She took on the Indian [material's] darkness in her canvases, closing them in with weighty and darkened skies, or with claustrophobic forests even when fidelity to her subject did not require her to do so. . . . She was drawn deeply into nature's dark side."[37]

It was Lawren Harris who prompted Carr to embark on her greatest and most distinctive phase. In 1931 he suggested to her in a letter that underlying her intense feeling for Indigenous art was her own deep response to the West Coast landscape itself. "The totem pole is a work of art in its own right and it is very difficult to use it in another form of art. But how about seeking an equivalent for it in the exotic landscape of the Island and coast, making your own form and forms with the greater form."[38] Carr took his advice, but she never let go of her deep love for Indigenous forms and culture. Some years later, while convalescing from a heart attack, she jotted down brief memoirs of her encounters with different groups. Published in 1941, *Klee Wyck* won the Governor General's Award for Non-fiction. In her own lifetime, she was better known for this slender book of short stories than for the paintings that today overwhelm us with their sophisticated compositions and raw energy.

Carr now sought to capture on canvas the mystery and movement of nature. The Group of Seven's style of the 1920s was the new orthodoxy; she took only what was needed from them for her own adamantly personal aesthetic. Her canvases are infused with what art critics have called "vitalism." Rainforests, beaches and driftwood, logged hillsides, sky, open fields—her eye was omnivorous and her rapture like Wordsworth's. She described in notebooks and her journal what she wanted to achieve, and these entries reflect the role religion played in her art. "A picture equals a movement in space. Pictures have swerved too much towards design and decoration. . . . The idea must run through the whole, the story that arrested you and urged the desire to express it, the story that God told you through that combination of growth. The picture side of the thing is the relationship of the objects to each other in one concerted movement, so that the whole gets up and goes, lifting the looker with it, sky sea trees affecting each other."[39]

Sometimes the movement is flowing and serene; in other canvases there are coils and cascades of growth. Skies pulsate with energy; seas swirl. Carr's paintings reflect her own violent mood swings and intensity. One painting that is almost lasciviously sensual is *Tree Trunk* (1931)—yet her contemporaries chose to ignore its eroticism. Elsewhere, particularly in the euphoric sky paintings or the depictions of churning forests, there is a note of mysticism. I have too many favourites to catalogue; I am in awe at the way she captures not just wild nature but also Gothic, mysterious grandeur.

Carr loved to sketch in the woods. Each summer, she would rent a cabin or have a rickety trailer (which she called "the Elephant") towed to an isolated spot on the edge of the forest. In the mornings she would pack up her folding stool, easel, notebook, and materials, and stomp off to find a good vantage point; then she would sit down, look around, light a cigarette to keep off the bugs, and let the scene enfold her. "Slowly things begin to move, to slip into their place. Groups and masses and lines tie themselves together. Colours you had not noticed come out, timidly or boldly. In and out, in and out, your eye passes."[40] In order to achieve the freedom of watercolour with the colour fixity and depth of oil, she began to thin her oils with gasoline and paint on inexpensive manila paper. (This technique was also cheaper than oil on canvas but would prove a nightmare for conservators trying to preserve her best work.)

At last! Public acclaim began to come her way (although it was critical, not commercial: the wolf was never far from the door). Launched into this final, triumphant stage of her career, Emily Carr was almost oblivious to it. In 1938, the Vancouver Art Gallery mounted a solo show of her work that became an annual event. Months later, four of her paintings went on display at London's Tate Gallery in a show entitled *A Century of Canadian Art*. Eric Newton, art critic of the Manchester *Guardian*, suggested she was a genius. He noted how Carr had dug much deeper into Canada's vast wilderness than the Group of Seven had done. "Where the Eastern Canadians have been content to stylize the outward pageantry of the landscape, she has symbolized its inner meaning, and in doing so has, as it were, humanized it. Her trees are more than trees: they are green giants and slightly malevolent giants at that."[41] Carr brushed off accolades and praise, fretting that they might make her "smug and stagnant."[42] In 1943 there were solo exhibitions at the Vancouver Art Gallery, the Art Association of Montreal, the Art Gallery of Toronto, and the Seattle Museum.

Carr died in Victoria in 1945, aged seventy-four, after producing her best-known and most powerful work in the last fifteen years of her life. She had proved, as Doris Shadbolt put it, that "art of great strength and conspicuous individuality could be produced in a remote corner of the country if the artist had the necessary qualities and a little bit of luck."[43] It was even more remarkable that in this case the artist was a woman who grew up without either colleagues or an audience in a proudly colonial and horribly philistine city on the far edge of the empire. Her strength of character and vision were extraordinary. "This is my country. What I want to express is *here* and I love it. Amen!"[44]

◈

Why did I choose Emily Carr to be part of this book? Why not Tom Thomson, Lawren Harris, or any other member of the Group of Seven pantheon, since they were recognized a decade before Carr and their work is equally well-known? These were all artists who wrenched the attention of Canadian art lovers away from pallid imitations of European art and focused them on the dramatic spaces of our own country.

I asked myself "Why Carr?" recently as I stood in front of one of her best-loved works, *Scorned as Timber, Beloved of the Sky* (1935), in the Vancouver Art Gallery, which now holds the bulk of her paintings. The canvas shows a lone, spindly tree, surrounded by brutally logged land, reaching up to a pearly pale sky painted with undulating circular strokes. The scorned tree could almost be a self-portrait for this defiant artist—her solitary, single-minded reach to self-fulfillment, while the landscape is desecrated around her.

Carr is here partly because she had a pioneer's resolve to make this land hers and to become part of it herself. Thomson and the Group of Seven were evolving their nationalist mission with the support of each other and the new nation's small cultural elite. Carr developed her vision in isolation, while on the other side of the country. Once she was discovered by the eastern establishment, her art and her national reputation exploded.

But she's also here because she tells Canadians, then and now, about far more than the awesome magnificence of Canadian space. By looking inward, she gave us an outward identity. She began with a terrain denser and wilder than anything seen in Algonquin Park; her forests were brooding and claustrophobic. In mid-career, she painted the carvings and cultural artifacts made by the Indigenous inhabitants of North America, who were ignored by the Group of Seven. In her later works, she infused her works with an erotic sensibility that few Canadian artists have equalled. And she captured not only the lush colours of the Pacific rainforest but also its despoliation by the logging industry. Carr never romanticized the wilderness, and she recorded how the resource industries—the basis of Canada's prosperity—were already gobbling up the scenery.

In the 1990s, Emily Carr's depictions of coastal Indigenous culture were criticized as cultural appropriation. Marcia Crosby, a Haida/Tsimshian art critic, argued that Carr invested carved poles with "a meaning that has to do with her national identity, not the national identity of the people who own the poles. . . . The colonization of images in order to create a new Canadian mythology is parasitic."[45] But these days, scholars are more likely to point out that Carr had great empathy for dispossessed peoples, even if she romanticized their culture. Gerta Moray, a Carr scholar, points out that Carr championed First Nations in the face of Anglo-Canadian derision and asserted "their honour, dignity and the coherence of their traditional way of life and beliefs."[46]

Today, there is a certain ennui with our national wallpaper—a feeling that our obsession with landscape stifled any Canadian shift to the new kinds of art that Carr had seen in Paris in 1910 and 1911. Perhaps that is why no Canadian artists from the early twentieth century ever established international reputations or foreign sales: while they were still painting landscapes, the art world moved on. It took a completely different group of artists—the Quebec intellectuals and artists, including Paul-Émile Borduas and Jean-Paul Riopelle, who in 1948 published *Refus global*—to launch surrealism and abstraction in Canada.

Yet Emily Carr's reputation has quietly grown. In 2012, a small selection of her work was included in Documenta XIII in Kassel, Germany, in an international exhibition of pioneering female modernists. In 2014, the first European solo exhibition of her work, mounted by London's Dulwich Picture Gallery, was ecstatically reviewed: "The best artist nobody knows," according to one British headline writer; "Canada's very own Van Gogh," according to another.[47] An exhibition entitled *Radiant Visions: From Monet to Carr* will be shown at the Musée d'Orsay in Paris in 2017.

As a child, Carr developed her artistic vision of this "wonderful new land"; today, her vision is recognized as richer and more complex than that of her contemporaries. By finding her place, she gave Canadians then and now a larger sense of ours.

CHAPTER 4

Beaver Tales

Harold Innis and the Ties That Bind

The present Dominion emerged not in spite of geography but because of it.
—Harold Innis, *The Fur Trade in Canada* (1930)

Harold Innis felt that he must work for Canada. Canadians must explain their new nation to the outside world. Above all, Canadians must understand themselves.
—Donald Creighton, *Harold Adams Innis: Portrait of a Scholar* (1957)

B y the early twentieth century a distinct Canadian identity had started to germinate. There was still not much to work with—no flag, no national anthem, no military heroes. But the dawn of Confederation was a fading memory; fears of being swallowed by the United States had shrunk. Thanks to determined individuals like Cartier, Steele, and Carr, the country was starting to develop a sense of its uniqueness. The Dominion could boast a federal system of government that was proving both durable and flexible, a police force that was rapidly morphing into a national symbol, and artists obsessed with the northern landscape.

And then, in August 1914, ties to the motherland abruptly tautened. Britain declared war on Germany, and Canada automatically signed on, alongside other colonies in the British Empire, including both settler colonies like Australia and New Zealand and colonial acquisitions like India. Canadian loyalty to Great Britain appeared rock-solid, and young men from Vancouver to Halifax rushed to enlist.

Today the war is recognized as a turning point in Canadian history: a conflict conducted on foreign soil that would accelerate the growing collective self-consciousness. Excellent historians like Tim Cook and J. L. Granatstein have written extensively about political decision makers, military strategists, key battles, and the Canadian soldiers who faced the horrors of trench warfare. My interest lies in exploring how the war shaped the intellectual development of one individual, who would then help mould the Canadian imagination.

But first let's consider the dramatic changes in Confederation's first few decades.

The Dominion's population exploded in the first years of the twentieth century, and by 1914 it was nearly eight million. Particularly since 1900, momentum seemed unstoppable. Most of the coast-to-coast growth consisted of British immigrants, eager to exchange the dirty, overcrowded streets of industrial cities for brick row houses or prairie farms, but many of the newcomers came from elsewhere and spoke German, Ukrainian, Yiddish, or Italian. The surge of immigrants into Canada and the rapid spread of roads, railroads, and industrial development generated momentum and optimism, and proud talk about the potential of a "young country." In 1904 Sir Wilfrid Laurier, the Liberal prime minister (and the first French Canadian to hold the office), lit a spark with his famous prediction that Canada's history "is only commencing. . . . The nineteenth century was the century of the United States. I think we can claim that it is Canada that shall fill the twentieth century."

Tinted lithographs of the monarch still hung on parlour walls in many homes, and the motto "One Flag, One Fleet, One Throne" appeared on the flyleaf of the 1910 *Ontario Fourth Reader*, beneath the Union Jack. But there were intimations that the Dominion might flex its own muscles. A whiff of mutiny against the imperial centre arose when Britain embarked on overseas adventures. In 1899, when Britain had been at war in South Africa against the Boers, many Canadians resented Britain's assumption that Canadian soldiers would automatically rush to enlist under the Union Jack. What quarrel did North Americans have with Afrikaner settlers? Now, a decade later, as naval competition between Britain and Germany heated up, Westminster asked for colonial contributions to the cost of expanding the British navy. Laurier, sensing resistance among his supporters, dodged this controversy by establishing Canada's "pocket navy": its own miniature fleet (in fact, two former Royal Navy ships) that might sail alongside Britain's Royal Navy. Jackie Fisher, Britain's bullying First Sea Lord, harrumphed that Canadians were "an unpatriotic, grasping people who only stick by us for the good they can get out of us."[1]

Quebecers were keenly sensitive to Quebec's interests in both federation and empire. There were now two million residents of the province, almost all of whose families had been in North America for generations and four out of five of whom spoke only French. For some Quebecers, the western expansion of Canada (Manitoba became a full province in 1870, Saskatchewan and Alberta in 1905) aroused all the same fears of French Canadians being swamped in an English-speaking ocean that George-Étienne Cartier had expressed in the Confederation Debates. In 1904 the editor of the Quebec newspaper *La Vérité* complained that "megalomania and the mania for constant growth [would] slowly [strangle] the autonomy of the French-Canadian nationality."[2]

Although Canada had been a self-governing Dominion since 1867, it still deferred to Britain for its foreign policy. This did not sit well with Quebecers like Henri Bourassa, a politician who was an outspoken critic of the British Empire. In 1912 he did not mince his words when he spoke to the Canadian Club. He pointed out that the Canadian cabinet had less voice in Britain's foreign policy than "one single sweeper in the streets of Liverpool, or one cabdriver on Fleet Street in London,"[3] since a Canadian had no vote in British elections. Instead Bourassa lobbied for more autonomy for a bicultural country based on the Cartier vision. "My native land is all of Canada, a federation of separate races and autonomous provinces. The nation I wish to see grow up is the Canadian nation, made up of French Canadians and English Canadians."[4]

But 1914 was different. When "that great black tornado" (in the words of former U.S. president Teddy Roosevelt) broke over Europe, a wave of enthusiasm to stand at Britain's side swept Canada. Prime Minister Robert Borden promised London all assistance possible. From the opposition benches, Sir Wilfrid Laurier proclaimed, "It is our duty to let Great Britain know and to let the friends and foes of Great Britain know that there is in Canada but one mind and one heart and that all Canadians are behind the Mother Country."[5] Everybody was convinced that it was going to be a short, sharp conflict: newspapers repeated the cliché that it would be over by Christmas, and men flocked into recruiting stations across English Canada. Within two months of the declaration of war, Canada had thirty-two thousand volunteers in uniform—with one thousand from Quebec.

Canada's contribution to the Allied war effort was considerable: 620,000 people would serve in the Canadian Expeditionary Force. The cost would be horrendous in lives and would strain national unity—but the country survived.

On July 7, 1917, twenty-two-year-old Harold Adams Innis was bored. After eight months as an artillery signaller in the trenches of northern France, the gangling young Canadian was tired of laying telephone lines, manning observation posts, and listening to the more or less continuous roar of guns. In a letter home, he described "working in mud, sleeping in mud and eating mud if the grub happens to touch anything." The assault on Vimy Ridge had begun twelve weeks earlier, and since then waves of bombardment had ebbed and flowed, ebbed and flowed. The signallers laboured on, conscious that, despite horrific losses, the Canadian unit was slowly consolidating its position close to the town of Vimy itself.

Private Innis was accustomed to monotony: there had been endless routine chores (collecting eggs, weeding round the rows of turnips and mangels) when he was growing up on the hundred-acre family farm in southwestern Ontario. Only books had insulated him from boredom. When he was twelve his parents had made considerable sacrifices to pay the train fare that allowed him to attend high school in Woodstock. Throughout his teens he had studied hard: after high school he had crammed a two-year teaching course into one year, then taken three years to do a four-year bachelor of arts course at McMaster University (then in Toronto). In the yearbook, he gave his motto as "Push on—Keep moving."[6]

Innis was self-disciplined and single-minded as a student, and his idea of relaxation was to join a debating club. But once war broke out and casualties in Europe mounted, the call for more volunteers intensified. He could not avoid the recruitment posters with such guilt-stirring slogans as "Your Chums are Fighting, Why aren't YOU ?"[7] English Canadians, particularly those with British family ties, continued to volunteer, but recruitment in Quebec quickly fell off: only about one in twenty of the troops sent overseas came from French Canada, although Quebec constituted one-third of the Canadian population. Pressure mounted on Prime Minister Borden to impose conscription, but he knew it could split the country.

As soon as Innis graduated in May 1916, he enlisted. The passage from

Harold Innis volunteered for military service in 1916 out of a sense of loyalty to Christian principles and democracy rather than to Britain.

clever student to weary, mud-spattered foot soldier was swift and demoralizing. First, as a new recruit, he was drilled by British officers and non-commissioned officers whose "insolence and brutality" and overt contempt for colonials he found intolerable. Next he was overwhelmed by the tedium of war.

That July night Private Innis wanted some action. "Since I was anxious to get out of the ordinary rut of signaling and one of the men was missing," he recalled in his memoir, "I served double duty." He joined a handful of "spotters" who cautiously climbed toward the top of the ridge and across the bleak landscape of barbed wire, dead bodies, and ditches to check out enemy installations. Suddenly a German shell exploded behind them. The Canadians realized that a German observation balloon was immediately above them, alerting a German battery to easy targets. Seconds later, a shell landed in their midst and Innis felt a piercing pain in his leg as blood gushed from his right thigh. It would have gushed from his back too, if a second piece of shrapnel had not lodged in a notebook in his rucksack rather than tearing into his flesh.[8]

Innis's fellow signallers quickly bandaged his leg and carried him to the dressing station. He was in horrible pain, but to his comrades he was lucky—he had scored a "Blighty," a flesh wound that would allow him to escape from the front. Within a few days Innis was on a hospital train, en route to England. But in the era before antibiotics, the wound was slow to heal and Innis suffered from fever and a succession of painful boils. Once again, the intense young Canadian began to chafe at monotony—this time, the routine of life in a Hampshire hospital. While the men around him revelled in trips to the local pub or London's West End, Innis yearned to get back to his studies at McMaster University and brooded over what he should write his master's thesis on. What impact, he asked himself, should the European carnage have on his own future, and that of his country?

The scars left on Canada by the war were deep and diverse; it changed the country forever. Harold Innis was also changed forever by the British condescension and senseless skirmishes he had witnessed, and by the unexpected upsurge of yearning he had felt for the land of his birth. The ideas that began to form as he lay under those rough army blankets in a Basingstoke hospital, his swollen leg throbbing, would shape his career and a new kind of nationalism in Canada.

⌖

Today, looking at photographs of Harold Innis, his shoulders hunched in a threadbare tweed jacket, I am struck by the rigid jaw and expression of skepticism on his face. Innis's background was classic English Canadian: he could have walked out of a short story by Alice Munro (who, like Innis, grew up in a rural township in southwestern Ontario). He was the brainy farm boy whom a Munro heroine meets in the local one-room schoolhouse and then watches escape from grinding field labour thanks to his parents' sacrifices. But although he had a background similar to many of the high achievers of his generation (farm boys who prospered thanks to their educations), he also retained a sense of being an outsider. That is one reason why John Watson entitled his biography of Innis *Marginal Man*.

Harold Innis's parents, William and Mary Innis, farmed a hundred acres of crops, pasture, and woodlot on Oxford County's checkerboard landscape of townships and fields, north of Lake Erie. It was just enough to feed their family of four children, but they struggled to find the right mix of produce (turkeys, pigs, hens, lumber) to keep enough bread on the table. The rhythms of the farm influenced young Harold for life. He could look at a chestnut or hickory nut and tell which tree on his father's property it had come from; he claimed that he could distinguish the source of a bucket of maple sap by its flavour. He knew he didn't want to replicate his forebears' lives of hard manual work, but he absorbed from his parents the no-nonsense stoicism and capacity for hard work typical of his Scots ances-tors,[9] and he never abandoned the austere self-discipline drilled into him every Sunday in Otterville's bleak little Baptist church.

As a student at McMaster, he could barely afford to eat, let alone dress up in a linen jacket and mingle with pedigreed students attending more fashionable institutions, such as the University of Toronto or Osgoode Hall. Once he was in France, his childhood memories provided psycholog-ical solace in the mayhem. "At present I am wielding . . . a pick and shovel," he wrote home a month after he had arrived at the front. "It reminds me of digging post holes in the clay during a dry summer as we had when putting up the line fence."[10]

If his rural origins moulded Innis's personality, his war experiences were so searing that he almost never spoke about them. Although he felt comradeship with fellow vets, he rarely attended Remembrance Day cere-monies, and he shuddered at platitudes about glorious sacrifice or wicked Huns. Only as he was dying, thirty-four years after his return from France, did he reveal his loathing of it to a fellow veteran, George Ferguson. Innis spoke, Ferguson would recall, "with real bitterness . . . bitterness I've never seen in another man about the stupidity of the whole performance."[11]

There were several reasons for that bitterness, but resentment against British attitudes was high on the list. As he told his sister, his faith had obli-gated him to fight in defence of Christian and democratic principles: "If I had no faith in Christianity, I don't think I would go."[12] But when he got to Eng-land he discovered a casual assumption among British officers that the colo-nials were there to defend the British Empire. "I remember the resentment which many of us felt when we were publicly thanked in England for coming over to help the Mother Country," he recalled at the end of his life. "We had

The Canadian National Vimy Memorial in France, finally unveiled in
1936, is dedicated to the memory of Canadians killed or injured in the
First World War—a conflict that changed Innis's life.

felt that we were concerned with fighting for Canada and Canada alone."[13] He
was also shocked by military discipline that was so rigid it sapped soldiers'
initiative and morale. He would later describe the "hated subservience to
officers. This cramping of individuality and the enforced idleness . . . have
eradicated many of the characteristics that marked the ordinary civilian. . . .
A man who has been over the top taking chances with life and death has become carefully indifferent to the mere happenings of everyday life."

Horrified by the senseless carnage and the manipulation of public opinion by government propaganda, Harold Innis began to think that his country should focus on itself rather than scrambling to serve Britain's needs.
While he was still in hospital in England, Innis scribbled down what his own
and his fellow countrymen's ambitions should be: "Work, work of brain and
of brawn, co-operation, organization and determination to heal the sores . . .
and to start again along the lines of sound national progress, is the hope of
the Canadian people . . . that she may take her place among the nations of
the world for the privilege of which her best blood had been shed."[14]

After a long and stormy transatlantic voyage from Britain, Harold Innis came limping home on Saturday, March 30, 1918, and stepped off the train at the little South Norwich railway station into his mother's waiting arms. Nobody present needed to remark that, despite his injury, he was one of the lucky ones. The bodies of thousands of other Canadian soldiers had been left behind in the blood-soaked mud of northern France. Harold spent that first night back in the bedroom he had always shared with his brother Sam. In the quiet darkness of his childhood home, he imitated for his younger brother the ear-splitting whines of shells of various calibres that had been lobbed toward him by German troops.

Innis's physical wound would take seven years to heal; the psychological damage lasted much longer. He showed all the symptoms of what we now recognize as post–traumatic stress disorder. In public, he could be thin-skinned, short-tempered, and obsessive, exasperating colleagues with frequent threats of resignation. In private, he could be remote, and he suffered recurring bouts of depression. He drove himself so hard that in the mid-1930s he would collapse from nervous exhaustion. His sense of urgency was obvious as soon as he set foot on Canadian soil. After only forty-eight hours at home, he headed back to Toronto to take his master's degree exams and get his discharge from the army. Of the latter, he would write, "It is hard to express adequately my feelings just at that point but 'glad' is a very poor word."

But what should he do next? Shrugging off his mother's dream that he would become a Baptist minister, he decided to take his discharge money and study a subject of which he felt painfully ignorant: economics. Settling on the University of Chicago because it offered a summer course, he arrived there in early July, bristling with resentments and exhaustion, and found himself in the middle of the celebration of Independence Day. Now he found new targets for his critical eye. He developed an acute antipathy to "American behavior on that occasion," he wrote in his memoir, because it consisted of "disgusting bragging and boasting."

Yet the University of Chicago was a congenial place. It was far less pretentious than the East Coast Ivy League schools. Like McMaster University, it had Methodist roots, and many professors came from small midwestern towns similar to those in Ontario. Chicago's political economists rejected such fashionable and abstract isms as Marxism or individualism in favour of sociological analysis of how communities function. Innis continued to recoil at American triumphalism ("What spoils everything is the ever lasting clapping of hands"[15]), but he found his economics courses so absorbing that he remained in Chicago to do a doctorate.

His thesis supervisor, the economic historian Chester W. Wright, recognized that this workaholic young Canadian was not just brilliant; he was also fiercely committed to his own country. So Wright suggested that Innis should write his thesis on the Canadian Pacific Railway.[16] The completion of the CPR less than four decades earlier was already recognized as a defining moment in Canadian history. What had driven its construction, and what had been its impact?

By July 1920 Innis had found his direction in life. He had acquired the analytical tools of economics and applied them to a Canadian history that had generally been seen exclusively in political terms. Moreover, he had met a good-looking student from Ohio called Mary Quayle, whose warmth and spontaneity softened his clenched-fist severity. They were soon engaged. When he finished his thesis, he wrote Mary, "Chester gasped when I wheeled the trunk load—comprising over six hundred pages—into his office. I was somewhat afraid that he would be obliged to move to other quarters. . . . Until it is accepted or rejected I shall more or less hold my breath."[17] He didn't have to hold it long. The University of Toronto offered him a lectureship in economics for $2,000 a year, providing financial security he had never known up until then. Two months later he was back in Canada, settling into his new job and preparing a course of lectures on economic history.

A History of the Canadian Pacific Railway, his thesis published in 1923, is a laborious work of scholarship. Filled with statistics about the number of ties and spikes used in the construction of the CPR, it did not represent an intellectual breakthrough; it simply repeated the conventional wisdom of the time that Canada was composed of four distinct regions—the

Maritimes, the St. Lawrence Basin, the Red River Settlement, and the Pacific Coast—that had developed independently and autonomously. I doubt that many people have ever read it.

But it was the starting point for Innis's most important work: *The Fur Trade in Canada*. Innis was now home, in the country for which he had, in the words of Donald Creighton, his first biographer, "a great and compelling affection."[18] Sojourns in Europe and Chicago had convinced him that Canada had a unique character—unknown and unappreciated, but one that he far preferred to those of Britain or the United States. "He felt obscurely that he must work for Canada," Creighton wrote. "Canadians must explain their new nation to the outside world. Above all, Canadians must understand themselves."

Mary Quayle and Harold Innis were married in 1921 and would have four children. Mary Quayle Innis would become a well-known economic historian and literary writer. The family spent summers in Muskoka, where Harold introduced his two sons and two daughters to the delights of sailing, canoeing, and *Alice in Wonderland*. His daughter Mary Innis Cates recalls a jovial parent who enjoyed family holidays, and regrets that "his biographers never describe him as a happy person." To outsiders, Innis remained a dark and forbidding figure. Nevertheless, the young academic was going to give his generation a reason to believe that an independent Canada made more than simply political sense. Its geography and its history mattered.

～

Huge skies, an eerie quiet broken only by the gurgle of fast-flowing water, the occasional glimpse of bear or moose—there are few experiences so quintessentially Canadian as a trip down a wide northern river. When I rafted down the Yukon River a few years ago, both the beauty of the landscape and its soft menace overwhelmed me. The loudest noise to break the silence was the rumble and splash of full-grown birch trees toppling into the water as the riverbank, undermined by powerful currents, collapsed. It was so different from the scenery I know best: the well-tilled neatness of

Europe, the small towns of central Canada, the commercial bustle of North America's eastern seaboard.

Most Canadians never visit the North; we huddle along the forty-ninth parallel, peering south across the border at a wealthier, more muscular country. Yet even the newest immigrant is aware of Canada's vast and often uncharted geography, reaching to the North Pole. Those who have spent time in Canada's North are rarely unmoved by its remote magnificence and the resilience of those who survive its harshness: Indigenous peoples, missionaries, fur trappers and traders, speculators and gold miners. The author Farley Mowat became a passionate champion of northern life with books like *Never Cry Wolf*. The pianist Glenn Gould found the "incredible tapestry of tundra and taiga" irresistible, as he said in his 1967 radio documentary *The Idea of North*. Both Gould and Mowat are among those for whom the North was a refuge as well as an inspiration.

In Innis's day, much of the North was uncharted. The ambitious professor, still limping from his war wound, was fascinated by the way that northern rivers sculpt their sinuous curves. "Channels are constantly changing, islands are being built up or cut down. . . . Large trees constantly under-

"Dirt research" took Innis down the Peace River in northern Alberta in 1924.

mined slap into the river. These are carried down and piled into great heaps on the heads of islands."[19] However, there was a subtext to Innis's enthusiasm. He was already working on a new approach to Canadian history that emphasized the North as a defining trait of Canadian identity.[20]

Harold Innis described his trips as "dirt research." They were a part of a much larger project: an economic history of Canada. During his doctoral investigation into the Canadian Pacific Railway, he had come to a conclusion that challenged conventional wisdom. Construction of the CPR was not the extraordinary, nation-building achievement that had glued Canada together, he argued. Instead, the railway had simply recaptured, through the new rail technology, a much older Canadian economic unity based on water communication. Now he wanted to get behind more recent, political milestones such as Confederation, the National Policy's erection of tariff barriers in 1879 to protect Canadian manufacturers, and western settlement, and chart the history of Canada's economic activities before 1867. He believed that if Canadians wanted to understand their country in the twentieth century, they had to study what had happened here in the seventeenth century.

For four hundred years, Canada had been exporting to Europe its primary products, or staples, as they were called in Innis's day: fish, fur, lumber. Yet the commerce had rarely been studied. Innis investigated documents about this trade that had lain unexamined in Canadian archives, and he insisted that his students in Toronto write long research papers about them. Frustrated by the way that map-makers focused on railway lines rather than interlocking river systems in their cross-Canada maps, he demanded that they cut new plates that reflected older trade routes. None of this made him popular. "Endless controversies developed between the bookstores, the map producers, the importers and myself," he remembered grimly—and he didn't include in his list colleagues exasperated by his constant rant that Canada should have its own history, not a borrowed British one. As he embarked on this enterprise, he realized that the history of the fur trade should be his topic, and he decided that "in a country of such vast extent I must begin immediately and try each summer to cover some new part of the country."[21]

Innis was not the first academic to study the fur trade: William A. Mackintosh from Queen's University was looking at staples, and the Scottish geographer Marion Newbigin was exploring French colonization in the St. Lawrence Valley. But Innis's thesis was more ambitious, and he was the only one whose research requirements included a tent, woollen underwear, leather hiking boots, and an eighteen-foot canvas-covered canoe. In May 1924, the pale, lanky twenty-nine-year-old packed his gear with his head "in very much of a whirl," as he put it.[22] Then he said goodbye to his wife and newborn son, Donald, and together with John Long, a high school teacher, took the train from Toronto to the West.

By mid-June, the two men had enjoyed several long days paddling between the steep banks of the wide, silty Peace River in northern Alberta, and short nights (it was nearly the summer equinox) camping on sandy beaches. Next, they canoed across Lake Athabaska into the Slave River, and then toward Great Slave Lake, a huge body of water in the Northwest Territories that is the deepest lake in North America and the tenth-largest lake in the world. Before they even reached the river mouth, they became aware of a hubbub. "I am looking out over Great Slave Lake," Innis wrote to Mary, "through a maze of tents and teepees. The Indians are all over the place— they are coming in for 'Treaty money.' And of course they all have dogs so that you can imagine what the place is like."[23]

Innis and Long now loaded their canoe onto a Hudson's Bay Company supply ship, the *Liard River*, for the next stage of the journey—on Canada's longest river, the Mackenzie, as it meandered north for nearly eighteen hundred kilometres through unbroken wilderness, finally disgorging its icy waters through a maze of channels into the Arctic Ocean. From the steamer's sunlit deck, Innis surveyed the dramatic northern panorama. Every chance he got, he peppered the captain, crew, and everyone they met at fuelling stations with questions about climate, supplies, hunting, travel, and habits. Typed up on his return to Toronto, those field notes were eighty-nine pages long.[24]

It is easy to romanticize Innis's northern adventures: he certainly did. One of his favourite books had always been Jack London's Klondike story

The Call of the Wild, and weeks before he left on his first trip, he and his wife watched a movie adaptation at the local cinema.[25] (Innis loved movies, particularly those starring Charlie Chaplin and the Marx Brothers.[26]) In his published account of the Mackenzie trip, he implied that he had made the whole journey by canoe, rather than mentioning that most of it was by supply ship. Donald Creighton adopted the same exultant tone when he described these travels: "The long summer, with its wind and sun, its space and peace and friendly companionship, had done him an immense amount of good. He had, as it were, shaken off the last evil effects of the war. . . . He never used his stick again. His limp disappeared."[27] In the years ahead, "dirt research" would take Innis to the Yukon, the northern regions of Ontario, Quebec, and Manitoba, the Maritime provinces, and Newfoundland and the Labrador coast. Although his face retained its skeptical expression in repose, his frame filled out, he began to laugh more, and his appetite for physical endeavour grew.

Yet his adventures were carefully planned and narrowly focused—"not as wild as all that," in the words of the geographer Matthew Evenden.[28] All details were arranged in advance; he carried letters of introduction from government officials; the overwhelming majority of Innis's informants were white men—HBC agents, railway company officials, missionaries. Indigenous peoples were observed from a distance, admired for their skills, but rarely interviewed.

These travels, and particularly the 1924 Mackenzie trip, provided Innis with the on-the-ground information he wanted about the region's geography, and in particular the crucial relationship between water routes and the fur trade. The Peace and Mackenzie Rivers had provided the highways for commerce: "The rivers hold sway."[29] In later trips he would spend more time on other activities, including mining, lumbering, and fishing, and the developments in transportation that would allow more northern exploitation. His improved health was mirrored by his optimism about the future, repeated frequently in numerous public lectures. "[Canada is] THE country of the twentieth century on account of her vast mineral resources," he told an audience in the small Ontario town of Hespeler in February 1926, according to a report in the *Mail and Empire*. "[I feel] perfectly safe in saying 'Go sell your boots and buy Government Bonds.'"[30]

The 1920s was a key decade for Harold Innis. When he wasn't furiously paddling through the North, he was teaching in the university, giving public lectures, burrowing through archival records, and establishing a new approach to Canada's economic history. His thinking was distilled into several scholarly books and articles. In 1927 he described the contemporary fur trade in *The Fur-Trade of Canada*. (The crucial difference between this title and that of his best-known book is the difference between "of" and "in.") Three years later, he published a brief biography of an almost forgotten eighteenth-century American trader, *Peter Pond: Fur Trader and Adventurer*. He also played a major role in two monumental volumes of *Select Documents in Canadian Economic History*.

But the culmination of all this activity, and his most important achievement, was the launch in 1930 of *The Fur Trade in Canada*. In this book, Innis launched a fundamental reinterpretation of our history and shaped a different perspective on Canada.

One of the most original aspects of *The Fur Trade in Canada* was Innis's starting point. He began with *Castor canadensis*. He quoted descriptions of the beaver from early explorers, such as David Thompson ("His meat is agreeable to most although fat and oily: the tail is a delicacy"). He described its two layers of fur, and why it was so attractive to furriers and felt makers. He explained how the trade network, based on waterways, predated the arrival of Europeans. Once the Europeans had arrived, demand for furs increased and First Nations became more adept at killing beavers, thanks to better weapons supplied by the newcomers. This meant that beaver populations in the East declined and the trade pushed westward across the continent. "The problem of the fur trade," he wrote, "became one of organizing the transport of supplies and furs over increasingly greater distances." In this movement, the "waterways of the beaver area were of primary importance and occupied a vital position in the economic development of northern North America." And those waterways ran east-west. "The northern half of North America remained British because of the importance of fur as a staple product."[31]

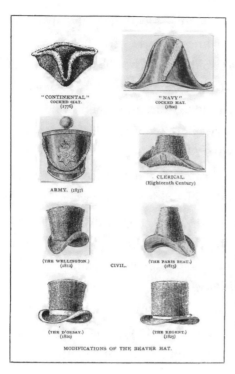

MODIFICATIONS OF THE BEAVER HAT.

The European enthusiasm for hats made from felted beaver fur fuelled colonial expansion in Canada from the sixteenth to the nineteenth century.

Starting his narrative in 1497, Innis relied on extensive quotations taken from his primary sources, including the Jesuit Relations and Samuel de Champlain's accounts of his voyages up and beyond the St. Lawrence River, to describe the earliest years of the fur trade. He emphasized that it was not simply a one-way flow to feed European demand for pelts: First Nations demand for manufactured goods had significant impact on European industries. "The fur trade was a phase of a cultural disturbance incidental to the meeting of two civilizations with different cultural traits," and alongside Indigenous-settler conflict, it caused dramatic disruptions in the relations among various Indigenous peoples.[32]

Innis recounted the struggle between groups of merchants, who entered beaver country through one of two natural corridors—either the St. Lawrence River route, controlled by the French until 1759, or Hudson Bay, gateway for the English. He did not ignore the important roles played by Indigenous guides, trappers, and middlemen. French coureurs de bois travelled north and west from Montreal while their British rivals, the Hudson's

Bay Company, built trading posts around Hudson Bay and its southern tip, James Bay. After the fall of New France in 1759, a group of aggressive Montreal merchants established the North West Company as a rival to the HBC and pushed their way across the continent, north to the Arctic Ocean along the Mackenzie River and west to the Pacific. Eventually, the two companies merged in 1821, the fashion for felt hats evaporated, and by the time of Confederation the fur trade was starting a slow collapse. However, British demand for another Canadian staple had already taken over. British shipbuilders needed lumber, and the transport infrastructure that had been developed by the fur trade was adapted to this new commerce. Enormous rafts of fresh-cut logs now floated down Canada's rivers. Throughout his book, Innis augmented his narrative with an avalanche of statistics about distances, costs, regulations, and loads.

In the 1930s many elements of the history of the fur trade would have been familiar to Innis's readers, who learned in school about "Gooseberry and Radishes" (Groseilliers and Radisson, the two French traders who explored the Lake Superior region in the 1650s and were involved in founding the HBC). But Innis had turned the story on its head. He did not write history from above, chronicling the doings of great men directing great events. Europe-based explorers, managers, and traders do not dominate his narrative: instead, he focused on the life cycle of the beaver, the technical details of river transportation, and the importance and skills of various First Nations (among them—using his terminology—Algonquins, Hurons, Montagnais, Cree, Blackfoot, Dogrib). Without the birchbark canoe, "Indian agriculture, Indian corn, and dependence on Indian methods of capturing buffalo and making pemmican, no extended organization of transport to the interior would have been possible."[33] At a time when Indigenous peoples were almost invisible in Canadian public life, Innis argued, "We have not yet realized that the Indian and his culture were fundamental to the growth of Canadian institutions."[34]

Innis revealed how geography had dictated the first European business venture to span the continent and draw the diverse regions into a single economic network extending from Labrador to the Alaska border. Canada constituted the most northerly of three distinct economies striped across the North American landscape. The southern states were the cotton belt. In the middle lay the widely diversified economic territory including New England and the coal and iron areas of the Midwest. Only in the North, and particularly on the inhospitable Canadian Shield where beavers thrived, could the fur trade prosper, and it had prospered thanks to the region's river highways. Coast-to-coast, argued Innis, it was all about beavers. "Canada emerged as a political entity with boundaries largely determined by the fur trade."[35]

This geographic framework profoundly influenced later economic developments. First, the fur trade laid the foundations for an economy almost entirely dependent on the export of staples to a rapidly industrializing Britain. Innis's "staple theory" argued that Canada's reliance on exports of its natural resources made the country dependent on more industrially advanced countries and vulnerable to market forces over which it had no control. Only when a new staple, such as lumber, wheat, or minerals, replaced older exports (cod and furs) would the economy keep growing.

And second, the transcontinental, centralized structure of the fur trade became the model for the Canadian banks, financial houses, and transportation companies that subsequently developed as national enterprises. "No such tendency toward unity of structure in institutions and toward centralized control as found in Canada can be observed in the United States."[36] The United States had regional railways and local banks; Canada had national railways and national banks.

The Fur Trade in Canada confirmed the thirty-six-year-old professor of political economy as a profoundly original thinker. No more great men; no more "colony to nation"! Ever since Confederation, the history of Canada had been presented as the fight by a handful of disparate British colonies to resist annexation by the United States and, through extraordinary human leadership, to achieve constitutional government. Now Harold Innis had produced an alternative explanation that presented Canada as the product of four centuries of intensive labour rather than a few years of constitutional negotiation.

His friend and colleague Donald Creighton was one of the first to recognize the significance of Innis's staple theory; he popularized Innis's ideas in his own 1937 book, *The Commercial Empire of the St. Lawrence*, as well as his two-volume biography of Sir John A. Macdonald. Thanks to Creighton, Innis's ideas morphed into the larger Laurentian thesis: the argument that Canadian economic and national development depended on the gradual exploitation of products such as fur, timber, and wheat by the merchants living in the cities scattered along the north bank of the St. Lawrence River system.

Harold Innis was a towering figure in Canadian academic life for thirty years, until his death in 1952. At the end of each decade, he produced a book of original analysis. With each publication, his arguments became more abstruse, and his prose denser (one critic has written of his gift of snatching "obscurity from the jaws of clarity"[37]). But none of his subsequent work had the same impact as *The Fur Trade in Canada*, first published in 1930 and continuously in print since then. The copy of *The Fur Trade* that my family owns is extraordinarily well thumbed. Unlike Innis's later publications, its prose is readable. It contains information that will not fail to enlighten Canadians who spend their summers near rivers and lakes and marvel at the industry of local beavers. From Innis's first chapter, "The Beaver," I first learned how *Castor canadensis* constructed the two lodges near our cottage, as part of its extraordinary adaptation, in Innis's words, "to the seasonal changes of a northern climate."

But most important, *The Fur Trade in Canada* provides a compelling argument for Canada's coherence as an independent country. This axiom sums up the entire book: "The present Dominion emerged not in spite of geography but because of it." Canada, which had already survived for more than half a century, was not an artificial political construction but a cohesive unit based on the Canadian Shield and the river systems and historically defined by the fur trade. Nationalist arguments about the historical integrity of Canada could now be based on a theory of territoriality as well as weaker myths of blood and political heroism.

This was a message that Canadians were ready to hear in 1930.

❧

Harold Innis's timing could not have been better.

Many of the boys who came limping home had, like Innis, learned in the trenches to see themselves as more than loyal subjects of the British Empire; now they were rethinking Canada's (and their own) colonial status. It helped that the 1920s was a prosperous decade: the population grew by 20 percent, to ten million, cities expanded, manufacturing boomed, and capital poured into the infrastructure required to bring mineral resources from the North. Canadians passed a crucial milestone in 1921: after that date, more of the population lived in towns and cities than in isolated farms and rural villages. City dwellers enjoyed a standard of living unthinkable for the Innis family and so many others before the war: electric lighting, radios, household appliances, cars. In the Roaring Twenties, possession of a flush toilet divided the haves from the have-nots.

In Ottawa, politicians quietly severed Canada's remaining links with Britain. For the Paris Peace Conference in 1919, Prime Minister Robert Borden had insisted that Canada should have its own seat at the table (although Britain ultimately signed the final treaty on behalf of the empire). The Imperial Conference of 1926, chaired by British prime minister Lord Balfour, issued a declaration that the various Dominions were "autonomous Communities within the British Empire, equal in status, in no way subordinate to one another in any aspect of their domestic or external affairs." Effectively, Canada could now conduct its own foreign affairs instead of falling into line behind British policy. Canada acquired even more muscle with the 1931 Statute of Westminster, which granted former colonies full legislative freedom from Westminster. (The only shackle on this constitutional advance was that the Statute of Westminster didn't cover the British North America Act, because the Canadian provinces and the federal government could not agree on an amending formula for it. Perhaps it seemed like a small point at the time, but it would become a festering wound.)

At the same time, a new self-consciousness flowered within the English-speaking regions of the Canadian Shield. On July 1, 1927, more than fifty thousand people gathered on Parliament Hill to celebrate Canada's Diamond Jubilee, and the country's first coast-to-coast broadcast allowed millions more Canadians to hear the speeches, the Peace Tower carillon, and a spirited rendering of "O Canada."[38] Desire for a national culture began to bubble, to match the country's economic growth and constitutional autonomy. This was a challenge in a country with an intellectual veneer as thin as a fingernail: there were fewer than twenty universities scattered through the nine provinces. But there was a rush to establish journals, professional organizations, national networks: the *Canadian Forum*, the Canadian Authors Association, the Canadian Historical Association, Canadian Clubs.

On the West Coast, Emily Carr grappled with the challenge of seeing rainforests, Pacific skies, and Indigenous artifacts through new eyes. In Toronto, Group of Seven painters deliberately established a style of landscape painting that owed nothing to Old World images of windmills and cows. In literature, a handful of novelists planted the seeds of a new northern realism. Frederick Philip Grove's *Settlers of the Marsh* and Martha Os-

Crowds gathered on Parliament Hill on July 1, 1927, to celebrate the country's Diamond Jubilee. A sense of national identity was finally developing.

tenso's *Wild Geese* described with harsh authenticity the struggles of immigrants on the prairies. Frank Scott, a McGill professor of law and a poet, caught the mood in 1926 with his poem "New Paths," which included these evocative lines:

> *Child of the North*
>
> *Yearn no more after old playthings....*
> *And all the burdensome inheritance, the binding legacies,*
> *Of the Old World and the East.*
>
> *Here is a new soil and a sharp sun*
>
> *Turn from the past*
> *Walk with me among these indigent firs*
> *Climb these rough crags ...*

The Fur Trade in Canada was well reviewed. The *Times Literary Supplement* described it as "learned and admirably worked out,"[39] and the *New York Times* commented, "Though his details are overwhelming, [he] has never lost sight of the grand cultural and economic considerations that are involved."[40] The *Boston Globe* wrote admiringly that "while painstakingly authentic [the book] is at the same time pungent with the good smell of the woods, the thrill of pioneering, of quick death, narrow escapes."[41] Reviewers within Canada paid more attention to Innis's analysis. In the *Canadian Forum*, Innis was praised for rescuing Canadian history from "those badly over-worked heroes, the French Catholic Church and the United Empire Loyalists.... Our political historians ... keep refining upon their chosen theme of the relations of ... a colony to a mother country, [and] they have practically neglected all those internal forces in the colony which have given to our Canadian civilization what distinctive concrete qualities it possesses."[42]

Despite the enthusiasm, *The Fur Trade in Canada* was no bestseller: it took fifteen years to sell the first printing of one thousand copies. But its thesis and approach seeped into popular culture more rapidly. First, Innis's thesis coincided with the new nationalism. The idea that Canada's uniqueness was shaped by the country itself, with its powerful rivers, boreal forests and rainforests, swirling skies and granite heart, began to take hold.

Next, as economic conditions within Canada changed, Innis's analysis gathered momentum. After the American stock market crashed in 1929, world demand for Canada's staples—wheat, lumber, mining products—plunged. By 1933, one-fifth of Canadians were dependent on government assistance, and prairie farm families were starving. As the historian Carl Berger points out, "The Depression made the economic interpretation of the past seem more appropriate than the Britannic idealism of the previous generation."[43] The sense of fatalism and economic determinism in *The Fur Trade* reflected the mood of helplessness in the thirties, when people felt themselves at the mercy of overwhelming forces beyond their control.

However, when the university professor, now balding but more self-assured, strode onto public platforms to discuss the country's economic ills, he never offered any solutions. "Let me warn you," Innis once said, "that any exposition by any economist which explains the problems and their solutions with perfect clarity is certainly wrong."[44] *The Fur Trade* had made him the greatest Canadian national historian of his day, yet he had reached his conclusion independently of the increasingly fashionable nationalism. He scorned academics who left universities to get involved in elected politics (although he threw himself into policy debates), and he never argued that the federal government should intervene to alleviate suffering during the Depression. "Baptists are always suspicious of control," he told his Winnipeg colleague, the noted historian Arthur Lower.

Harold Innis himself was in as much of a hurry as ever. By the 1930s he had already shifted his attention to a different staple: cod, which had predated fur as North America's biggest export to Europe. Determined to extend his economic analysis to another staple industry, fisheries, he arrived in St. John's, Newfoundland, in June 1930, where, he discovered, "One breathes, eats, sees, and talks nothing but cod." He would spend a month doing "dirt research" in Gaspé and Labrador, exploring the European dom-

Atlantic cod predated fur as a major North American export to Europe. The cod fishery still thrived in the 1930s and 1940s.

ination of the North Atlantic fishery.[45] In 1940 he published *The Cod Fisheries: The History of an International Economy*, which looked at how another staple had linked the eastern seaboard of North America to Europe. But he remained a northern booster, enthusiastically extolling the potential of northern development.[46]

When he was forty-six, he achieved one of his greatest ambitions: he was appointed head of the Department of Political Economy, an achievement that had appeared unthinkable twenty years earlier, when the department was dominated by Oxbridge-educated anglophiles. Now he demanded that Canadians should fill academic posts where possible, and he reacted angrily if anyone cast aspersions on standards within Canadian ivory towers. When the Carnegie Endowment for International Peace commissioned a series on Canadian-American relations, he insisted that Canadians should edit Canadian material.[47]

Harold Innis's scholarly output continued to be astonishing: he edited volumes on economic history, he delivered keynote addresses, he wrote introductions to volumes by other scholars, he contributed to essays in honour of colleagues, he spoke at international conferences. Whenever he travelled through a university town, he made a point of visiting faculties of history and economics.[48] However, he was in such a rush to publish that his written work became increasingly inaccessible.[49] His habit of dumping undigested blocks of statistics and lengthy quotations into his text bewildered and exasperated readers.

By the time Innis's landmark study on cod was published, the author himself was racing off in a new direction. So were events beyond the university. Innis was horrified by the outbreak of war in Europe in September 1939 and appalled at the idea that universities might be ransacked for soldiers and government advisers. He insisted that a scholar should focus on scholarship: "He must either do this or throw in his hand to the enemy."[50] Innis had lofty values of human freedom in mind when he said this, but it also captured everything he had thought a quarter of a century earlier, under the scratchy hospital blankets in Basingstoke. As he wrote in 1943, "Scholarship provides the essentials for that steadiness and self-respect by which Canada can become a nation worthy of those who have fought and given up their lives in the last war or in this."[51]

And he launched himself in yet another new direction. Starting with an interest in the pulp and paper industry, he widened his scope first to the world of newspapers, and then to the universe of communications. In his final three books, *Empire and Communications* (1950), *The Bias of Communications* (1951), and *Changing Concepts of Time* (1952), Harold Innis explored the ways in which technologies of communication distort the cultures in which they are embedded. It was a stupendous challenge: he ranged over Egyptian, Babylonian, Greek, and Roman civilization, the British Empire, and into the present. He covered oral and written traditions, technologies that dominate space, and those that survive time. His obsessions took him on an intellectual journey far beyond Canada, staples, or economics; as he thrashed around on philosophical terrain, few of his economics and history colleagues followed him. The few who did were dismayed by his maddening obscurity. As the *Economist* noted in its review, "Incoherence, indeed, is Professor Innis' besetting sin."[52]

However, the last laugh was on Innis's critics. Although Innis's writing style was aphoristic, fragmentary, ambiguous, and clotted with obscure references, his work was carried forward by an admiring colleague. The literary scholar Marshall McLuhan, undoubtedly one of the most charismatic academics Canada has ever produced (and the only one to appear in a Woody Allen film), built on Innis's communication theories in books like *The Mechanical Bride* (1951), *Understanding Media: The Extensions of Man* (1964), and *The Medium Is the Massage* (1967) that were far more lucid than his mentor's. And a new generation of Innis scholars recognizes Innis as a thinker ahead of his time, whose later books anticipated communications studies. According to his biographer John Watson, "Working before the invention of the transistor, the microchip, the personal computer and the Internet, Innis was approximating their effect on thought and research in the use of primitive photocopying, a pastepot, and a long pair of scissors."[53]

⁀⌣⁀

So how did Harold Innis help shape his generation's image of Canada? The idea that Canada had emerged because of its geography, and not in spite of it, boosted the self-confidence of a country that, like Innis, had emerged from the First World War ready for more autonomy. His insight pierced the narrative chatter from the 1930s onward as Canadians sought to construct their nationhood and turn a settler culture in the imperial hinterland into an independent hub. As Watson puts it, "His theory moved marginal man, particularly the 'colonial' intellectual, to the centre stage of Western culture." By the time of his death in 1952, aged only fifty-eight, Innis was acknowledged as the dominant figure in Canadian historical studies of the interwar generation. "To Professor Harold A. Innis," announced the London *Times*, "the Canadian social sciences owe a greater debt than to any other man."

His impact on the next generation of history students was enormous. Many had avoided Canadian history in university because it was branded "boring." *The Fur Trade in Canada* was a revelation—compelling and important. Rod Macleod, a young graduate student from Alberta, reluctantly enrolled for a course at Queen's University, in Ontario. "Innis was like a light bulb going on for me," he recalls. "*Fur Trade* actually explained the disconnected anecdotes that passed for the Canadian history I'd learned at my Edmonton high school. [I finally grasped] why New France did not thrive as the New England colonies did . . . why the fur trade beyond the St. Lawrence valley promoted peaceful relationships with the First Nations . . . how the timber trade created the first large-scale wave of immigration." Macleod went on to become a leading historian of western Canada, Sam Steele's biographer, and chair of the history department at the University of Alberta in his hometown.

Today, Innis is almost forgotten outside universities. Within his own lifetime, other scholars contested his attempt to screen Canadian history exclusively through an economic lens. Prairie historians like W. L. Morton objected vociferously to Innis's assumptions that Canadians were homogeneous and that the West was peripheral in importance. Later historians have rejected the notion that the staple theory is sufficient to explain our country's evolution, while economists subsequently railed against Innis's insistence that economics should be approached through history. At the college named after him within the University of Toronto, a favourite song is "Who the Hell Was Harold Innis?"

Nobody is writing national histories for general readers in Canada any longer, and although primary products still play a major role in our economy, the great rivers of Canada have little impact on our politics. But at a crucial moment in our history, Innis provided a compelling intellectual framework for a country struggling to free itself of imperial ties while fighting off American domination. He also dragged Canadian attention toward the North, making it a defining part of our identity. No wonder that, in every federal election campaign these days, party leaders always don their parkas, head north, and do a photo op with a backdrop of ice floes. Maybe it's political window dressing, but it certainly says something primal about our country.

PART 2

A Different Kind of Country

CHAPTER 5

Caring for Each Other

Tommy Douglas Kick-Starts Medicare

What do you say to a woman whose family is on relief, whose husband has died because they couldn't get the kind of medical and hospital care he needed, a woman who has no prospects for the future and very little in the way of social welfare assistance? It is awfully hard to know what to say to people like that.

—Tommy Douglas, interviewed by Chris Higginbotham (1958)

I don't mind being a symbol but I don't want to become a monument. There are monuments all over the Parliament Buildings and I've seen what the pigeons do to them.

—Tommy Douglas (1984)

So far I've written about people who, building on their own experiences, skills, and imaginations, helped lay the foundations for the way their contemporaries saw this country: a federation held together by its political structures, its respect for the law, and its geography; a vast and beautiful land that had been peopled for centuries and had an internal cohesion. In their different ways, Cartier, Steele, Carr, and Innis all contributed to a collective vision of Canada. Their ideas slowly took root in the deepening soil of nationhood. They were not alone; other homegrown intellectuals, artists, and politicians (many of whom I've mentioned) also struggled with this perennial source of angst: what does it mean to be a Canadian? There are many threads in this tapestry.

Fast-forward to the Canada that emerged from the Second World War. The country that was almost lethally split by Quebec's hostility to conscription in the First World War had come through the next war apparently intact. Pride in Canada's extraordinary contribution to the Allied effort in the Second World War nurtured a more robust self-confidence (tinged by mounting resentment of American muscle). This was a different Canada from the fragile entity that in 1918 had reached for autonomy and the self-knowledge sought by Harold Innis. Over a million Canadians (out of a population of 12.5 million) saw service between 1939 and 1945, and by war's end Canada had the third-largest navy among the Allied powers, the fourth-largest air force, and the fourth-largest army. Members of Canada's armed forces had brought credit to themselves and to their country.

Canada was solvent, thanks to efficient price and wage controls, heavy taxation, and war-bond drives, and its economy now boomed. Compared with the war-ravaged countries of Europe and Asia, it was an untouched utopia—a magnet for refugees. By 1960 the population had swelled to eighteen million. The benefits of the social safety net (including family allowances and pensions) were a beacon for others too. In 1949 Newfoundlanders voted in a referendum to become the tenth province of Canada, completing the nation that sprawled from Atlantic to Pacific. It was a case of the irrepressible selling the irresistible. Premier Joey Smallwood proclaimed with typical hyperbole: "Our very manhood, our very creation by God, entitles us to standards of life no lower than our brothers on the mainland."[1]

Snip, snip, snip: a flurry of activity in Ottawa cut Canada's ties with Britain. A new citizenship act enabled immigrants to become citizens of Canada, as opposed to "British subjects." When legal appeals to the Judicial Committee of the Privy Council in Great Britain were abolished, Canada's Supreme Court became supreme in fact as well as name. The patrician Vincent Massey became Canada's first Canadian-born governor general, and the first GG to be appointed by the government of Canada, in 1952. The most important symbolic step would be taken in 1964, after a bruising debate, when a Liberal government headed by Prime Minister Lester Pearson replaced the old Red Ensign (featuring the British flag in the corner) with the bold new Canadian Maple Leaf flag.

Was Canada now a major international power? Hardly. But it was a player in global affairs, nonetheless: a "middle power" with an impressive war record and outsized microphone, whose diplomats played a leading role in drafting the United Nations Charter. It became an inveterate joiner of every international organization it could, and it established an image as an international peacekeeper and benevolent donor of foreign aid. It was prosperous, democratic, eager to help. Yet there remained a sense of unrealized potential and undefined identity, with not much more than a shared passion for hockey, doughnuts, and savings accounts, and a distaste for guns, to unite most French and English speakers, old-timers, and new immigrants.

✢

In 2003 Tommy Douglas was voted the "Greatest Canadian" in a CBC Television competition. He beat out not just the man I championed in the contest, Canada's first prime minister, Sir John A. Macdonald, but also such luminaries as Prime Minister Pierre Trudeau and the hockey great Wayne

Gretzky. Douglas achieved this status because he led the campaign for state-funded health insurance in his province, Saskatchewan. His success provided the model and momentum to the federal Liberal Party to do the same for the whole country. Today, in the words of the political columnist Jeffrey Simpson, medicare is "the third rail of Canadian politics. Touch it and you die. Every politician knows this truth."[2] Canadians regularly tell pollsters that our health care system is our most important defining national characteristic. (It is linked to another cherished Canadian value: not being American.) "Tommy," as he is universally known, is an icon within the national imagination and a symbol of deeply held Canadian values.

Douglas bridges two eras in the history of modern Canada. He began life here shortly after the First World War, during the pioneer years on the prairies, when most Canadians had only their own meagre resources to draw on and anticipated little help from governments, federal or provincial. By the time he died, after another world war and the explosive growth of the Canadian economy, Canadians were wealthy and expected government to provide for the public good. Tommy Douglas had a lot to do with this transition in expectation. He had established the model for our political leaders in the second half of the twentieth century: he gave voters a taste for high-flying "visions." Plodding, grey-flannel government was not enough.

Before I delve into Douglas's story, I want to describe the pre-Tommy years when medical care was out of reach of most Canadians. Health crises that today are dealt with almost routinely (appendicitis, difficult childbirths, broken limbs) could be killers. If you got sick, you had only your family, your neighbours, and your church to turn to. The doctor was likely kilometres away, and anyway you couldn't afford him. In the 1920s Canadians had a life expectancy of fifty-five years, compared with well over eighty today.

The governments of most European countries had already decided that citizens' health was a collective responsibility. Germany adopted a health insurance system as early as 1883, only twelve years after its various principalities had joined together in a federation, to provide some glue for the new state. (Such a notion was beyond the imaginations of our Fathers of

Confederation in 1867: in the view of George-Étienne Cartier and his colleagues, railways, not social programs, would knit the infant Dominion together. How times have changed!) The British government implemented a similar health insurance scheme in 1912, in order to meld a hodgepodge of private arrangements between doctors and workers' organizations.[3]

But here in Canada, provincial governments did not have the money to get into health care, and successive federal governments argued that Ottawa's role was confined to running the armed forces and the post office and erecting tariff barriers to foreigners. Serious lobbying for a national health care system began only when the boys came marching home from war in 1918. After sacrificing friends and health in the carnage, they found themselves facing unemployment, poor working conditions, and minimal medical help for their wounds. Soon government-funded health care was one of the several demands voiced by a rash of new political protest parties, including Alberta's Social Credit Party, Progressives in Manitoba, and United Farmers parties in Ontario and Alberta.

At first, Ottawa continued to resist the demand: federal politicians insisted that social assistance was the responsibility of the provinces. But then the wiliest politician in Canadian history became prime minister, in 1921. Liberal leader William Lyon Mackenzie King was a man who proclaimed himself a reform leader while marching behind the troops. With his finger in the political winds, he immediately endorsed a national sickness plan. However, he then did nothing about it. Only the imminent defeat of his minority government forced him to take action on another of his progressive promises: a twenty-dollar-a-month pension for those over seventy years of age who were destitute.

The 1920s was a prosperous decade in Canada, and debates about health and welfare programs simmered down. Few Canadians realized how shaky were the foundations of the postwar wealth, which rested on a handful of staples—wheat being among the most important by this time, alongside lumber and minerals. Between 1925 and 1929, the prairie provinces supported an astonishing 40 percent of the world's wheat export market.[4] Then the New York Stock Exchange collapsed in 1929, and the continent was plunged into the Great Depression. By 1933 hardship and starvation stalked the land: around 20 percent of the Canadian labour force was unemployed. These were the years when the significance of Harold Innis's ideas began to sink in and Canadians glimpsed the dangers of a national economy based on staples.

Nowhere was the catastrophe so great as on the prairies, where one-crop farming had robbed the land of its ability to regenerate and turned it into a bleak Sahara. Calamitous droughts soon transformed Manitoba, Saskatchewan, and Alberta into a dust bowl: hot, dry winds blew the topsoil off in black clouds. Farm incomes shrivelled and farm families faced starvation across all three provinces—but southern Saskatchewan was affected hardest and longest.[5]

Accounts of those years are almost as horrifying as memoirs of life in the trenches during the First World War. For two successive summers, the clouds of grasshoppers were so thick that they blotted out the sun. The hoppers ate *everything*—not just thistles and tree bark and the new shoots in the fields, but even lace curtains and clothes hung out to dry. The entire province headed toward bankruptcy. Shoeless children wept with hunger. Mrs. Thomas Perkins, a desperate farmer's wife in Kingdom, Saskatchewan, wrote to Prime Minister R. B. Bennett in 1933, begging for help. "My husband will be 64 in Dec. and his nuritis [sic] very bad at times in his arms and shoulders. We have had very little crop for the last three years: not enough at all to pay taxes and live and this year crops around here are a complete failure. . . . I really don't know what to do. We have never asked for anything of anybody before."[6] Enter Thomas Clement Douglas.

❧

One recent summer's day, I flew over southern Saskatchewan and through the airplane window looked down on a landscape that might have been painted by a child: vast rectangular fields occasionally bisected by meandering coulees; brilliant yellow and green crops ripening in the summer sunshine; a handful of tiny vehicles moving along roads as straight as rulers. Wheat, oats, alfalfa, barley, canola, lentils—from this height, I couldn't

ARTISTIC VISIONS OF CANADA

Logging, 1888. George Reid, who was born in Ontario and studied in Paris, applied the classical techniques of painting to quintessentially Canadian themes.

The Flood Gate, 1900–1901 (*above*). Another Ontario painter, the self-taught Homer Watson, was admired as "the Canadian Constable" because his work was similar in subject matter and style to the British painter's. In *Indian Church*, 1929, Emily Carr's depiction (*right*) of a missionary church encircled by lush Pacific rain forest was uniquely Canadian.

Emily Carr's raw intensity and concern for the changing landscape, as shown (*above left*) in *Scorned as Timber, Beloved of the Sky*, 1935, speaks to contemporary artists such as Douglas Coupland (*above right*).

The West Wind, 1916–1917 was completed by Tom Thomson shortly before he drowned. One of our most widely reproduced images, this painting encapsulates the idea of survival in a harsh landscape that the Group of Seven would collectively promote.

For What?, 1918. Frederick Varley served as a war artist and was horrified by the brutality of trench warfare. He returned to Toronto, became a founding member of the Group of Seven, and directed his attention to a different kind of wilderness.

Untitled, 1944. Pegi Nicol MacLeod was one of the few women to be offered an official commission as a war artist. Although she was antiwar, she was eager to showcase the importance of Canadian women's contribution to the war effort.

Paul-Émile Borduas and Jean Paul Lemieux were two of the foremost painters of twentieth-century Quebec. In Montreal, with works such as *Leeward of the Island*, 1947 (*left*), Borduas challenged the establishment by introducing abstraction and denouncing the influence of the Catholic Church. In Quebec City, Lemieux employed a modernist aesthetic in powerful evocations of figures, landscapes, and urban scenes, often from his own childhood or Canadian history. *Charlottetown Revisited*, 1964 (*above*) captures the weight of the past.

Hauling Job Sturge's House, 1979. The community strength of Newfoundland's outports is caught in David Blackwood's prints. Here, a fisherman's home is hauled across the ice as part of a government attempt to consolidate scattered and isolated communities.

Reason over Passion, 1968. Inspired by a remark from the newly elected prime minister Pierre Trudeau, Joyce Wieland drew on the traditional female skill of quilting for this arresting piece of conceptual art. A similar quilt, with the words *La raison avant la passion*, hung at 24 Sussex Drive.

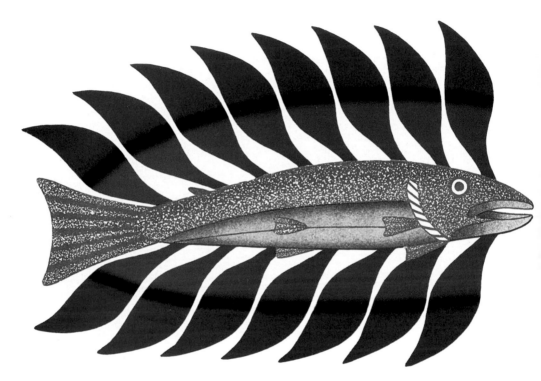

Luminous Char, 2008. Contemporary Indigenous artists combine modern techniques and materials with traditional images. After a printmaking co-operative was established in Cape Dorset, Kenojuak Ashevak developed a distinctive graphic style.

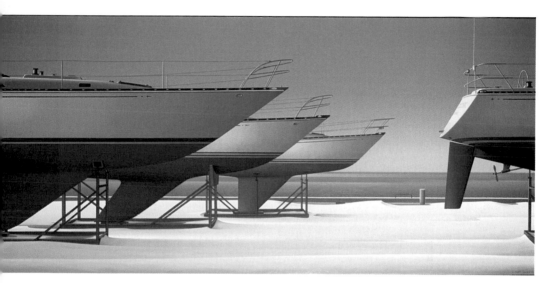

Four White Boats: Canadian Gothic, 2002. With extraordinary precision and light effects, Newfoundland artist Christopher Pratt captures the Atlantic province's uniqueness in this eerie depiction of sailboats, locked in winter.

Cree artist Kent Monkman constructs this ironic commentary on how Indigenous culture has been misrepresented. In *The Academy*, 2008, references to classical sculpture and early Canadian portraits jostle together with European stereotypes of "Indians" in a longhouse.

Explosions, 2011. Our continued fascination with the sublime North, and concern about ecological damage there, are caught in Sarah Anne Johnson's photo-based work.

identify which crop filled which rectangle. But the impression of luxuriant fertility was unavoidable. No wonder the province was once known as the breadbasket of the empire.

But today's lushness is thanks to intensive technological farming methods that have been around for only a few decades: soil conservation, water management, and (amid controversy) genetically modified crops. During the 1930s Depression, this landscape was a bleached desert of blowing topsoil, tumbleweed, and poverty. If you want to see what Saskatchewan's early years were like, take a look at *Drylanders*, a 1963 National Film Board production directed by Don Haldane.[7] This black and white feature film, still regularly shown to Saskatchewan schoolchildren, traces the fortunes of the Greer family as the father laboriously develops a farm from the virgin prairie, then watches drought destroy all his efforts. It is unbearably grim—a story of dashed hopes and tragedy that was shared by thousands of immigrants on the prairies back then. I defy anybody to watch *Drylanders* without thanking their lucky stars that they've never had to pull a plow across virgin grassland or watch crops wither in the field.

Saskatchewan is no different from many regions of Canada, including the Yukon, Newfoundland, and Alberta. Its economy (and its population) has yo-yoed across the decades, driven by business cycles, climate shifts, and world markets beyond its control. Family farms like the Greers' have gone today, replaced by the massive agribusiness enterprises that I saw from the air. Even more significantly, agriculture now constitutes less than a tenth of Saskatchewan's economy; sales of potash, oil, and natural gas fill the provincial coffers. But Saskatchewan is unique in one respect. In the mid-twentieth century, it was an incubator for "prairie socialism." This political ideology spawned not only social programs that improved the welfare of individual Canadians but also an attitude to government that seeped into the national psyche.

One thread in the mid-twentieth-century tapestry of national identity was a shared belief that government can be a force for good, improving life for everyone. Canadians no longer embrace this idea wholeheartedly; too many political scandals and government-bashing politicians in recent years have eroded confidence that governments are always efficient or even be-nevolent. Nevertheless, we share a residual faith in government that, according to political scientists, makes Canadians more like Scandinavians than like Americans. And where did this faith come from? Saskatchewan's Tommy Douglas can claim much of the credit.

As premier of Saskatchewan from 1944 to 1961, Douglas headed an interventionist government that introduced a web of social programs. From the hopelessness and despair of Saskatchewan in the 1930s, as depicted in *Drylanders*, Douglas forged help-the-other-fellow frontier radical-ism. He laid the groundwork for a government-run public health insurance system in his province. He didn't stop there either: he moved into federal politics and lobbied Ottawa to make medicare a coast-to-coast program.

Douglas is an unlikely hero, a chirpy bantam of a man who spent eleven years as a Baptist minister before entering the bare-knuckle world of politics. He was obviously a mesmerizing presence. The passion and poetry of

Tommy Douglas's oratorical skills, legendary while he was a young Baptist minister in Saskatchewan, served him well in politics.

his oratory, with its revivalist-meeting resonance, are undimmed in recordings of his speeches, although at the end of his life he would bomb on television because he looked like an old geezer. And he strategically deployed a weapon rare in Canadian politics: a sense of humour. "The Liberals talk about a stable government, but we don't know how bad the stable is going to smell," he remarked in the 1965 election.[8]

What lay behind the showmanship? When did he decide that he could serve his God more effectively in politics than the pulpit? Where did he get the mental toughness required to face down some mean opponents (several of the most ruthless were in his own party)? How did he persuade Canadians to adopt a different vision of society, and to prefer co-operation to survival-of-the-fittest individualism? What drove Tommy?

＋∾＋

Tommy Douglas found himself immersed in a political clash as soon as he set foot in Canada as a fourteen-year-old in January 1919. He arrived in Winnipeg from the gritty Scottish shipbuilding city of Glasgow, along with his mother and two younger sisters. They were awaiting his father, Tom, a taciturn iron moulder who had served in France and not yet been discharged from the British army.

Homeless, unemployed veterans roamed Winnipeg's streets that chilly winter; unlike Harold Innis, most had neither means nor the opportunity to pursue their educations, even if they had wanted to. "There was no unemployment insurance and no orderly transition of the economy from war to peace," Douglas recalled years later.[9] His father, an early supporter of the British Labour Party, had bred in young Tommy a healthy contempt for the class system and skepticism about capitalism. Now the scrappy fourteen-year-old began to attend some of the meetings at which protesters demanded decent wages and the right to organize unions. Employees in the building trades had seen living costs jump 73 percent since 1913, while wages had risen only 13 percent. The demands were echoed by metalworkers, street-railwaymen, telephone operators, city police officers.

The protest meetings had little impact. So on May 15, more than thirty thousand workers walked off the job and Winnipeg, a city of two hundred thousand people, came to a standstill. Winnipeg's employers and city council were seriously rattled. With the 1917 Russian Revolution fresh in their minds, they decided that dangerous Bolsheviks were about to take over the city, so they started sacking striking public employees and ramming through new laws permitting the deportation of "enemy aliens."

On June 21, 1919, a day that became known as Bloody Saturday, Douglas was in the thick of events. "We had a very bad situation," Douglas recalled. "Several other young fellows and I climbed up on the roof of a building to see the mounted police charge the workers in Market Square in front of City Hall. The police opened fire and killed a man . . . not very far from where we were." As bullets whistled around their ears, Douglas and his pals watched demonstrators overturn a streetcar and the Mounties shoot into the crowd. Then they heard that the police had thrown into jail a revered local hero: J. S. Woodsworth, the former Methodist minister who ran the All People's Mission in Winnipeg's overcrowded North End.

The bitterness generated by the strike (despite the brief interruption for Sam Steele's funeral) left Winnipeg a class-divided city for generations to come.[10] Such police brutality leaves a lasting impression on young activists; anyone who participated in protests at the 2001 Summit of the Americas in Quebec City or the 2010 meeting of the G20 political leaders in Toronto can probably still taste the raw anger of those moments. Young Tommy never forgot the 1919 clash, and in subsequent years he would perceive a pattern to such events. "Whenever the powers that be can't get what they want, they're always prepared to resort to violence or any kind of hooliganism to break the back of organized opposition."[11] Douglas's sympathies were always with the common man standing up for his rights rather than the (often badly trained) police, under orders from frightened or angry politicians, trying to restore order.

If the Winnipeg General Strike reinforced Douglas's solidarity with blue-collar workers and distrust of "the powers that be," a childhood injury had taught him the precariousness of health care among the underprivileged. When he was six, he fell and cut his right knee; osteomyelitis devel-

During the 1919 Winnipeg General Strike, the Royal North West Mounted Police charged on horseback, swinging truncheons, then fired on demonstrators. Thirty lay injured after the fracas, and two men died.

oped in his leg. A few years later, during a preliminary trip the Douglas family made to Canada, the knee problem flared up again. The child was in constant pain, and doctors told his mother, Ann, that the leg would have to be amputated. Then a prominent orthopaedic surgeon decided this little boy would make an ideal teaching project for his students. The surgery was a complete success, and the Douglas family were overjoyed and deeply grateful. But as an adult, Tommy Douglas would reflect on the cruelty of a system where a rich kid could buy a top surgeon, but a poor child would keep his leg only if the physician chose to use him as a teaching aid.

Today Tommy is a legend, and these two events—the near loss of his knee and his front-row seat at the Winnipeg General Strike—are seen as inspirations along his political journey. Both happened before his fifteenth birthday, and it would be years before he ran in an election; I'm sure that a career in politics would have seemed unthinkable to a new immigrant who had left school at fourteen. It certainly would have been almost impossible if he had stayed in Britain and tried to enter British politics. His father's hero, Keir Hardie, a Glasgow miner who became Britain's first Labour MP, was the rare exception to the rule that most Westminster politicians had professional backgrounds and private school educations. Thanks to Hardie's union-building activities, Douglas's birthplace, Glasgow, earned the nickname "Red Clydeside." (Glasgow remains an independent-minded community: witness its sturdy vote in favour of Scottish independence in the 2014 referendum.)

In Canada, Douglas started his adult life in the printing trade. He worked in a print shop all day and attended night school one or two nights a week to sharpen his skills. In his mid-twenties he would abandon the Linotype machine and enter the Baptist ministry. Eleven years working within the church gave Tommy Douglas his moral compass and his faith that ordinary people could achieve a New Jerusalem. But he started out in Winnipeg as just another immigrant with a bit too much attitude for his own good.

Tommy was always a go-getter. In his late teens and early twenties, he earned extra dollars by giving recitations at concerts while using his print-shop wages to pay off his parents' mortgage. Winnipeg audiences loved this wiry young man, with the build and toothy grin of a kid, who gave spirited renditions of the poetry of Robbie Burns, Rudyard Kipling, and Pauline Johnson. Timing, phrasing, inflection—Douglas acquired all the skills of a master performer long before he reached a national audience. He also channelled his combativeness into competitive boxing. He later admitted that he was never a champion: "I was too short in the arm to be a good boxer, but I was fast on my feet and could hit fairly hard." More skills that came in handy in political debates.

But beneath young Tommy's compelling voice and flashing fists there were deeply rooted convictions about an individual's duty to help the less fortunate. He was born into a family and society that remained steeped in the do-good Christian faith of the nineteenth century (in its twilight, but still tenacious) while simultaneously acquiring the new twentieth-century ideology of socialism. This was the milieu that gave his life its contours.

"I was a bit of an oddity in the print shop," he later admitted. "I was always good friends with everyone, but I didn't join the lads in the evenings. I didn't go to the drinking parties and didn't play poker, as most printers do." He read widely as he tried to get his mind around tough political questions, such as "Why are some people poor?" As a child, Tommy had watched his father's and uncles' growing interest in socialism, and once in Canada, he picked up books about rural co-operative initiatives. Western farmers were banding together to experiment with co-operative schemes like wheat pools (the Saskatchewan Wheat Pool was set up in 1923), and the young man could see that farmer-owned marketing systems worked well.

At the same time, Douglas had inherited his mother's Baptist faith, and he now spent a lot of time around the Beulah Baptist Church, where he organized prayer meetings, a Boy Scout troop, and a church youth group. The young idealist was drawn to J. S. Woodsworth, the preacher who had been arrested during the general strike. A distant, bearded figure who could have walked straight out of a Tolstoy novel, Woodsworth was a pacifist and leading exponent of the social gospel, a radical Christian movement of the time that tried to deal with problems like poverty and unemployment through the application of Christian principles. Woodsworth lived among Winnipeg's poor, helping newly arrived immigrants from central Europe find jobs, housing, and companionship. Consciously or unconsciously, Tommy Douglas absorbed from the union movement and the social gospel both a sense of responsibility to his fellow humans and a belief in the potential of collective action.

Tom and Ann Douglas were thrilled when their only son announced that he was going to study for the ministry. Although it would require years of training and Tommy would earn less than he did as a printer, his parents shared a Scottish respect for education and community leadership. So in the spring of 1924, Tommy Douglas enrolled in the theology program at Manitoba's Brandon College, a small hive of intellectual activity in the middle of the vast, flat prairies. For the next six years, he would be immersed in theological questions about the literal interpretation of the Creation and in practical debates about how best to serve God in twentieth-century Canada. He scraped together the money for his fees by waiting tables, charging five dollars for recitations at fund-raising suppers, and preaching sermons at a Presbyterian church (the congregation settled for a Baptist because no Presbyterian was available).

At Brandon, Douglas worked hard and emerged a big man on campus: star debater, president of the student body, and a member of the dramatic club. Wiry, compact, and neatly dressed in worn suit and well-polished shoes, the young student was always ready with a quip to break the ice, and he made friends easily. When he graduated in 1930, he quickly found a job as minister at the Calvary Baptist Church in the dusty little town of Weyburn, Saskatchewan. With Douglas in charge, the church's congregation expanded and the number of activities for young people multiplied.

By now Douglas was married to Irma Dempsey, a fellow Baptist whom he had met at debating contests. The new Mrs. Douglas frequently found herself swept up in her husband's missionary work. One day he brought eleven delinquent boys home for lunch. "They were dirty, wore cast-off clothing, needed haircuts and were really scruffy," recalled Douglas. "My wife nearly went home to her mother." The police magistrate had been about to send them to reform school but had decided to call the minister instead. While Irma Douglas fed them and cleaned them up, Tommy badgered members of his congregation for some decent clothes and after-school jobs. Then he realized that the boys didn't know how to play. "They could pick a lock. They could get into a building and out again, and you'd never know how they got there. They could fight at the drop of a hat ... but they couldn't play games." So he organized boxing and basketball sessions for them.

That was Tommy all over—an idealist, not an ideologue. But as the Depression tore holes in the social fabric of the prairies, he was increasingly frustrated by the limits of his profession and his church. In one of his speeches from this period, he argued, "The religion of tomorrow will be less concerned with dogmas of theology and more concerned with the social welfare of humanity. When one sees the church spending its energies on the assertion of antiquated dogmas, but dumb as an oyster to the poverty and misery all around, we can't help recognize the need for a new interpretation of Christianity. We have come to see that the Kingdom of God is in our midst [only] if we have the vision to build it."[12]

As the 1930s rolled on, more businesses failed, more marriages and families were postponed. Farmers lost money on every bushel of wheat they tried to harvest and faced the loss of the family farm to the bank. Ninety-five percent of farmers in the Weyburn area were on relief.[13] Douglas's store of heartbreaking anecdotes from these years fuelled his political speeches for the rest of his life. He watched bright youngsters surrendering dreams of a university education. He saw hard-working families clothing their children in flour sacks and eating gopher stew as they spiralled into debt. The energetic young minister lobbied the local council to help the poor and distributed food and clothing from the Calvary Baptist Church basement. He knew he was treating only the symptoms of the problem and not the cause. But what *were* the underlying issues? Why had the economic system broken down? In Alberta, the Social Credit leader William Aberhart and his protégé Ernest Manning were asking the same questions.

Looking for answers, Douglas began part-time studies in the summer of 1931 toward a Ph.D. in sociology at the University of Chicago. He never completed his thesis, but as part of the fieldwork, he undertook the kind of project that Chicago's pioneering sociology professors far preferred to analysis of charts, graphs, and statistics: close attention to the day-to-day existence of powerless people. Douglas immersed himself in the lives of some of the seventy-five thousand vagrants who lived in shacks on the Chicago waterfront. He was appalled. "There were boys who had been bank clerks, medical students, and law students." Many were laid-off railroad workers. Douglas discovered "poverty, misery, want, lack of medical care, and lack of opportunity for a whole generation of young people who were frustrated and denied their right to live a normal decent life."[14] He was outraged that, far from taking action to help these men, the powers that be blamed them for their own misfortunes and pretended that there were plenty of jobs for those who were prepared to work. There weren't. When he returned to Saskatchewan, he redoubled his efforts to secure more assistance for the needy. As he shifted from offering charity to demanding government action, he noted, "I was labelled as a rather dangerous radical in the community."

The Depression provided a spur to labour union organization right across Canada. Some of the new unions were more militant than others: after a forceful strike, the United Auto Workers in Ontario successfully negotiated an agreement with General Motors for its Oshawa plant. In Quebec, the Confédération des Travailleurs Catholiques du Canada, formed in the 1920s, proved effective despite the Catholic Church's suspicion of socialism. But in the West, the RCMP (which provided provincial as well as federal policing) was often called in at the slightest suspicion of labour unrest.

Douglas had a ringside seat on what was going on. In Estevan, just down the road from Weyburn, there were coal mines in which many new immigrants worked in deplorably unsafe conditions while living in squalid housing and accepting wage cuts. In 1931 the miners joined the Mine Workers'

Members of the Single Men's Unemployed Association marched through Toronto in 1930, demonstrating their helplessness in the face of economic collapse.

Union of Canada and called a strike. The RCMP, which was the provincial police force and represented the concerns of the employers, moved in with rifles, revolvers, and machine guns, and after a three-hour street battle two miners were dead and several badly injured. Some of the injured miners were taken to the Weyburn hospital, where Douglas visited them and organized a truckload of food for their starving families. The Estevan strike confirmed his distrust of the powers that be. They certainly distrusted him: around this time the Mounties opened a file on Tommy Douglas as a suspected Communist that in time would be thicker than the New Testament. His repeated denunciations of Communism were ignored.[15]

In later years, Douglas mused on roads not taken; maybe he would have ended up as preacher in a large Baptist church in the United States or Canada, or perhaps he would have gone to teach social ethics at the University of Chicago. However, I find it hard to believe that this forceful young activist could have confined himself to a pulpit or classroom. He himself remarked that there were plenty of other men eager to take on prestigious positions, "but there weren't any, at that particular time, who were prepared to enter the dust and the din of the political arena."[16] They lacked Tommy's fiery indignation.

Douglas's new direction began with invitations to address meetings of the United Farmers of Saskatchewan. This was a group that had started out as resolutely opposed to party politics, but it soon learned that politics was the only way to create change and secure assistance for farmers. Douglas contacted Woodsworth, his early hero from North Winnipeg, who was now an MP in Ottawa, as a member of the short-lived Independent Labour Party. (In 1927 it was Woodsworth who had forced a squirming Mackenzie King to introduce an old-age pension initiative, in order to save his minority Liberal government.) Could Woodsworth suggest how the farmers might work with the labour unions?

Woodsworth put the young minister in touch with M. J. Coldwell, a member of Regina's city council and co-founder of the grandly named but sketchy Independent Labour Party of Saskatchewan. Coldwell, an earnest British-born school principal who looked like Mr. Chips, was deeply committed to the advancement of social justice and the defence of civil liberties. He quickly realized that in Saskatchewan, the farm vote carried more weight than the union vote. So he was happy to accept an invitation from Douglas to come and speak in Weyburn. It was the start of a lifelong friendship and political alliance.

Tommy and Irma Douglas enjoyed their years in Weyburn, despite the tough times they watched envelop the community. Their daughter, Shirley, was born here. The Calvary Baptist Church was foursquare behind its pastor, supporting his welfare efforts and nodding appreciatively at sermons with titles like "Jesus the Revolutionist." The congregation did not object when Douglas got involved with the new party that westerners like Coldwell and Woodsworth had worked so hard to establish: the Co-operative Commonwealth Federation. At the CCF's first national convention in Regina in 1933, delegates approved a document that was instantly tagged the Regina Manifesto. The thrust of the manifesto's fourteen-point program was that society's goal should be to address human needs, not just to make money.

For the farmers, union members, and central Canadian academics who attended the convention, the manifesto was a clarion call for more progressive policies. For the established Conservative and Liberal Parties, it was a revolutionary document that flirted with Communism.

Douglas managed to attend the final day of the Regina gathering and was buoyed by the enthusiasm expressed for social change. When the CCF failed to find a candidate to run in Weyburn in the 1934 provincial election, he agreed to let his name go forward—but only because he was convinced he could never win against the Liberal candidate, a popular local physician. He insisted at the start of the campaign that this would be his only foray into elected politics. He had too much else on his plate. (His other projects included an unfortunate side trip into eugenics, on which he wrote a thesis. By the time the Nazis had demonstrated the horrendous implications of such a theory, Douglas had rejected it completely.)

It's funny how politics gets in your blood. As the campaign gathered speed, the rookie CCF candidate discovered that he enjoyed explaining to people how the economic system worked. Douglas always loved a fight.[17] Adrenalin coursed through his veins as he watched the crowds grow at election rallies (there were few alternative sources of entertainment), and he began to think he might win the seat. In the end, he came third. But he was hooked. "As Jonah said when he was swallowed by the whale," he told his election-night audience, "you can't keep a good man down."

The following year there was a federal election. The CCF came knocking, but Douglas insisted that his future lay in the pulpit. However, when he told the superintendent of the Baptist Church for the West that he was being pressed to run again, the latter told him firmly that if he didn't stay out of politics, he would never get another church in Canada. "And I'll see to it," warned the superintendent.

What a mistake! Tommy Douglas, the bantamweight boxer, replied, "You've just given the CCF a candidate."

It was a rough campaign: the Liberals attacked the CCF as a Communist organization that would confiscate farmers' property. Douglas averaged three campaign stops a day, ducking the rotten vegetables occasionally pelted at him. At one meeting he even smashed a water jug so that he had a jagged glass weapon against some drunken toughs. But on October 14, 1935, Weyburn voters gave Tommy Douglas 44 percent of their votes and he easily beat his rivals.

On their way to a new life in Ottawa, the Douglas family stopped in Winnipeg to see Tommy's parents. Tom Douglas had always had high hopes for his son. "Now remember, laddie," he said on this occasion, "the working people have put a lot of trust in you. You must never let them down."

↜↜↝

The Regina Manifesto is a wonderful document to read today. I found a copy at one of my favourite Canadian libraries: the Bruce Peel Special Collection at the University of Alberta in Edmonton. I know the Peel's wooden reading tables well because Sam Steele's papers are lodged there. I recall with pleasure the days I spent poring over Sam's illegible scribbles in a small leather-bound diary, and the sloping script of his lengthy letters from

Dawson City to his wife, Marie, in Montreal. The artifacts told their own story of frontier adventures; the diaries had a fusty dampness and some of the Mylar-protected letters displayed traces of immersion in the Yukon River, during outward dogsled journeys from Dawson City. Using those papers was a sensual as well as a literary experience.

These days, I can access many historic documents online, so the Regina Manifesto came to me via the Peel Special Collection's website.[18] Sitting at my Ottawa desk, I could flip through its eight pages on my laptop screen, noting the old-fashioned typeface and blocky design. But I could not hold the dog-eared, orange-covered pamphlet in my hands, feeling its vibrations of idealism. Archival research is no longer a tactile journey into history.

Nonetheless, to read the pamphlet is to time-travel backwards into a very different Canada. This was an era when political statements were written in plain English, rather than massaged by pollsters and spin doctors into sound bites and bumper stickers. The manifesto, with its echoes of the 1848 Communist Manifesto, stridently endorsed a new approach to government. The aim of the new Co-operative Commonwealth Federation party was to "replace the present capitalist system, with its inherent injustice and inhumanity, by a social order from which the domination and exploitation of one class by another will be eliminated. . . . The present order is marked by glaring inequalities of wealth and opportunity, by chaotic waste and instability; and in an age of plenty it condemns the great mass of people to poverty and insecurity. Power has become more and more concentrated into the hands of a small irresponsible minority of financiers and industrialists and to their predatory interests the majority are habitually sacrificed." Capitalism was cruel and unjust, argued the manifesto's authors, and should be replaced by social planning and public ownership of the most important economic levers.

Some of this has a familiar echo nearly eighty years later. In the economic meltdown of 2008–09, there were plenty of newspaper columnists and academics willing to talk about "chaotic waste" and "predatory interests." However, in the twenty-first century, no North American political party or media columnist would launch such an overzealous broadside on their country's financial elite. But the CCF was an upstart protest party grasping for remedies to the desperate circumstances of the 1930s. It was not alone; in Alberta the Social Credit movement and in Ontario the United Farmers party were also gaining traction. And the horrors of what was going on in Stalin's Soviet Union, ostensibly justified by the Communist Manifesto, were still hidden.

The main authors of the Regina Manifesto were well-known university teachers, including Frank Underhill (a colleague of Harold Innis at the University of Toronto) and Frank Scott, the McGill University constitutional lawyer who also wrote poetry. They belonged to the loftily named League for Social Reconstruction, which played an important role in the CCF's foundation. The Regina get-together was an intriguing hubbub of tweed jackets, dog collars, and farmers' overalls.

The Regina Manifesto lets us glimpse how far we have travelled. Reading it eighty years after its composition, I am struck by its appealing mix of hard-headed analysis and rosy dreams. Most of its demands are part of the fabric of our lives today: publicly funded health care, workplace safety standards, free speech, a Canadian central bank, minority rights, crop failure insurance, adequate public pensions, an end to protectionism. It specifically abjured violence. Other demands—abolition of the Canadian Senate, eradication of public debt, and a foreign policy focused on disarmament and world peace—seem as utopian today as they seemed then. The document ends with a rousing flourish: "No CCF government will rest content until it has eradicated capitalism and put into operation the full programme of socialized planning which will lead to the establishment in Canada of the Co-operative Commonwealth."

This call to arms was too piercing for some readers, including Prime Minister Bennett, who promptly branded the CCFers as Communists.[19] The sentence quietly vanished in 1956, at the height of the Cold War, when the Regina Manifesto was redrafted as the more moderate Winnipeg Declaration. Yet the manifesto's drafters were not the only people calling for more government planning. Similar prescriptions for economic recovery floated around in all the countries afflicted by nosediving economies. In

Britain, the economist John Maynard Keynes urged the government to drop austerity measures and start spending. In the United States, Franklin Roosevelt instituted a raft of new programs after he became president in 1933, many of which were exactly the kind of initiatives that both the CCF and Keynes wanted. Roosevelt's New Deal, as it came to be called, focused on relief, recovery, and reform. Washington made major public investments in bridges, dams, airports, and roads to provide jobs; improved farmers' lives by artificially raising prices for agricultural products; and launched rural welfare projects. The New Deal gave a major dose of hope to Americans as the U.S. economy began a slow crawl to recovery.

But in Ottawa, the federal government under Conservative prime minister R. B. Bennett dragged its heels rather than get involved in what it regarded as provincial responsibilities and irresponsible debt financing. People like Tommy Douglas, who saw the suffering first-hand, raged against Bennett and his cautious, tight-fisted advisers.

Douglas was only thirty-one years old when he arrived in Ottawa in 1935 to join the seven-person CCF caucus. The CCF members had offices in "Socialist Alley," as their corridor in Parliament's Centre Block was known. The threadbare group was led by J. S. Woodsworth, already a revered (if antiquated) figure in Canadian politics. Douglas, thirty years younger than Woodsworth, still looked like a student, with his infectious grin and crinkly hair. Another member of the caucus was Agnes Macphail, who had run for the United Farmers of Ontario. Macphail, the first woman to be elected to the House of Commons, thought Douglas was "brash."

Brash works. In the next nine years, Douglas convinced Canadians that they should sit up and take notice. His speeches were well prepared, his delivery lively, his convictions—Canada's need to have an independent foreign policy and a social safety net—rock-solid. He had a particular gift for explaining economics in everyday terms. He talked to audiences inside and outside Parliament about economic cycles, the need for both capital and labour in any enterprise, the role that government could play if it was prepared to do so. In *Maclean's* magazine, the journalist Bruce Hutchison commented that "at times, he could penetrate even the rhinoceros skin of the Government."[20] But it was all just words: the CCF had little impact on government policy during this period. Mackenzie King was back in power as Liberal prime minister and met tales of prairie hardship and demands for relief programs with a concerned smile and deaf ear.

As war approached in Europe, Douglas's party faced a painful split. On one side, Woodsworth and M. J. Coldwell were staunch pacifists. On the other side, there was no way that the scrappy kid from Winnipeg could renounce war, much as he deplored evidence of war profiteering by Canadian manufacturers. "If you come to a choice between losing freedom of speech, religion, association, thought, and all the things that make life worth living, and resorting to force, you'd use force."[21]

Once Canada declared war against Germany in 1939, most of Douglas's rhetoric was directed toward the defence of civil liberties in the face of war hysteria. But he was impatient at his lack of impact: the CCF was almost invisible within Ottawa. The heartland of CCF support was Saskatchewan, and the party began to press him to run for provincial party president. It

With the declaration of war in 1939, Douglas and the CCF were invisible in Ottawa, as most Canadians lined up behind Prime Minister Mackenzie King and the war effort.

wasn't much of a job. After the drought and despair of the Depression, Saskatchewan remained Canada's poorest province, and the party was broke. Yet public support for the CCF was beginning to build nationally as the old-line parties—Liberals and Conservatives—appeared mired in inertia. By 1942, after some adroit manoeuvring through nasty internal party battles, Douglas emerged as the CCF leader in his province.

In the words of Bill Waiser, a Saskatchewan historian, "Tommy Douglas, by the sheer force of his personality, had an immediate impact on the fortunes of the provincial CCF party."[22] It wasn't simply that Douglas was sharp-witted and energetic. All those years as a Baptist minister had reinforced his natural optimism and faith in people's capacity to work together for the common good. He had integrity, and he inspired others with his sense of mission. In the provincial election two years later, he convinced an electorate wearied by first the Depression and then the war that innovative planning could put the provincial economy on a firmer footing. Farmers, blue-collar workers, and urban immigrants listened carefully to a politician who offered more than the usual bromides.

The province's governing Liberals dismissed CCF candidates as dangerous Bolsheviks, and the *Regina Leader-Post* warned that a CCF victory "may start Canada on the road to strife and devastation."[23] Corporate Canada supplied dollops of cash for scaremongering. (The retailer Simpson's offered to distribute anti-CCF propaganda alongside its catalogue.[24]) But this was not enough to shake the faith that more than half of Saskatchewan voters had in Tommy and his commitment to their welfare. The CCF won forty-seven of the fifty-two seats in the legislature in 1944. A party that had never been in power won a landslide victory—and North America had its first avowedly socialist government.

Douglas soon had his cabinet in place. He himself took the health portfolio, and he asked his Liberal predecessor for a briefing on the department's activities. The former minister retorted that Douglas had made lots of promises: "Go ahead and see what you can do." Douglas replied, "I'll just give you a tip that we plan to do more in the next four years than you've done in the last twenty-five."

+∿+

Many observers expected Douglas and the CCF to be a one-term wonder. Instead the party won five straight majority victories between 1944 and 1960. Tommy managed to establish an almost-personal rapport with each of his voters. When I hear a scratchy recording of one of his weekly broadcasts, I understand how he did it. His warm, reassuring voice would reach out through the cold prairie night to the most isolated farmhouse as he signed off, "Good night, and good luck." His folksy manner made people feel he was their best friend, although in private he could be aloof.

As Douglas had predicted in 1944, his first term was extraordinarily busy. He drove his staff, his cabinet, and himself hard. In its first sixteen months in office, the CCF government approved 192 bills and created several new departments (Social Welfare, Labour, Co-operation). Despite having inherited a huge public debt, it went on to fulfill many of the Regina Manifesto's practical promises. It created the publicly owned Saskatchewan Power Corporation, which brought electricity to the province's more isolated regions (forty thousand farm families were finally liberated from the dangerous tyranny of oil lamps). It established Canada's first publicly owned car insurance scheme, the Saskatchewan Government Insurance Office, with rates twenty dollars cheaper than its private-sector competitors'. In this and subsequent mandates, the CCF government spawned numerous Crown corporations that operated utilities, an airline, and a sodium sulphate plant, among other enterprises (some of which were hopeless). It founded the first arts board in North America and passed Canada's first bill of rights, which prohibited discrimination based on race, colour, or religion. It reformed the public service so that it became a meritocracy rather than a patronage pool. Public servants were granted the right to unionize.

This was government at its most sleeves-rolled-up interventionist, but how could the province afford all this? Every great premier or prime minister needs a good money manager, and Douglas had one of the smartest in his treasurer, Clarence Fines. The Douglas-Fines partnership was a classic good-cop/bad-cop routine: charismatic Tommy whipped up a can-do spirit within cabinet while stodgy Fines, fund-raiser extraordinaire and former school vice-principal, applied the brakes. Fines also relied increasingly on private enterprise to finance industrial and resource development, especially for oil exploration. One observer described Fines as "a dedicated socialist with the acumen of a tycoon."

The booming postwar economy helped, and so did the fact that, in Ottawa, Prime Minister Mackenzie King was also talking about the need for a planned economy in the postwar world. And Douglas was no wild-eyed Marxist. He knew that his government had to demonstrate financial stability to maintain credibility in financial circles, and he publicly announced that the government would not start expropriating or nationalizing any new ventures. (Wardrobe was also important. "You can be as radical as you like," he told his daughter, "but you must dress like a banker."[25]) Despite a handful of fiscal misadventures, Clarence Fines would develop sixteen balanced budgets in a row and steadily pay down the public debt.

The Liberal government in Ottawa made various attempts to undermine the prairie socialists, including calling in loans and threatening to disallow Saskatchewan legislation. But Douglas went on radio to attack "a government of tired old men who are merely holding onto the spoils of office with a hope of finding a final resting place in the Senate," and he invited his listeners to make their opposition known to the federal government. Soon the federal mailbags were overflowing with protests, and Ottawa backed off.[26]

Prairie socialism turned out not to be so scary. What's more, academics inside and outside the province were fascinated by the Douglas experiments, and an increasingly urban Canadian population embraced the idea that government should look after its citizens. Within Saskatchewan, kilometres of dirt tracks were turned into blacktop roads, and new municipal water and sewer systems gave rise to one of the best sights in Canada: the ritual burning of smelly old outhouses. By 1960 Douglas's government was getting glowing reviews in even the American press. *Time* magazine reported that Saskatchewan had not only a balanced budget but also North America's "most comprehensive welfare state . . . cradle-to-grave security that matches anything in such better-known socialist Edens as Sweden, Uruguay and New Zealand."[27]

However, it still didn't have what had been promised in every election platform: a comprehensive, publicly funded health insurance system. One of the principles of the Douglas government was that new services were introduced only as they became affordable. A program that would provide complete medical care for every Saskatchewan citizen, regardless of ability to pay, was a much more expensive proposition than any of the other CCF promises.

The CCF government was not starting from scratch. Dozens of rural districts already had community-funded hospitals staffed by salaried doctors. But from 1944 onward, the Douglas team started improving access to medical care. Canada's first air ambulance service was introduced for the province's 907,000 scattered inhabitants, many of whom lived far away from medical services. Free medical care was provided for 30,000 single mothers, widows, and old people. Patients with venereal diseases, tuberculosis, psychiatric illnesses, and cancer were treated free. Thirty-three hospitals were renovated or built; by 1954 the province had gone from having the fewest hospital beds per capita in the country to having the most, and the provincial government was picking up the tab for hospital care.

Canadians outside Saskatchewan watched these innovations with interest. Why couldn't they too enjoy these benefits? In 1957 the Conservative government in Ottawa agreed to pay half the costs of such provincial hospital insurance, and the other nine provinces signed on. But that was as far as Ottawa was prepared to go. Despite vigorous lobbying by Douglas, the feds refused funds for a pilot project in Saskatchewan in which *all* medical care would be covered.

Saskatchewan would have to go it alone. With fifteen successful years as premier behind him, Tommy Douglas had had enough of caution. The province's finances were in good shape; revenues from uranium mining and oil and gas production had helped achieve the CCF goal of a diversified economy. "The CCF's early-days loud talk of 'eradicating capitalism' is not even a whisper now," reported *Time*, reflecting the muted approval for this government (if not its politics) that had affected even Bay Street and Wall Street. "Saskatchewan's Deputy Minister of Travel and Information now makes a dozen trips yearly to Eastern Canada and the US luring new industry to the province." The premier decided it was time to deliver full health coverage. In a radio broadcast in December 1959, he let loose his soaring rhetoric of hope: "If we can do this—and I feel sure we can—Saskatchewan [will] lead the way. Let us therefore have the vision and courage to take this step . . . toward a more just and humane society."[28]

The medical care insurance scheme proposed by the CCF government was based on five principles: the state would pay costs; everybody would be covered; there would be no cuts to other services; the plan would be operated by government, not private insurance companies; and the legislation would have to be acceptable to both physicians and patients. The doctors balked. Although Douglas assured them that nothing would be done without their approval, their professional body, the Saskatchewan College of Physicians and Surgeons, made it clear that they would co-operate only if they continued to be paid on a fee-for-service basis, and if they controlled the plan. Although the CCF would have preferred to put all physicians on salary, Douglas agreed they could retain their status as independent professionals, paid a fee for each service rendered. He had watched the Labour government in Britain give way to the same pressure from British doctors in order to establish the National Health Service in 1948. But Douglas insisted that the government would be in charge.

Still the college refused to play ball. For the first time since his election as premier in 1944, Douglas now faced a powerful, organized opposition within the province. Ever optimistic, he continued to assume that he would be able to bring the physicians over to his point of view. But the Saskatchewan college was dominated by recent arrivals from Britain—doctors who had left Britain specifically to escape the National Health Service and had no interest in the province's co-operative traditions. They were unyielding. So Tommy decided to give as good as he got. He called an election in June 1960 with medicare as the key CCF promise. "The people of this province will decide whether or not we want a medical care program," he declared.

Douglas's CCF government faced opposition across the province, particularly from doctors, when it introduced public health insurance in 1962.

It was one hell of a fight. Physicians' professional associations throughout North America viewed as an attack on their professional autonomy what was happening in the underpopulated and (despite CCF efforts) still relatively poor province. During the 1960 campaign, the Canadian Medical Association and the American Medical Association poured money into a propaganda attack, claiming that patients would be "reduced to a number," that doctors would leave the province, that the government would have access to patients' confidential records.

The sturdy Saskatchewan voters trusted Tommy Douglas. They disregarded these hysterical claims and gave the CCF government 69 percent of their votes and its fifth consecutive majority. But still the physicians refused to yield. A group of Regina doctors expressed widely felt anger in a letter to a special advisory committee: "This socialist garbage is an insult to any normal human being. Yours in bitter hatred."[29] The Medical Care Insurance Act became law in late 1961, but implementation was delayed in the hope of getting the doctors onside. No deal. On July 1, 1962, the province's physicians went on strike: only emergency services were available to Saskatchewan citizens.

Today Tommy Douglas's name is the only one mentioned as the medicare champion. In fact, he had resigned from provincial politics, after a remarkable seventeen years in Regina, before the doctors' strike began. It was left to his successor as premier, Woodrow Lloyd, first to pursue negotiations with the physicians and then to face the hysteria after July 1. "Keep Our Doctors" committees organized noisy demonstrations, and provincial Liberals vented their outrage. But Premier Lloyd was just as tough as Tommy. At the first whiff of strike action, he had cabled the province's agent in England: "Get some British doctors. Fly them in."[30]

The strike lasted twenty-three days, during which support for the physicians gradually evaporated. In the end, the Medical Care Insurance Act was amended to eliminate the suggestion that the government controlled the doctors, but all the other principles (universality, quality, public administration, fee for service) remained intact. A year later, Lloyd was named an "outstanding citizen" by *Maclean's* magazine.[31] When the provincial Liberals finally toppled the CCF government in 1964, they made no changes to the plan.

+∿+

Why had Tommy Douglas, already regarded as Saskatchewan's most successful premier ever, decided to leave the final stage of the medicare fight to Woodrow Lloyd? Because his sense of duty was even stronger than his relish of a good fight. He had reluctantly agreed to become first leader of a new federal party: the New Democratic Party, offspring of a union between the federal CCF and the labour movement. It was an uncomfortable decision as well as an ill-assorted marriage. When the federal election was called in 1962, he ran as the NDP candidate in Regina City. Caught in the medicare battle whiplash ("I'll shoot you, you red bastard," yelled one voter at Douglas's campaign manager[32]), he suffered a humiliating defeat.

What a blow after all those triumphant victories in provincial elections! A riding was quickly found for him in British Columbia, and he won a by-election for the NDP, but it was a rocky start for both him and the new party. And when he and Irma moved to Ottawa, he found he was back to being a minor player on the national scene. In Regina he had enjoyed having his hands on the levers and a professional, highly motivated public ser-

At the founding convention in 1961, Tommy Douglas was
elected the first leader of the federal New Democratic Party.

vice to help him navigate toward his New Jerusalem. In Ottawa the NDP
was in backbench Siberia—not a propitious launch pad for its ideals of
democratic socialism.

Douglas spent the next seventeen years in Ottawa. During those years the
NDP never made the electoral breakthrough its founders had anticipated;
Douglas's vision of the New Jerusalem did not catch on. The much-loved
bantamweight fighter for social justice and medicare failed utterly to connect
with Canadians as a national leader: fewer than one in five Canadians voted
for his party. His preacherly, down-home style didn't work with urban Canada and appealed still less to French Canada; he had nothing to say about the
emerging national unity crisis as the *indépendantiste* movement took off in
Quebec. Federalist Quebecers such as Pierre Trudeau and Jean Marchand
chose to join the federal Liberal Party, despite their union backgrounds.
Douglas's New Democrats were dismissed as "Liberals in a hurry"—good for
floating new policy ideas, but too radical to be trusted with power.

Yet Douglas's impact is undeniable, because his policy ideas were
adopted and implemented by the governing Liberal Party, first under Lester Pearson and then Trudeau. The Canada Pension Plan, the national

system of health care insurance, and a smorgasbord of new government agencies were established. In the 1970s, under NDP pressure, Prime Minister Pierre Trudeau's minority government set up Petro-Canada, a publicly owned oil company to defend Canadian energy interests in an industry dominated by foreign capital. From the sidelines, Tommy Douglas watched Canada become a country in which the ties binding the country together, sea to sea, were not the old CPR rails but the new promise of access to health care for all.

By now, Douglas was the grand old patriarch of the New Democrats, with a peace button on the lapel of his old-fashioned boxy suits as he took his place among the hippie lefties of the 1960s. He spoke out against nuclear missiles and the U.S. war in Vietnam, and he championed the new generation of Canadians, telling the NDP old guard in 1970, "Do not be fooled by beards and mini-skirts and long hair. This is a generation of young people who have a greater sense of social responsibility than any generation I have seen. . . . [They] are not thinking of how they can be president of General Motors. . . . [They] are going down into the slums and ghettos to fight the battles of the underprivileged."[33]

I wish I had been at the NDP's national convention in 1983, held in Regina to mark the fiftieth anniversary of the manifesto. This was Tommy Douglas's last hurrah. Already weakened by cancer, he was wheeled into the hall on a golf cart, pulling a cake with fifty candles. After a couple of triumphant laps, he was helped to the podium. The years fell away as he began to speak: the old evangelical appeal was as powerful as ever as he reminded the crowd of all that the party had achieved, and all that remained to do. Winning votes was not enough, he told the party faithful. What was needed was recruits "who are willing to dedicate their lives to building a different kind of society . . . a society founded on the principles of concern for human well-being and human welfare."[34] The applause began before he had even sat down. Despite every effort from the organizers to move on, it continued for half an hour.

꘎

The paradox of Tommy Douglas is that the one national contest he ever won was long after his death. He was a brilliant and transformative leader in Saskatchewan, but he never succeeded at the national level. So how did he win the CBC title of "Greatest Canadian"? Was it because of medicare? Or because of his larger significance in the way that Canadians like to differentiate ourselves from Americans? Ironically, even his beloved Saskatchewan has turned its back on its New Democratic traditions: its electors are now among the most conservative in Canada.

The fight to introduce medicare into Saskatchewan remains a turning point in Canadian history. Other countries might regard homicidal clashes as founding moments in their national psyches. In Canada, the battle was fought with stethoscopes. Douglas himself recognized that Saskatchewan was probably the only province in which the forces of organized medicine could be defeated. His personal popularity as premier of a dirt-poor province and sixteen years of good government from the CCF meant that voters trusted him rather than insurance companies and medical associations.

Perhaps Newfoundland, in the days of Premier Joey Smallwood, might have managed it. Elsewhere, however, there were skirmishes throughout the process of implementation. The most bitter resistance exploded in Ontario, then the wealthy heartland of Canada and headquarters of the big insurance companies, who had done very well out of private health insurance. It took until 1972 for every province and territory to get full coverage.

Tommy Douglas would not be happy with today's Canadian health care system, which has been squeezed and pummelled by rising medical costs, political pressures, and changing demographics. But we do have a universal, accessible health care insurance system with a single payer: government. If you are rushed to a hospital emergency department anywhere in Canada, you need your government health card, not your credit card. It would be electoral suicide for any party to change the basic principles on which health care is funded and provided.

Medicare established the most dramatic split between Canada and the United States. Tommy Douglas had convinced a nation, in the physician Vincent Lam's words, "that in a civilized society, health care should be

Only Joey Smallwood, who served as premier of Newfoundland for twenty-three years, enjoyed the levels of support on his home turf that Douglas enjoyed in Saskatchewan.

considered essential to individual and social well-being, and viewed both as a public right and a collective obligation."[35] A few years ago I attended a seminar on health care at a small liberal arts college in Vermont. Prompted by President Barack Obama's determination to establish a national health care system in the United States, the Americans there, including physicians and health economists, got into heavy discussions about incentives, opportunity costs, capital investments, moral jeopardy, and a whole lot of other business-type jargon that would have made Tommy Douglas howl with rage.

One of the participants turned to me and asked if the same kind of debates took place in Canada. "Not really," I replied. "We've settled these questions. Health care is recognized as a 'public good.' We agree that our elected governments should look after us." The doctor smiled grimly. "Here in the States," she said, "wellness is an 'aspirational good.'" Most Americans must still make their own arrangements and decide for themselves where health care "fits" on their list of priorities. A new roof on the family home versus speedy access to a new kidney; a car or a new knee. Not a choice any Canadian has to face.

CHAPTER 6

Landscaping a Literature

*Margaret Atwood and the
Geography of the Mind*

I'm talking about Canada as a state of mind, as the space you inhabit not
just with your body but with your head.

—Margaret Atwood, *Survival: A Thematic Guide to Canadian Literature* (1972)

CanLit might not exert the fascination of—say—a venereal wart.

—Margaret Atwood, in conversation (2014)

In spite of the triple handicap of being a token "feminist" author, a Canadian, and a poet, Margaret Atwood manages to be a true novelist. She
opens our eyes to ways in which we think and behave, irrespective of sex
and nationality.

—Philip Howard, review in the *London Times* (1980)

In the mid-twentieth century, Marshall McLuhan, our best-known intellectual, observed, "Canada is the only country in the world that knows how to live without an identity."[1] As the psychic distance between Canada and Britain yawned, a tsunami of American pop culture swept north. How could this country resist being *I Love Lucy*-ed to death? A new uneasiness arose: a fear that Canada was doomed to become a decaffeinated annex to the United States. In the words of our best-known writer, Margaret Atwood, "The beginning of Canadian cultural nationalism was not 'Am I really that oppressed?' but 'Am I really that boring?' "

I'm in a Toronto café, talking to Atwood about Canadian culture. Her shock of frizzled grey hair is wild against the intensity of her gaze from those fierce blue eyes. In her mesmerizing drawl, she tells me one of her favourite stories, set in Toronto in the early 1970s. It is a story she has frequently told before, and to which she enjoys adding a cheeky twist. "I was on the board of the House of Anansi," she explains, "and we all knew we needed to publish books other than poetry in order to support the poetry. Anansi had done quite well with *VD*, which was the first guide to venereal disease for the general reader. We thought about other books that might sell as well. I pointed out that there was no popular, accessible book about Canadian books. There was a bunch of academic articles, but nobody had pulled them together for the ordinary reader. I said, 'Why don't we do a handbook . . . a sort of *VD of Canadian Literature*?' "

Her colleagues on the Anansi board agreed. Dennis Lee and Dave Godfrey, two University of Toronto academics, had founded the House of Anansi in 1967 to publish and promote Canadian literature. But it was a thankless task, and the pioneering basement publishing company was hurtling toward bankruptcy. Then aged thirty-three, Atwood quickly mapped out a literary handbook as "a sort of grown-up version of Girl Guide cookies"—a stopgap solution to help Anansi pay the rent. "We thought it might sell three thousand copies, which would have been sufficient for our needs. We were so excited when Mr. Britnell ordered two copies for his bookstore: he usually ordered only one of anything, so around the office we called him One-Book Britnell. I remember somebody saying, 'It's going to be a hit!' "

Margaret Atwood sips her coffee (regular, with cream *and* milk) and gives a high-pitched giggle. The book she is talking about is *Survival: A Thematic Guide to Canadian Literature*, her first non-fiction prose publication. It asked the question "What have been the central preoccupations of Canadian poetry, fiction, and non-fiction?" This was an important question, according to Atwood, because "literature is not only a mirror; it is also a map, a geography of the mind. Our literature is one such map, if we can learn to read it as the product of who and where we have been." For far too long, Canadian readers had looked at other nations' maps while treating their own authors as inconsequential. But Atwood helped change all that when she declared boldly that Canadian authors should be treated seriously because they "are also transmitters of their culture."

When the book appeared in 1972, it was an instant bestseller, and it remains the ur-text of CanLit, with sales to date of 150,000 copies.[2] *Survival* secured Anansi's survival, and it also sparked controversy. While one reviewer hailed it as "a fine example of what happens when a first-rate intelligence takes on a task usually carried out by literary morons,"[3] another took umbrage at Atwood's focus on "the negative aspects of the Canadian imagination."[4]

Meanwhile, more than four decades later, Atwood has become the world's best-known Canadian writer. Alice Munro may have won the Nobel Prize for Literature, but type "Queen of CanLit" into a Google search, and Atwood's name dominates the first page. She has been an icon, a brand, a pundit within Canada for as long as most of us can remember, and in the past two decades she has taken that public persona global. The author of more than seventy volumes of fiction, essays, poetry, reviews, lectures, and plays, she tweets regularly to over half a million followers. Her name and her books crop up in works by other bestselling novelists, including the Americans Carl Hiaasen and Mark Jarman. Several of her books are required reading in schools as far afield as Germany and Japan. To mark

Atwood's seventy-fifth birthday in 2014, CBC Radio devoted a lot of its books website to her, including "75 Surprising Facts about Margaret Atwood." Atwood's steely humour was visible in the entry: "She has no problem eating bugs, especially giant locusts."

Atwood's fearless footprint is so large that sometimes it feels as though she invented Canadian literature. However, because she studied literature, she knows better than most of us that there were significant authors and books in this country long before *Survival* appeared. Atwood has written about the elusive Canadian literary tradition, which predates Confederation, and she has also used it in her own work. Why did *Survival* sell so well from the moment it appeared? "Because people were finally ready for it. You cannot create a [public appetite for new ideas] out of nothing, but you can channel it." Cocking her head to one side, she resorts to one of her favourite teaching stratagems—a scientific metaphor—to explain why in 1972, after decades of indifference, Canadians finally began to celebrate our distinct literary imagination. "If you think of mushrooms . . . that mushroom you see as you're walking along is merely the fruiting body. The real mushroom is under the ground."

Survival's thematic approach helped a generation of Canadians look at our culture with new eyes. Atwood examined various patterns that recur in Canadian novels and poetry and suggested that they were woven into the national DNA. She announced that the dominant obsession was with survival. She contrasted this with the ideas that she suggested drove other literary traditions: the frontier as the dominant symbol of American literature, for example, and the island for much British literature. Suddenly, English Canada's literati were chattering about what made Canadian writing different from that of other countries—and, more fundamentally, how it reflected the national character.

Atwood herself, unshackled by academic inhibitions, told us who we were. "Our stories," she wrote, "are likely to be tales not of those who made it but of those who made it back, from the awful experience—the North, the snowstorm, the sinking ship—that killed everyone else. The survivor has no triumph or victory but the fact of his survival; he has little after his ordeal that he did not have before, except gratitude for having escaped with his life." She linked the survival theme with the enduring anxiety of her fellow citizens. "Canadians are forever taking the national pulse like doctors at a sickbed: the aim is not to see whether the patient will live well but simply whether he will live at all."

Atwood is in enormous demand as a speaker and travels incessantly; although she graciously agreed to give me an interview, her assistant could only schedule our conversation three months after my request. In 2014, at age seventy-five, she published her short story collection *Stone Mattress* and then went on the road for six weeks, to promote it in Italy, France, Greece, and Britain. When I arrived at the Bloor Street café, she was already seated with a friend in the busiest, most crowded section, with her back to the window. I found myself part blinded by the wintery sun behind her, and I worried that the surrounding noise would drown her voice on my recording (it didn't). From the start, she was in control of our conversation; transcribing it later, I realized that previous interviewers had heard most of her answers during the previous fifty years (she has an excellent memory, for her own words and others').

Nevertheless, the wait was worth it: she was generous with time and insights. Erudite and witty, she chatted about the years leading up to the CanLit explosion of the 1960s, 1970s, and 1980s. She held me in her gimlet gaze, sometimes pressing her lips together—with suppressed humour or exasperation, I was never entirely sure. But I did not see the frosty, perhaps sarcastic side of her public persona that I've heard about. (One Atwood anecdote concerns the man who said to her, "You're Margaret Atwood, aren't you? My wife reads your books." Atwood is said to have replied, "And what are you reading, Big Boy?") Perhaps she has mellowed. At one point, I commented that she had been kind to a young scientist with whom she had appeared onstage. "Why not, at my age?" she said, smiling.

Atwood was still in her teens when she decided to be a writer. In Toronto's Leaside High School yearbook for 1956–57, her fellow students wrote, "Peggy's not-so-secret ambition is to write THE Canadian novel—and with those English marks, who doubts that she will."[5] I ask if she had ever

While still in high school, Margaret Atwood was determined to be a writer—although she never assumed she could make a living with her pen.

felt any tension back in the 1960s and 1970s between that career ambition and the role she played in getting CanLit off the ground. Her eyebrows lift incredulously. "Back then, nobody thought in terms of a 'career.' You thought in terms of writing," she admonishes. "We didn't feel entitled. You needed a job, and then you were going to do the writing in the spare time."

But then the CanLit explosion happened, and Margaret Atwood was at the centre of it both as an author and as an activist. The success of CanLit encouraged Canadians to feel that perhaps, even as this northern land entered its second century, there was a unique, post-colonial national identity. Margaret Atwood's books have given us maps of who we are, where we have been, where we live—and where we may be going.

✦

Before there was Atwood, there was Susanna Moodie. Both these CanLit matriarchs are stars in my own universe: I read Atwood's fiction as soon as it is published, and I have written about Susanna Moodie in *Sisters in the Wilderness* (1999). There is a tight link between them.

Moodie, a well-educated Englishwoman who arrived in Upper Canada in 1832, is the author of one of Canada's earliest classics: *Roughing It in the Bush*. Published in 1852, fifteen years before Confederation, this memoir described Moodie's painful experiences as a pioneer in the Canadian backwoods and her sense of geographical, cultural, and social dislocation. Sharp-tongued Moodie was an established writer in Georgian London before she crossed the Atlantic. Once here, she was never one to minimize her misery:

> *Oh! land of waters, how my spirit tires,*
> *In the dark prison of thy boundless woods;*
> . . . .
> *Though vast the features that compose thy frame,*
> *Turn where we will, the landscape's still the same.*[6]

Roughing It sold so well that Moodie's publisher urged her to rush out a sequel. A year later, *Life in the Clearings versus the Bush* appeared. Partly because Moodie's revelations about the squalor of pioneer life (pigs! skunks! Yankees!) had scandalized her well-to-do family in the Old World, she now insisted that she had come to terms with the New World—although her protests reek of dutiful resignation. "The homesickness that constantly preyed upon me in the Backwoods has long yielded to the deepest and most heartfelt interest in the rapidly increasing prosperity and greatness of the country of my adoption."

Moodie deserves our sympathy: she was homesick and she made little money from her literary efforts. When the Dominion of Canada was launched in 1867, there were still no copyright protections for works published here, and the publishing industry consisted largely of fly-by-night printers who made their money from scurrilous newspapers and handbills. The population was too small to offer any hope of profit from less populist fodder, and the few Dominion citizens who boasted bookshelves filled them with the likes of Shakespeare and Molière, Charles Dickens, and Alexandre Dumas. Canadians with literary ambitions had to find publishers in New York, Boston, London, or Paris. Moodie's two books were both published in London, then reprinted (without permission or any payment to Moodie) in the United States.

Yet there were always a handful of men and women like Moodie scribbling away in the backwoods and the mountains, or on the prairies or along the shore. In the 1830s, Thomas Chandler Haliburton of Nova Scotia achieved international fame with his humorous bestsellers about a wisecracking character called Sam Slick. But most authors enjoyed only local success. Nevertheless, as newcomers flooded into the Dominion, the number of publications grew and a national consciousness began to stir. A group of young poets, born in the 1860s and including two New Brunswickers, Charles G. D. Roberts and Bliss Carman, earned themselves the label of the "Confederation poets" with their verses about classic Canadian themes: water, winter, and woods. Quebec authors writing in both French and English romanticized New France's history. Pauline Johnson, with her mixed English and Mohawk ancestry, recited bloodthirsty ballads about Indian warriors and patriotic chest-thumpers like "Canadian Born" (1903), celebrating her country's British links:

> We first saw light in Canada, the land beloved of God;
> We are the pulse of Canada, its marrow and its blood;
> And we, the men of Canada, can face the world and brag
> That we were born in Canada beneath the British flag.

By the early twentieth century, some Canadians were winning huge readerships in Britain and the United States. Ralph Connor would sell over five million copies of his first three books, including *The Sky Pilot* (1899), during his lifetime; altogether he would publish three dozen stirring tales of life in western Canada. Little girls all over the world would fall in love with a plucky orphan in rural Prince Edward Island in Lucy Maud Montgomery's *Anne of Green Gables* (1908) and its sequels. After the First World War, Stephen Leacock (author of *Sunshine Sketches of a Little Town*, 1912) became the most popular humorist in the English-speaking world, thanks to his ironic treatment of pretensions in Ontario's small towns and among Montreal's plutocrats. The animal stories of Ernest Thompson Seton, often told from the animal's point of view, sparked an interest in the natural world throughout North America. I recall coming across in my English school library several dog-eared volumes from Mazo de la Roche's sixteen-volume saga of the Whiteoaks family, beginning with *Jalna* (1927)—although I always assumed the author was male and the Lake Ontario landscape was American.

So there were successful Canadian authors, writing books with Canadian themes and settings. But fiction was regarded as a frill of dubious value, and distances were so vast that writers rarely met. As Atwood remarks, "There was plenty going on, but nobody knew each other." Most Canadian writers of fiction, non-fiction, and poetry continued to be published outside the country, by publishers such as Macmillan, Thomas Nelson, or Oxford University Press, and then distributed in Canada by a subsidiary of the parent company alongside the latest British or American bestsellers. No publisher could survive by publishing Canadian books alone.

However, there are a few silver linings to the dark cloud of colonial gloom. Lorne Pierce was one Toronto publisher determined to nourish a distinctly Canadian culture, despite the country's vast size and modest population. Dapper and earnest (quintessentially Canadian characteristics at the time!), Pierce was editor from 1920 to 1960 of the Ryerson Press, a division of the United Church Publishing House.[7] Like the ordained Methodist minister he was, Pierce felt a calling—a mission to foster Canada's "development of an inward life [and] the evolution of a collective spirit."[8] Pierce nearly killed himself with exhaustion as he criss-crossed the country, selling books and spotting talent. In 1922 alone, he travelled close to eighteen thousand kilometres by train, in trips to the Maritimes and western Canada, all the while editing manuscripts in jolting railcars.[9] Among the poets and novelists whom he discovered and promoted were E. J. Pratt, Dorothy Livesay, Louis Dudek, Frederick Philip Grove, and Laura Goodman Salverson. The authors drew on major Canadian themes: the Newfoundlander Pratt, for instance, wrote narrative verse about the Last Spike.

How many Canadians today know these names? Not many, I'm sure, but they, and Pierce, were slowly building a Canadian literary tradition.

The key to profitability for a Toronto publisher was the school textbook market. Thanks to Pierce's efforts, Ryerson and Macmillan Canada joined forces to co-publish textbooks for elementary and high schools that covered Canadian history, prose, and verse. Designed as "the cement to bind us [as] a people to one another," they sold well.[10] The intention was overtly nationalist: in 1942, Pierce wrote, "It is my belief that only by a deep immersion in . . . the political, social, scientific, and literary history of the country can an 'education for citizenship' be achieved."[11]

The readers gradually introduced Canadian students to the existence of Canadian texts, although until the 1950s, British books continued to dominate schools in English Canada, and Quebec educators stuck to French classics. Most English-Canadian and French-Canadian schoolchildren grew up assuming that real history and real literature happened elsewhere. Atwood herself recalls an overload of English Romantic poets, plus *Hamlet* and Thomas Hardy's *The Mayor of Casterbridge*, in high school reading lists. ("I don't think it did us any harm. And we did get a poem by E. J. Pratt in grade thirteen.") National indifference to Canadian writers pushed English-Canadian publishers into dire straits; in 1948 they issued a mere fourteen books of fiction and thirty-five works of poetry and drama.[12] The same year, eighteen hundred works of fiction were published in Great Britain and over eleven hundred in the United States. Meanwhile, a tidal wave of American movies, music, and magazines washed north.

Another glint of silver within the philistine gloom was the Montreal author Hugh MacLennan, who declared his determination to "hammer out a literary pattern for Canadian life." The McGill professor was appalled that Canada was "apathetic about herself, neither a colony nor a nation, and in the literary world she was a little better than a dumping-ground for foreign books."[13] MacLennan incorporated Canadian preoccupations and settings in *Barometer Rising* (a novel about the 1917 Halifax Explosion, published in 1941) and *Two Solitudes* (the 1945 bestseller inspired by English-French tensions in Quebec). Still, when Canada emerged from the

Second World War with a new self-confidence and a strong economy, the question remained: why was this country's artistic life so stunted?

The bleakness of the situation drove several writers in the pre-Atwood generation to leave the country. Mavis Gallant turned her back on Montreal in the 1950s: she was living in Paris when she wrote the brilliant short stories that were frequently published in the *New Yorker*. She rarely came home. Margaret Laurence, born in Manitoba, chose to live in England during the 1960s; there she wrote most of her greatest work, *The Stone Angel*. Mordecai Richler, a Montreal native, spent much of his twenties and thirties in Paris and London because "Canada was a big and lonely place . . . at the end of the world."[14] He published his first seven novels in England, including his breakthrough bestseller, *The Apprenticeship of Duddy Kravitz*.

Yet apathy about Canadian literature was slowly evaporating. In 1949, alarmed at the anemic state of Canadian culture, the Liberal government in Ottawa appointed the Royal Commission on the Development of the Arts, Letters and Sciences, with a future governor general, Vincent Massey, as chair. The Massey Commission was a turning point for this country's writers and artists, as well as for Canadian citizens generally. The five commissioners went on a hand-wringing cross-country tour. They heard that the arts were starved, and that the country was "hostile or at least indifferent to the writer." The commission's report argued that if Canada was to fully mature as an independent country, it needed state support for the arts in both English and French. "It is in the national interest to give encouragement to institutions which express national feeling, promote common understanding and add to the variety and richness of Canadian life, rural as well as urban."

It was a eureka moment in our history. Action took a little longer. (Louis St. Laurent, Liberal prime minister at the time, is said to have responded in shock: "Fund *ballet* dancers?!"[15]) However, in the postwar fizz of national self-discovery, support for cultural distinctiveness had gained enough momentum to persuade even potential critics that government patronage was a public good. The most important initiative was the establishment in 1957 of the Canada Council for the Arts, with a mandate to "foster and promote the study and enjoyment of, and the production of works in, the arts." Canada Council dollars were directed toward education, travel, commissions, awards, and grants for artists. The long-term effect was to build support not just for artists but also for the *idea* of the arts as an important element in national identity. Finally, it seemed that the "Great Canadian Novel" might be a worthy purpose for an aspiring writer—such as Margaret Atwood, whose ambition had just been noted in her high school yearbook.

So what is the direct link between Moodie and Atwood?

In the Bloor Street café, Atwood is in instruction mode. She stonewalls any probe into her private life in interviews, preferring thoughtful analysis conducted through rhetorical questions. I soon learn to let the pauses after these questions drag on: I am not expected to answer, because she will likely answer them herself. Right now, she is explaining how women have played a major role in Canadian literature from the earliest years.

In any examination of North American literature, she tells me, "a curious thing emerges. It's possible to cover American literature from, say, 1625 to 1900 without spending much time at all on women writers.... Attention focuses on the 'great' and overwhelmingly male American writers of the period: Melville, Poe . . ."[16] But what happens when you look at early English-Canadian literature? "You can't ignore the women." This is partly because Canada was settled later than the United States, and "women were literate when they arrived here," she notes. "Those pioneer women like Moodie, or the nuns who landed in Quebec—they came, they saw, they wrote. Also, in a pioneer society, the arts were a girly thing because the men went out and did the heavy work."

That's why, argues Atwood, if Canadian literature could be described as rich in anything, it would be considered rich in women's novels and memoirs. "The percentage of prominent and accomplished women writers, in both prose and poetry, is higher in Canada than it is in any of the other English-speaking countries." Atwood observes that women writers also dominate Quebec's early literature. The hurdle that Canadian women had to overcome if they were going to be published, as Moodie and her successors including Atwood had discovered, was not their gender but their nationality—the same hurdle that men faced too. The battle in the literary arena was not between the sexes but against stifling indifference. For metropolitan critics elsewhere, all Canadian writers were second-rate.

Margaret Atwood had been aware of Susanna Moodie's work from childhood; a copy of *Roughing It in the Bush* was in the family bookcase, and an extract from it had appeared in her grade 6 reader. At the time, she could not have been less interested: the label "Canadian classic" was repellent to a child in love with medieval castles, ray guns, and (later) Jane Austen novels.[17] But while she was a graduate student at Harvard, she had a vivid dream that she had written an opera about Susanna Moodie. "I could barely read music, but I was not one to ignore portents." At Harvard's Widener Library, Canadiana was shelved close to another of Atwood's favourite haunts: the shelves devoted to witchcraft and demonology. Atwood, who had already impressed classmates with her originality, immersed herself in the Moodie memoirs.

Susanna Moodie fuelled Margaret Atwood's insight into Canadians' ambivalence toward their own country. In 1970, two years before the ground-

In her poetry, Atwood captured the misery that Susanna Moodie, a nineteenth-century immigrant, experienced in the bush. The poet herself felt at home in the backwoods.

breaking *Survival,* she published a sequence of poems entitled *The Journals of Susanna Moodie.* A further edition of *The Journals* would appear in 1980 with extraordinary hand-printed illustrations by Atwood's close friend the artist Charlie Pachter.

In these poems, Atwood describes Moodie's profound alienation from the unfamiliar North American landscape. "I am a word / in a foreign language," states the wretched narrator in Atwood's opening poem, "Disembarking in Quebec." Elsewhere, Atwood's Moodie describes how

We left behind one by one
the cities rotting with cholera,
one by one our civilized
distinctions
and entered a larger darkness.

It was our own
ignorance we entered.

Atwood explored in an afterword how Moodie "claims to be an ardent Canadian patriot while all the time she is standing back from the country and criticizing it as though she were a detached observer, a stranger." Perhaps, continued Atwood, contemporary Canadians were like Moodie: they failed to embrace this country as their own.

How was Atwood able to plumb a nineteenth-century immigrant's terror of the wilderness? Because she knew this landscape so well herself—and, unlike Susanna Moodie, she revelled in it. As a child, she had learned to love the bush that Moodie had hated; it was life outside the backwoods that was alien. As Atwood writes in a 2014 edition of *The Journals,* "She was appalled by the wilderness: I by the city. . . . Both of us were uprooted. Both of us were far from home, both anxious, both scrabbling for cash, both under pressure. . . . I said for her what she couldn't say, and she for me."[18] In the words of Atwood's biographer Rosemary Sullivan, "As she worked on the poems, Margaret discovered that Moodie and she were each other's obverse. Moodie was a kind of anti-self."[19]

Margaret Atwood's own childhood has become almost as mythologized as Susanna Moodie's pioneer hardships. Born in Ottawa in 1939, she was only a few months old when she was tucked into a backpack and, along with her older brother, Harold, taken north for the first of many summers in the backwoods. Until she was a teenager, her default existence was life in the bush.

Her father, Carl Atwood, was a forest entomologist who was never happier than when building cabins and tracking bugs kilometres from the closest settlement. Her mother, Dorothy, was a university-educated nutritionist who adapted easily to constant change. Between 1936 and 1948 the Atwoods moved twenty times—sometimes between fixed points (city in winter, forest in summer), sometimes from one city (Ottawa, Sault Ste. Marie) to another (Toronto). "Home," for both of them, was Nova Scotia, but after their marriage they never lived there. "My mother was from a small town," says Atwood, "and though she was homesick for it all her life, she couldn't wait to get out of it." Instead of a cozy community where everybody knew each other's business, the typical features of Margaret's childhood homes were "a chunk of pink granite sticking out of the ground, a kettle bog, a horizon line of ragged black spruce: ah! There you are! Home ... Not a place but a trajectory."[20] A trail through the trees was home from late April until early November: both Carl and Dorothy Atwood were nomads who liked to be as far as possible from "civilization." The smells of Margaret Atwood's childhood were not of kitchen cleaners, bubble gum, and roast beef dinners but of campfires and fish guts.

"We did not have television, electricity, radio, libraries, or other people," Atwood told a standing-room-only audience at a 2014 conference, "Women as Public Intellectuals," at Mount Allison University in New Brunswick. "But I had an older brother and we grew up with edged tools and outboard motors. When we took our high school aptitude test, I did well in garage mechanics."

Atwood did not complete an entire school year until she was in grade

8. Instead, she learned self-sufficiency and wilderness skills from her parents. Dorothy Atwood home-schooled her children; Carl Atwood taught them how to identify the genus and species of birds and insects. The children (a second daughter, Ruth, was born in 1951) kept frogs, snakes, crayfish, and jays as pets; they later built a birchbark tepee and mapped the surrounding woods.[21] Atwood became a voracious reader: animal stories, comic books, girls' adventure stories, mysteries, and (her favourite) Grimm's fairy tales. Her first novel, written when she was six, featured an ant floating down a river on a raft.

Sullivan writes, "The young girl who surfaced from those months spent in the forest was an outsider to female conventions." Atwood never assumed that the way boys and girls behaved in 1940s Toronto was the only way people would ever behave. Nor did she ever sentimentalize nature: "I hate to break it to you," she tells me, one eyebrow raised, "but toads don't wear waistcoats." Mr. Toad of *The Wind in the Willows*, an old friend from my bourgeois British childhood, is instantly banished to never-never land.

When Atwood was seven, her father was appointed a professor in the University of Toronto's Department of Zoology. The family moved into a modest home in the Leaside district, close to one of the city's wooded ravines. Many of Atwood's most vivid childhood memories—memories reworked in her fiction—are of adventures in the overgrown, damp ravines dense with wildlife, or among the cluttered, dusty showcases of the Royal Ontario Museum, with its diorama of sabre-toothed tigers. Atwood explored a handful of conventional rituals: she attended Sunday school, although her parents were not churchgoers, and she joined the Brownies, where she aced the wood-lore tests. But she remained that detached observer.[22]

Every spring it was back to the woods for the tight-knit Atwood clan. Far from suburban expectations, Margaret was free to think for herself and read what she liked. Twenty-five years after those idyllic summers in the bush, the Canadian filmmaker Michael Rubbo would make a documentary about the Atwood family at its northern Ontario cottage. He intercut interviews with Dorothy and Carl Atwood with shots of Atwood herself paddling across the lake with her partner, Graeme Gibson, or reading to their daughter, Jess, by lamplight. Rubbo is obviously frustrated that there appears to be no trauma in the now-famous novelist's childhood—no dark secret of repression, guilt, or family dysfunction. Instead, the Atwoods display humour and good sense as they quietly mock the man behind the camera.[23]

At Leaside High School, Peggy shocked her friends by announcing she was going to be a writer. In addition to penning passion-filled Brontë-esque verses, she also used her obvious talents to satirical effect—including in an operetta for her home economics class about synthetic fabrics, starring King Coal's daughters, Princesses Orlon, Nylon, and Dacron. Aged eighteen, she enrolled at Victoria College, in the University of Toronto, and immediately began to publish poems and articles in the college literary journal.

The impact of Northrop Frye—Vic's éminence grise, author of *The Bush Garden* (which would be published in 1971) and one of Canada's greatest literary critics—was immense. In Sullivan's words, "Margaret made the astonishing discovery that Frye took Canadian literature and young writers seriously." She absorbed his theories about the importance of stories, as a way that humans understand themselves and others, and his argument that all stories, whether Shakespearean or comic book, are hewn from the same plot lines. His idea that Canadians shared a "garrison mentality"—a sense of isolation from cultural centres, besieged within a hostile landscape—would inform her *Survival* argument. And she saw how he remained in Canada, despite his global stature and offers from other, more "important" universities, because he found both Toronto and its academic community congenial. Atwood too would decide that, as an artist, she preferred to remain in her own city.

By now there was a bumptious group of long-haired Canadian poets, which included Al Purdy, Irving Layton, and Earle Birney. Atwood made her mark among them as a sharp-witted and talented regular at one of Toronto's scruffier and more subversive hangouts, the Bohemian Embassy in Gerrard Street Village—an area that, as Atwood herself would write, was "morphing from whitebread quasi-slum to cool pre-hippie hang-out."[24] The Embassy, serving no alcohol and run as a private club, was established in reaction to Toronto's stifling conformity; poets, folk and jazz musicians,

By the 1960s Toronto streets such as Gerrard and Yorkville (*above*) boasted hippie hangouts.

playwrights, and actors congregated here. Atwood gave her first reading in the Embassy's black-walled second-floor space in November 1960. Her low-pitched monotone had to compete with the whoosh of the espresso machine and the flush of the toilet.

Despite the sexism of the surrounding culture, Atwood discovered a sense of solidarity among the poets. "The coffee-house stuff was all self-generated, people just did it. Nobody said, 'You can't do this because you're a girl'—except a few people like Irving Layton when he was being naughty in public. The rest of them, including those that you might think would be Mr. Macho like Al Purdy or Earle Birney, treated you as a poet. They were genuinely interested in your work." That was the significance of the Bohemian Embassy: "We knew there was a community. You went there and read your poetry, under the auspices of John Robert Colombo."

It was the energetic impresario and poet Colombo who told the young Atwood, "You've got to change your name! Nobody will take you seriously if you call yourself Peggy." Fifty years later Atwood still thinks he was right. "Peggy is a frivolous name, you've got to admit. You can get away with being an actress or a folk singer . . . but to be a poet . . . You can see his point."

First she went to gender-free initials—M. E. Atwood ("Why do you think J. K. Rowling is J.K.?")—and then to Margaret.

The network of poets developed. They learned of each other's work in the Bohemian Embassy and on CBC Radio, where Robert Weaver had Canada's first literary program, *Anthology*. "That's where many of us, including Alice Munro, Gwendolyn MacEwen, and I were first heard. It was the first time anybody actually paid us for our work. Weaver knew everybody in the country so he gave us the sense that there was a continuum out there."

Atwood decided to follow the example of many of her fellow poets who, faced with publishers' disregard for Canadian poetry, had started to hand-print and promote their own work (a slim volume of poetry being more manageable than a lengthy novel). She designed and printed her first book of poetry, *Double Persephone*, on a friend's press: seven pages long, with a lino-block cover and a print run of 250, it sold through local bookstores for fifty cents. Her friend the poet Gwendolyn MacEwen wrote admiringly of Atwood's "clean-cut, uncompromising slant on things."[25] In 1964 her second poetry collection, *The Circle Game*, would be published by Contact, one of the small Canadian presses that had begun to spring up. It was printed in such a small edition that when it won the 1966 Governor General's Award for Poetry, it was already out of print. It would be reprinted by the House of Anansi.

When she graduated from the University of Toronto, Atwood radiated a confidence rare among women and Canadians in that era. She also impressed contemporaries because, "in a world of impractical poets and artists, she was worldly-wise in the extreme."[26] She told Frye that she intended "to run off to France and live in a garret and work as a waitress and write masterpieces," she recalls today. "He said I might get more writing done if I got a Woodrow Wilson [scholarship] and went to Harvard."

Atwood would spend two years in Cambridge, Massachusetts, studying early American literature and Victorian novelists, drafting poetry, and playing with ideas for future novels. From the intellectual historian Perry Miller, she absorbed the idea that books needed to be seen within their historical context: writers write out of their physical and cultural circumstances. It was a new experience for Atwood to look at literature through a political lens. She began to ponder whether Canadian writers had not yet found a way to reconcile their aesthetic sensibilities with the northern landscapes.

Most important, Atwood glimpsed Canada from the outside as a country with a shape and a culture of its own. In the United States, she discovered, Canadians were invisible, and as a result, many Canadian expatriates became flamboyantly nationalist, trying to assert their difference by bragging about (usually fictional) encounters with bears, Indigenous people, or frostbite. "It wasn't the American national identity that was bothering us; nor was it our absence of one. We knew perfectly well we had one, we just didn't know what it was."[27] But Atwood was never going to adopt a knee-jerk defence of her country. Instead she was more interested in unmasking the hypocrisies of both countries. The young and sardonic Atwood noted that the Canadian national animal is the beaver, an animal that spends its time constructing earthworks and is said to chew off its own testicles when attacked. (This defensive tactic is actually a myth, but it served her purposes.) In contrast, the American eagle is a bird of prey.

Atwood returned to Canada in 1963. (She would spend more time at Harvard in the mid-1960s.) By now, she had begun to brood about both Susanna Moodie and the issue of Canadian identity. Moreover, she had absorbed the idea that literature is *always* political.

～

The noise level in the Bloor Street café has subsided, as the pre-office espresso clientele gives way to mid-morning hipsters looking for lattes. Many of the café's clients have recognized Atwood. With characteristic Canadian deference, they show no interest in asking for selfies with the star. However, breaking all the self-service rules, a server comes over to ask if we would like more coffee. Atwood, in black pants, sweater, and long brightly coloured silk scarf (a uniform, I've noticed, favoured by senior poets), seems surprised by this special attention.

We return to the narrative of her writing life and how it unfolded within the context of the growing Canadian self-consciousness. We are firmly in the turbulent 1960s now—the decade not just of anti-war flower children and feminism but also of a surge of nationalism. Canadians began to fall in love with their own country, as governments led by the Liberals Lester Pearson and Pierre Elliott Trudeau introduced new national programs and symbols: a national health insurance system, the Maple Leaf flag, and, most exhilarating of all, Expo 67. The massive celebration for the one-hundredth anniversary of Confederation drew millions of foreign visitors to Montreal.

Not every Canadian embraced the new symbols: this was also the era of the Quiet Revolution in Quebec. Under the slogan "Maîtres Chez Nous," Quebecers demanded more control of the province's resources. By the end of the decade the Parti Québécois, under the charismatic leadership of René Lévesque, would begin to push for sovereignty. The shiny new national pride seemed on the brink of being punctured.

Meanwhile, the United States was tearing itself apart over its war in Vietnam. Hundreds of draft dodgers streamed across the U.S.-Canadian border,

Born in Alberta and raised in Saskatchewan, singer-songwriter Joni Mitchell was a major figure in Toronto's downtown folk scene in the 1960s.

including musicians and writers who swelled the crowds in the coffee houses of Toronto's Yorkville district. There were many reasons for Canadians to start differentiating their country from its macho southern neighbour.

When Atwood arrived back in Canada in the summer of 1963, she took a job with a market research company called Canadian Facts. The job suited her because her duties took little time or mental energy; by noon most days, she had completed her reports on clients' products and was quietly thinking about her own work. Yet the company's questionnaires elicited answers from Canadians that fascinated her. One of the questions was "Is Canada different from the United States?" The majority answered no. The next question was "Do you think that Canada should join the United States?" And the majority answered no.

Atwood smiles as she describes this conundrum. "So what that meant was that [Canadians] knew there was a difference between the two countries, but they didn't know what it was. The disjunct between the two responses fitted in with a lot of other disjuncts that I knew about." She had already learned that publishers insisted that they could not publish a Canadian author unless they had a British or American partner: publication in Canada alone was too expensive, and the audience here too small. But this usually meant changes. "On the one hand, we were told that Canada doesn't have an identity. But on the other hand, when we submitted those manuscripts, those British or American partners would say, 'It's too Canadian.'"

By the mid-1960s, with a Governor General's Award to her name, Atwood was acknowledged as a rising talent. After a year teaching grammar to engineers at the University of British Columbia, she spent the summer writing a novel in UBC exam booklets and sent it to the Canadian publisher McClelland & Stewart. Unknown to her, it lay forgotten for some time in a desk drawer, but it was finally published in 1969 with the title *The Edible Woman*.

The Edible Woman had secured an American publisher because it conformed to the unwritten rules about Canadian literature; it was set in a city that is rarely named (although its mysterious ravines and snowy weather are familiar to most Canadians). The novel is a dark comedy about Marian

McAlpin, a young woman working in a market research company who develops an eating disorder. It is biting social satire—I laughed out loud as I read about the "coast-to-coast sanitary napkin survey" that had gone terribly wrong. One questionnaire was returned "with 'Tee Hee' written on it, from a Mr. Leslie Andrewes." Another respondent claimed to have been pregnant for seven years. " 'Oh *no*, poor thing,' gasped McAlpin's colleague. . . . 'Why, she'll ruin her health.' " In the final chapter, McAlpin finally asserts herself.

Surfacing, Atwood's next novel, was written before Atwood's non-fiction analysis of Canadian literature, *Survival*, but it was published the same year, 1972. In this novel, the narrator and a group of friends travel to a wilderness cabin in northern Quebec to search for her father, who has disappeared. The book is full of details that resonate with Canadians who head north each summer: rutted roads, pink fireweed, logjams, herons, hokey ornaments at remote gas stations. But there is also a layer of menace, plus acknowledgement of a vanished Indigenous people. Atwood brazenly outed herself as a Canadian this time, and the *Toronto Star* reviewer described *Surfacing* as "a Canadian fable in which the current obsessions of Canadians become symbols in a drama of personal survival: nationalism, feminism, death, culture, art, nature, pollution."[28] It is vintage Atwood in more ways than one. Although this narrator, like Marian McAlpin, is nearly submerged by her neuroses, like McAlpin she regains control. The final chapter begins: "This above all, to refuse to be a victim. Unless I can do that I can do nothing. I have to recant, give up the old belief that I am powerless and because of it nothing I can do will ever hurt anyone." Not a bad metaphor for Canada's literary tradition finally rejecting its colonial status.

Despite its Canuck character, *Surfacing* also found an American publisher. Atwood recalls how the New York publisher asked her if there were any good quotes he could put on the back cover. "I said, 'Well, I've got all these wonderful ones from Canada.' He said, 'Oh no, that won't do. Canada is death down here.' " Her head tilts to one side as she grins at me: "It's not anymore, but that's the way it was back then. Same in England. Total dismissal." However, the novel was not dismissed—in fact, it attracted continent-wide attention. The *New York Times* described it as "thoroughly brilliant" and the newspaper's reviewer concluded, "Atwood shows the depths that must be explored if one attempts to live an examined life today."[29] The Quebec director Claude Jutra turned the book into a film, released in 1981.

It was a short step from *Surfacing* to the provocative statements about Canadian literature in *Survival*, in which Atwood wrote that "Canada as a whole is a victim, or an 'oppressed minority' or 'exploited.' . . . In short, Canada is a colony." Canadian gloom, she suggested, might be because "Canadians have a will to lose which is as strong and pervasive as the Americans' will to win." She illustrated her argument with a crisp catalogue of recurrent themes in Canadian novels and poetry, including the idea that nature is menacing rather than romantic, that Indigenous people are persecuted rather than savage, that families are claustrophobic ("ingrown-toe-nail family-as-trap"). But the thirty-three-year-old author was determined that Canadian writers, like her own heroines, did not have to remain trapped in colonial passivity. She offered a bracing alternative: "A tradition doesn't necessarily exist to bury you: it can also be used as material for new departures."

From now on, Atwood's writing career went from strength to strength. Between 1976 and 1983, she would publish six books of fiction, two of non-fiction, three of poetry, and two for children. While at Harvard University she had begun a relationship with her fellow student Jim Polk, an anti-war American who was also an aspiring novelist. They married in 1968, but the marriage did not survive Atwood's short-term contracts at various universities (University of Alberta in Edmonton, Sir George Williams University in Montreal, York University in north Toronto). They divorced in 1973 and she formed a relationship with Graeme Gibson, a Canadian writer.

Gibson and Atwood moved to a classic old Ontario farmhouse in Mulmur Township, north of Toronto; their daughter, Jess, was born in 1976. Atwood had achieved the balance in her life that for years had seemed unobtainable: total commitment to her writing, and a partnership with "a large man who likes kids and cats, and has an ego so solid it isn't threatened by mine."[30] Such an egalitarian relationship was still an anomaly in those days: despite the inroads of feminism, wives deferred to husbands within most marriages.

Equally important, Atwood had demonstrated that it was possible to be a self-supporting professional writer in Canada. By the mid-seventies she was making a comfortable income, and in 1976 she incorporated herself under the name "O. W. Toad" (an anagram for "Atwood"). She also acquired a New York agent. Until then, she recalls, "there wasn't enough of a literary culture here to think about having a literary agent. They wouldn't have made enough money out of it." She hired an assistant to handle correspondence and all the requests that had begun to fill her mail slot: the "Atwood-criticism industry," as Sullivan describes it, was taking off.[31] Today articles about Atwood's work fill scholarly journals, while the Margaret Atwood Society, an international association of scholars, teachers, and students, holds well-attended annual conferences and publishes a journal called *Margaret Atwood Studies*.[32]

It wasn't only Atwood's career that was flourishing. Thanks in part to the Canada Council, the performing arts (ballet companies, theatre festivals) and art galleries blossomed. But it was creators like Atwood who were massaging the Canadian identity into shape. "The Canada Council fed the activity, but the poets had provided the yeast," she tells me. With *The Journals of Susanna Moodie*, she herself had helped launch the career of Charlie Pachter—Canada's Andy Warhol, whose tongue-in-cheek paintings of subjects like the Maple Leaf flag and the Queen on a moose have reinforced these national symbols over the past half century.

Demand for Canadian books rose, and a Canadian publishing industry steadily took root. After co-founding the House of Anansi, Dave Godfrey had joined forces with his fellow writers Roy MacSkimming and James Bacque to start New Press. By the 1970s, there was an explosion of new small publishers right across the country: besides Anansi and New Press, there was Coach House, Oberon, Hurtig Publishers, Tundra, Talonbooks, blewointment Press, Fiddlehead, Breakwater, and others. Established publishers like Oxford University Press and Macmillan Canada also took a

British ballerina Celia Franca arrived in Canada in 1950, founded the National Ballet of Canada, and remained its artistic director for twenty-four years. Canada Council grants were crucial to the company's growth.

keen interest in the literary turmoil. The West was bursting with new talent: Patrick Lane, George Bowering, Pat Lowther, John Newlove, bill bissett, Eli Mandel. In Montreal, Irving Layton and Leonard Cohen read their poetry to crowds of adoring young women. In Edmonton, the passionate nationalist Mel Hurtig founded Hurtig Publishers, which released another provocative examination of Canadian identity, *The New Romans: Candid Opinions of the United States*, by the poet Al Purdy. More overtly anti-American than *Survival*, it was also less successful, but it still sold more than twenty thousand copies because, as Atwood explained to me, the appetite was there. Writers boarded Greyhound buses for cross-Canada book tours and got to know each other. There were plenty of power struggles and romantic intrigues (the couch at Anansi was particularly well used). Meanwhile, readership for Canadian books blossomed.

The great impresario of the CanLit explosion was the publisher Jack McClelland, who published almost everybody and decided that Canada's literary scene needed pizzazz. McClelland was "a swashbuckler," recalls Atwood. "He returned from the war and put so much energy into Canadian publishing." McClelland decided that McClelland & Stewart, the publishing house founded by his father, should stop depending on imports from its American partners and should make money from its own impressive list. "He looked for a niche that wasn't filled," Atwood explains admiringly, and he realized (as Lorne Pierce had done before him) that schools needed Canadian texts. A few universities had created a new market by finally launching some courses in Canadian literature. In 1957 McClelland founded the New Canadian Library series, classics in inexpensive paperback format that became the yardstick of quality writing for generations of students. Oxford University Press jumped on the same bandwagon and commissioned a Canadian poetry anthology for students from the editors Dennis Lee and Roberta Charlesworth.

Next McClelland invented the book tour. Thanks to lavish book launches and publicity stunts right across Canada, he won media coverage and sales for his stable of homegrown authors, which included Atwood, Mordecai Richler, Farley Mowat, Pierre Berton, Irving Layton, Leonard Cohen, and Margaret Laurence. In 1972, for example, a swag bag for reviewers and booksellers accompanied the publication of Berton's book *The Great Railway: Illustrated*. It contained cut plug tobacco, a cigar, pemmican, and moustache wax. Another stunt, on the ides of March in 1980, involved McClelland, clad in a toga, driving down Toronto's Yonge Street in a chariot with Sylvia Fraser, to publicize Fraser's novel *The Emperor's Virgin*. Even a late snowstorm could not smother the chariot's progress or McClelland's bravado.[33] In the words of the writer Matt Cohen, McClelland was "a man who gave Canada a unique and priceless gift: a series of visions of itself and the words through which . . . Canada defined itself as a nation."[34]

McClelland's showmanship paid off in sales. But his success caused international publishing conglomerates to look north, where they saw, as Atwood puts it, "there's gold in them thar hills." They began to acquire Canadian publishers and to establish their own subsidiaries that developed publishing lists in both English and French. Canadian ownership shrank, and McClelland & Stewart lurched from crisis to crisis. A debate about foreign ownership of Canada's cultural industries erupted, as writers and readers realized they had something of value that they didn't want to lose to Yankee carpetbaggers.

Atwood had never embraced the Romantic notion that a true artiste should be aloof from grubby reality, and she now emerged as a formidable leader within the writing community. In *Survival,* she had noted that "the same people who would not dream of asking a musician or actor to perform without a fee often expect a writer to do just that. Writers have to eat too, and at the moment there is no union to protect their interests."[35] She and Graeme Gibson pushed for a union of authors from across Canada to win some control over the way writers were seen and treated.

The result was the Writers' Union of Canada, which lobbied aggressively on behalf of authors. Its first chair was Margaret Laurence, newly returned from England. "Writers are a tribe," she announced at TWUC's founding meeting in 1973, and from then on, the tribe had a collective presence in the English-Canadian consciousness. Four years later, Quebec writers launched UNEQ, the Union des Écrivains Québécois. As TWUC's historian, Christopher Moore, has noted, "Formed to promote the very idea that cultural policy was necessary to Canada, the Writers' Union [has] become one of many institutions participating in the making of cultural policy." Public lending rights, copyright law reform, tax changes, digital rights—the Writers' Union relentlessly went to bat for its members in these long-running debates.

Atwood herself wrote the entry on the Writers' Union for *The Canadian Encyclopedia.* It concluded, "One of the most important achievements of the union is to have fostered a spirit of professionalism and self-respect among writers. . . . Since the 1960s the public's image of the Canadian writer has changed . . . from defective freak to acceptable member of society, and the union has reflected and fostered that change."

TWUC was just the beginning. Together, Atwood and Gibson invested time and money in causes that would strengthen ties within the literary community. In 1976 they were among the founders (along with Pierre Berton, Margaret Laurence, and the playwright David Young) of the Writers' Development Trust (now the Writers' Trust of Canada) to advance interest in Canadian literature and to support Canadian writing. In 1984 the first meeting of the English-Canadian centre of PEN International, the organization that fights on behalf of writers whose right to freedom of expression has been violated, was launched in their dining room. Atwood served as its first president from 1984 to 1986 and also came up with the idea for the first PEN fund-raising project: a CanLit cookbook. It made enough money for PEN to hire an executive director.[36] Far from "defective freaks," as Atwood had put it, Canadian writers were now flexing muscles and earning decent livings. British and American publishers and critics paid attention to Canada's emerging literary stars.

By the end of the twentieth century, CanLit's big names had their own glitzy recognition system: a series of prizes and awards that boosted both sales and image. There had been literary awards since 1937, when Lord Tweedsmuir (better known as the bestselling British novelist John Buchan) inaugurated the Governor General's Literary Awards. But the GGs, as they are known, were always a dowdy affair: there was no flashy ceremony, and not until 1951 did they include an honorarium of $250.

However, in 1994 the businessman Jack Rabinovitch decided the writing world needed a bit more glamour. On the advice of his old school friend Mordecai Richler, Rabinovitch founded the Giller Prize, initially with a purse of $25,000. According to David Staines, editor of McClelland & Stewart's New Canadian Library series and an adviser to Rabinovitch, "It was a great time to launch a prize because there was now a critical mass of good writers. Yes, Atwood was a blazing star, but it was a full firmament." Awarded at an exuberant extravaganza in Toronto each November, the Giller lifted sales of the winning novels by up to four or five times, while boosting interest in CanLit. Today the award is sponsored by Scotiabank, the purse is $100,000, and the gala is televised. As Staines notes, "The Giller's impact has been huge. For the first time, Canadian writers were not looking elsewhere for approval." Atwood won the award in 1996 and has been on the jury four times, more than anyone else other than Staines.

Other glamorous awards for Canadian fiction and non-fiction followed the Giller, including the RBC Taylor Prize for literary non-fiction, the Writ-

Jack Rabinovitch founded the Giller prize in 1994 in honour of his late wife, Doris Giller. From left to right, Esi Edugyan (the 2011 winner), Jonathan Lethem, Margaret Atwood, and Jack Rabinovitch.

ers' Trust of Canada Awards, and the Griffin Poetry Prize. Each helped create excitement around books. In the meantime, Canadian authors were also picking up international prizes: Margaret Atwood won the Arthur C. Clarke Award in 1987 and the Booker Prize (now called the Man Booker) in 2000; Jane Urquhart became the first Canadian winner of France's prestigious Prix du Meilleur Livre Étranger in 1992; Michael Ondaatje won the Booker Prize in 1992 and Yann Martel won it ten years later; Carol Shields won the Pulitzer Prize in 1995; Timothy Findley was named Chevalier de l'Ordre des Arts et des Lettres in 1996; Lawrence Hill won the Commonwealth Prize in 2008; Alice Munro won the Nobel Prize for Literature in 2013. Canadian culture was celebrated outside Canada.

The business side of CanLit is not such a happy story. Publishers grapple with the same challenges that faced their predecessors a century ago: the audience is too small, the distances too vast, the market too flooded with foreign books. Canada's bookstores wilt under the pressure of online sales, and global pressures on the industry rock publishing companies.

Nevertheless, the literary community is firmly established. On average, about 1,500 new trade titles are published each year, including nearly 200 novels.[37] These days, anybody who agrees to be a juror for one of the big awards finds herself facing an avalanche of new publications to speed-read before the deadline for the long-list and short-list announcements.

So what characterizes CanLit today? Is survival as strong a theme as it was when Atwood described it in 1972? Or do different literary themes reflect the Canadian identity in the twenty-first century?

Today's literary culture reflects a different country. As Canadian writers and readers relinquished the colonial mentality, and as the population evolved from bicultural to multicultural, says Staines, "all directions are open to us." Indigenous writers, including Richard Wagamese, Joseph Boyden, and Thomas King, are major prizewinners. Many of today's literary stars were born elsewhere and set their fictions in their childhood homes: Vietnam for Kim Thúy, Germany for Dan Vyleta, Lebanon for Rawi Hage. In Staines's opinion, "Writers here have the freedom to write about whatever, and wherever, they want." Yann Martel, author of *Life of Pi*, has described Canada as "the greatest hotel on earth." He meant it as a compliment: that this country "welcomes people from everywhere" and has no problem if immigrant writers prefer to reside here while their imaginations roam across landscapes they left behind.

Thanks to the sturdy foundation of the 1960s CanLit explosion, David Staines suggests, our literary culture today "has solidity without shape. There is no single umbrella idea." Yet contemporary Canadian bestsellers often share particular characteristics. Atwood comments, "If you're writing in Canada, you can't avoid the weather." Multigenerational families continue to loom large, although now they may be Indigenous or immigrant. Raw nature continues to be an important motif, although fragility rather than menace is the angle. At the same time, certain genres remain largely absent from our bookshelves. Unlike Britain, Canada has no creamy layer of middle-class social realism ("Maybe there isn't a big enough readership for it," suggests Atwood). And when Canadian crime writers set their novels within Canada, there may be a tinge of gentility to the murders (think

Louise Penny or Maureen Jennings). "Mean streets" is not a cliché with so much salience here, so grittier writers such as Ian Hamilton or Peter Robinson set their stories offshore.

Atwood once described herself as "a curious, often bemused, sometimes disheartened observer of society."[38] Introduced relatively late to social conventions, she became an expert at deadpan observation. She is not alone. Her predecessor Susanna Moodie was an astute observer of a country and population to which she never felt she belonged. And the novelists based in Canada who are now snapping at Atwood's heels continue to be "great observers," says Staines, although their gaze may be directed beyond our borders.

In the introduction to *Moving Targets*, a collection of pieces written between 1982 and 2004, Margaret Atwood divides her own career into stages. Until the mid-1980s she was "world-famous in Canada." Then she published the chilling novel *The Handmaid's Tale*, about a bleak near-future after a fundamentalist takeover. Set in a Puritan New England, it depicts a totalitarian society where pollution has caused widespread infertility, and young women are enslaved and turned into breeding machines. Like any Atwood novel, it is filled with stiletto insights, but these are darker. "A rat in a maze is free to go anywhere, as long as it stays inside the maze."

This chilling vision catapulted her into stage two of her career, with an international readership.

The Handmaid's Tale continues to haunt imaginations worldwide; it has been made into both a movie and an opera, and it regularly appears on university reading lists. Atwood calls it "speculative fiction" rather than science fiction, since it is a nightmare version of our world rather than a fantasy of spaceships and extraterrestrial beings. She enjoys describing international reaction when *The Handmaid's Tale* was published in 1985: "In Britain they thought it was a jolly good yarn, in Canada they asked, 'Could it happen here?' but in America, I heard, 'How long have we got?' " The novel played on public anxiety about the right-wing backlash to feminism and the impact of chemical contaminants.

Atwood herself now lives in Toronto, but her fingertips remain on the pulse of a larger world. From the start, all her novels have focused on contemporary social and political issues, although often in the guise of particular genres. After *The Handmaid's Tale*, alongside poetry and short stories, she published a Gothic romance, a feminized fairy tale, a ghost story, and a piece of historical fiction, in each of which she scrutinized relations between men and women, and the way that women construct their identities. These universal themes were set firmly within Canada: Toronto's postwar growth, for example, is charted in both *Cat's Eye* and *The Blind Assassin*. Readers beyond Canadian borders were immersed in the sociology of Canadian girls' friendships or the geography of nineteenth-century Ontario. When Atwood did book promotion tours outside this country, she championed other writers, "sprinkling," as she puts it, "Canadian authors hither and thither—you should read this and that person, and you should publish this and that person."

Given the diversity of twenty-first-century Canada, it is perhaps inevitable that such a brilliant, productive, and commercial novelist has now moved beyond her own Canadian context. In 2003 Atwood returned to speculative fiction, laced with satire, with *Oryx and Crake*. For years she had been clipping items from newspapers and popular science magazines; now she wove them into a warning: don't trust scientists and big corporations to run the world. *Oryx and Crake* is the first in the *MaddAddam* trilogy of novels that takes readers on a wild ride through a post-human landscape. National boundaries blur again as she paints a grim picture of climate change, pollution, and the risks of biotechnology—a picture that warns her widening international readership about its complicity in the problems. A mysterious worldwide plague has destroyed human civilization and all but a handful of humans. Mutant monsters like wolvogs (wolves crossed with hogs), liobams (lions crossed with lambs), and pigoons (pigs with partly human brains) roam around, threatening the few human survivors. There is also a mysterious tribe of bio-engineered humanoids called Crakers, which smell like citrus fruits and wave blue penises when they want to mate.

The *MaddAddam* trilogy is, to put it mildly, pessimistic—which means it catches the public mood perfectly. As a character in *Oryx and Crake*, the first volume in the trilogy, says, "Anyway, maybe there weren't any solutions. Human society, corpses and rubble. It never learned, it made the same cretinous mistakes over and over, trading short-term gain for long-term pain." So it is no surprise that an HBO series of the *MaddAddam* books is already in the works; Atwood has tweeted about her interest in how they will portray those penises. She has also published another "speculative fiction" novel, *The Heart Goes Last*, in which she turns her fierce wit on where organ retrieval schemes and privatized prisons might take us.

By my reckoning, Atwood is now in stage three of her career. She is one of Canada's most important cultural exports. (Who else is in that rather small category? My list includes Alice Munro, Drake, Cirque du Soleil, Jim Carrey, Céline Dion, Mike Myers, Justin Bieber, Robert Lepage, The Weeknd, and various hockey heroes.) In 2016 her version of *The Tempest* appears as part of a prestigious British series of books marking the four-hundredth anniversary of Shakespeare's death, with other contributions by some of the best-known writers in the English-speaking world. She is part of Canada's international image. Does she still feel embedded in the Canadian literary tradition?

The eyebrow goes up: the drawl becomes more pronounced. "You can say of the author: short, female, curly-haired, old, Canadian, Ontarian, Torontonian. . . . You can say all those things, but just one of [those words] is not going to do it. It's just one descriptor." And by now there are so many more descriptors for Atwood, the wildly successful writer whose sensibility has been shaped by the cultural traditions within which she grew up, who played a vital role in nurturing our literary tribe, and who herself is now helping to shape the Canadian imagination.

Margaret Atwood did not achieve all that alone. But she certainly gave us confidence in our collective imagination, and—like Emily Carr and Harold Innis before her—helped us understand the space we inhabit. Without her, Canadian literature would be a more fragile plant on our boreal landscape.

CHAPTER 7

Establishing Our Rights

Bertha Wilson Champions the Charter

In some . . . areas of the law, . . . I think that a distinctly male perspective is clearly discernible and has resulted in legal principles that are not fundamentally sound and should be revisited as and when the opportunity presents itself. . . . Some aspects of the criminal law in particular cry out for change since they are based on presuppositions about the nature of women and women's sexuality that in this day and age are little short of ludicrous.

—Bertha Wilson, "Will Women Judges Really Make a Difference?" (1990)

In 1982, she was a pioneer, the first woman appointed to the [Supreme] Court. By 1991, she had become a hero, especially to a generation of women law students and young lawyers.

—James MacPherson, eulogy for Bertha Wilson (2007)

E xpo 67, which galvanized national pride from coast to coast, confirmed Canada's status as a mature nation. What a birthday party! Planners had expected twenty-six million visitors to the sixty national pavilions; fifty-five million came. As Margaret Atwood puts it, Expo 67 was "a high point for Canada's belief in itself, a sort of, 'Hey, we can do this on the world stage. What do you know, we pulled it off.' "[1] Thanks to Expo planners and people like Atwood, Canadians welcomed the idea of themselves as citizens of a prosperous, open-minded young country with a distinct culture and unlimited potential as it entered its second century. By now the term "Dominion" had been deliberately erased.

Nobody symbolized Canada's new-found self-confidence more colourfully than the Liberal leader who became Canada's fifteenth prime minister the following year. Pierre Elliott Trudeau—brash, bilingual, sophisticated, and brainy—held power for fifteen years between 1968 and 1984. The first prime minister to embrace the power of televised images, he was cool before most of us realized the word had been reinvented. I was living in London in 1977 when the photo of him pirouetting behind the Queen's back at Buckingham Palace was splashed over front pages. The insouciance of this guy! The un-Canadian charisma! The London *Daily Sketch* named him the world's seventh-sexiest man.[2]

Pierre Trudeau was and remains a deeply polarizing figure within this country, one who has inspired every emotion except indifference. Because I am not putting a spotlight on prime ministers, Trudeau (like his predecessors, both Liberal and Conservative) has only a background role here. However, he was a transformative leader. And he led the country during years when that buoyant Expo 67 self-confidence would be severely shaken. At the moment when the Canadian identity appeared to be at its most vigorous, fault lines began to emerge.

Throughout his years in power, Trudeau was preoccupied with Quebec's demands for autonomy, inside or—if English Canada wouldn't budge—outside the federation. He advocated a strong and united Canada even as his critics, both French- and English-speaking, argued that Ottawa had too much power. It was a struggle that came close to tearing Canada apart. Yet today Quebecers' demands for a separate North American state have faded from the national dialogue. Subsequent federal governments have recognized the uniqueness of La Belle Province. Although about one-third of Quebec voters continue to register separatist sympathies, a new generation of Quebecers is less engaged in the *indépendantiste* movement than their parents.

What is the legacy of Pierre Elliott Trudeau? I would include a united Canada with its own constitution, a strong commitment to bilingualism, and a place for francophones in the mainstream. He also left a reservoir of ill feeling in the West, whose interests he consistently treated with disdain. However, beyond the Ottawa–Quebec City axis he is remembered today for his passionate support for progressive values and social justice. One of the best-known statements in Canadian history is "The state has no place in the bedrooms of the nation"—the words he uttered in 1967 while still the federal minister of justice. He caught the mood of the times as he de-criminalized gay sex, legalized contraception, and liberalized divorce laws.

As prime minister, he went even further. He entrenched the Charter of Rights and Freedoms in the 1982 Canadian Constitution, so that it was in-corporated into Canada's constitutional framework. The Charter was Trudeau's baby: he had promoted the idea in academic articles before he went into politics. In his memoirs he insisted that it would enhance unity among Canadians because it should create a "society where all people are equal and where they share some fundamental values based upon freedom."[3]

More than three decades later, the Charter is embedded in the Cana-dian imagination as a guarantee of this country's tolerance and respect for individual rights. It is a document that inspires national pride: we regularly cite it as a defining characteristic of our country. How many of us have ac-tually read it? I'm not sure. Nevertheless, most of us know that it guarantees a long list of individual rights, including democratic rights, legal rights, and mobility rights, along with an equally long list of fundamental freedoms:

freedom of conscience, religion, thought, belief, expression, the press, peaceful assembly, and association. It specifies that Indigenous rights should be protected, and it recognizes the diversity of Canadian society.

Yet few predicted the Charter's iconic status back in 1982. When the Canadian Parliament passed the Constitution, much of the Charter was words on the page—a tossed salad of terms still untested in court. It would be up to the judiciary to decide how to interpret these words. Would our courts stick to narrow definitions of all these brave promises, or would they interpret them expansively so that the rights of individuals were increased at the expense of the powers of the state? How far would the Charter limit parliamentary supremacy?

We know now that the courts would prove generous (too generous, in critics' opinions) in many cases involving the application of Charter guarantees to both individual and group rights. The tone was set by the nine justices of the Supreme Court of Canada as soon as the first few test cases worked their way up through the legal system to reach our top court. No single judge set this direction, but one judge in particular was an extraordinarily effective advocate for the rights of individuals.

Bertha Wilson had a formidable reputation as a judicial thinker before she donned the scarlet robes of a Supreme Court judge, but she was never regarded as a radical. She was appointed largely because it was finally time for a woman on the court. Yet anybody who studied her biography might have predicted that this quiet, determined Scot would use the new tool to maximum effect on behalf of underdogs enmeshed in legal travails. Wilson helped flesh out Pierre Trudeau's vision of a country where the institutions of the state could not arbitrarily trump the rights of individuals. Not only has the Charter become national bedrock, but it has replaced the American Bill of Rights as the constitutional document most emulated by other nations.[4]

✦

In a spacious, hushed office in Ottawa, surrounded by shelves packed with leather-bound volumes of statutes and tables piled high with legal briefs

When Bertha Wilson graduated
from Dalhousie University Law
School in 1956, there were few
opportunities for women lawyers.

and drafts, I'm learning how judges think. Across the desk is David Stratas,
a judge on the Federal Court of Appeal who as a newly qualified lawyer in
the 1980s had been a law clerk in the Supreme Court, working for Justice
Wilson. A jovial man whose enthusiasm conceals a sharp intellect, Stratas
leans forward as he shares with me his classification system for judges who
populate the upper reaches of our judiciary.

I am engrossed. Like most Canadians, I tend to think of judges as remote figures entirely removed from humanity, thanks to years closeted together in the hothouses of law school, academe, and practice. Now this
senior judge is giving me a glimpse into their rarefied world.

"Category one judges are those who rely on their good instincts. They
argue from practicality and the gut and don't think in terms of rigid rules
or concepts," Stratas explains. "Category two includes the rigid rule observers. They revel in the tangibility of law. They are not particularly daring, and
they are temperamentally conservative, but they are detailed, technical,
and reliable.

"And then there's category three: the judges who understand the rules but are more interested in the concepts that prompted the rules in the first place. Has the rule evolved away from the concept underlying it? Does the concept need to be re-examined for its application to a changing society? These are the judges with intellectual curiosity.

"Courts need all three types, but Bertha Wilson was a classic category three." That wasn't all: Wilson had backbone too. "She was a front-of-the-roller-coaster person: very courageous and keen for the ride, preferably with others but alone if need be."[5]

I can tell that Stratas is a full-on fan of his former boss, and that he esteems category 3 judges, especially if they sit on the Supreme Court. Yet when Bertha Wilson was a little girl in Scotland, nobody would have predicted her ascent to Supreme Court eminence. As a child she never voiced the ambition to become a lawyer; as a young minister's wife, she appeared content to play self-deprecating second fiddle to her more sociable husband. She was consistently underestimated, perhaps because she never sucked all the air out of a room when she entered. Nevertheless, like many immigrants, she grasped new opportunities in a new land. And then she went on to help shape a core Canadian institution.

Born Bertha Wernham into a comfortable Scottish working-class family (her father was a stationery salesman) in 1923, she enjoyed the excellent free education available in Scotland. She studied philosophy at the University of Aberdeen, an old and prestigious university well-known for its links to the Scottish Enlightenment and its strong philosophy faculty. By the time she graduated, she had absorbed both the up-from-the-bootstraps self-reliance on which Scots have always prided themselves and a framework for intellectual analysis. (Both her brothers became philosophy professors.)

At her mother's insistence, Bertha Wernham moved on to teachers' college. However, she didn't really want to be a teacher, and she further exasperated her parents by becoming engaged to a young theology student, John Wilson, who was too left-wing and working-class for her mother's tastes. She never finished her teacher training. Instead Bertha married John as soon as he was offered his first parish, a remote fishing village called Macduff that faced the chilly North Sea. She seemed set for

Growing up in Scotland, Bertha Wernham and her two brothers all studied at Aberdeen University, an excellent university with no tuition fees.

a life as a Presbyterian minister's wife, the parish's unpaid and selfless welfare worker.

Macduff, with a population of one thousand, was a dour, insular community, with a granite church and a drafty Victorian manse. While John ministered to his recalcitrant flock, Bertha kept chickens and learned how to cook over an open fire. The minister's pay was so small that she depended on gifts of fish and oatmeal for their diet. Together, the Wilsons instituted a range of activities to enliven parish life. Bertha was soon fully occupied with youth groups, the Women's Guild, the Girl Guides, the Women's Missionary Society, and the Nursing Association.[6]

In retrospect, Bertha acknowledged that Macduff was where she developed an empathy for others: "I discovered how complicated people are, how lonely proud people are, how dependent on the rest of us old people are, how very hurt sensitive people can be by what seems to us like nothing." She learned to listen carefully and develop deeper insights into what makes people tick. She saw "how most of us are locked up tight inside ourselves, much of the time pretending to be something we are not." It was the beginning, she would later acknowledge, "of my education for living."[7]

Life in the bleak little village was a dead end for both Wilsons, and within a couple of years, they knew they needed to move on. As usual, it was John who took the initiative. He saw in a Church of Scotland paper an advertisement placed by a Presbyterian congregation in Canada. A little logging town called Renfrew, not far from Ottawa, wanted a Scottish minister. A few weeks later, Renfrew's new thirty-year-old minister was boarding a crowded transatlantic liner called the *Aquitania*, with his twenty-six-year-old "accompanying spouse" at his side. In September 1949, the *Aquitania* steamed into Halifax Harbour.

As I imagine the Wilsons' arrival in Canada, I can almost hear the medley of British accents—Scots, Scouse, Cockney, Yorkshire—as the newcomers lean over the scarred deck rails, chatting excitedly as they seek a glimpse of their new country. A picture of the Wilsons from these years shows an attractive woman with a shy smile and curly brown hair, dressed in a sensible woollen coat and plain leather shoes, smiling broadly at her husband, a compact figure who (even in the dated black and white photograph) almost vibrates with energy. Altogether, there would be ninety-five thousand new arrivals in Canada in 1949, and for many of them, including the Wilsons, Pier 21 in Halifax would be the gateway. They were part of the postwar bulge of emigration into Canada. From 11.5 million in 1941, the population would jump to 18 million by 1961, of whom one in six had been born outside the country. British immigrants dominated the influx, but thousands more came from the shattered nations of southern and eastern Europe. Italians, Greeks, Poles, Ukrainians, and Latvians arrived, bringing with them exotic new tastes and customs to liven up the homogeneity of "old-stock" Canada.

However, non-Europeans needed not apply: racism had characterized Canada since before Confederation, and it persisted at official as well as unofficial levels. In 1914 hundreds of Sikh and Hindu would-be immigrants, aboard the steamship *Komagata Maru*, were refused entry in Vancouver and sent back to India. A few years later the Chinese Immigration Act stopped Chinese immigration entirely (previously, would-be immigrants had faced a punitive head tax). Although the act was repealed in 1947, few Chinese immigrants were allowed in the country. In the 1930s

Canada closed its doors to Jewish refugees fleeing Hitler's Third Reich; 907 desperate Jews aboard the *St. Louis,* for example, were forced to head back to Europe in 1939. Most perished in the Nazi death camps. Immediately after the war, Prime Minister Mackenzie King insisted that "the people of Canada do not wish, as a result of mass immigration, to make a fundamental alteration in the character of our population. Large-scale immigration from the orient would change the fundamental composition of the Canadian population."[8]

The entrenched racism extended to people within Canada's borders too. Indigenous peoples were treated as second-class citizens and denied many rights, such as the right to vote. In 1942, after the Japanese attack on Pearl Harbor, Canadians of Japanese origin (most of whom were born in this country) were forced to leave homes, farms, and businesses along the British Columbia coast and move to crowded, shabby internment camps elsewhere.

But British immigrants, like John and Bertha Wilson, were welcome. What did this young Scottish couple see, after they had disembarked and an immigration officer had stamped "Landed Immigrant" on their identification cards? Probably not much, since they immediately boarded a train. If they had glanced at the local paper, Halifax's *Chronicle-Herald,* they would have been surprised to see that more column inches were devoted to baseball scores and American news than to stories from Britain. But they would have been reassured by an article headed "Canadian Employment Is Better," which recorded that the unemployment rate here was only 2 percent, compared with 6 percent in the United States.[9]

Soon Bertha and John Wilson were finding their feet in Renfrew.

Years later Bertha Wilson described her first impressions of Canada to her biographer Ellen Anderson, author of the well-researched and informative *Judging Bertha Wilson: Law as Large as Life.* "I recall the [Robbie] Burns supper in our first January in Canada," Wilson told Anderson. "We had haggis and bagpipes and all that! I felt the country to which I had come was more Scottish than the one I had left behind." There is a hint of exasperation in this statement.

There were other reminders of Scotland. Once again, the minister's stipend was stingy and the minister's lodgings inadequate. Moreover, in this parish there was no role for the minister's wife—no Women's Missionary Society or Ladies' Aid. Bertha Wilson ended up working as an unpaid housekeeper for an elderly parishioner. For a university-educated woman accustomed to being an energetic community leader, it was deadly. But she wasn't ready to rock the boat.

The Wilsons lasted no longer in Renfrew than they had in Macduff. John Wilson did not particularly enjoy traditional ministry work, and when the chance to serve as a naval chaplain came up in 1952, he grabbed it. While he was on active service on the destroyer HMCS *Cayuga*, Bertha Wilson moved to Ottawa and took a job as a receptionist for two dentists. She was an anomaly for her times: a twenty-nine-year-old chaplain's wife living as a single woman. She was often lonely, but there were compensations. "I developed a new sense of confidence in myself and was intensely proud of every new hurdle that I crossed. I know that this first experience on my own was a necessary prelude to my career in law."[10]

The Wilsons were reunited in Halifax a year later. John was still the breadwinner, and his unassuming wife was soon working, once again, as a receptionist in a dental office. However, now she had a goal: she was saving in order to pay university tuition. Attracted to the study of law because of her undergraduate interest in philosophy back in Aberdeen, she applied to the law school at Dalhousie University although she had no plans to practise. The dean barked, "We have no room here for dilettantes. Why don't you just go home and take up crocheting?"[11] Wilson persisted. Shy, and one of only five women in the class of sixty, she was older than nearly all the others.

"From my very first day of classes," she told the writer Sandra Gwyn in 1985, "I knew the law was my thing. I just sopped it up like a sponge."[12] She discovered the legal framework to our lives that is invisible to many of us: "I was fascinated by the history of the law and how it had developed over the years as social conditions changed and I marveled at its flexibility. I wondered how I could have lived this long without realizing the large part it plays, behind the scenes, in everything we do. I acquired a whole new perspective on life."[13] Soon she was winning prizes, and classmates were borrowing her notes.

But this was still Canada in the 1950s. Bertha Wilson remained an "accompanying spouse." The national health insurance system, the CanLit explosion, and the women's movement were way beyond the horizon, and so was her future role in the country's legal system.

✦

The Supreme Court of Canada is housed in one of the most imposing buildings in Ottawa—an art deco temple, with massive bronze doors and a steep copper roof, on the capital's main government thoroughfare, Wellington Street. To its east are the handsome Gothic buildings of the parliamentary precinct, noisy with debate about the country's future. To the west is the bleak office tower that houses Library and Archives Canada, silent custodian of our past.

Sandwiched between yesterday's records and tomorrow's legislation, the Supreme Court radiates a timeless and purposeful dignity. Nobody who walks through those bronze doors, into the marble-lined entrance hall, can escape the knowledge that this is the keystone of the Canadian justice system. It is the court of last resort, where cases arrive for final determination only after they have worked their way through several lower-level courts of trial and appeal.

These days the Supreme Court is a judicial Mount Rushmore to many Canadians: a magnificent and solemn monument vital to the national sense of self-worth as well as a brake on governmental excess. Given the reverence in which we hold it, I was surprised to discover that for much of its life it was almost irrelevant. Created in 1875, it began as a sideshow; the Judicial Committee of the Privy Council in London, on the far side of the Atlantic, was the court of last appeal for the Dominion of Canada. The Canadian top court's first members (six back then, including two from Quebec) met rarely, in a Parliament Hill committee room. They were a motley lot, better at infighting than at legal arguments. Decisions rendered by one judge, according to two colleagues, were "long, windy, incoherent masses of verbiage, interspersed with ungrammatical expressions, slang and the veriest legal platitudes."[14]

A low point was reached with the launch of the famous Persons Case in the late 1920s, when the first wave of feminism was still bubbling away. Five prominent women from Alberta, including the redoubtable Nellie McClung, asked the Supreme Court if women could be considered "persons" and therefore eligible under the British North America Act to be appointed to the Senate. The whiff of male chauvinism in the converted horse barn that housed the court at the time almost blotted out the stench of manure as the chief justice announced his decision in 1928. The act specified that "qualified persons" might sit in the Senate, and that meant men. The judges had resorted to "originalism": the principle (still popular on the U.S. Supreme Court) that the words in the text mean what was in the brains of the BNA Act's authors. Since no women held office in 1867, the act's authors could not have intended to allow them in the Senate, and the 1928 court saw no need to take account of the massive social changes in the intervening years.

Prime Minister Mackenzie King confided to his diary that the chief justice was "a laughing stock and an ass"; he encouraged the women to appeal the decision to London. In October 1929, bewigged British law lords contradicted Canada's top judges. They argued that the BNA Act was an organic document, like "a living tree capable of growth within its natural limits," rather than frozen in time, and they decided that Canadian women were persons after all. The British lord chancellor added that, unlike the unimaginative Canadian judges, he and his colleagues wanted to give the BNA Act "a large and liberal interpretation" rather than "a narrow and technical construction."

The most significant event in the court's history over the next two decades was the move into its splendid new building, designed by the Montreal architect Ernest Cormier, in 1946. Three years later, the Canadian Supreme Court severed ties with Westminster (it took the Imperial Privy Council itself to nudge the Supreme Court out of its dependency) so that

In 1946 the Supreme Court of Canada moved into its new courthouse,
one of the most impressive buildings in Ottawa.

Canada now enjoyed full judicial independence. The number of judges was
raised to nine, with three from Quebec in recognition of its different system
of law. In general, the court remained relentlessly conservative, rarely issu-
ing decisions that challenged the status quo.

During these years, the Progressive Conservative government led by
John Diefenbaker took the first important step toward guaranteeing individual rights. The 1960 Bill of Rights protected numerous rights, including
freedom of speech and religion and the right to life, liberty, and security.
(Indigenous people finally got the vote in 1960, thanks to Diefenbaker.)
But Diefenbaker's bold move had limited application because it was an act
of Parliament, rather than part of the Constitution, and because the Supreme Court was so timid in interpreting it. According to one legal academic, by the late 1960s, a gloomy malaise hovered over that art deco
copper roof because the majority of the elderly and grumpy judges shared
"an outdated and unduly narrow conception of the role of law in courts."[15]
Their critics grumbled that the court dealt today with the problems of tomorrow by applying the solutions of yesterday.[16]

And then, in 1970, Prime Minister Pierre Trudeau threw a rock into this sluggish pool. He appointed the brilliant Bora Laskin, a University of Toronto law professor, to be the court's first Jewish member. Three years later, Trudeau vaulted Laskin over five more senior judges into the seat of chief justice. Laskin, who was known as a civil libertarian and an aggressive supporter of federal over provincial powers, began to flex the court's muscles. According to Jim Phillips, co-editor of the Osgoode Society for Canadian Legal History, Laskin believed that judges must be more than technicians: they should "shape the law to reflect reality and improve society."[17] Laskin constantly challenged his colleagues to think more deeply about legal principles and introduced a view of the law that lawyers would soon be calling the "purposive approach."

There was more to come when the British Parliament severed its last legal ties with Canada and in 1982 passed Canada's new constitution, which included the Charter of Rights and Freedoms. In the words of Philip Slayton, a former Supreme Court law clerk and dean of law, "After more

In April 1982 Queen Elizabeth and Prime Minister Pierre Trudeau signed the new Canadian Constitution, with the Charter of Rights and Freedoms securely embedded in it.

than a hundred dull and undistinguished years, the Supreme Court of Canada was transformed from, at best, a peripheral presence in government to a supremely powerful institution at the heart of Canada's affairs. Now things got exciting. Now judges had the power to strike down legislation that they considered incompatible with the constitutionally guaranteed rights and freedoms of each individual."[18]

This was a new world, and Canadians started to notice what was going on in our top court. For almost the first time in the institution's history, camera crews could be seen hauling their cumbersome equipment up its granite steps. And this was also the moment when Bertha Wilson donned the scarlet robes of a Supreme Court judge.

꙼

Whenever Bertha Wilson was asked how she had achieved her remarkable ascent through legal ranks, she would reply, "Good work habits"—or, as the phrase sounded in her pronounced Aberdeen accent, "Guid wurrk habits."

She was hardly alone in this: Canada has benefited from waves of diligent Scottish immigrants who became bank presidents, heads of universities, or, like John A. Macdonald and Tommy Douglas, inspirational political leaders. There were significant other factors in Bertha Wilson's success, including a supportive husband (who took early retirement to make her life easier) and no family distractions (the Wilsons' childlessness was a source of regret). Most important was something over which she had no control: timing. The women's movement was about to challenge the limited roles allowed to educated women throughout North America. Wilson herself lived through a revolution within her profession. Today women constitute more than half of each graduating class in many of Canada's twenty-three law schools. But when Wilson graduated from Dalhousie's law school in 1956, she quickly discovered there was no market for women lawyers in Halifax: the profession there was an old boys' club.

Wilson finally found a spot as an articling student with a colourful solo practitioner named Fred Bissett (father of the poet bill bissett). "From the dizzy heights of academia I was plunged into the stark reality of the police court, with its daily roster of drunks and prostitutes. . . . And when I became too insufferable in my new-found legal knowledge, Fred would say to me, innocently, 'How would you like to work up a defence on this buggery charge?' "[19]

Bertha Wilson was not destined for a career in the Nova Scotia criminal courts. When John Wilson took a job in Toronto with the fund-raising arm of the United Church, his wife followed him. Once again, she faced the challenge of finding an articling position. Leafing through the Yellow Pages, she looked for a really big firm "because in a small firm they could always fob you off with excuses about not having a ladies' washroom." She applied to and was grudgingly accepted by Osler, Hoskin & Harcourt, a corporate-commercial giant—although a senior partner later recalled a long and solemn debate about whether women were really suited to be lawyers. She proved her worth so effectively that, after her articling year, Osler's quickly hired her on a permanent basis—the first woman lawyer on the prestigious firm's roster.

Wilson was still an anomaly. Many of Osler's pinstriped partners, whose wives were traditional homemakers, didn't know what to make of the new hire, and many clients at the time were uneasy working directly with a female lawyer. So Wilson beavered away on legal research in the bowels of the firm and discovered she had a flair for it. She analyzed judgments, read law reports, wrote opinions, and established a reputation for rigorous analysis and sound advice on any area of law. She became the firm's specialist in estate planning, particularly for the wives of wealthy clients. She put Osler's ahead of its competitors by setting up the first centralized information retrieval system in a Toronto law office in the days before Quicklaw and LexisNexis.

Young lawyers looked to Wilson for guidance; older lawyers turned to her for reassurance about the warp-speed modernization of legal practices in the sixties and seventies.[20] Over the years, she became the ultimate law geek, who understood the whole fabric of the law and how it fit together. Yet to most of her colleagues, she was the reserved woman with a Scottish accent. Some assumed she was a librarian.

She was finally made a partner in 1968, yet she remained little known outside Osler's thickly carpeted corridors. While other partners golfed or attended baseball games with clients, she sat on the boards of the Clarke Institute of Psychiatry and the Toronto School of Theology. She tackled difficult social issues as a member of United Church policy committees. At a converted boathouse in the Kawartha Lakes area east of Toronto that the Wilsons rented year-round, she and John spent their weekends quietly reading.

By the time Wilson reached her fifties, she knew how good she was at her job. As she watched the women's movement begin to take off across North America, a sense of dissatisfaction crept in. She grew tired of being invited to client meetings on Bay Street to provide information to senior partners, while being derisively tagged "the skirt" behind her back. In later years she suggested to women law students that they might well find themselves stuck because "the powers that be have a vested interest in keeping you at the level you're at simply because you are so good at assisting your superiors and making them look better than they really are!"[21] It was certainly true in her case. When she accompanied one of her colleagues into court, she didn't even sit at the lawyers' table. Instead she would watch from the back and listen to her colleague make the arguments that she had helped develop. She admitted to Sandra Gwyn in the mid-1980s, "I would think to myself, 'I could do that. Why didn't I ever take a crack at it?' But by then, you see, it was too late."[22]

It wasn't. Political pressure was building in Ottawa for more female faces on the bench, and Wilson was one of the few eligible women. In 1975 she was invited to join the Ontario Court of Appeal—the first woman to join a court of appeal in any Commonwealth country. After some hesitation, she agreed. She knew that not everybody was thrilled by the appointment: there were muttered questions about her lack of courtroom experience, her suitability, and, of course, her gender. One judge protested, "No woman can do my job!"[23] Some Osler partners were thrilled for her, others were just plain jealous. She took it all quietly in her stride but made her own position clear at her swearing-in ceremony. "Perhaps the unusual nature of my practice has helped me to . . . remember that people and the law are inextricably intertwined, and that the role of the profession is essentially to serve the needs of the people."

Wilson sat for seven years on the court of appeal, writing judgments in every area of the law—commercial, torts, contracts, property, family, criminal, and human rights law—and developing original legal arguments. Once again, her peers learned to look beyond her quiet manner. According to her friend James MacPherson, former dean of Osgoode Hall Law School and now a judge on the Ontario Court of Appeal, "She was a prolific, principled, and superb writer." And she didn't duck controversy as she pushed the law to adapt to contemporary challenges. Kent Roach, like Stratas a former law clerk to Wilson, later observed, "There was a bit of shyness to her—it wasn't like you were immediately confiding in each other personal secrets or anything. But there was real determination . . . a fearless sense of principle. She really just called them as she saw them."[24]

In one case, involving the division of property after a marriage breakdown, Wilson came down firmly on the side of the wife, using an argument hitherto applied almost exclusively to business partnerships. Her opinion was upheld. In another case, she wrote a spirited defence of the right of a nine-year-old girl to play on a boys' softball team. She pointed out that the girl "was refused registrations simply because she is a girl. Her case seems to me therefore to be on exactly the same footing . . . as the case of a boy denied registration . . . because he is black." This time, she could not carry her colleagues with her. In a third case, Wilson pushed the legal envelope even more firmly. The case involved Pushpa Bhadauria, an East Indian mathematician who claimed that she was prevented from getting a job at Seneca College in Toronto because of her race. Wilson argued in favour of Bhadauria's claim. It was a bold argument, involving a new "tort of discrimination," and the Supreme Court disallowed it. But Wilson's argument and approach were widely admired.[25]

Wilson's decisions on the Ontario Court of Appeal demonstrated that she was aware of the evolution of attitudes in our society and committed to rethinking the way legal principles should apply to changing social practices. But that's not why her name came up when a vacancy appeared on the Supreme Court. It was because she was a woman—and until then, no woman had served on the bench there.

Judy Erola, minister for the status of women, supported by the health minister, Monique Bégin, lobbied Prime Minister Trudeau within cabinet for Wilson (whom neither knew personally). "It was tough," recalls Erola. "Bertha wasn't part of the establishment, and Trudeau had never heard of her. She was picked apart from every angle." The prime minister had a male candidate whom he preferred; he had no particular expectation of how Wilson might interpret the law if she was appointed to the Supreme Court. But public pressure grew, and finally Jean Chrétien, then justice minister, told the prime minister, "Boss, the girls are right." When Pierre Trudeau signed the order-in-council appointing Wilson, he turned to Erola and asked, "Are you happy now, Judy?" Trudeau's patronizing tone still enrages Erola. "It was never about me. It was about having a court that represented as many points of view as possible."[26]

In the 1982 photograph taken in her first year on the court, Wilson is conspicuous among the nine scarlet-robed judges for her gender. She was conspicuous in many other ways too. She took a different approach to her job from most of the men she now joined. She always tried, she would later explain, "to enter into the skin of the litigant and make his or her experience part of your experience and only when you have done that, to judge."[27] Moreover, none of her new colleagues came from such modest backgrounds: they all had glittering CVs, with impressive war records, prestigious educations, or dazzling courtroom careers. Only seven of the fifty-seven judges appointed to the top court before Wilson were born outside Canada, and none had arrived here as an accompanying spouse. As she said in a speech in 1995, five years after she had stepped down from the court, "An immigrant is someone who lives always on the boundary between two worlds. She has, in a manner of speaking, been born twice; and this personal duality colours and shapes all her thoughts and actions."[28]

But there she was, aged fifty-nine, sworn into a court she had never dreamed of joining. She took her place as the newest judge at Chief Justice Bora Laskin's far right. His doubts about her appointment were well-known: he bristled at the label "feminist" (a label that made Wilson herself uncomfortable) and was one of those who had asked, "Is she *ready*?" Her brief remarks on the occasion were designed to reassure him that she was not hungry for confrontation. "I trust that within the collegial structure of this national court I can be a faithful steward of the best of our legal heritage."

Immediately after she was sworn in, the court heard an excruciatingly complicated intellectual property case. The chief justice turned to Wilson and said, "Bertha, you have come out of a great big corporate-commercial law firm—you must know all about . . . the law of patents. Why don't you write it?"

"Fine," said Wilson, smiling politely and looking around at the raised eyebrows and steely expressions of eight men hell-bent on testing her. She had no expertise in this area of law. Undeterred, she set to work learning everything she needed to know. Her clearly written decision, which her colleagues supported unanimously, is still frequently quoted.[29]

Nineteen days after her swearing-in, on April 17, 1982, the Canadian Charter of Rights and Freedoms became law. As former Supreme Court justice Frank Iacobucci has said, the Charter "is not written like an income tax code, which is very precise. . . . The Charter is written in general language and so the judges have to interpret the legislation."[30] It would be the Canadian judicial system's job to flesh out the Charter and say what its vague promises and value-laden terms actually meant.

Wilson knew she had to pay her dues to escape the cold universe of belittlement. In her first two years in Ottawa, she buckled down and wrote one decision after another in difficult commercial cases. Little by little, she gained respect for her hard work and clear thinking; little by little, she got the measure of the men around her. She gritted her teeth when, consciously or unconsciously, they excluded her from lunchtime conversations by talking endlessly about baseball or hockey scores. Her only sport was curling.

A creature of habit, Wilson had a daily work routine that was utterly predictable. Each morning she arrived at the court at eight o'clock sharp, driven by John in their little silver Toyota. In her second-floor office, she would lay her papers neatly on her desk, next to a row of freshly sharpened pencils. The door was closed as she made notes in her small, careful script, then dictated her decisions onto a Dictaphone for her secretary to type later. When the court was sitting, she would join her colleagues on the bench to hear the lawyers who were presenting cases, and once the lawyers had finished their arguments, she followed the other judges out to the conference room to exchange preliminary opinions.

At five o'clock, the silver Toyota was back. Her law clerks would load a stack of books and papers into the trunk, knowing they would see them the next day, festooned with yellow stickies. She was a stickler for detail. It must have been like working for a rather severe schoolmarm, yet her clerks revered her, and they imitated her Scottish burr and quiet humour with an unalloyed affection that not many Supreme Court justices earn.

The first Charter cases began to arrive at the Supreme Court in the mid-1980s, presenting it with a whole new responsibility: scrutinizing legislation to ensure it did not infringe the rights of individuals. In 1984 Brian Dickson had succeeded Laskin as chief; now he and his colleagues were, as Wilson would say in a speech in 1987, "somewhat in the position of space travellers leaving the gravitational comfort of earth: we [had] to learn new ways to cope with unfamiliar and uncharted horizons."[31] The Charter forced the nine judges to be more imaginative and creative than most of their predecessors would have wanted or dared. At the same time, the court's decisions had to conform to legal principles. Wilson herself often spoke about judges' obligation to remember that they were appointed, not elected. "There is no plausible justification for us to substitute *our* personal values and *our* moral choices for those of the elected legislature."[32]

Wilson's own inclination to give Charter provisions some punch was quickly evident in the famous *Singh* case, which concerned the rights of refugees. Harbhajan Singh was one of seven Sikhs seeking refugee status who argued that the Charter required they should have a full oral hearing, rather than simply submitting a written claim to anonymous officials. Wilson penned the majority Supreme Court decision: Singh was right on the grounds that "fundamental justice . . . requires an oral hearing." Immigration officials were soon tearing out their hair because thousands of other refugee claimants now demanded expensive hearings. But Wilson, an immigrant herself, was adamant: "The guarantees of the Charter would be illusory if they could be ignored because it was administratively inconvenient."

Bertha Wilson was not alone in her determination to make the Charter meaningful. There was, to use Stratas's terminology, at least one more category 3 judge in the art deco temple: Wilson's colleague Brian Dickson. The son of a banker, he began his legal career as a wealthy corporate lawyer in Manitoba and was originally regarded as very traditional. But according to Jim Phillips, he had "become more compassionate and radical as he became more senior." Dickson now shared the "purposive" (a word lawyers use interchangeably with "expansive") approach to his judicial role. He argued that the Supreme Court had a duty to be creative in its Charter interpretations and, if necessary, shift the law so it reflected contemporary social values and meant something for ordinary Canadians. He and Wilson made a formidable duo. According to Dickson's biographer Robert Sharpe, "They developed a very close relationship. Brian Dickson admired her because she was a rigorously logical, principled thinker. And she worked so hard."[33] They did not always agree with each other; they could not always persuade their colleagues to be as bold. But at a crucial moment in the Supreme Court's history, they gave its deliberations real intellectual punch. Rosalie Abella, a friend of Wilson who now sits on the Supreme Court herself, has called them "the Fred and Ginger of the Charter."

By the mid-1980s, Charter cases occupied a large part of the court's attention. The judges were immersed in hearings about Sunday shopping, mandatory retirement, spousal benefits, tobacco advertising, tax law, street soliciting. Observers noted that the Charter was profoundly changing Canadian political culture, making it more American because our Westminster-style Parliament was now subject to judicial oversight.[34] The volume of work was almost overwhelming: the court was hearing over 150 appeals a year (today the number is around seventy), and Wilson's law clerks staggered under the weight of the legal briefcases that they hauled down to the Toyota. Wilson wrote and wrote and wrote, often finding herself either dissenting from the opinion held by the majority of her colleagues or agreeing with the final decision but writing what are called "concurring reasons," which meant she had arrived at the same conclusion via a different route. She would never go along with a decision that did not reflect her view of the law; she was, in the words of one observer, "not so much stubborn as implacable." She did not care if others disagreed with her reasoning.

These were the years when Charter cases triggered intense media interest. Canadians got used to seeing black-robed lawyers solemnly entering the courthouse, while television reporters tried to explain what they might hear or say. Activists hovered at reporters' elbows, eager to grab the microphone. Some were Charter supporters, like the Canadian Civil Liberties Association, talking about the need to give the Charter "teeth." Others were Charter critics, like the anti-choice group REAL Women, fulminating about the court's "judicial activists" usurping parliamentary supremacy—as though the federal Parliament itself plus nine of the ten provincial legislatures hadn't presented this responsibility to the court when it incorporated the Charter of Rights and Freedoms into our constitution.

By the time the Supreme Court had ruled on its first hundred Charter cases, Wilson had emerged as the judge most sympathetic to people who claimed a Charter right to protection from established laws. In general, the nine judges upheld about one-third of Charter claims, but there was a great deal of individual variation. Wilson supported Charter claimants more than half the time, which meant she was frequently in dissent—and often alone.[35] Her dissents and concurring reasons were anchored in the text of the law, while reflecting her unique viewpoint. She pushed her colleagues to go beyond the nuts and bolts of case law into the context of a case, and to incorporate the insights of sociology, philosophy, and history into their discussions.

Nowhere was this more evident than in the Supreme Court's ruling on one of the most controversial issues of the period: abortion. Although Wilson did not write the Supreme Court's decision in the famous *Morgentaler* case in 1988, her concurring reasons to support it are the opinion best remembered today.

The case revolved around a woman's right to terminate a pregnancy and the liability of a physician who performed abortions. Since 1969 abortion had been legal in Canada under very restricted conditions: it could be performed in a hospital only if three doctors decided that if the woman continued her pregnancy, she would endanger her life or health. The restrictions forced many women to resort to illegal and dangerous backstreet abortionists. Henry Morgentaler, a Montreal physician and Holocaust survivor, was a passionate advocate for every woman's right to end an unwanted pregnancy, and in 1968 he founded a free-standing clinic in Montreal to provide safe abortion services. For the next two decades, while police continuously harassed him because his clinic was illegal, public support for him grew. Morgentaler became a champion of women's

Demonstrations about women's access to safe, legal abortions regularly erupted in the 1970s and 1980s; the issue reached the Supreme Court in 1986.

rights and opened more clinics in Toronto and Winnipeg. Four times he was taken to court and four times juries acquitted him because they decided the law was unjust, while justice ministers in Quebec and later Ontario strove to uphold the law. In 1975 he spent ten months in jail, where he suffered a heart attack.

Morgentaler appeared at the Supreme Court in 1986 to watch his lawyers appeal a decision by an Ontario court that he should be convicted of providing illegal abortions. This was a huge story: I remember the footage of the short, grey-bearded physician being grimly escorted through placard-waving supporters and shrieking opponents. Still the only woman on the court, Bertha Wilson found that she suddenly had a bulging mailbag dominated by anti-abortion rants. Her secretary was so upset by gruesome pictures of mutilated fetuses that Wilson insisted on opening all the letters herself.[36]

Over a year later, in the depths of winter, the court released its long-awaited decision. Seven judges had heard the case; five had ruled in Morgentaler's favour. For his supporters, all that mattered was that he had won. The Criminal Code clause that restricted access to abortion services had been struck down because it violated the Charter of Rights and Freedoms.

But that wasn't what rippled through Canada's legal community and twenty-three law schools. Legal observers were intrigued that the five justices in the majority had written three different opinions. As James MacPherson observes, "If ever there was a case where the court would have wanted to speak with one voice, this was it. But in the end, although five judges agreed what the proper result should be, they couldn't agree on the reasoning behind the decision."

Two of the five judges who supported Morgentaler's acquittal wrote a technical, follow-the-rules opinion that the Criminal Code clause violated the Charter on procedural grounds, because it contravened principles of fundamental justice. Two more judges, including Chief Justice Dickson, went much further than this cautious approach: they reasoned that forcing a woman to carry a fetus to term "is a profound interference with a woman's body and thus a violation of her security of the person." All four of these male judges indicated that Parliament could still set limits on access to abortion.

Wilson's reasoning pushed the supremacy of individual autonomy still further. "Is the conscience of the woman to be paramount or the conscience of the state?" For Wilson, taking away a woman's ability to make the decision and giving it to a committee was a clear violation of the liberty and security of a person. She wrote that, as a constitutional matter, it was unlikely that any formulation could be found that did not interfere with a woman's fundamental freedom of choice at least within the first trimester of her pregnancy. She set the whole issue into the larger context of women's lives in the late twentieth century. "The right to reproduce or not to reproduce . . . is properly perceived as an integral part of modern woman's struggle to assert her dignity and worth as a human being." And just to reinforce her point, she suggested that "it is probably impossible for a man to respond, even imaginatively" to the dilemma women face in dealing with an unwanted pregnancy because he can relate to it "only by objectifying it, thereby eliminating the subjective elements of the female psyche which are at the heart of the dilemma."[37]

MacPherson recalls the general surprise at Wilson's fearlessness. "She could have just gone along with the majority, but that wasn't Bertha. She showed that she had a totally different mindset from all the men. There was a sort of collective gasp from younger members of law faculties, particularly the women. It was like, 'Oh my gosh, finally there is someone who knows how we think, feel and live.' It was beautiful."

The same kind of reasoning, rooted deeply within Wilson's life experiences, was visible in another case from this period: the *Lavallee* case. Angélique Lavallee had shot her boyfriend in the back of the head after years of abuse. Her lawyer argued that she had acted in self-defence, and brought in expert testimony on the newly articulated and controversial condition of "battered woman syndrome." The Supreme Court faced the question of whether such expert testimony was acceptable.

This time Bertha Wilson volunteered to write the opinion for the majority. She knew that her colleagues were not inclined to admit the testimony: after all, Lavallee had shot her partner when his back was turned, and anyway, why hadn't she just left the home months earlier? As Dickson and Wilson rode up to their second-floor offices in the court elevator, the chief justice turned to Wilson and asked in amazement, "Why on earth would you volunteer to write on that one?" He thought it was an open-and-shut case for dismissal.[38] But Wilson was steeped in new sociological research about the powerlessness of women in abusive situations and quietly persuaded her colleagues to see the situation from the battered woman's point of view. "A man's home may be his castle, but it is also a woman's home— even if it seems more like a prison in the circumstances." In the end, Lavallee was acquitted, and only one judge dissented from the Wilson decision.

Morgentaler and *Lavallee* were only two of the many cases in all areas of law on which Wilson prepared reasons, but they were the ones that attracted the most attention. Her admirers applauded her for incorporating women's perspectives into her opinions; her detractors (especially REAL Women) railed against her "feminist bias."

In 1987 a second woman was appointed to the Supreme Court: Claire L'Heureux-Dubé, from Quebec. L'Heureux-Dubé found Wilson "reserved and a bit distant by nature, and not very talkative either. But in her own way, I knew she was a friend." L'Heureux-Dubé spent a couple of hours with her colleague after her swearing-in ceremony. "'They are set in their ways,' [Bertha] told me, meaning that I should not try to change things. Probably she had tried." The younger judge developed enormous respect for the colleague whom she describes as "the most brilliant and profound of all the judges there at the time and also the most reflective on the nature of law and its direction in the long run. Her decisions in *Lavallee* and *Morgentaler* are masterworks and their spirit is still alive today."[39]

Two years later a third woman donned the scarlet robes: Beverley McLachlin. At McLachlin's swearing-in, Wilson impishly whispered, "Three down, six to go." McLachlin would become chief justice in 2000, presiding over a court that regularly includes four women among its nine judges. None would experience the isolation that Wilson, the pioneer, had known. These days, the idea of a top court without a single woman on it is unthinkable.

Bertha Wilson retired from the Supreme Court in January 1991. Although she wrote relatively few majority decisions in her eight years on the court, she wrote dozens of dissents and concurring reasons, signed her name to more than 160 decisions, including at least fifty Charter rulings, and delivered more than sixty speeches. She was sixty-seven and not in good health; she told friends she wanted to spend more time with her husband. But John Wilson got less of her time than they had hoped. First she got involved in two demanding and unwieldy projects: the Canadian Bar Association's Task Force on Women in the Legal Profession, and the Royal Commission on Aboriginal Peoples. And soon after they were finished, Alzheimer's disease dulled her razor-sharp intelligence. With her husband of sixty-one years at her side, she died in Ottawa on April 28, 2007.

↜↝

Along with the flag, the Mounties, and medicare, the Charter of Rights and Freedoms is one of Canada's best-known national symbols.[40]

Chief Justice Brian Dickson and Justice Bertha Wilson together led the effort to make the Charter meaningful for the most vulnerable members of Canadian society. Conservative politicians and some legal academics fulminate about "judicial activism," and during her lifetime Wilson was often the focus for such critiques. In 1995 two academics from the University of Western Ontario, R. E. Hawkins and Robert Martin, made a direct attack on Wilson in a legal journal for "promoting her personal, ideological agenda. . . . She did not simply transgress the boundaries that restrain the behavior of judges in a liberal democracy, she denied their existence."[41] The article triggered outraged debate within the legal community. These days, Canada's leading constitutional scholar, Peter Hogg, considers that "on balance, we have improved our country's governance by having the Charter of Rights."[42]

I spent a day reading the hefty tome of Wilson's speeches in the red-carpeted library of the Supreme Court itself. For most of the time, I was the only person at any of the solid pale-oak tables placed in the alcoves between shelves of leather-covered volumes. When today's clerks want to check statutes and case law, they never come here because everything is available online—an option not open to Stratas and Phillips when they clerked for Justice Wilson.

As I read the speeches, in which Wilson's acute intelligence shines through her straightforward language and clear diction, I could feel her presence all around me. Under the glass top of each library table were copies of the Canadian Charter of Rights and Freedoms. At the top of each copy was the Canadian coat of arms, the title of the Charter, and the Maple Leaf flag. At the lower edge was a drawing of Parliament's Centre Block. But when I looked more closely, I realized that each copy was in a different language. Of course our official languages, English and French, were there, and also a handful of the sixty Indigenous languages spoken in Canada, including copies printed in Cree and Inuktitut syllabics. But there were also versions in Polish, Russian, Chinese, three different Arabic scripts, Dutch, Swedish, Indonesian, and ones I couldn't identify. If you are a newcomer to Canada today, as the Wilsons were over half a century ago, you will almost certainly be able to read one of our foundational documents in your own language.

The way that the Dickson court, and Bertha Wilson in particular, interpreted the Charter to align the law with social change has had global impact. According to Jim Phillips, "In many countries, legal academics and judges are still largely technicians, who see their job as expounding not expanding." But in countries reaching beyond that model, our Supreme Court is a beacon. Justice Albie Sachs, who was appointed to the Constitutional Court of South Africa by Nelson Mandela, describes how the post-apartheid South African court looked to the Canadian Supreme Court as "our first port of call," because its decisions were "modern in spirit, carefully articulated, and imbued with the kind of values that permeated our own Constitution."[43] Justice Michael Kirby, who sat on the High Court of Australia from 1996 to 2009, describes the Canadian Supreme Court as "one of the great final national courts of the English-speaking world (a comment made with due deference to Quebec). Justice Wilson wrote many decisions that have proved influential in Australia, particularly in the field of public law, administrative law, statutory interpretation, antidiscrimination law, and refugee law. I count myself lucky that I met her."[44] Mark Tushnet at Harvard Law School recently suggested that, since the year 2000, the international influence of Canada's Supreme Court and its Charter has overtaken that of the U.S. Supreme Court and the U.S. Constitution.[45]

When I first included Bertha Wilson on my list of Canadians who have helped shape our sense of who we are, many people expressed surprise. Unlike Harold Innis, she did not explore what forces in the past had given coherence to Canada; unlike Tommy Douglas, she did not inspire Canadians to cluster around a new national vision for the future. Unlike others I've written about, she did not articulate, write, or paint large statements about what kind of country we live in. She was a lawyer, which almost by definition means that her public pronouncements were carefully limited to the case in question or to the specific topic on which she had chosen to speak. I read seven hundred pages of major speeches that she delivered across Canada but found only a handful where she widened the focus.

The most moving was the retirement speech she gave as she shed her scarlet robes forever. "I have found my role on the Court challenging, exhilarating and enjoyable and never more so since the advent of the Charter gave Canadians an awareness of the rights and freedoms which make this country such a wonderful place in which to live," she told the assembled dignitaries. "Our Charter is and must continue to be a vital force in molding the lives of Canadians." The Charter put the law into its true perspective, she insisted, as "a set of values that we, as a civilized, cultured and caring people, endorse as the right of all our citizens of whatever colour or creed, male or female, rich or poor to enjoy."[46]

By giving legal effect to Pierre Trudeau's vision of the Just Society, Justice Bertha Wilson protected vulnerable minorities from over-intrusive state power and defended the individual rights of all citizens. I don't think that Wilson would give a second thought to the fact that almost nobody in Canada today would recognize her, and the vast majority don't even know her name. I am sure that she would take enormous satisfaction from the fact that, in the thirty-five years since Prime Minister Pierre Trudeau made the Charter part of the Canadian Constitution, this legal document now ensures tolerance and fairness within our noisy, complicated, and diverse society.

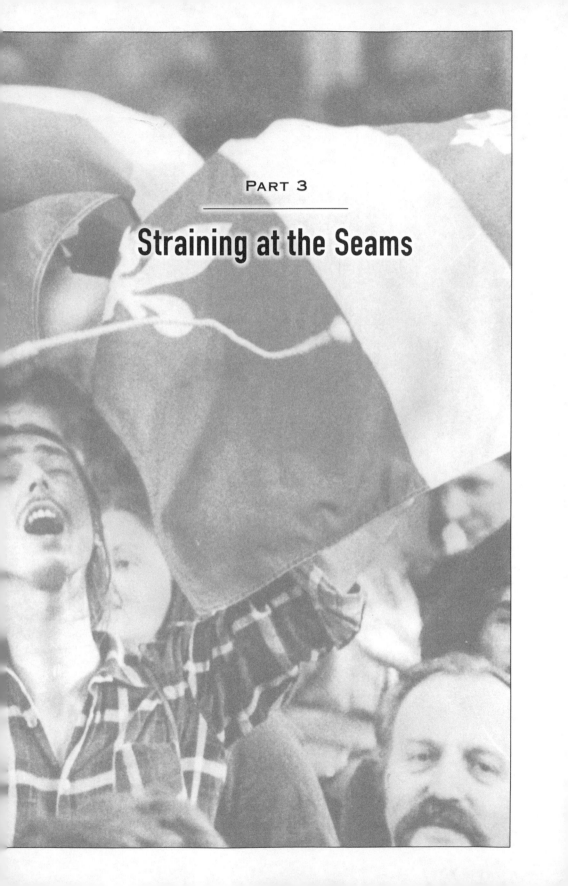

PART 3

Straining at the Seams

CHAPTER 8

Silent No More

Elijah Harper and the Power of No

Aboriginal people want to be part of this country and want to be recognized as being the First Nations and for the great contribution made by the citizens of this land in the development of this country.

—Elijah Harper, quoted in Pauline Comeau, *Elijah: No Ordinary Hero* (1989)

Every land claim, every barricade, every protest is less a harangue for rights and property than it is a beseeching for the promises offered in that flag, represented by it. Equality, shared vision, a shared responsibility. A wish, a held breath waiting to be exhaled.

—Richard Wagamese, *One Native Life* (2008)

As a survivor, I respectfully challenge you all to call for a national inquiry into missing and murdered Indigenous women. And I ask everyone here remembers a few simple words: love, kindness, respect, and forgiveness.

—Rinelle Harper, statement to the Assembly of First Nations (2014)

U ntil this point, my biographical approach to Canadian history has been as sunny as Sir Wilfrid Laurier's rhetoric, as I looked at people who helped cultivate its endless promise. And superficially, there was much to be upbeat about. Changes to immigration and refugee policies had made the total population (nearly twenty-eight million by 1990) increasingly diverse. In 1979 and 1980, over fifty thousand people who had fled from Vietnam were welcomed here as refugees—a dramatic contrast to the way that Sikhs, Chinese, and Jews had been treated in previous years. Along with newcomers from Indonesia, India, and Somalia, they were absorbed without too much resentment. Mosques and temples became familiar sights within Canadian cities. The Expo 67 anthem sung by Bobby Gimby—"Ca-na-da"—appeared in retrospect to launch a new confidence. The country that had championed the United Nations peacekeeping force now enjoyed its reputation for pluralism and non-violence. What could make Canadians prouder than our country's constant position at or close to the top of any international index of human development?

But the exuberance and pride, not to mention all the benefits of Canadian citizenship, were not shared equally. There were other, darker aspects to Canada's evolution: the widening cleavages between regions, Quebec's demand for more autonomy, the alienation of and mistreatment of Indigenous peoples. By the late twentieth century, simmering discontents had turned into open conflicts. There were strong and contradictory visions for the country; in retrospect, the collective euphoria of Expo 67 seemed naive. Successive governments fought to accommodate several different groups with competing priorities. The national unity crisis triggered by Quebec was the most critical, and it occupied centre stage in the national news. Yet it was part of a much larger fragmentation that had been affecting Canadians as far back as Confederation.

By 1979 Canada was welcoming immigrants and refugees from all over the world, including some fifty thousand "boat people" from war-torn Vietnam.

Thursday, June 14, 1990. In Winnipeg, the prairie sun beat down mercilessly on noisy throngs of people as television crews set up their equipment outside the Manitoba legislature. Inside the imposing Tyndall-stone building, an uneasy hush gripped the legislative chamber. A stocky man hunched forward, clutching an eagle feather in his right hand. Elijah Harper's brow and cheeks shone with nervous perspiration; sweat trickled down his neck under his dark ponytail; his bulky shoulders and arms strained against his suit jacket.

Then the former chief of the Red Sucker Lake First Nation rose to speak. His voice was so soft that many of those present strained to hear it. But his words were blunt. "Our relationship with Canada is a national disgrace," he said. "What we are fighting for is democracy, democracy for ourselves and democracy for all Canadians. . . . Most of all we are fighting for our rightful place in Canadian society."

Disgrace. A shocking word. Who was this unknown provincial politician, berating a country that prided itself on tolerance?

On that day, in that place, Elijah Harper was uniquely placed to make

Elijah Harper's act of defiance in the Manitoba legislature symbolized First Nations' frustrations and their growing clout in Canadian politics.

history. A small group of Indigenous strategists working alongside him had crafted his message and had begun the day together by burning sweetgrass.[1] But the speech was delivered by this nervous, self-conscious chief. And the messenger himself embodied in his own story the whole painful history of relations between Indigenous and non-Indigenous Canadians.

For three straight days, the New Democratic member of the Legislative Assembly—the first member of a First Nation elected to the Manitoba legislature—had snarled up parliamentary process simply by saying no each day. No, he would not agree to unanimous consent to rush a motion through the House. The motion under consideration would have allowed public hearings in the province on a new federal constitutional deal, the Meech Lake Accord. The hearings were essential to secure cross-Canada approval for the deal. Now, on this hot June day, Elijah Harper followed up his fourth no with remarks about why he wanted the motion—and therefore the accord—to die.

The accord was part of a broader, white-knuckle constitutional drama that convulsed Canada in the late twentieth century. At this moment in Winnipeg, the country seemed to be coming apart at the seams.

To understand how the fate of Canada came to be in the hands of a lone Manitoba MLA, we have to go back to the 1970s and 1980s, and the constitutional wrangles triggered by Quebec's sovereigntist movement. Elijah Harper's role in the constitutional drama did not emerge until the second act.

Act one, stage-managed by Prime Minister Trudeau, unfolded between 1980 and 1984, as the final ties between Britain and its former colony were cut. Canada got its own constitution, laid out in the 1982 Constitution Act. This new constitution incorporated and amended the 1867 British North America Act, for which George-Étienne Cartier had worked so hard. The Charter of Rights and Freedoms, on which Bertha Wilson would expend so much judicial effort, was embedded in the Constitution Act. So was a new amending formula that required unanimous consent by all ten provinces (an improbably high hurdle) for any further changes.

While act one of the drama had finally given Canada a constitution that was not a simple act of the British Parliament, the document smacked of an elitist compact that shunned the interests of women, new Canadians, and minorities. And although article 35 gave constitutional recognition for the first time to "existing aboriginal and treaty rights," this fell far short of the various demands of Indigenous leaders. Moreover, Quebec premier René Lévesque had rejected Trudeau's package, which meant that the new constitution lacked Quebec's signature. Lévesque, leader of the sovereigntist Parti Québécois, had refused to sign in part because the new Constitution Act did not include a veto power for Quebec over future constitutional amendments.

The Meech Lake Accord was act two. In 1984 a Conservative government replaced the federal Liberals, and Prime Minister Brian Mulroney became the new constitutional choreographer. Mulroney promised to bring Quebec back into the Constitution "with honour and enthusiasm." Three years later, he and the ten provincial premiers embarked on the Quebec Round of negotiations. Next to a small, shallow expanse of water in the Gatineau Hills called Meech Lake, the politicians hammered out an agreement that included recognition of Quebec as a "distinct society." The prime minister, who had a dangerous penchant for hyperbole, announced that this deal was going to "save Canada" by ensuring Quebec's place in the federation. Yes, yes, yes, Canada's Indigenous peoples had concerns, first ministers acknowledged. But they must wait. Right now, the very existence of Canada was at stake.

However, the accord was an even greater disappointment to Indigenous peoples than the Constitution Act, since it had nothing to say about their rights and history. They were not alone in their opposition. Former prime minister Trudeau accused Mulroney of being a "weakling" who had sold out to the provinces.

The provinces had three years to ratify the deal. Despite the disagreements, most provincial legislatures voted their consent. By early June 1990, only Manitoba and New Brunswick were not on board. The prime minister persuaded New Brunswick to sign on, which left only Manitoba—although Newfoundland was wobbling in its commitment.

And now this rumpled Oji-Cree MLA was sabotaging the whole thing. Suddenly people across Canada were asking, "Who is Elijah Harper?"

Harper had never made much of a political splash outside his province. When reporters looked for comments from Indigenous leaders, they gravitated toward Phil Fontaine, the brainy silver-haired leader of the Assembly of Manitoba Chiefs, or Ovide Mercredi, vice-chief of the Assembly of First Nations and master of the acerbic retort. Elijah Harper? He mumbled, and he took too long thinking about what he would say. His hesitancy led some players in the 1990 Meech Lake crisis to write him off as a bit slow, and perhaps manipulated by his colleagues. Now his face was on national television every night, and his tone of quiet reason served as a contrast to the belligerence of some of the other Meech Lake actors. As his widow, Anita Olsen Harper, remembers, "He didn't ask for this role, but it was the only path he could take because otherwise he would have been betraying his people."[2]

There was something both noble and discomforting about press photographs of the forty-one-year-old man. With his long hair and bolo tie, a thunderbird on its beaded clasp, he looked and behaved like no other elected politician in Canada. Most of the time he seemed reluctant to speak. It was as though a Roman senator were sitting there, clad in his toga amid besuited businessmen and lawyers, or (given the sporadic drum-beats beyond the building's walls) as though a *Game of Thrones* hero had come to life.

Within hours of his first no, Elijah Harper had become a champion to anybody who felt unsettled or betrayed by the Meech Lake Accord, and a menace to politicians and provincial leaders determined to see it pass. As the deadline approached, the pressure was intense. The chiefs had pre-sented Harper with the eagle feather, symbol of the bravery of a warrior, to help him withstand it. It rarely left his hand. As his biographer, Pauline Comeau, points out, "Elijah was so authentic. He knew he was just one piece of a larger struggle." The following day, Harper would drive a final nail into the accord with a last no: he refused to give unanimous consent to forgo the required public hearing and thus allow ratification by Manitoba.

This was a watershed moment in Canadian history. The Meech Lake Accord was dead. In Ottawa, as I well remember, there was shock, anger, and a deep dread that the centre could not hold. When Newfoundland realized that Manitoba had effectively killed the deal, it aborted its own vote on the accord. The Mulroney government went into fibrillations when several Quebec MPs defected to join a new sovereignty movement, the Bloc Québécois, headed by Mulroney's former friend and cabinet minister Lucien Bouchard.

In Winnipeg, by contrast, thousands of Indigenous people from all across the province (where more than 17 percent of the population is In-digenous) converged on the lawns outside the legislature to dance, drum, and dream of a better future. A few non-Indigenous people joined in the exuberance, while others offered support from the sidelines. All the fights over the Constitution, culminating in the arm-twisting of the final dramatic week, had upset many Canadians. Outside Quebec, there had been a wave of sympathy for the First Nations' rejection of the Meech Lake Accord. As Elijah Harper had said earlier in the week, "What we have accomplished... is that we have made the general public aware of Aboriginal issues." Many

Canadians realized for the first time how little attention we had paid to the story of Indigenous peoples.

Elijah Harper had quietly implored Canadians: "Look at the relationship with Canada in terms of when the Europeans came here. We shared our land and resources with strangers, the people who came to our homeland. . . . The Canadian constitution doesn't even mention this, not even as a founding nation of this country. There are only the French and the English."[3] It was the first time that many of us started learning in any detail about the disgraceful actions perpetrated in our lifetimes, as well as in the distant past.

That awareness had been a long time coming. The standoff in the Manitoba legislature reflected far more than frustration with Brian Mulroney's constitutional deal, which had put Quebec's agenda ahead of all other issues. Since 1867 Canada's Indigenous groups had been pushed to the margins of Canadian society. But by 1990 a generation of forceful Indigenous leaders had emerged who argued that legal promises made to them had been broken: their rights had been ignored, their health impaired, their children taken away, their place in Canadian history suppressed, and much of their land stolen. Mulroney's threat that the accord's collapse would trigger a crisis of national unity did not intimidate them. They had little left to lose.

"Everything came together at that moment," recalls Phil Fontaine, then an intense radical who went on to serve three terms as national chief of the Assembly of First Nations. "It was a no to denial and to the exclusion of all First Peoples. It was a no to Ottawa's standard way of dealing with important issues. We weren't opposed to Quebec, but we weren't prepared to be an afterthought." Elijah Harper, eagle feather in hand, immediately became a powerful symbol. Harper, Fontaine, and the other Indigenous leaders did not want to break up the country, and they sympathized with Quebec's concerns. But they knew this was a pivotal moment in relations between the federal government and Canada's Indigenous peoples, and they had to grab it. "Every night," Fontaine remembers, "Canadians could watch Elijah—decent, respectful, and extending his hand to the whole country.

"Since Elijah spoke up for us," adds Fontaine, "we have had a far larger public presence. Sometimes the stories are less than positive, and improvements have been less than we hoped for, but Aboriginal issues are in the media every day. Elijah forced people to pay attention."

✦

Today there are about 1.4 million Indigenous people in Canada, including 850,000 First Nations people (still legally known as Indians), 450,000 Métis, and 60,000 Inuit.[4] They speak more than thirty languages and constitute 4.3 percent of the total population, and their share of the population is increasing rapidly because their birth rate is much higher than that of other Canadians.

Their stories begin several millennia before the birth of the Dominion of Canada in 1867, my opening point for this book. In past accounts of this country, this meant that Indigenous peoples were often covered in the early chapters of history textbooks, dealing with explorers, the fur trade, and the contest between England and France. In the sixteenth century, when Europeans first arrived here, there were as many as two million people living in what is now Canada, in diverse and complex societies. But almost invariably textbooks described early contacts from the European point of view, and Indigenous people were mentioned only because they were useful to the newcomers as fur trade partners and military allies. Their usefulness to Europeans had faded by the nineteenth century. The newcomers first divided the land, assisted by their theodolites and section markers; next, assisted by their racial categories, they divided up the people. Indigenous history slipped out of sight as the colonial narrative gathered speed and Indigenous-held land became more important than the Indigenous people themselves. By 1871, after three centuries of epidemics and conflict, the census reported only 100,000 Indigenous people in Canada.

During the first century after Confederation, "Indians" barely surfaced in the construction of Canadian identity, except as an exotic flourish. Those of European descent were almost oblivious to the First Peoples, the vast majority of whom lived on reserves or on the outer edges of the country.

Government policy was overtly paternalistic and mean-spirited. "Indians" registered under the 1876 Indian Act ("status Indians") were treated not as fellow citizens or adults but as dependants of the federal Crown. They did not have the right to vote or buy liquor unless they gave up their Indian status. The federal government's goal was assimilation of Canada's Indigenous people into the settler mainstream. The fact that this would blot out their unique systems of governance, cultures, and languages was not a concern. Canada avoided the worst excesses of violence and exploitation that characterized treatment of Indians to the south, but the Americans had set the bar low. Ottawa remained largely blind or indifferent to Indigenous people's poverty, unemployment, and ill health.

Indian bands that had signed land treaties with the federal government in the first half century after Confederation found that the land allocated to them for reserves was marginal and food rations were inadequate. One glimpse of the resulting hardship is noted in an 1880 report by the North West Mounted Police surgeon John Kittson, which mentions that the Cree around Fort Macleod were receiving less than half the provisions provided to state prisoners in Siberia.[5] NWMP officers like Sam Steele realized that the Indigenous people were starving and reported this back to Ottawa, but the protests were ignored. According to the historian James Daschuk, author of a devastating analysis of federal policies in the West in the late nineteenth century, "Once regarded as the saviours of the indigenous population of the west, the police became the ambivalent agents of their subjugation."[6]

Under the 1876 Indian Act, most First Nations were entitled to a wide range of government services because they were "status Indians." However, many others did not have status, and the provisions did not cover any Métis people. By the mid-twentieth century, there were all kinds of problems. A large proportion of status Indians now lived in cities, far from their traditional communities but still poorly integrated into the larger society.

Indigenous activism mushroomed in North America in the 1960s and 1970s, alongside (but less loudly than) black activism and the women's movement. After the Second World War, Canadian Indigenous peoples had finally been granted the federal vote without the requirement to surrender Indian status. The National Indian Brotherhood was established and rapidly became the voice of First Nations people on reserves, where poverty was rife and infant mortality high. And then the activists were given a target. In 1969 the government of Pierre Trudeau published a White Paper that argued that the Indian Act was discriminatory and should be abolished, and that First Nations should be given the same rights as all other Canadians.

Along with powerful provincial Indigenous organizations in Alberta and Manitoba, the brotherhood whipped up a high-profile campaign against the White Paper. Despite its stated intention of enabling First Nations citizens to be "free to develop Indian cultures in an environment of legal, social and economic equality with other Canadians," it was seen as another strategy to achieve the goal set long ago: assimilation. First Nations wanted no part of it. Harold Cardinal, a Cree from Alberta and the most articulate Indigenous leader of his generation, insisted that the proposals would lead to "cultural genocide." Such a move would rob Indians of their land, their treaties, and their unique traditions. Cardinal and other leaders wanted Indian status to be preserved but based on a different model: they would have preferred to become what Cardinal called "citizens plus." But giving one group of Canadians special privileges did not sit well with most non-Indigenous people. The White Paper proposals died.

The federal government continued to look for solutions. It committed itself to negotiating new treaties in parts of the country that had none, and to addressing claims for violations of existing treaties. It promoted "self-government" on reserves (although there were extensive restrictions). However, the standard of living for most Indigenous people was far below that of other Canadians, and First Nations leaders remained deeply discontented about slow progress on rights and inadequate controls of their own affairs. By 1990, when Elijah Harper played his historic role, the old model of relations between Indigenous and non-Indigenous Canadians had clearly broken.

The shifting relationship between Indigenous and non-Indigenous communities brought sensitive issues to the fore. There were so many minefields: growing disparity in the standards of living of Indigenous and non-Indigenous communities, disagreement over Canadians' clashing versions of events, the difficulty of dealing with ugly aspects of our shared past.

Even language can become a barrier. As a historian, I recognize that Indigenous people are not homogeneous, but as I wrote this book I was aware that appropriate terminology was constantly evolving. "Indigenous" is now the collective adjective that covers all the different peoples, from Mi'kmaq in the Maritimes to Haida on the West Coast, from Métis on the prairies to Inuit in the North. ("First Peoples" is sometimes used as a similar umbrella term, but the term "Aboriginal" has fallen out of favour. "First Nations" covers only "Indians," the legal term that some still use themselves. "Natives" seems acceptable in some circumstances, and cool urban Indigenous people sometimes call themselves NDNs.)

And what should I call non-Indigenous Canadians like myself? The author Thomas King (of Greek, German, and Cherokee descent) suggests that if we call First Nations people "Indians," we might refer to ourselves as "Cowboys." Perhaps not. Euro-Canadians? Yet many of the ancestors of those who were once called "Whites" left Europe generations ago. And anyway, non-Indigenous Canadians come from all over the globe: the majority of today's immigrants are non-white.

How much easier it sometimes seems for non-Indigenous Canadians to look away from this troubled history, with a mumbled apology for the cruelty of our forebears. Or to be hyper-rational about it and focus on words like "healing" and "going forward," as if the historical slate can ever be wiped clean. Or to rant about the hideous attitudes of the past, as though every action of non-Indigenous people was motivated by conscious racism. There is no issue in Canadian history more complicated and painful than relations between this land's original inhabitants and the larger community of Canadians.

Difficult questions persist—questions about why some Indigenous groups have flourished and others seem helpless, mired in poverty and trauma. Or how to make Canadian voters and governments attach greater priority to acknowledging and correcting historic wrongs. Or how to accommodate the demands of fewer than 5 percent of Canadians in a way that most of the other 95 percent of the population will accept. Or even . . . is such accommodation possible in the twenty-first century, given both the diversity of Indigenous peoples and the extraordinarily heterogeneous nature of the Canadian population overall?

✦

What an unlikely hero! As I consider the way that Elijah Harper was shaped by his upbringing and went on to grab our attention, I'm struck by how he personified First Nations history. He'd seen it all. Even without the eagle feather, he symbolized the dreadful consequences of colonization and the extraordinary resilience of its victims. Yet he also expressed his culture's struggle to find solutions that were not rooted in revenge.

There are more than six hundred First Nations bands and 3,100 reserves across Canada, including dozens of small ones scattered across the watery northern reaches of Ontario, Manitoba, Saskatchewan, and Alberta. Few reserves are as remote or as poor as the Red Sucker Lake First Nations reserve in northeast Manitoba, where Harper was born in March 1949. Named after the fish that spawn locally, Red Sucker Lake perches on the inhospitable Canadian Shield and is surrounded by spruce and Jack pine. In winter it is a full day's drive on an ice road from Winnipeg; in summer, it is accessible only by small bush planes. It is a small speck on the district map covered by Treaty 5, signed in 1875.

To an outsider, this community of seven hundred Oji-Cree looks scruffy and depressing. It takes only twenty minutes to drive along the rutted, garbage-strewn clay road from one end of the reserve to the other. Rusty skeletons of abandoned pickup trucks litter the yards, their dead batteries bleeding acid into the surrounding land. The houses are mainly one-storey, shabby clapboard; the school is often closed; there is no cellphone service, and few residents enjoy running water or indoor toilets. Contamination of nearby waterways triggers regular water alerts. The community's only regular source of income is transfer payments from Ottawa.

But that's the perspective of a middle-class urban outsider. To an insider, like members of the extended Harper clan, this has been home for generations—a place of much-loved landmarks, great blueberry crops, and good hunting. Abject poverty cannot extinguish the sense of belonging. Most children grow up here as young Elijah did, confident that they are welcome in every house and cherished by relatives; visitors always mention the quiet laughter and gentle teasing that characterize social events. Residents don't particularly enjoy the conditions: food and travel are expensive, and who wants to face the challenges of personal hygiene, laundry, child raising, and cooking with such inadequate facilities? Yet this is their land, with which they enjoy a deep spiritual connection. Its residents feel whole and accepted here. Nobody is judging or crowding them.

Red Sucker Lake was Elijah Harper's world from the moment of his birth, on March 3, 1949. The eldest son in a family of thirteen children, he was taken by dogsled to his father's trapline in the bush when he was only two weeks old, and he was rapidly absorbed into the seasonal rhythms of reserve life. His father's father taught him how to fish and trap; his mother's father passed on Indigenous creation stories and memories of ceremonies that were no longer permitted. The annual fall moose hunt would become a fixture on Harper's calendar for the rest of his life. Not only was it a way to feed his family; it was his chance to shrug off political stress. Anita Olsen Harper recalls, "He was happiest there. He loved to put on his gumboots and go tramping around."

Those rhythms constituted the upside of traditional Oji-Cree culture. The twentieth-century downside came when Elijah was five years old. He found himself wrenched away from his warm, loving family and heading five hours west, alone on a plane, to Norway House Hospital. His parents knew only that there was something wrong with his neck; they were never told that Elijah had contracted tuberculosis. (He learned the truth only decades later when his biographer, Pauline Comeau, looked at the hospital records.) The child spent the next six months in a TB sanatorium on Clear Lake in The Pas, on the other side of the province. He was cured of tuberculosis, but his links to his own people had been damaged. When the little boy stepped off the plane and ran into his mother's arms, she could barely understand him at first. He was speaking Swampy Cree rather than the Cree dialect spoken on his home reserve.

Three years later, Elijah and his younger brother Fred were packed off to the United Church's residential school in Norway House. The boys were reluctant, but their father wanted his sons to be able to function in the larger world. "He told me that although he would miss us and everything, he knew that we had to get an education," Harper told Comeau.[7] But it felt like exile to the eight-year-old, who protected himself by keeping a psychological distance from what was happening. Suggests Comeau, "Such detachment would become a constant in Harper's life, eventually becoming a self-defence skill to be called upon when a situation was too stressful or painful."[8]

Harper would spend most of the next decade in residential schools in Norway House, Brandon, and Birtle, Manitoba. He suffered the humiliations and miseries of institutionalization. His hair was clipped short; his freedom to roam curtailed. He was punished when he spoke his own language. "You feel like you don't have any say, no rights, nothing," he later

Making Good Canadians of the Children of the Red Man

This is an Indian school at Mellapolla, four miles from Prince Rupert, B.C., where only within quite recent times have the Indians of that part of the country come within close touch of civilisation. Now there is a well-equipped little school for the Indian children, with a young lady teacher from England in charge. The photograph was specially taken for the "Pictorial" by the first man to penetrate far north of Prince Rupert with a moving-picture camera—in the interests of a Franco-Belgian concern. The expressions on the faces of the Indian children are worth studying.

From 1880 onwards, residential schools were an important element in Ottawa's assimilation policy for Indigenous people. Harper was mistreated and abused, and he never completely recovered from the experience.

recalled.[9] He saw classmates being humiliated. Two teenage boys who ran away from the Birtle residential school were made to bend over a table and pull down their pants and shorts; then they were strapped repeatedly. "We just stood around the room, stood at attention and watched. It was to let you know not to break the rules." He was taught that his culture and language were inferior and that the Oji-Cree way of life on the land was dying. He was deliberately devalued and his sense of self-worth damaged.

He was also subjected to sexual abuse. This was something he never told his biographer, and even now Anita Olsen Harper, his widow, prefers simply to mention that it happened but not to elaborate. Elijah Harper's reticence on this painful subject was the standard reaction within his generation and previous ones: the abuse was so taboo that victims rarely discussed the experience even among themselves. Instead they suppressed the anguish and internalized the shame. Only when First Nations issues began to boil in 1990 did the bitter silence crack and survivors begin to talk about it. That's when Phil Fontaine, then head of the Assembly of Manitoba Chiefs, revealed on CBC Television that he had been sexually abused in a church-run residential school. But the trauma and collective denial still linger, as the 2009–15 Truth and Reconciliation Commission discovered when it held hearings about the impact of residential schools.

Despite the brutal residential-school experience, Elijah Harper—now fluent in English—was seen to have potential. In 1967 the taciturn student arrived in Winnipeg to stay with a foster family and attend high school. He got involved with one of the earliest First Nations political organizations of this period: the Manitoba Association of Native Youth. Most Indigenous youngsters in his generation failed to graduate from high school, but Harper had larger ambitions. After getting the necessary credits in night school, he enrolled at the University of Manitoba in the fall of 1971. He was one of the first Indigenous students to gain access to higher education.

At the University of Manitoba, twenty-two-year-old Harper was one of a handful of Indigenous students within a sea of younger, non-Indigenous faces. Lonely and insecure, he felt his heart lift when he noticed a poster about a proposed student association. The organizer was Ovide Mercredi, an articulate Cree activist. Harper became one of the first members of the newly launched Manitoba Indian and Eskimo Association, where he met representatives from other communities and forged alliances that would last a lifetime. The association was soon organizing demonstrations, helping students elsewhere set up similar organizations, and drawing attention to the blatant racism that was pervasive in the student body.

These were the years that followed the Trudeau government's 1969 White Paper. After the failure of that first major attempt to reform the 1876 Indian Act, Indigenous concerns disappeared from the headlines. Canadians fired up about human rights abuses joined freedom marches in Alabama rather than noticing what was happening in their own backyard. However, educated and politically astute Indigenous leaders were now emerging both on reserves, where self-government provided employment and salaries for band chiefs and councillors, and within cities like Winnipeg with large Indigenous populations.

Harper spent the summer after his first year of university with the Manitoba Department of Education, researching and writing on various Indigenous projects. On evenings and weekends he frequented the Manitoba Indian Brotherhood offices. There he met Phil Fontaine, then chief of the Fort Alexander Reserve, and the two young men reviewed together the latest federal proposals to reform administration of reserves. The Department of Indian Affairs had abandoned the idea of assimilation: now it wanted First Nations organizations to run the reserves while Ottawa controlled the spending. This proposal was a long way from the type of self-government that the new Indigenous associations had begun to demand, and they were uncompromising. As Harper told his biographer, "What I saw was that they would establish a brown bureaucracy for Indian Affairs to administer all that misery. Over four or five years, the money . . . would be reduced and eventually the bands would be supporting their tribal council."[10]

Harper dropped out of university in his second year and retreated to Red Sucker Lake, overwhelmed by the demands of family, school, and activism. Within six years, he and his wife, Elizabeth, would have four children: Marcel (from Elizabeth's first marriage), Bruce, Tanya, and Holly.

Next Harper started working for the Manitoba Indian Brotherhood as a community development officer; eventually he was hired by the Manitoba Department of Northern Affairs. He learned his way around bureaucracy, quietly observing why and how decisions were made in the system.

But Red Sucker Lake kept pulling him back. When he heard that the position of band chief was coming vacant in 1978, he decided to run. He promised that, if elected, he would create jobs. It was a big promise, but it brought victory. Aged twenty-nine, Elijah Harper was elected chief.

Harper did not manage to solve his reserve's fundamental problems of poverty and isolation. How could he? For those not involved with the band council, there was no meaningful employment available, beyond winter trapping or perhaps some government contract work, and there was no prospect of establishing any. But thanks to his bureaucratic experience, the new chief did secure two key improvements: satellite television and a better winter road. Both involved adroit manoeuvring with government officials. He purchased a television satellite dish and arranged for it to be flown to Red Sucker Lake, without asking permission from the Department of Indian Affairs in Ottawa. The dish broke all Ottawa's broadcasting regulations because it allowed the reserve to capture American programming. However, by the time Ottawa realized what the chief had done, it was a fait accompli. In order to secure grants for the winter road, Harper played a three-way game of chess with various government departments, allowing each to think that one of the others had already approved the financing. His success in gaming the system encouraged him to develop bigger political ambitions. And then the provincial New Democratic Party came knocking, looking for an Indigenous candidate.

NDP leader Howard Pawley flew to the remote reserve for Harper's nomination meeting. He was appalled to discover that he and Harper were the only people in the community hall when the meeting was scheduled to begin. But the nominee just chuckled. "Don't worry," he reassured Pawley. The new satellite dish was broadcasting from Detroit a John Wayne cowboys-and-Indians western, "and everyone in the community is watching." A couple of hours later, when the program was over, the community hall filled up. Harper received enough votes to become the NDP candidate for the sprawling northern riding of Rupertsland, where 90 percent of the thirteen thousand voters spoke either Cree or Ojibwa. In 1981 he was elected to the provincial legislature. The same election brought the NDP to power, with Howard Pawley as premier of Manitoba.

༺༻

As I explore Harper's career, I realize how often he felt immobilized, strung between two poles. It wasn't just the clash of loyalties between his own people and his New Democratic colleagues in the Pawley government. It was also the tension between two different styles of government. As a chief, he had followed the traditional practice of slowly working toward consensus through long discussions and respectful consultations with elders. This process suited both his temperament and the politics of a community of fewer than a thousand people. But it doesn't work in our parliamentary system, which answers to millions of people and requires deals and decisiveness. It also makes negotiations between Indigenous organizations and federal politicians time-consuming and difficult, as a handful of First Nations can always block a deal by simply refusing to compromise.

In the Manitoba legislature, Harper was a fish out of water. A colleague saw him ambling down a hallway "and my heart went out to him." She described her reaction to Pauline Comeau: "I could relate to how he was feeling, how he must be trying to adjust to it—this big brick-and-cement building and all the rules and regulations that go along with the position he had just been elected to."[11] An imposing institution, racist barbs from some members of the Conservative opposition, and the corrosive sense of being an outsider awakened unhappy memories of residential school.

Elijah Harper began as a backbench MLA. He gave part of his maiden speech in his native tongue, the first time Cree entered the legislature's official record. He spoke about the pressing issues facing First Nations: poor housing and health, extremely high unemployment rates, the damage done by residential schools. But Harper could do little for his constituents other than draw attention to the problems. First Nations education, fishing pol-

icy, health care, the need for economic development policies on reserves—
these were all Ottawa's responsibility, not Winnipeg's. He insisted, "We as
Indian people must take steps to control our destiny." But it was not clear
how they could do that.

However, Manitoba now had a critical mass of Indigenous leaders. Par-
adoxically, most, like Elijah Harper, were products of residential schools.
They had first crossed paths in the offices of Ovide Mercredi's native student association or in the Manitoba Indian Brotherhood. Harper had a
sturdy network that included Phil Fontaine, Moses Okimaw (a lawyer who
headed the Manitoba Indian Brotherhood), Murray Sinclair (then
vice-president of the Manitoba Métis Federation, who would go on to head
the Truth and Reconciliation Commission and now sits in the Senate), and
Mercredi, as well as chiefs throughout the province. They would congre-
gate out of sight of legislators at the St. Regis, a downtown Winnipeg hotel
that was soon dubbed the "Indian Embassy." There they honed their demands for a larger role in the conferences of first ministers that were held
in Ottawa, and for a significant say in constitutional discussions. Determined, as Harper had said in his maiden speech, to "take control" of their
destiny, they intensified their campaign for self-government—the very
opposite of nineteenth-century Ottawa's goal of assimilation.

But what did self-government mean? When Harper raised the issue
often in his own NDP caucus, he met hostility and incomprehension from
some members. He would explain, "What it is all about is to take control of
your lives, manage your own affairs, and determine your own future." He
would insist: "We have never relinquished that right, even by signing the
treaties." None of this made much sense to Harper's colleagues in the Manitoba legislature, or to Canadians watching the same demands made at four
First Ministers' Conferences that met in Ottawa in the 1980s to define Indigenous rights. Which Indigenous organization or leader would speak for
all the different peoples, would negotiate resource rights, would handle the
substantial budgets that the federal Department of Indian and Northern
Affairs administered? By now, the appalling social conditions on many reserves were widely acknowledged. But was there enough capacity in the

hundreds of small bands to take on responsibility for housing, child care, education, roads, and water systems? Handing these services over, as Harper, Mercredi, and Fontaine now seemed to be demanding, might open the door to further deterioration and corruption. And all politicians balked at the price tag that such reforms would carry.

In the Manitoba legislature, Elijah Harper watched and listened. It was hard to have much impact when so many issues belonged to the federal government. "Elijah's strength was that he was not interested in grandstanding," Howard Pawley said later. "He was interested in gradually working his way up." But Harper didn't develop even such basic political skills as networking or public speaking. And he was unpredictable. As his former deputy minister told Comeau, "He can be tremendously effective or a complete bomb. If there is an Indian in the audience, the man is unbelievable. An all-white audience and he gets uncomfortable and he tries to deliver a message he thinks the white audience wants to hear—and he fumbles."[12]

Harper was never a cabinet star. After four years as a provincial legislator, he was finally made a junior cabinet minister in 1986. The following year he was promoted to minister of northern affairs and, with the help of a seasoned bureaucrat, scored a minor success. He asked cabinet for $2 million for an Aboriginal Development Fund that would centralize information on Indigenous program activities within the Manitoba government. Many of Pawley's fractious and unsympathetic ministers erupted with protests. Harper listened and watched. Then he quietly interrupted: "I am getting pretty tired of being the token Indian." He won the vote.

There were additional stresses: his marriage was unravelling, his finances were a mess, and there was a drunk-driving charge. Elected representatives at every level of government face similar crises, but in a culture saturated with negative stereotypes, Harper was branded. When it all got too much, he would disappear. He needed the silence of the northern bush, the rich swampy smell of the land where his family had their trapline. A week or two later he would re-emerge after a therapeutic retreat on Red Sucker Lake Reserve. His behaviour drove his officials nuts.

These were the years when Brian Mulroney's Meech Lake Accord was making its way through provincial legislatures. Each month saw new uncertainties, especially because other issues were souring the political environment. The 1988 free trade deal, the federal election the same year, budgetary cutbacks, distrust of Prime Minister Mulroney, blistering criticism from former prime minister Pierre Trudeau (the accord, he raged, "should be put in the dustbin"[13])—all contributed to a cross-country hardening of attitudes. While Quebec insisted that not a word in the accord could be changed, demands for amendments piled up from women's groups, trade unions, anti-poverty groups, and the premiers of New Brunswick and Newfoundland. And in Manitoba, the ratification process was delayed, first by deteriorating relations between Winnipeg and Ottawa, and then by a provincial election that saw the defeat of Pawley's NDP.

In June 1989, Elijah Harper attended an Assembly of First Nations conference in Quebec City. It wasn't a particularly newsworthy event, and most media outlets ignored it. Pierre Cadieux, the newly appointed federal minister of Indian and northern affairs, had reluctantly agreed to address the chiefs. Cadieux watched impatiently as a thickset man in a buckskin jacket whom he did not recognize made his way over to the microphone. "I am a member of the Red Sucker Lake First Nation," Harper announced softly, "and . . . I am also a member of the Manitoba legislature. Are you prepared to include in the Meech Lake Accord protection for Aboriginal treaty rights and recognition of native self-government?" The minister waffled. Harper told the minister he would not support the accord when it came through the Manitoba legislature. His remark had no impact. "They didn't take me seriously."[14]

A year later, people took Elijah Harper very seriously indeed as he stood, eagle feather in hand, and killed the Meech Lake Accord. It might have foundered even without Harper's no if the Newfoundland legislature had decided to withdraw its support at the last minute. Many of the accord's opponents were relieved that its demise was triggered by Indigenous concerns rather than hostility to Quebec.

However, Harper had permanently marked the country. He not only put the spotlight on Indigenous claims but also ensured that first ministers alone would never again conduct constitutional negotiations behind closed doors. He had defied the political elite, and he made us acknowledge that the way that Canada treated its Indigenous people was "a national disgrace." The Canadian Press voted him newsmaker of the year, and (more meaningful to him) Red Sucker First Nation named him honourary chief for life.[15]

Despite Prime Minister Mulroney's dire warnings, Canada did not fall apart when the accord died. Most of us got on with our lives, went to the lake, and lit the barbecue, eager to shrug off constitutional fatigue. The dollar rose and foreign investors increased their holdings of government bonds. In the words of the political journalist Andrew Cohen, "After all the shouting, wailing, crying and bawling, after all the recriminations and lamentations, it was as if the radio had suddenly died. . . . Finally, there was silence."[16]

Yet for Elijah Harper, the moment when he helped to defeat the Meech Lake Accord was a personal triumph. The humiliations and setbacks of his own life had been forgotten in the sense of empowerment he enjoyed as he spoke for Canada's Indigenous people. It was a "feeling of unity, togetherness and solidarity."[17] He determined to share it. A few weeks after the death of Meech Lake, a land dispute erupted in Quebec, between the Mohawk community of Kanesatake and the town of Oka over the expansion of a golf course onto land claimed by the Mohawks. The dispute quickly turned ugly; a police officer was killed and the Canadian Armed Forces deployed. One morning Elijah Harper emerged like an apparition from the Oka pine forest to offer support to the Mohawk warriors. He now saw himself as an Indigenous ambassador at large.

Prime Minister Mulroney made one final attempt to reconcile Quebec and the other provinces by convening a marathon session of the premiers, representatives from First Nations, Inuit, and Métis organizations, and various interest groups. The 1992 Charlottetown Accord included concessions to everybody in the room. Its provisions dealing with Indigenous peoples were the most generous and detailed ever to appear in a constitutional proposal; the accord included a recognition of their right to self-government. But this new deal was defeated in a national referendum. Many

In 1990 the violent confrontation at Oka between Mohawk residents and
Sûreté du Québec officers showed Canadians that First Nations would
fight to protect their land.

Canadians from different backgrounds voted against it because (among
other reasons) they thought it gave Indigenous peoples too much. Senior
Indigenous leaders supported the deal, yet about 60 percent of First Nations people on reserves voted no—and so did Harper—because they said
it didn't give them enough. While another wave of sovereigntist sentiment
built in Quebec, the Indigenous fight for self-government seemed permanently stalled.

Elijah Harper, perhaps the only politician to emerge from the Meech
Lake fracas with his reputation enhanced, now found his own career was
stalled too. He resigned from the Manitoba legislature and switched parties. In the 1993 federal election won by Jean Chrétien's Liberals, he became the Liberal MP for the northern Manitoba riding of Churchill.

Ottawa provided an even greater culture shock than the Manitoba legislature for this soft-spoken man. Once again he was an outsider. And once
again, First Nations were falling below the radar. The Royal Commission
on Aboriginal Peoples had been appointed in 1991 in the hope of recasting
the relationship between Indigenous people and government; Bertha Wil-

son, now retired from the Supreme Court, was one of the seven commissioners. But "RCAP," as it soon became in Ottawa jargon, went way over budget and took six years to produce its five-volume report. Most of its recommendations would be ignored.

All 295 MPs, along with every chief in Canada, were given copies of the 1996 report. Harper's office on Parliament Hill quickly became a dumping ground for the five volumes. "He was so disappointed," Anita Olsen Harper recalls. "Some of his colleagues would drop their copies on his desk and say, 'I have no use for this. There are no Indians in my riding. Here, you take it. Give it to a friend.' They didn't even read it. They felt no obligation to the issues." Indigenous matters were still not mainstream political concerns.

Defeated after one term, Harper continued to be in demand as a public speaker, but his health slowly deteriorated. In May 2013 he died in Ottawa, of heart failure due to complications from diabetes. Hundreds of supporters filed past his open casket as he lay in state in the Winnipeg legislature. Then his body was loaded into a small plane and flown to Red Sucker Lake First Nation for burial.

Elijah Harper is in many ways a tragic figure. Although he overcame tuberculosis, residential school abuse, political setbacks, and money and marital problems, he never achieved enough for Red Sucker Lake Reserve, from which he derived his sense of identity. The reserve continues to be one of the poorest in Canada. And the First Nations leadership were unable to resolve their own internal differences and take advantage of the opportunity that his courage created for them in 1990.

Yet Harper's impact on Canada lives on. His eagle feather gesture and soft-spoken no marked an indictment of all those attempts, over a century and a quarter, by governments, churches, and the population at large "to change Indians, Métis and Inuit into just another ethnic group in the multicultural mosaic," in the words of the historian J. R. Miller.[18] Elijah Harper had demonstrated the will of Indigenous peoples to live on their own cultural terms, whatever the challenges.

Has anything changed since that snapshot moment, more than a quarter of a century ago? Yes and no.

On the negative side of the scales is the catalogue of bleeding sores. Red Sucker Lake Reserve is not alone in its problems. The number of reserves where there is insufficient housing, no school, or a school requiring repairs never seems to budge. One in five First Nations communities are under drinking water advisories. Nearly half of reserve communities need a new school; nearly thirty thousand First Nations children are in care. Schools on reserves receive proportionately far less funding than schools elsewhere: between $3,000 and $4,000 per child.[19]

Off reserve, it often seems, the story is equally bleak. The catalogue here includes the glacial pace of land claim negotiations, the disproportionate number of Indigenous people living in urban poverty, high suicide rates among Indigenous young men, the generational damage caused by residential schools, the corruption of a handful of band leaders.

Since Elijah Harper's death, particularly grim issues have emerged. Harper's old friend Murray Sinclair became chair of the Truth and Reconciliation Commission, which was set up as part of the 2007 Indian Residential Schools Agreement that also secured compensation for residential school survivors. Sinclair and his two fellow commissioners heard from 7,000 former students, and much of the testimony was profoundly shocking. Since the 1880s, more than 150,000 Indigenous children had been removed from their families, and the commission revealed that at least 6,000 had died. Witnesses spoke of a degree of physical, psychological, and sexual cruelty that few non-Indigenous people had ever imagined occurring behind the schools' grim brick walls.

At the same time, nearly 1,200 Indigenous women were killed or went missing between 1980 and 2012, according to the RCMP. A great-niece of Elijah Harper very nearly joined that macabre statistic. In late 2014 sixteen-year-old Rinelle Harper was attacked and left for dead on the banks of the freezing Assiniboine River in Winnipeg.

The ugly stories breed pessimism, and some cynicism—a sense that nothing changes, that Indigenous people are trapped in their own self-perpetuating pathologies. Frances Abele, professor of public policy and administration at Carleton University, suggests, "Articles about tragedy, dysfunction, failure—they fit into a narrative in the news of how bad things are for Indigenous people that drives out the rest of the story." Indigenous communities are viewed as tax burdens rather than being seen as fellow Canadians or potential partners in resource wealth production. As Phil Fontaine says, "That kind of racism accepts Indigenous poverty."

There have been no significant political deals: for most Indigenous people living south of the sixtieth parallel, the goal of self-government appears an increasingly unreachable objective. Only in the three northern territories do Indigenous peoples, who form a substantial percentage of the population, have more control over political decisions. Elsewhere, the ideal of following a traditional way of life while enjoying a twenty-first-century standard of living appears unrealistic.

Indigenous frustration welled up once again in late 2012 with the Idle No More movement, the largest Canada-wide social action movement since the protest marches of the 1960s. Organized by four women lawyers (three of them from First Nations), the grassroots movement had many targets. A key complaint was the Conservative government's disregard for treaty rights and environmental protection laws as it sought development of resources and construction of petrochemical pipelines. As Elijah Harper did in 1990, participants found a lot of support from non-Indigenous groups. What did Idle No More achieve? Nothing specific, although Phil Fontaine suggests, "It was another key moment—like the 1990 moment with Elijah—which embodied hope of change."

So was Elijah Harper's brave gesture futile? Did his refusal (backed up by most chiefs) to assent to the Meech Lake Accord process achieve nothing for Canada's Indigenous population?

It is always hard to link cause and effect. However, there has been significant change since 1990.

Far more Indigenous students receive some post-secondary education. Elijah Harper was one of only a handful of such university students across Canada in 1970. Today, close to thirty thousand Indigenous students, in academic gowns and with big smiles, file across university and college stages and collect certificates on graduation day each year. (The jump in numbers is huge, but as a percentage of the demographic group, it is still much lower than the figure for the whole Canadian population. Fewer than one in ten Indigenous people go to post-secondary institutions, compared with one in four of other Canadians.) Elijah Harper's widow, Anita Olsen Harper, has a doctorate in education from the University of Ottawa; a couple of his grandchildren are heading toward college.

Indigenous history is now one of the hottest humanities disciplines on our campuses. Ethnohistory, post-colonial scholarship, economic and demographic analysis, Indigenous studies—according to the Carleton University historian Michel Hogue, "Aboriginal history has moved into the academic mainstream. There's a critical mass of scholars writing it from the point of view of the peoples themselves."

Law schools have been particularly attractive to Indigenous students: Canada now boasts over two thousand Indigenous lawyers. Why law? Because it has been our judicial system rather than our political system that has started to take Indigenous rights and demands seriously. This trend has created a demand for lawyers from these communities. Although there were protests in 1982 that the protections granted to Indigenous peoples in the 1982 Constitution Act and the Charter of Rights and Freedoms were completely inadequate, those clauses have proved powerful weapons. They have opened up new avenues of political participation. Since 1982 more than forty Indigenous rights cases have gone to the Supreme Court of Canada.[20] Indigenous oral histories have been given the same weight as the written histories of colonizers.

Some of these cases have breathed life into the wording of the eleven treaties signed between First Nations in Canada and the Crown between 1871 and 1921, treaties that covered most of present-day Alberta, British Columbia, Manitoba, Ontario, Saskatchewan, and the Northwest Territories. These agreements provided the Dominion government large tracts of land and access to resources in exchange for promises (often ignored) to the original inhabitants. Indigenous communities now have far more muscle when negotiating any developments not only on their reserves, but also on any lands that have been their traditional hunting or fishing grounds. If a corporation wants to exploit the resources (logs, rocks, minerals, oil) on those lands, it cannot go ahead without extensive consultation.

Many of these legal decisions have made politicians, public officials, and business leaders grind their teeth in frustration. But Chief Justice Beverley McLachlin made it plain in May 2015 that the Supreme Court had no intention of backing off (and in the process, she proved that she shared with Bertha Wilson that great Canadian characteristic: empathy with the underdog). In a public speech, she said, "The most glaring blemish on the Canadian historic record relates to our treatment of the First Nations that lived here at the time of colonization." Echoing Harold Cardinal, nearly half a century earlier, she went on to describe assimilation policies as "cultural genocide against Aboriginal peoples."

Off and on reserves, there are economic success stories. At least one-third of reserves have pulled themselves out of the cycle of dependency, and another third are on their way.[21] The Cree in northern Quebec, the Osoyoos in British Columbia's Okanagan, the Athabasca Chipewyan First Nation in northern Alberta, the Dene in Saskatchewan—with good leadership, these reserves have taken control of their own resources and developed thriving wage economies. There are now forty thousand businesses in Canada owned and operated by Indigenous entrepreneurs. In 2009 Phil Fontaine, now a white-haired businessman, founded his own company, Ishkonigan, a consultancy and mediation company that actively supports collaboration between Indigenous communities and corporate Canada. Explains Fontaine, "The challenge is to balance economic development and environmental protection. There is great resistance to the extractive industries because they have been so destructive, and that does not sit well with our people."

There are hopeful political initiatives too. The Idle No More protests prompted the birth of Canadians for a New Partnership. Headed by the Dene leader Stephen Kakfwi, former premier of the Northwest Territories, its partners include two former prime ministers, Progressive Conservative

Joe Clark and Liberal Paul Martin. Its goal is to build trust through a true commitment to Indigenous treaties and rights. The number of Indigenous MPs is slowly rising: ten were elected in 2015. Prime Minister Justin Trudeau gave Canada its first Indigenous justice minister, Jody Wilson-Raybould, a lawyer with Kwakwaka'wakw roots who had been a British Columbia regional chief for the Assembly of First Nations. The 2016 federal budget included $8.4 billion to improve the lives of Indigenous Canadians.

In the past decade, perhaps the biggest change is a quiet acknowledgement of First Peoples' presence in our national life. At cultural or political events, recognition of First Nations land claims is routine in the opening remarks. In November 2015, when Justin Trudeau's cabinet was sworn in, the ceremony began with First Nations drums, Inuit throat singers, and a message of thanks to the Algonquin people on whose territory it took place. *Meegwetch!*

I am particularly struck at the way that artists have now made Indigenous themes, stories, and visions part of the artistic mainstream in Canada. Indigenous writers have been winning major awards for several years now. The novelist Joseph Boyden (Irish, Scottish, and Anishinaabe heritage) has taken readers deep into First Nations communities and history, most recently in *The Orenda*. In fiction and poetry, Lee Maracle (of Métis and Salish heritage) has explored what it means to be an Indigenous woman living in two cultures. One of the most successful non-fiction books of recent years is Thomas King's *The Inconvenient Indian: A Curious Account of Native People in North America*, which is a First Nations history that manages the extraordinary achievement of being both devastating and hilarious.

A whole catalogue of other artists from every Indigenous group in Canada is achieving international success by challenging stereotypes. The work of Indigenous visual artists is now in collections of contemporary art, rather than hived off into Indigenous art ghettos. High prices are paid for work by Kent Monkman (Cree and Irish ancestry), Jane Ash Poitras (Cree), Brian Jungen (Swiss and Dane-zaa), Carl Beam (Ojibwa), and Gerald McMaster (Plains Cree and Blackfoot).

Joseph Boyden won the 2008 Scotiabank Giller Prize for his novel *Through Black Spruce*, which dealt with the insidious decline of the Cree community in Moosonee.

In 1991 the Kwakwaka'wakw artist David Neel silkscreened a portrait of Elijah Harper holding his eagle feather, entitled *Just Say No*.[22] Neel went on to represent Canada at the prestigious Venice Biennale in 1999 with an installation of contemporary carved masks and a twenty-six-foot dugout canoe in the Grand Canal. He was followed at the Biennale in 2005 by Rebecca Belmore (Anishinaabe), an artist who in performance, installations, and photographs has taken apart several Canadian clichés. One of her earliest pieces was *Twelve Angry Crinolines*, in which she satirized the 1987 visit to Thunder Bay of the Duke and Duchess of York. The royals had visited a pioneer fort and paddled in a canoe for the press's benefit.

Musicians? It's a long list, which includes Tanya Tagaq, the Inuit throat singer who has collaborated with the Icelandic singer-songwriter Björk and whose eerie, passionate sounds won the 2014 Polaris Music Prize. And then there's A Tribe Called Red, three Ottawa musicians who mesh the pounding beats and chants of First Nations music with hip-hop and electronic music. Their "electric powwow" events have made them the face of an urban Indigenous youth renaissance as they champion their heritage.

Tanya Tagaq, a throat singer from Nunavut known as "the polar punk," is a passionate defender of the traditional Inuit way of life, including the seal hunt.

Commenting on the visionary trio's appearance at the massive South by Southwest music festival in Texas in 2013, the *Washington Post* wrote, "There wasn't anything like it at SXSW. There probably isn't anything like it on earth."

Video, printmaking, film, poetry, children's books—the list of successful works by Indigenous artists exploring their own cultures for diverse audiences lengthens every year.

Sometimes the message these artists deliver is combative or reproachful. Often it has a dark humour. And at other times it suggests a new route to reconciliation. At the Lakefield Literary Festival in 2014, I heard a presentation by the Ojibwa writer Richard Buffalo Cloud Wagamese. Wagamese's novels *Indian Horse* and *Medicine Walk* feature First Nations men traumatized by their childhoods. A tall, good-looking man in his late fifties, the author spoke about the pain of children who grew up without fathers, of families torn apart by residential schools, of the lack of real communication between Canada's Indigenous residents and settlers from elsewhere. His tone was warm as he implored us to engage Indigenous Canadians on

This appeal to make Canadian history included maple leaves and a beaver on the flag, although Canadians in the First World War fought under British command.

Food and machinery, in addition to thousands of troops, were part of Canada's massive contribution to "the Motherland" and her allies between 1914 and 1918.

Canada's agricultural exports were a backbone of the economy in the early twentieth century, although few farmers looked as dapper as the boots-and-breeches one featured in this poster.

The female rider waved a Union Jack over the returned Canadian soldier in 1919, but she was clad in provincial flags and her horse was garlanded with maple leaves for the victory parade.

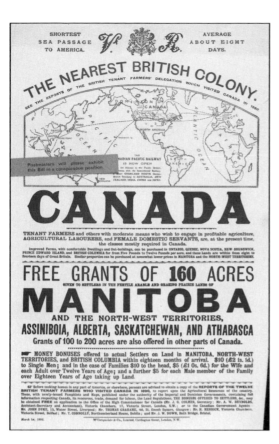

From the late 1800s to the 1920s, the Canadian government lured settlers to the prairies with promises of free land and images of plentiful crops and healthy children.

In the first half of the twentieth century, Canadian Pacific made brilliant use of colour posters to advertise their railways, steamships, and airline . . . and incidentally, the country itself.

In 1930, Prime Minister Mackenzie King posed as a blacksmith as he appealed to French Canadians not to allow the links in the chain that he had forged to rust. Although he lost the election, King would pay careful attention to national unity and enjoy a further thirteen years in power.

By 1930, the Mounties and their glossy black horses were recognized as Canadian icons wherever British shoe polish was sold.

GET YOUR TEETH
INTO THE
JOB

Issued by the WARTIME INFORMATION BOARD, OTTAWA.   Printed in Canada.

In the Second World War, the Canadian government was happy to use a cartoon beaver to suggest that Canadian hard work and guile could defeat Adolf Hitler.

NEWFOUNDLAND

CANADA'S *Newest* PROVINCE

invites you

FOR MORE INFORMATION
NEWFOUNDLAND TOURIST DEVELOPMENT OFFICE
ST. JOHNS, CANADA

Roger Couillard

When Newfoundland joined Confederation in 1949, a new image entered
Canadian iconography: a sou'westered fisherman welcoming mainland visitors.

L'Exposition universelle
de 1967—
Le Spectacle du Siècle

The 1967
World Exhibition—
Show of the Century

expo 67

28 AVRIL–27 OCTOBRE   APRIL 28–OCTOBER 27

MONTREAL CANADA

Expo 67 and Captain Canuck captured the nationalistic exuberance as Canada entered its second century.

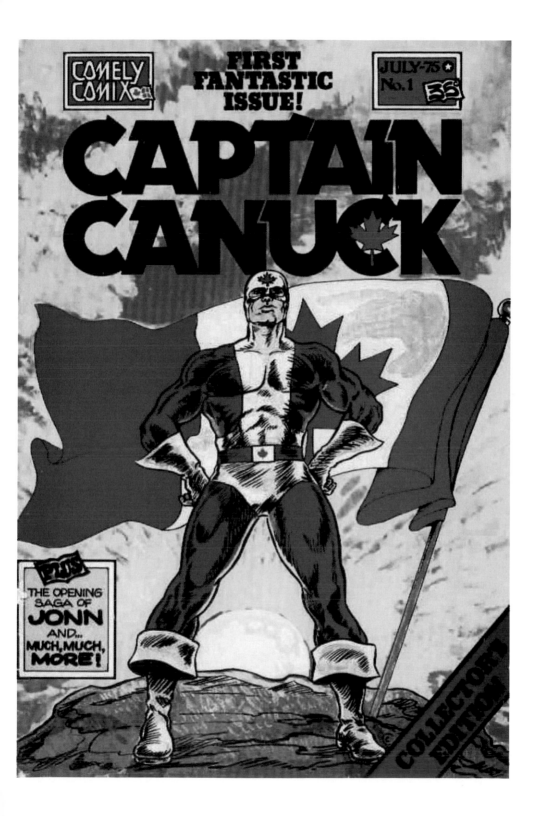

Artists—Athletes 1976 Olympics. Inuit imagery became popular throughout Canada after several Inuit communities established printmaking co-operatives.

All politics is local: a Toronto icon is thrust into an
international protest in this 2011 poster.

NO KEYSTONE XL

FrankeJames.com

OH NO CANADA!
www.OhNoCanada.com

By the twenty-first century, well-established imagery—the red maple leaf alongside the dome of the U.S. Capitol—crosses international borders, as Canadian concern about the global environment mounts.

a spiritual level rather than through laws and logic. He talked of the power he draws from contact with the land, and he explained the need of Indigenous peoples to stay deeply connected with it. His message was inclusive rather than polarizing. "People ask me what they should call me—Aboriginal, native, Indian? But anybody born in this country is native to it, and therefore when I talk about natives, I am talking about all of us."

Wagamese's audience was mesmerized. The author is without doubt a great performer, but there was a deeper magic than that. His listeners were ready to hear Wagamese's stories and perspective. There was a feel-good revivalist-meeting quality to the whole event that made me uncomfortable. Yet I was impressed at the way he brought us into his world without making us squirm in our seats with guilt.

Elijah Harper played a fleeting role in our history, but his image—the bolo tie, the eagle feather—pops up in any national accounting of Canada's political evolution. How that image is interpreted depends on the viewer.

With its electronic "powwow-step" music, A Tribe Called Red was the featured headliner at the Electric Fields Festival in 2013. The musicians are vocal supporters of the Idle No More movement.

For the cynical, it is a romantic but naive gesture: a colourful counterpoint to conventional power politics, and a reminder that Indigenous people can be exasperatingly uncompromising. But for an increasing number of Canadians, both from Indigenous communities and at venues like the Lakefield festival, Harper is the symbol of Indigenous peoples' 150-year-long battle to shed the role of victims and become part of the national dialogue. Although many of the issues remain unresolved, Canadians can no longer avoid or ignore them. Elijah Harper enlarged our field of vision.

CHAPTER 9

What Does the West Want?

Preston Manning and Populist Power

There are hundreds of Canadian communities that have given more thought to hiring their rink manager than they have to electing their Member of Parliament.

—Preston Manning, *The New Canada* (1992)

The habit of treating Alberta as an exploitable and resource-rich hinterland goes back three hundred years. And why should a self-centred Canada change its attitude? Canada as a country is an act of imagination so unlikely that it is hard to believe its actual success. . . .

—Aritha van Herk, *Mavericks: An Incorrigible History of Alberta* (2001)

Preston Manning is one of the most consequential and intellectually creative political figures of the past twenty-five years. Which other politician who never got to be prime minister has had so much impact on the national political conversation?

—Jeffrey Simpson (2015)

At the start of the twentieth century, Prime Minister Wilfrid Laurier predicted that the century would "belong to Canada," and as the country matured, there were times when such confidence seemed justified. The anthem, flag, and literary culture had boosted a quiet patriotism. Youngsters who explored the world sewed maple leaf badges on their backpacks. By the end of the century the population had soared to over thirty million (five times the number of people in Laurier's Canada) as immigrants and refugees from South America, Africa, and Asia continued to arrive.

However, the last years of the twentieth century saw growing tensions that challenged the Canadian talent for compromise and "muddling through." How could one country accommodate the rural-urban split, the divide between resource-based western economies and others, Quebec's secessionist movement, and the Indigenous peoples' campaign for self-government and Indigenous rights? Was this country going to dissolve, and all its promise go to waste?

Populist movements in different regions have challenged the status quo ever since George-Étienne Cartier introduced federalism as the solution to regional tensions. However, in the late 1980s the Macdonald-Cartier political bargain that had kept the different provinces tenuously glued together was fragmenting. Not only had the Meech Lake Accord failed, bringing Quebec nationalists into the streets and shattering the Progressive Conservative Party, but the brushfire of a new populist movement had ignited in the West. It was carefully nurtured by Preston Manning, a soft-spoken preacher and management consultant who was Alberta born and bred.

Populism has a long and complicated history in Canada. It has flourished when large numbers of citizens feel that the game is rigged against them and they are being ignored. Unlike American populist movements, Canadian populism rarely deteriorates into racist demagoguery; in common with American populism, it frequently involves hostility to an economic order dominated by "money power." In Canada, "money power" always means the moguls of central Canada.

Some populist protests simply fizzle out, when the naïveté of their policies meets the reality of governing such a sprawling country. But others have had a profound impact on the national agenda. In the early twentieth century, farmers' parties in Ontario, Alberta, and Saskatchewan pulled political debate leftward with their anti-business rhetoric and their demands for participatory democracy and farmers' collectives. This was the world from which Tommy Douglas drew his political inspiration. A similar tug to the left came from two initiatives in the Maritimes in the 1920s: the Maritime Rights Movement, which demanded better economic treatment by Ottawa, and the Antigonish Movement, led by Father Moses Coady, which concentrated on strengthening the local economy through co-operative action.

Other populist movements yanked debate to the right. The Social Credit League of Alberta, born in the bitter Depression years, promoted conservative social values as well as raging against big business and the banks. Similar right-wing populist movements emerged in Quebec too, from the 1940s: first Maurice Duplessis's provincial Union Nationale party, then the federal Créditiste party, led by Réal Caouette.

Populist leaders like to claim they speak for "regular folk"—"the little guy" for Tommy Douglas; "ordinary Canadians" for Preston Manning. The authority of populist leaders comes from a direct bond with their supporters. They promise that government will be closer to the people, and that "regular folk" far from centres of power will get a break.

Leaders of surging populist movements have become provincial premiers—William Aberhart in Alberta, Maurice Duplessis in Quebec, Joey Smallwood in Newfoundland—but none has ever become prime minister. However, successful populists can redirect the way we think about our country, shake up the other political parties, and jump-start new initiatives, as Tommy Douglas did by championing a national health insurance program. Preston Manning founded a populist party dedicated to asserting western demands and pruning Ottawa's powers. Just as Elijah Harper forced Canadians to pay more attention to the way Indigenous peoples were treated, so Manning would try to rebalance the Canadian federation and give the West more power.

⁓

"Never say 'Whoa' in a mudhole!"

My neighbour roars with laughter as he sees the incomprehension on my face. I have no idea what this western expression means. It is March 2015, and we are at a black-tie dinner at the Ranchmen's Club, a posh private establishment in Calgary that ripples with financial muscle. Founded in 1891, the Ranchmen's is similar to such clubs in wealthy cities across North America. Tonight's dinner guests are as urban, educated, and affluent as their counterparts in the Toronto Club or the Vancouver Club. But wait . . . How about the stuffed buffalo heads in the foyer, or the outbreak of cowboy boots among the patent leather pumps? Yes, this is Alberta—our petro-province, quietly regarded by some Canadians elsewhere as overstuffed with XXL-sized Stetsons and right-wing swagger. The Ranchmen's Club was founded before this city had sidewalks.

The overflow crowd at this exclusive event is enjoying itself: there are frequent toasts, punctuated with hoots of laughter. You would hardly know that Alberta's economy is tanking, because of a calamitous global drop in oil prices, until the premier of the day rises to speak. Jim Prentice has entered provincial politics only six months ago, after a successful career as a lawyer, federal politician, and banker. Personable and self-deprecating, he has just become sixteenth premier of the province as it enters its eightieth year of deep-dish conservatism, first with Social Credit governments and then with Progressive Conservative governments. This is a province that embraces one-party rule, free enterprise, low taxes, and a deep distrust of central Canada.

Prentice is speaking tonight to his kind of people: bankers, oilmen, businessmen, entrepreneurs. As we tuck into grilled Alberta beef with plum and fig polenta, my dinner companion (a former chair of the Calgary

Stampede) gives me a quick rundown on other guests at our table. Most of them, he points out with pride, started with "zip" and have made it big. Then Premier Prentice is on his feet, giving his audience the bad news: looming deficits and job cuts. I look around, noticing a mix of blank stares and sage nods.

A few weeks later, with polls running in his favour, Prentice calls a provincial election. But then the unthinkable happens: a massive shift of opinion across the province. Two months after the Ranchmen's dinner, the Alberta electorate turfs Prentice and the Conservatives and triggers shock waves across Canada. The left-wing New Democrats sweep aside nearly eight decades of right-wing supremacy. Our petro-province will be under socialist rule.

"Never say 'Whoa' in a mudhole." What my neighbour had meant was that Albertans never wallow in a slough of despond: they dig their spurs into their horses' flanks and keep moving. Alberta's Conservative Party, as Jim Prentice had discovered to his cost, had become intellectually and politically bankrupt—a mudhole. The electorate had decided en masse to gallop off in another direction, whatever the risk.

A couple of weeks after the provincial election, Preston Manning, these days an elder statesman for many conservatives, gave me his opinion of the result. "I wasn't really surprised," he responded, in his distinctive nasal drawl. "The NDP win fits into the Alberta pattern of one-party government. Change comes when Alberta's voters turn against a tired old bunch and toward a fresh new bunch." Provincial NDP leader Rachel Notley had won the election not because of her socialist ideology, he said, but because she connected with the grassroots.

Manning knows all about triggering political change by connecting with the grassroots. For decades, during political campaigns and conventions, he stood on platforms in church basements and convention halls, a skinny, slope-shouldered man with a bemused expression, waving an index finger in the air and appealing to "ordinary Canadians." He reckons that a distinguishing characteristic of Alberta's political culture is its willingness to accept a "new party" as an instrument of change.

From the mid-1980s to the political upset of 2015, thanks to population changes and the fossil fuel economy, power in this country shifted westward. The populations of Alberta and British Columbia grew faster than those of most other provinces; major oil companies relocated their Canadian head offices from Toronto or Montreal to Calgary. In the process, some of the old liberal (large-L and small-L) assumptions about this country were shaken. Granted, Canadians continue to regard our health care system, the Maple Leaf flag, and the Charter of Rights and Freedoms—all achievements of Liberal governments during the second half of the twentieth century—as intrinsic to our national identity. But Canadian opinion swung toward greater acceptance of free markets and more skepticism about government interventionism.

This shift reflected larger global swings, but Manning certainly pushed Canadians to move in this direction. Since Confederation, federal politics had been dominated by our two "big-tent" parties, which were often largely indistinguishable on issues such as state intervention or law and order. They took turns governing, depending on leadership and how well they brokered regional and religious cleavages. The parties were most successful when they hewed to the centre of the political spectrum and paid closest attention to the two largest provinces in the centre of the country, Ontario and Quebec.

This was certainly true of Brian Mulroney's Progressive Conservatives when, in 1987, Preston Manning planted the seeds of a new political movement in western Canada that would grow into a national and far more conservative organization, the Reform Party. The political analyst Robin Sears, from Earnscliffe Consulting, suggests that Manning was the Canadian version of an American "states' rights" politician. "He accepts Ottawa's role, but he's anti-centrist, perhaps because he grew up as an outsider. Nobody ever loses that sense of being excluded and disrespected."

Preston Manning would lose control of the changes he had triggered and would limp away from the reborn ideological Conservative Party that emerged from the Reform Party chrysalis. But his movement and vision for Canada coloured Canadian attitudes to government, gave the Liberal Party

Preston Manning (*left*) and his adviser Stephen Harper (*far right*) arrived in Ottawa together in 1993 determined to reshape Canadian politics.

a free ride for two elections, and eventually led to the emergence of a new Conservative Party with a strong base in the West.

So although Manning failed in his own political ambition, his role has been critical. Where did this vision come from? It was deeply embedded in the DNA of both his province and Manning himself.

⌁

Preston Manning is one of forty-six "mavericks" featured in a permanent exhibit, *The Story of Maverick Alberta*, in the Glenbow Museum, a Calgary museum that tells the story of southern Alberta and the West. What is a maverick? The story goes that a Texas rancher named Samuel A. Maverick did not wish to brand his cattle, so unbranded calves came to be called mavericks. According to the Calgary writer Aritha van Herk, author of the book *Mavericks*, on which the exhibit is based, "Albertans are mavericks, people who step out of bounds, refuse to do as we are told, take risks, and then laugh when we fall down and hit the ground. . . . Our history is different, our politics are different, our ways of thinking are different."[1]

Each of Canada's ten provinces and three territories is unique. (Don't ever confuse a Nova Scotian with a Prince Edward Islander, or think a Cape Breton accent is from Newfoundland.) When I first arrived in Ontario all those years ago, I noticed a certain curled-lip discomfort among my fellow central Canadians about Albertans. Mordecai Richler famously dismissed Edmonton as "the boiler room of Canada" and said that Calgary looked as though it had been uncrated yesterday. When I asked what it was like, I was frequently told, "Think Texas" (this was *not* a compliment), and there is indeed an American tinge to Alberta attitudes.

Yet there is an optimism about Albertans—a belief that you can reinvent yourself—that is a refreshing contrast to the pursed-lip caution that historically has characterized Canadians elsewhere. The province's residents take pride in their prickliness: to quote van Herk again, "Aggravating, Awful, Awkward, Awesome Alberta."[2] Land of the Rockies and the rodeo, booms and busts, Alberta boasts the tallest mountains, the oldest rocks, the fastest-growing population. It has become the country's wealthiest province, thanks to winning the geological lottery and discovering that it sits on top of vast oil fields. Yet in the first half of the twentieth century it was so poor that it twice flirted with bankruptcy.

Alberta's catalogue of grudges against central Canada is as colourful as it is long, and Preston Manning grew up steeped in them. He explored a century of fights in a 2005 academic paper entitled "Federal-Provincial Tensions and the Evolution of a Province."[3] In Manning's telling, relations with Ottawa went off the rails even before Alberta was born. Frederick Haultain, who between 1897 and 1905 served as premier of the North-West Territories (including present-day Alberta, Saskatchewan, and most of Manitoba), had lobbied for just one new province, to be named Buffalo. A united West, with a nice beefy name, would have more bargaining power against the centre. But the Liberal government in Ottawa opted to divide and rule. In 1905 it created two provinces and named the one that abutted the Rockies Alberta, after one of Queen Victoria's daughters, Princess Louise Albert. Moreover, it wasn't until 1930, after a fight with the federal government, that Alberta (along with Saskatchewan) won control of its natural resources—resources that would come to dominate Alberta's economy.

By the time Preston Manning was born in Edmonton in 1942, Albertans—still a largely rural people, toiling behind plows and on harvesters—had already demonstrated their predilection for maverick politicians and one-party landslides. First, the populist United Farmers of Alberta toppled the sitting Liberals in 1921 and endorsed policies like a provincial hail insurance scheme, a farm credit program, and the Alberta Co-operative Elevator Company. Next, in 1935, the UFA was toppled by another populist newcomer, the Social Credit Party, founded by the charismatic preacher "Bible Bill" Aberhart.

Today Alberta's Social Credit Party is remembered as the "funny money" party. It claimed it would loosen the grip of eastern banks and institutions on the money supply by promising to pay $25 to every adult Albertan in the form of a "prosperity certificate." A $25 dividend sounded pretty good to farmers facing bankruptcy. North America was in the middle of its worst depression ever, leading to a horrendous collapse in average farm income from $1,975 in 1927 to $54 in 1933. Alberta's debt-plagued farmers were burning wheat they couldn't sell and killing cattle while people around them were starving.

But the $25 prosperity certificates were of less value than Canadian Tire money: they turned out to be paper currency substitutes churned out by an Alberta printing press. And Aberhart's solutions defied the British North America Act's stipulation that Ottawa controlled the banking system: only the federal government could "prime the pump." Bible Bill never explained how his government would fund the $25 dividends. Instead, he ranted on CFCN Radio and in packed Calgary theatres against the "fifty big shots" and the "high mucky-mucks" in central Canada who kept Albertans in poverty. His provincial banking system was shot down by Ottawa, which reluctantly bailed the province out.

There is a lot not to like about Bible Bill. He was dictatorial, contemptuous of many aspects of democracy including a free press, and—like his economic mentor, the British engineer Major Clifford H. Douglas—anti-Semitic. Nevertheless, Social Credit's educational policies and labour legislation were among the most advanced in the country, and the Aberhart government created the Métis Settlements in northern Alberta—the first official recognition of the Métis as a group with Indigenous rights.

William Aberhart served as premier of Alberta from 1935 to 1943 and casts a long shadow over Alberta's history. In his memoir *Think Big: My Adventures in Life and Democracy*, Preston Manning describes him as "courageous, bombastic, and stubborn. . . . He was either loved or hated." Manning argues that the founder of Alberta's Social Credit party gave his voters hope in desperate times. "While a historical canard has taken root that he was a discredited and even despicable failure, in fact, Aberhart gave new life and expression to an axiom of Western politics that inspires many Westerners to this very day: If you find the economic or political status quo unacceptable, Do Something!"[4]

Which, if you think about it, is another way of saying, "Never say 'Whoa' in a mudhole."

One of the smartest things that Aberhart did was to recruit Ernest Manning, Preston's father, to be his aide, chauffeur, and co-worker. While still in his teens, Ernest Manning was drawn to Bible Bill's Christian evangelism; the Saskatchewan farmer's son built his own crystal radio set so that each Sunday he could listen to the old man's radio show, *Back to the Bible Hour*, on Calgary's CFCN radio station. In his early twenties Ernest Manning attended Aberhart's Calgary Prophetic Bible Institute and became its first graduate. The preacher started to treat his serious young acolyte as an adoptive son. Manning was soon spreading the fundamentalist gospel himself, while courting another of Bible Bill's disciples—Muriel Preston, the quick-witted, sharp-tongued pianist at the institute.

Aberhart dazzled the two prairie youngsters, both from hardscrabble backgrounds, with his vision of a better tomorrow. "My parents' lives and homes were infused with a panoramic sense of history and big ideas of economic and social reform, democratic processes, and populist politics," Preston writes in his book. Manning Sr.'s evangelism morphed into an antiestablishment political crusade alongside that of his mentor. In 1935, when Albertans voted en masse for Aberhart's folksy charms, twenty-six-year-old

Ernest Manning was elected in a Calgary riding and joined the cabinet as provincial secretary and minister of trade and industry.

Ernest Manning and Muriel Preston married in 1936. Preston, their second son, was born in 1942. A year later, Premier William Aberhart died and Manning succeeded him as party leader and premier of the province. He would be premier for the next quarter century, yet politics were rarely allowed to intrude on family. "My father never invited politicians into our home, and the media respected the separation of public and private life."[5]

Preston Manning's brief account of his childhood in his memoir is suffused with the impact of the Great Depression on the lives of his parents and thousands of homesteaders. Manning himself is not a particularly introspective man, and he resorts to anecdotes only to illustrate political or moral points. His mother's stories of families where children were fed on

The hunger and despair of the Dirty Thirties were vividly described in W. O. Mitchell's novel about a boy growing up on the prairies.

gopher stew and clad in garments sewn from flour sacks are quoted as parables to suggest our moral obligation as individuals to care for the less fortunate.[6] The Alberta writer W. O. Mitchell depicted the small-town scrimping, saving, and misery of the 1930s prairies much more vividly in the classic Canadian novel *Who Has Seen the Wind*. "Houses needed paint; cars on Main Street on Saturday night were older models; plate glass windows were empty where businesses had left. . . . [Hobos] left their penciled marks on doors of generous people: 'Champ 32', 'CPR 10', 'CNR Jos', '21-Circle.'"[7]

Mitchell's novel and Preston Manning's memories are tinged with a romantic view of prairie resilience to which many Albertans still respond; "old-timers" are featured at every Calgary Stampede. Yet by the time that Manning was in school and Mitchell's novel was acclaimed, Alberta was on fast-forward. The Second World War boosted the provincial economy; the discovery of oil in Leduc in 1947 changed everything. Cattle now grazed between oil rigs. By 1951 more Albertans lived in cities than on farms, and the province's population was close to one million, surpassing for the first time those of Saskatchewan and Manitoba.

Premier Ernest Manning, child of the impoverished West, lived every politician's dream; for most of the postwar period, the good times rolled. Aberhart's funny money theories were left in the dust as oil money transformed Alberta's standard of living. Big Chevrolets purred along newly blacktopped roads, and the Ranchmen's served sixteen-ounce steaks.

The Manning government kept its distance from central Canada. "Rightly or wrongly," Preston Manning observes, "many Albertans emerged from the Depression and War years with the conviction that when they and their province [were] in deep trouble they were largely on their own, but when the nation was in trouble, they were expected to come to its aid."[8] And even as Alberta's spending on education, health care, and roads became the highest in the country,[9] Premier Manning stuck to the rhetoric of frugality and forbearance. He reminded voters that "our material assets must be augmented by the greatest possible development of all spiritual and moral resources."[10] Alberta's minimum wage remained twenty-five cents an hour below the recommendations of the Canada Labour Code. Liberal initiatives like medicare and social housing were furiously resisted as unwarranted intrusions into provincial jurisdiction.

One day in 1963 Preston climbed the stairs of the legislative building to visit his father and discovered the premier frowning over a telegram from Prime Minister Lester Pearson. Troubled by the stirrings of Quebec's independence movement, Pearson was proposing a royal commission that would, he hoped, cement national unity. It would be called the Royal Commission on Bilingualism and Biculturalism, and it defined Canada as "an equal partnership between two founding races," the French and the English, "taking into account the contributions made by other ethnic groups."

Pearson's telegram outraged Premier Manning. He regarded this step as "worse than misguided," according to his son. German, Scandinavian, and central European immigrants had helped settle the prairies, and Chinese and Sikh Canadians clustered in the cities. In the Manning view, Pearson's attempt to impose "a central Canadian definition of Canada as a whole" was downgrading both Alberta and its people.[11] Why, he asked, should those French-speaking Quebecers take precedence over Edmonton's large Ukrainian population?

As the premier's son, Preston Manning himself never knew hardship; he grew up in a comfortable middle-class home in Edmonton, with weekends on the family farm where a foreman looked after seventy head of dairy cows. While in school, he often went to the legislature after class and sat outside his father's office, doing his homework as politicians and petitioners came and went. At home he watched his father, "my mentor and my hero," sit at the kitchen table, using a mechanical adding machine to prepare budget speeches. At his father's suggestion, his rock-ribbed reading choices included *The Revised Statutes of Alberta*, Will and Ariel Durant's multi-volume *Story of Civilization*, and Winston Churchill's *History of the English-Speaking Peoples*. Whether he realized it or not, Preston Manning was preparing himself to go into the family business.

For six days a week, Ernest Manning focused on politics; on the seventh, he spread God's word. Preston Manning describes his father as "the best preacher I had ever heard." The Mannings had taken over Aberhart's radio program and retitled it *Canada's National Back to the Bible Hour* (Muriel was music director), and Preston took notes of all his father's sermons. Alongside his parents, he attended the Fundamental Baptist Church—like the Social Credit Party, an independent, self-organizing unit rather than an established institution with a long tradition of rules and rituals. His commitment to free enterprise, self-reliance, and Christian values was absolute. It was a very Alberta approach, highlighted by an expression popular during the province's Golden Jubilee celebrations in 1955, when Preston was thirteen: "Places don't grow, men build 'em."[12]

By the time Ernest Manning announced his departure from provincial politics in 1968, his son had graduated in economics from the University of Alberta. Lanky and bespectacled, the boy who had memorized the periodic table of the elements in school was the very definition of a geek. He followed closely in his father's footsteps. He often spoke on the premier's radio broadcasts; he had run as a Social Credit candidate in the federal election (with no chance of winning); he wrote large chunks of Ernest Manning's book *Political Realignment: A Challenge to Thoughtful Canadians*, published in 1967, the year of Expo. This slim volume urged a shakeup of the traditional political establishment because "the distinctions between the Liberals and Progressive Conservatives are rapidly being reduced to the superficial distinctions of party image, party labels and party personalities." Ideology should replace the pragmatism that had helped Canada muddle through the previous century. *Political Realignment* foreshadowed Preston Manning's plans to re-engineer federal politics in Canada.

Several party insiders urged Ernest Manning to anoint his son as his successor, but the premier refused. Social Credit supremacy was about to be challenged by a young Harvard-educated Progressive Conservative lawyer, Peter Lougheed. ("A Madison Avenue glamour boy with the charm of an Avon lady," sniffed Manning Sr.[13]) Within three years, Lougheed's provincial Conservatives had swept aside Social Credit in the kind of landslide election victory in which Alberta specializes. "Another political tornado had dusted through the province," as Aritha van Herk puts it. "Alberta changed again, with Lougheed articulating a sophisticated and updated version of Alberta's pride and independence."[14] Social Credit was toast: both Ernest Manning and his son now seemed hopelessly fusty compared with the cuff-shooting Lougheed crowd.

Preston Manning would spend the next twenty years as a management consultant, in partnership with his father in Manning Consultants Limited. While his father joined eastern corporate boards and was appointed to the Senate, Preston sat in corner offices, explaining to executives how their organizations could be slotted into matrixes, charts, and models. His clients ranged from oil companies and public utilities to community development organizations; his particular expertise was retooling organizations from the bottom up. He also married the forthright and lively Sandra Beavis, a graduate of Alberta's Prairie Bible College and a student nurse who attended the same church as the Mannings. Preston Manning speaks frequently about his wife with unequivocal respect for her personally, and also for the sacrifices required of women who marry politicians. "Measured in terms of my future well-being, my family, and my business and political career, asking Sandra to marry me was the smartest decision I ever made."[15] The Mannings would have five children. But as Calgary sprouted glass towers and new subdivisions ate up the surrounding fields, Preston never stopped brooding about politics.

However, with his Social Credit roots, the younger Manning remained uncomfortable with the traditional political establishment. Climbing rungs was not his style. His fellow Albertan Joe Clark, who had joined the federal Progressive Conservative Party when he was sixteen years old, urged Manning to follow his example. "He kept saying to me that I should get in and change the party from within. But I could see that wouldn't work. As long as a party is successful, the old guard will block change."[16] He was confident another "prairie fire" would start smouldering, allowing him to challenge the establishment from outside the tent. It was all a question of timing: he could not "Do Something," in the Aberhart mode, until there was grassroots momentum. "Rather than getting in on the tail end of the populist movements produced on the Canadian prairies during the Depression, I would wait for the next one."[17] But he was already planning a western-based populist movement, committed to a small government agenda, that would evolve into a national party. He knew what he wanted to sell; he just needed an audience ready to buy. "You can't manufacture a third party: only when people are angry can you try and harness the energy."[18]

In the next few years, anger began to simmer. This was the era of the energy wars between Ottawa and Alberta. After the OPEC cartel raised world oil prices in 1973, Ottawa watched Alberta's oil revenues climb. When the second oil shock hit in 1979–80, tripling oil prices, Liberal prime minister Pierre Trudeau decided to introduce a tax on oil exports. This move would effectively lower prices for domestic consumers and raise revenues for Ottawa. It also created an incentive to shift to oil exploration in federally controlled regions offshore and in the North. The feds argued that this interventionist National Energy Program was in the national interest because it would allow Canada to have more balanced development and an equitable sharing of the benefits of oil.

Such an argument might have made sense even to some Albertans in the early twentieth century, when "nation building" for a precarious Confederation had included the idea of interregional subsidies. But now Albertans reacted with fury: the NEP forced them to sell their oil below world prices. It excited the most primal of their anxieties—the fear they would lose control to outside interests, and that those interests would rob them of their patrimony.

This was Alberta's resource, argued Premier Lougheed, for the province to use to strengthen and diversify its own economy. Many, like Manning, saw the NEP as an even more nefarious scheme: "a massive raid by a spendthrift federal government on the resource wealth of western Canada." Some Albertans plastered their cars with bumper stickers that read, "Let the Eastern Bastards Freeze in the Dark." Pierre Trudeau became a pariah in Alberta, and Lougheed, the "blue-eyed Arab of Saudi Alberta," beat back Ottawa's attempt to control a provincial resource. But the number of oil rigs operating in Alberta dropped from 400 to 130.[19]

The high price forecasts of the NEP were soon discredited as world oil prices tumbled and a recession further dented Alberta's economy. As he chatted to his corporate clients, Preston Manning heard their exasperation with Ottawa's policies, which, they argued, were bleeding money out of the West. All Ottawa cared about, they grumbled, was Quebec. With the election of a separatist government in Quebec in 1976, the burning issue in Ottawa was national unity. A proliferation of task forces and cabinet committees grappled with scenarios and sweeteners as a Quebec referendum loomed. The two-decade-long constitutional battles had begun, featuring the 1980 referendum, the Constitution Act, and the Charter of Rights, plus two failed attempts (the Meech Lake and Charlottetown Accords) to get Quebec to sign the Constitution Act. It was a volatile and uneasy period in national politics: Brian Mulroney would replace Pierre Trudeau as prime minister in 1984; Elijah Harper, speaking for Indigenous peoples, would scupper the Meech Lake Accord in 1990; the Charlottetown Accord would be defeated in a hard-fought national referendum in 1992.

Throughout it all, Albertans felt ignored.

There were now crabby little eruptions of western separatism, including the formation of the Western Canada Concept party. An Alberta farmer, Bert Brown, plowed the slogan "Triple E Senate or Else" into his neighbour's three-kilometre-long wheat field outside Calgary to demonstrate support for an "elected, equal, effective" upper chamber.

However, in Manning's view, Alberta's separatist initiatives weren't really serious. They were simply tactics to draw attention to western grievances. The prairie fire for which he was watching was not yet ablaze. He continued to wait.

Nobody was happier than the denizens of the Alberta oil patch when the Progressive Conservative leader Brian Mulroney became prime minister in 1984—even though he came from Quebec. The federal Progressive Conservatives won every single seat in Alberta, while the Liberals were almost completely shut out of the West. But enthusiasm soon soured. "The West expected spending to be controlled, the deficit to be dramatically reduced, [plus] tax relief and a new sensitivity to Western aspirations and concerns," explains Manning. Instead, Mulroney's government showed no interest in cutting taxes and was as focused on Quebec as its Liberal predecessor. Moreover, western conservative support for old-fashioned "family values" (which included hostility to abortion, homosexuality, and premarital sex) was shunned by Ottawa's Conservative power brokers. Manning recalls, "I heard the rumblings of disappointment in the boardrooms and on the streets as I made my consulting rounds. . . . The grass was dry—very dry. One spark, and who knew what might happen?"[20]

In Preston Manning's version of history, that spark was a federal decision—"in the national interest"—that a Montreal company rather than a Winnipeg corporation should get the maintenance contract for Canada's CF-18 jet fighters, even though the Winnipeg firm's bid was lower. The CF-18 decision convinced many westerners that a change of government in Ottawa hadn't changed anything. Preston Manning reckoned, "All the conditions for a full-blown prairie fire were now present. . . . It was time to act!"

Never say "Whoa" in a mudhole. Ernest Manning's son spurred his horse into a gallop.

≁

Preston Manning was ready to ride the wave of public discontent, and he had plenty of backing within Alberta—not least, Ted Byfield's newsmagazine *Alberta Report*, which presented a slick version of Manning's message. But were Canadians ready for him? Would they take seriously this rather prim introvert in badly cut suits, whose speeches consisted of reasoned arguments and to-do lists rather than soaring rhetoric?

The first test came at a gathering of the newly formed Reform Association of Canada in Vancouver in May 1987. Carefully devised by Manning, the event was billed as two days of lengthy discussions to develop "A Western Agenda for Change." Behind the podium, a large banner proclaimed, "The West Wants In." Over five hundred people from all four western provinces were happy to vent against central Canada.

At first, central Canada was less impressed. Manning had invited Prime Minister Mulroney to send a representative to Vancouver. "Mulroney sent a short, snarky response, saying he would forbid any of his members to attend."[21] Taking its lead from the Mulroney government, the Ottawa press gallery dismissed Manning as just another whining westerner and dubbed him "Parson Manning." Craig Oliver, chief political correspondent for the CTV network at the time, recalls that Manning's "utter faith in the rightness of his views and the conviction with which he expressed them seemed very like sermons from the pulpit." It wasn't just that Manning sounded like a preacher. He still *was* a preacher; his Christian faith was and remains a crucial part of his life. Similarly, *Alberta Report* promoted very conservative Christian values relentlessly. But for the secularized, irony-soaked Toronto intelligentsia, it was a bit much.

No matter. By the end of the Vancouver meeting, Preston Manning had got what he came for. Delegates voted to establish a new, broadly based federal political party with its roots in the west, which had moved beyond grievance toward demands for debt reduction and democratic accountability. In an anti-Quebec swipe, Manning supporters agreed that no province should have special status. Soon the new party was christened the Reform Party of Canada, and Manning had been elected leader.

The party had a slow start. In the 1988 federal election, all the Reform Party's candidates were defeated, and the party won only 2 percent of the vote. (Even in Alberta, it managed to get only 15 percent.) However, the "West Wants In" movement had smothered the cranks who were demanding that the West get out. "Reform was the relief well for that wildcat flow of separatism," comments Manning. "We channelled the energy into making the federation work better rather than kicking it apart."[22]

Manning methodically grew his party. He dropped the western rhetoric and began to talk of "Old Canada" and "New Canada" as he criss-crossed the country. His slight figure, with wire-rimmed glasses on his nose and a prairie twang in his voice, turned up in small-town halls and church basements, with little advance publicity other than handwritten notes nailed to telephone poles or circulated in general stores. The crowds seemed to appear out of nowhere to hear him talk about stuff from a viewpoint that they weren't hearing elsewhere, and to voice views that were barely admissible within mainstream parties. Manning's followers were tired of soaring federal deficits and feverish debate about keeping Quebec in Canada. They cheered Manning's denunciations of the policies of bilingualism and multiculturalism; they applauded his calls for an elected Senate, referendums, equality between provinces, and "bottom-up democracy" (whatever that meant). Many meetings ended with a passionate rendition of "O Canada." For all Manning's talk of New Canada, his audience—disproportionately older, male, and rural—looked awfully like Old Canada, nostalgic for simpler, more God-fearing times.

Manning lacked Tommy Douglas's oratorical magic. Yet Reform's appeal was unmistakable as it steadily rolled eastward into Ontario, surfing on the growing unpopularity of Brian Mulroney's Tories. Even if much of Reform's platform was dismissed by critics as naive, Manning's movement carried none of the historical baggage of the three established parties. In an era of unprincipled or bumbling politicians, nobody questioned Preston Manning's integrity.

By 1990 Canada's federal debt was swelling and some of Bible Bill's despised "high mucky-mucks" in the East decided that Manning was the only political leader paying attention to the crumbling economy. Preston Manning was invited to a private dinner hosted by the publisher Conrad Black and the financier Hal Jackman in their plush sanctuary, the Toronto Club. He explained to fifty financial heavy hitters that his party would ask voters to choose between Old Canada and New Canada. "Old Canada is a Canada where governments chronically overspend and where there's a constitutional preoccupation with French and English relations. In New Canada, governments would be fiscally responsible and we'd go beyond French-English relations as the centrepiece of constitutional discussion." Old Canada, sitting right in front of Manning and puffing cigars, "inhaled the words 'fiscally responsible' like a narcotic," according to Ian Pearson in *Saturday Night* magazine. The fifty big shots present that night gave Manning a standing ovation.[23] The western champion of "ordinary Canadians" had successfully recruited corporate support.

The first major gains for Reform came in the 1993 federal election. That election redrew the electoral map of Canada because the Progressive Con-

servative Party fell apart. While Jean Chrétien's Liberals swept into government, only two PCs were elected. Two upstart parties—Alberta-based
Reform, and the separatist Bloc Québécois—picked over the PC carcass.
The Bloc won fifty-four seats, catapulting it onto the official opposition
benches, while Reform, with more votes, was hot on its tail with fifty-two
seats, all but one in the West. Preston Manning was elected as the honourable member from Calgary Southwest, and one of his closest advisers, a
young economist called Stephen Harper, won Calgary West.

Reform overtook the Bloc Québécois in the 1997 election. The Liberals under Jean Chrétien once again coasted to victory, thanks in part to a
divided opposition. But Reform won sixty seats—all in western Canada—
and Preston Manning became the leader of the official opposition.

It was a stunning achievement. Within a decade, Preston Manning had
cannily steered his regional protest movement onto the national stage. The
Reform Party had become Canada's major right-wing party and started to
win votes, but no seats, in Ontario. There was still no sign that it could ever
form a government; its share of the vote remained below 20 percent, and it
had no support in Quebec and no MPs from east of the Lakehead. In an era
of ethnic and gender equity, party membership was dominated by English-
speaking older white men.

Nevertheless, Preston Manning had pushed his version of conservative
values into the mainstream. Public accountability and government debt
were now concerns from coast to coast; spending and tax cuts, and the
privatization of social services, were part of political debate. By and large,
he had managed to shut down the anti-gay, anti-abortion, anti-government
crazies in his party. ("If you turn on a light, you're going to attract bugs," he
reflects.) He had broken the mould of traditional two-party politics and
succeeded, he hoped, in achieving Frederick Haultain's 1903 goal of creating a strong western block that could challenge the centre.

Manning's sense of timing had been spot-on. The Reform Party was
born amid the constitutional conflicts of the 1980s, and the political fault
lines of this large and unwieldy country zigzagged across the map. Throw
in the visceral distrust of Brian Mulroney, the passions aroused by the 1988

free trade deal with the United States, high unemployment, and rampant inflation, and you have a toxic mix. As Keith Spicer, chair of the Citizens' Forum on Canada's Future, noted in the group's 1991 report, there was "a fury in the land." The national angst didn't subside after the Liberal electoral victory of 1993, because only two years later, Quebec held a second referendum on sovereignty. The separatist forces came within a heartbeat of winning.

Nevertheless, it wasn't just about timing. As Craig Oliver admits, "We in the media don't always recognize a game changer when we meet one."

~~

Those who come to Canada's national capital to participate in the business of government see Ottawa very differently from the way that long-time residents experience the city. Lifers enjoy stable house prices, free-flowing traffic, and a seasonal rhythm of skating on the Rideau Canal in winter and hiking in the Gatineau Hills in the summer. We love the Gothic Parliament Buildings as a landmark—a glorious Victorian gesture of optimism about the fragile new Dominion's future—but we rarely stroll across the grounds. We relish the big-city amenities (national museums, the National Arts Centre) but we cherish the homey atmosphere of our neighbourhoods.

In contrast, those who come here for politics—MPs, reporters, and eager young staffers—are often leery of a city that is periodically convulsed by scandal and tagged a "fat cat." New arrivals stick close to the parliamentary precinct and the surrounding palisade of government offices. Their loyalties are defined by their Sparks Street hangouts: their preferred reading is the *Hill Times*; they watch question period every day. Ottawa is not home: the Ottawa Senators are not their team. Most have no intention of settling here. MPs who commute home for weekends know the featureless road to the airport better than they know the colourful Byward Market.

Leaving Sandra and the family in Calgary, newly elected Preston Manning arrived in Ottawa in 1993 with an outsider's distrust of an established institution. During his first term in Parliament, he stayed in a drab room in the downtown Travelodge. He visited the museums or the National Arts

Centre only for government functions. Ottawa felt to him, he recalls, "like the capital of a nineteenth-century British colony. Even the flags were scrawny: Husky Oil gas stations out west have bigger, better Maple Leaf flags."[24] He regarded the flexibility required to balance the federation as symptoms of "Ottawa fever." Not only did the politics of compromise offend his fundamentalist principles, they also fed into his sense that, once MPs arrived in Ottawa, they too easily forgot why they were elected. "First the memory starts to go. Sufferers forget all those commitments that were made during the election. Then it's the hearing.... It gets harder and harder to hear the voices of the folks back home. After a little while the head starts to swell, and that can be fatal."[25]

Manning was determined to challenge every long-standing parliamentary convention. Reform, like Social Credit before it, presented itself as a "movement" rather than a morally compromised political party like the Liberals and the PCs. He sat on the second row of opposition benches to illustrate that there would be no hierarchy of frontbenchers and backbenchers; he renamed the party whip the caucus coordinator to avoid the traditional term's "authoritarian connotations."[26]As leader of the official opposition, he refused the keys to his official limousine and to Stornoway, the official residence. (He later relented when he realized this would put the driver and staff out of jobs.)

But the longer Manning remained in Ottawa, the more apparent it became that he could never be prime minister. Television made demands on politicians that the Fathers of Confederation never faced. On screen, "Parson Manning" came over as too earnest, too dull, and a magnet for mockers. "In the beginning, I was loath to give this subject much of my time," he admits, but under pressure from advisers he submitted to an upgrade: capped teeth, laser eye surgery, and a voice coach to iron out the squeak. Next came his wardrobe. "We started with the ties, enlisting the help of a 'tie consultant.'... There was the 'power tie'... the 'come-hither tie'... the 'back-off tie.'... We bought them all, but the problem was that I couldn't remember which tie did what." Reporters warmed to him when he made a very funny speech about the makeover at the annual press gallery dinner.

Most cartoonists and political commentators mocked Manning rather
than taking the rise of the Reform Party seriously.

But that was not enough. His religious convictions and Prairie Home Companion style did not cut it for young, urban Canadians.

Far more significant than dearth of charisma was his attitude to Quebec.
It wasn't simply that he didn't speak French. Steeped in western alienation,
he showed little sympathy for a province with a unique cultural and political
legacy that predated Confederation and that it wanted to protect. Every political strategist in Canada knows that to form a government, a party must
win two out of three regions: Quebec, Ontario, and the West. (Atlantic
Canada can mean the difference between a minority and majority government, but there are too few seats to guarantee a government.) This was why
party leaders since the days of John A. Macdonald and George-Étienne
Cartier have spent so much time balancing the interests of different regions:
this is how brokerage politics evolved. But Manning's attitude ensured not
only that he could never win any seats in Quebec, but also that his prospects
in Ontario—where voters cared about national unity—were significantly

reduced, and that he had no resonance in the Atlantic provinces. "He is a conviction politician," says the political strategist Robin Sears, "and there is a big gap to navigate between principles and power."

In fact, the only way that Reform could get a whiff of real power was if Quebec did separate. Jean Chrétien, prime minister at the time, suspected that "Manning knew he could never become prime minister of Canada because of Quebec and, consequently, that he wouldn't have been terribly sorry to see it leave the federation."[27] The fact that its departure would leave Canada looking like a doughnut, with a big hole in the middle, was not discussed by the Reform leader. Instead, he suggested that if "the *people* of Quebec and the *people* of the rest of Canada" were properly consulted about his New Canada, they could "be reconciled."[28]

By the 1990s Manning's railing against government debt had helped build public acceptance for the belief that government spending must be cut. This made it much easier for the Liberal government to pass a tough budget in 1995 and straighten out the nation's finances. At the same time,

Manning largely ignored the separatist fervor in Quebec.

constitutional fatigue had set in: nobody wanted to talk about rebalancing federal powers. Reform's populist tide and Manning's personal popularity began to ebb.

Manning recognized that he needed to attract a broader range of conservatives, particularly in Ontario. First he renamed his party the United Alternative; soon this transformed itself into a new party, the Canadian Alliance, with a platform that combined Reform and Progressive Conservative policies. (Brian Mulroney branded it "the Reform Party in pantyhose," and most seasoned PCs refused to join.) But at the Canadian Alliance's first leadership convention, in 2000, Manning was shocked to find himself cast aside in favour of a younger, more "electable" leader who might win votes in Ontario. Manning's immediate successor, Stockwell Day, quickly became a laughingstock after his evangelically inspired views on evolution were skewered on national television. Craig Oliver recalls the internecine struggle to oust Day as "a circus of intrigue and betrayal."

To Manning's distaste, the Alliance then merged with the remnants of the old Progressive Conservative Party, in 2003. Within a remarkably short time, Manning's one-time policy adviser Stephen Harper had elbowed aside all comers, won the leadership of the Canadian Alliance, and taken the helm of the new Conservative Party. The word "Progressive" was flung into the trash can.

The fiscal policies that Manning's Reform Party pushed were part of the late-twentieth-century wave of conservative economics sweeping Europe and North America: Margaret Thatcher and Ronald Reagan gave Manning an intellectual respectability that he didn't have in the 1970s. However, it was Manning who had strengthened the ideological spine of Canadians on the conservative side of the political spectrum. "Nobody in Canada was talking about balanced budgets until Preston Manning put them on the map," argues Tom Flanagan, who worked alongside Stephen Harper as a policy adviser to Manning. Flanagan is an American academic who served as head of the political science department at the University of Calgary until 2013, and who was a conduit of American neo-conservatism into the Reform Party since its birth. "He pushed the issue to the top of the Conservative agenda." Manning reframed the economic debate in a way that portrayed government as spendthrift and corrupt, making it difficult for any politician to discuss tax hikes or social programs.

Without the Reform Party and Preston Manning, Stephen Harper would never have become prime minister of Canada; he had neither the patience nor the personality to build a party from scratch as Manning had done. But he won three federal elections, which gave him two minority governments and one majority government. Once installed at 24 Sussex Drive, he stuck as close as he dared to the Manning agenda.

Harper championed trade liberalization, balanced budgets, lowered taxes, and constrained government spending (although the 2008 global economic crisis forced some deviation from Reform dogma). He moved the policy yardsticks rightward on foreign policy, criminal justice, and civil liberties. He re-engineered the federation by leaving the provinces to run their own health care, environmental, and education programs with little federal co-ordination or intervention. Canada reduced its support for multilateral organizations like the United Nations and for aid to less developed countries. Its official indifference to climate change debates made it an outcast internationally.

Some of this was straight cost-cutting. But many of the changes went way beyond the Manning legacy and were driven by more than a determination to reduce Ottawa's power. Harper wanted to challenge the Liberal monopoly on values that defined Canada: universal health care, peacekeeping, Charter freedoms, and diversity. His campaign to slash Ottawa's powers included direct attacks on institutions and programs that postwar Liberal governments had established to bind the country together, from the national broadcaster to university exchange programs. Harper tried to reinforce in the Canadian psyche overtly right-wing values, including a new respect for the monarchy and the armed forces, and an emphasis on military victories and sacrifice.

Harper had little patience for accountability or Manning's precious "bottom-up democracy." In Manning's words, "Stephen was never prepared to be a team player, [and the two minority governments] . . . reinforced his tendency toward iron control."[29] The goal of building a populist party that directly involved members in policy-making was doused by the hard reality of the deals required to govern Canada. It was always an unrealistic goal, according to Flanagan, who had left Manning's office and gone to work with Stephen Harper. "That's too unwieldy within our system. What you need in national politics is an armoured division, not a populist party. 'Top-down' wins in Canada."

The founder of the Reform Party watched his former lieutenant operate with an autocratic ruthlessness that shocked many supporters. In 2015 the *National Post* columnist Conrad Black, no friend of the Liberals, berated Harper for governing the country like "a sadistic Victorian schoolmaster."[30] In the election a few days later, Stephen Harper was defeated. Among the 5.5 million Canadians who stuck with the Conservatives (32 percent of all voters), the vast majority were older white westerners—the original Reform Party supporters.

After the election I asked Preston Manning if he felt Harper had betrayed his legacy by abandoning Reform Party populism and running such a top-down government. "I wouldn't use the word 'betrayal,'" replied the former leader of the Reform Party. "And I never like to talk about legacies. If you keep looking in a rear-view mirror you'll run into a tree." Manning is philosophical about his own failure to propel his creation to power. As he tells me over the telephone, "The first people to scale the walls of any fortress are those who get hot oil poured on them. It is usually the third wave that makes it."

༺༻

How did Preston Manning affect the promise of this still young, still growing nation?

He demonstrated the continuing appeal of populist movements within Canada, and he achieved a larger role for the West in our public life. Despite his aversion to "Ottawa fever," Manning was always committed to the idea that Canada is built on mutual accommodation among regions and interests; his objective was to change the terms of the accommodation. Almost single-handedly, he doused the flames of western separatism in the late 1980s. A decade later, he did not endorse the letter, signed by Stephen Harper among others, suggesting the construction of a "firewall" around Alberta to protect the province from Ottawa. Manning himself says that one of Reform's most important contributions is that "we shifted the geopolitical centre of gravity from the Laurentian Basin towards the West. The West cannot be taken for granted anymore."

At the same time, Preston Manning widened the political debate within Canada by destroying the old Progressive Conservative Party and spawning a much more right-wing option. He is a devotee of American political history, and many of his ideas have a distinctly Republican flavour—particularly distrust of the federal government. He likes to take credit for the fact that, in Canada today, "trade liberalization and balanced budgets are conventional wisdom. The new guys will be measured by those yardsticks."

But there is a more paradoxical way in which this Albertan has shaped our country. He clarified the choices ahead as Canada embarks on the next 150 years.

Preston Manning offered Canadians a different kind of Canada, a country of more modest ambitions that quietly minded its own business and looked to market forces rather than government for leadership. When I asked him what holds Canada together today, he offered only, "Democratic values and inertia. Nobody wants to make the effort to kick it apart." This narrow outlook is a stark contrast to the grand vision articulated by George-Étienne Cartier and John A. Macdonald in 1867, on which they based the new Dominion and with which subsequent prime ministers, from Wilfrid Laurier to John Diefenbaker, from Lester Pearson and Pierre Trudeau to Brian Mulroney, have rallied the country. It is also a contrast to the "Never say 'Whoa!' in a mudhole" optimism of which most Albertans are so proud.

In the 2015 election, the electorate voted against the limited vision offered by Manning and his protégé Stephen Harper. They had tried to lead Canadians in a different direction, and the majority of Canadians refused to be led. Harper's successor, Liberal leader Justin Trudeau, had campaigned on Canada's enduring potential with the line "In Canada, better is always possible." He emerged with a majority government, including MPs from every province and territory.

When the new prime minister and his cabinet were sworn into office by the governor general, I joined the several thousand people who streamed through the open gates onto the grounds of Rideau Hall. On an unseasonably sunny November day, we watched our new government promenade up the drive. It was like a carefully choreographed Hollywood moment as the youthful leader sauntered forward at the head of a team that was the personification of inclusiveness. This looked much more like the "New Canada" than Manning's definition of this phrase when he was building his party. Half the new ministers were women; top posts had gone to Indigenous Canadians and people from several non-traditional immigrant groups; one of the ministers had arrived here as a refugee from Afghanistan less than twenty years earlier. Next to me, in the crowd of spectators, women in hijabs posed for photos with Trudeau, and cab drivers in turbans held toddlers up to see him. Despite the regional, linguistic, and ethnic tensions, at that moment the country seemed extraordinarily united.

Preston Manning's failure to become prime minister, followed by the Trudeau victory, has not blunted the former Reform leader's evangelical urge to engage the grassroots in the political process. After he retired from federal politics in 2002, Manning turned his attention back to building a new conservative movement from the grassroots up. "Something has got to be done to get the democratic juices running again," he explains. "If you can't change the system, can you raise the calibre of the people in it?" In order to encourage more widespread participation in public life by those who share his views, he founded the Calgary-based Manning Centre, which runs annual conferences for conservatives and offers training courses in political activism. "These are the kinds of reforms that might restore public confidence in the system," he explains.[31] Robin Sears predicts, "His influence will be this last chapter, with his calls for a more principled approach to politics."

Today Preston Manning is busy promoting a conservative response to

Manning founded the Manning Centre for Building Democracy in 2005, and in recognition of his public service was appointed to the Privy Council in 2013.

environmental damage. "The argument I like to make," he explains, "is that core 'conservative' values include 'conservation.' Living within our means is a conservative concept. We should extend the concept to its ecological conclusion—we should live within our environmental means." Such a statement has won him surprising supporters: Margaret Atwood dubbed him "Man of the Future" in the *National Post*.[32] Manning continues to argue that solutions to global warming should be left to market forces rather than federal initiatives. "Why not harness pricing mechanisms to mitigate environmental destruction?" This approach may be far too gradual, given the speed of climate change. But at least Manning is talking about the issue within circles where some prefer to ignore it.

Preston Manning's reputation is not mortgaged to the death of the Reform Party. When he speaks at a university, the lecture hall is full. When he walks through an airport, strangers shake his hand. Mention his name, and Canadians who would never have voted for him will often admit affection for this westerner with a preacher's drawl, and agreement with some of what he writes these days. "He has mellowed in his old age" is a common sentiment. Perhaps. Or perhaps, over the past two decades, the centre of gravity in Canadian politics has shifted toward him.

I asked Manning what he thought of the 2015 election result, as I had asked him his reaction to the result of the election in Alberta earlier in the year. "I wasn't really surprised," he responded, in the now familiar nasal drawl. "You shouldn't read too much into the Conservative Party's defeat. The standard life of a government in this country is nine years: after that, it is always living on borrowed time. And the core Conservative vote held."

And in Canada, regional pressures never disappear. Preston Manning continues to watch and wait. "Justin should enjoy the 'swearing in,'" he tells me, "because, as my dad used to say, the 'swearing at' soon begins!"

CHAPTER 10

Secret Handshake

The Power of Now

Canada is a country that's basically brand new; we haven't had much chance to really establish who we are, what we are. In terms of the American experience, we're where they were in about 1911. Growing up, we always had this strange sensation that we were just one lap dance away from morphing into the US, and it was a very scary feeling.

—Douglas Coupland, interviewed by Hans Ulrich Obrist (2014)

> *Now when you're Third World born but First World formed*
> *Sometimes you feel pride, sometimes you feel torn . . .*

—Shad, "Fam Jam (Fe Sum Immigrins)" (2013)

The Canada that I love is the country that embraced my family when we arrived as refugees, fleeing the merciless regime in Haiti. We had nothing but the belief that we could reinvent ourselves in Canada. . . . What we discovered is a country where people are compassionate and constantly looking for solutions to better their collective destiny. . . . Such is the promise of Canada.

—Her Excellency The Right Honourable Michaëlle Jean (2016)

There is no single story. Canadians have never been a homogeneous people, and Canada has been under construction since its earliest days.

Today's Canada would be unrecognizable to most of the persons I've written about, frustrating to others. Sir George-Étienne Cartier would be astonished to hear, alongside the official languages French and English, over two hundred other languages on our streets.[1] Emily Carr would be awed by the success of Canadian artists (and appalled by the destruction of West Coast rainforests). Tommy Douglas would utter a cheer when he realized how much Canadians appreciate our health care system, despite its faults. And while slow progress on First Nations' demands for their rights would grieve him, Elijah Harper would applaud the confidence of today's Indigenous peoples as they claim their due. The shaky elite-driven Dominion established in 1867 has done more than hold together as the country has matured; political, cultural, and intellectual leaders in successive generations have spurred its transition into a cohesive democracy.

But what about Canadians who are shaping our country today? While it was an interesting challenge to select people from previous generations who contributed to our multi-layered identity, hindsight was my safety net. Most of my subjects have already had their impact (although in some cases it is barely recognized). What potential will be unlocked as we embark on the next 150 years? Thanks to travel and technology, Canada is more connected to the world than ever, and national identities are dissolving almost as fast as national boundaries.

In the nearly four decades that I've lived here, the composition of our population has changed dramatically. When I arrived, most immigrants still came from Europe. Today China, the Philippines, and India send us more people than any other country, and one in four Canadians in our population of thirty-five million speak languages other than English or French.[2] This shift would shock Canadians who grew up in the shadow of the British Empire, saw only faces like their own in their families, schools, and offices, and died before the end of the twentieth century.

Looking ahead, I sense that the demographic churn will be extraordinary. By 2031 almost half the adult population is expected to be foreign-born or have at least one parent born elsewhere, and most residents of big cities will be from visible minorities (Toronto has already raced past that point).[3] Diversity is not just about ethnic and religious differences: other aspects of identity, including gender and sexual orientation, are now part of the conversation. Ask Canadians under thirty-five how they think of themselves, one researcher told me, and their nationality is barely mentioned: they derive their identity from their sense of self rather than the dominant culture.[4] If this is true, what will continue to bind us together? And what does the future promise for Canada?

༺༻

One aspect of this country that has been established (in part by those I've spotlighted) during the past century and a half is a set of values and experiences that most people share, consciously or unconsciously. The writer and artist Douglas Coupland describes our collective sense of being Canadian as "a secret handshake."

I discovered Coupland's definition of Canadian uniqueness within the chaos of the interconnected world in his 2014 show at Toronto's Royal Ontario Museum, *everywhere is anywhere is anything is everything*. The pop culture commentator is a global figure, with shows in several countries, columns in both *VICE* magazine and the London *Financial Times*, and a 2015 residency at the Google Cultural Institute in Paris. However, he continues to call Vancouver home, and he explores his own country with shrewd glee. In his work he suggests that we have compiled and nursed our sense of identity carefully but privately, and that some aspects of it are not particularly pretty.

Coupland draws on his childhood to construct an image of Canada that is deliberately more like a scrapbook than a monument. Growing up during the 1960s and 1970s, he noticed, for example, that his family's backyard

Artist and author Doug Coupland describes being Canadian as "a weird identity."

was almost overshadowed by the mountains and trees that Emily Carr painted. "I remember the suburbs being built, and I clearly remember, and often dream of, the sounds of chainsaws leveling a forest to make space for the middle class homes of my youth," he has written.[5] He updated iconic landscape images created by Carr and the Group of Seven, "as if they might have been painted from today's perspective using contemporary tools," in the words of the curator Daina Augaitis.[6]

Take a look at the 2011 Coupland version of my favourite Carr painting, *Scorned as Timber, Beloved of the Sky*, now reworked into angular blocks of flat colour. The jagged geometry reflects the spiritual power of the terrain that Carr captured a century ago, while implying that this landscape is even more fractured by development these days. Coupland's prismatic renderings of some of Canada's most beloved images link our wilderness past to our technology-driven future. Nostalgia for the pioneer landscape flows parallel to endless curiosity about where technology will lead us; the artist acknowledges that history shapes expectations.

The young Coupland also noticed that, despite the overwhelming influence of the United States, there were stories and products that were unequivocally Canadian. From adolescence, he hoarded provincial number plates, Crown Royal bags, beer cans, Canuck cartridges, stubby beer bottles, macramé hangings, Ookpiks, and postage stamps. In his 2002 book *Souvenir of Canada* and his extraordinary 2003–04 project *Canada House*, he lovingly displayed some of his collection of "all those things that contribute to a sense of who Canadians are as a people," as Augaitis puts it. He continued this theme in the 2014 exhibition *everywhere is anywhere is anything is everything* by constructing a room out of one of our most enduring products, plywood panels. Then he filled it with furniture cobbled artfully together from uniquely Canadian paraphernalia: French-language advertisements for Pepsi-Cola, distressed "Eskimo" paintings, a partially scorched model of the CN Tower.

This is the "secret handshake" section of the exhibition.[7] The furniture and household objects, vibrant with meaning for Canadians, convey our singular history and self-image. Touring the show, I watched visitors pause in front of the *Trans Canada Hutch*, which is a tribute to Terry Fox's 1980 cross-country run, on a prosthetic right leg, to raise funds for cancer research. It includes green highway signs from northern Ontario and a replica of the runner's healthy left leg. It was like a "Spot the Canadians" test: non-Canadian visitors stared blankly at the disconnected limb while the rest of us marvelled at its bulging muscles. The same room contained coded references to some of the uglier passages in our shared past: the violence of Quebec's October Crisis in 1970, the cruelty directed at Indigenous peoples, the desecration of natural resources.

Doug Coupland is best known for work that has universal themes and no particular national references; the writer who invented the viral phrases "Generation X" and "McJobs" is an international art star working in a post-national world. As one of the posters in his installation *Slogans for the 21st Century* reads, "Everyone on Earth Is Feeling the Same Way You Do." But he has not let go of his roots—literally. He created a collection for the clothing firm Roots, with its über-Canadian beaver logo. His "secret handshake" embraces some of our country's competing narratives—the good and the bad—and its condition as an unfinished and perhaps unfinishable project. It is a great metaphor for how we relate to each other. Yet most of us cannot articulate our Canadianness. "Only Canadians care about Canada. It's a weird identity. It's like being the youngest of fifteen children: you don't get as much attention but you do get away with a lot."[8]

Coupland could take his Canadian identity for granted as he developed an international renown. His family had lived in this country for generations and his father was a physician with the Canadian Armed Forces. But what about a first-generation Canadian, who arrived with his parents after Canada opened its immigration doors wider in 1976? What does being Canadian feel like when it is obvious you aren't descended from one of those doughty Fathers of Confederation? What does Canada promise you then?

Shadrach Kabango—or Shad, as the Juno-winning rap artist is known to his fans—is a quintessentially twenty-first-century Canadian. Born in Kenya, where his Rwandan parents were living as refugees at the time, he was eleven months old when he arrived with his family as a landed immigrant in London, Ontario, in 1983. As he puts it in his 2013 rap "Fam Jam (Fe Sum Immigrins)":

> *From donated clothes to caps and gowns*
> *It's a little shout to my black and brown*
> *Folks that know the game, not in class to clown*
> *Had the funny accent, look who's laughing now.*[9]

In the YouTube video of the song, Shad wears the standard rapper uniform of T-shirt, hoodie, and back-to-front baseball cap, and protest songs figure large on his albums. But he doesn't reflect the raw anger of much American rap. His lyrics are studded with Canadian references (First Nations rights, colonialism, Quebec separatism, immigration policy), but the tone is more humorous, and the Maple Leaf flag is painted on a bare brick wall behind him.

Several decades ago writers like Alice Munro and Margaret Atwood

Musician Shadrach Kabango finds that Canadians can be too guarded.

confirmed Canada on the page. Today it is musicians who give the country its own beat. Music festivals rock Canada from coast to coast; anybody under forty looks naked without earbuds or headphones. And Shad has more than his music with which to explore Canadian identity. Since mid-2015, he has hosted CBC Radio's cultural affairs show *q*, which has a total of three million listeners in Canada and the United States for its broadcasts and podcasts. When Shad got the job, he told the *Toronto Star*, "My mission in music has always been to make a unique and positive contribution to culture and to people's lives. This is an exciting opportunity to pursue that same mission in a new way."[10]

One day, in a control room in the Toronto CBC Broadcast Centre, I sat next to the *q* producers and watched Shad chatting with his guests. Sporting a cap bearing the logo of a Montreal skateboard company, DIME, he interviewed Kanwer Singh (a spoken-word artist known as Humble the Poet), a Dutch municipal politician, and the Winnipeg Métis writer Katherena Vermette. Most at ease when talking about music, he treated everyone with the same respectful, curious, and confident manner. That's his personality—but it is also almost a parody of the Canadian archetype.

Like everybody else I've written about, Shad owes much to his background: family and education are key to his quiet self-assurance. Like most immigrants, Shad's Rwandan parents wanted their children to benefit from the stability and opportunities that Canada offered and that they themselves had never known back home. Although people of African descent have always represented a small fraction of the Canadian population, they have included some gifted artists. The poet and playwright George Elliott Clarke comes from the well-established black community in Nova Scotia. The novelist Lawrence Hill has written extensively about the black experience, past and present, in bestsellers like *The Book of Negroes* and *Black Berry Sweet Juice*, a memoir about growing up black in Canada.

Unlike Scottish immigrants such as Bertha Wilson (who found herself celebrating Robbie Burns Night in the Ottawa Valley), the Kabangos did not slip effortlessly into an émigré or African-Canadian network. When Shad's older sister, Charity, was first enrolled in a London public school, she recalls, "I was the only black there: Shad joined me three years later, but we still represented the school's entire cultural diversity." She often felt out of place in the French-speaking Catholic school that her parents (both English-speaking Protestants) chose for their children: "People wanted to touch our hair."

Shad recognizes that the transition was not easy for his parents, but he says, "I had a good time in school." Being smart helped. So did his equable temperament. Charity was more aware of discrimination: "Once everybody in Shad's class who got an A for a project got a sticker—except him. My mum remembers that . . . but he doesn't. He shrugs stuff off." Shad's father founded the African Association of London and organized community talent shows and Christmas parties, to tie together the various African families scattered across pale-skinned London. Soon Charity and Shad had more aunties and uncles than anybody else in their school. Soon, too, a new wave of Africans arrived, including more families from Rwanda. Canada was changing fast, opening up space for immigrants from Africa and Asia.

Shad appeared to be following the classic model: a child of immigrants achieving the educational success for which his parents had hoped. He studied business administration at Wilfrid Laurier University and then took a graduate degree in liberal studies at Simon Fraser University. But he changed direction after noticing that "hip-hop was where I saw people who looked like me doing something proud, positive, and political." He liked the immediacy of rap, and the way it could be funny and serious and rooted in his own experience. "I found a voice." By 2013 he had released four albums, the latest of which is *Flying Colours.* It doesn't bother him that hip-hop began among disaffected black dropouts in American ghettos—a very different place than the one he comes from. "My feeling is always—if I can just make music, I'll be happy." But Shad's music is much more than that: this is not a perfect place, his songs make clear, and we can do something about it. There is a moral edge to his message. So Canadian.

I first heard of Shad when he appeared on CBC Radio's *Canada Reads* programs in 2012. He was championing Carmen Aguirre's *Something Fierce,* a memoir of resistance to the Chilean military dictatorship in the 1980s. The contrast between Aguirre's passion and the cerebral, cool style of her champion was striking. Who *is* this well-spoken, thoughtful musician, I wondered, as I heard him deftly dispose of the arguments of Aguirre's critics. Another of the *Canada Reads* panellists insisted Aguirre was "a bloody terrorist." Shad jumped straight in: "If you consider her a terrorist, you have to consider Nelson Mandela a terrorist." The audience loved it.

I'm not sure what my mental image of a rap star was, but it certainly wasn't somebody who sounded like he could deliver a TED Talk.

Although he rarely listened to CBC Radio as a child, Shad is steeped in the importance of our public broadcaster as a forum for coast-to-coast discussions. "Our country's borders may be secure," he reflects, "but there's not so much internal cohesion. This is a fragmented, polarized society divided between urban and rural, clashing points of view, different regions. The Internet locks us into individual Facebook feeds. At its best, Q can provide a broader, open conversation where everybody's at the table." Shad shrugs off negative feedback because he's proud, for himself and the CBC, that "people *care.*"

Shad's parents have returned to Rwanda, so they can contribute to its rebirth after the horrors of the tribal massacre that took place there in 1994. Shad frequently visits them: "Canada is my country, but Rwanda gives me a larger world view and a connection with my roots." The dual nationality "makes me appreciate Canada even more." There is much to appreciate here: democracy, long lifespans, relatively low crime levels, high educational levels, and (despite the growing gulf between rich and poor) a deep commitment to equality. Our three oceans have largely insulated Canadians from the overcrowded cities, murderous conflicts, and searing poverty that characterize much of the rest of the world.

But, as Shad points out, our comfortable lives can make us smug. "We are not a perfect country," he observes. "Sometimes we take pride in our great ideals but we don't progress them. Our treatment of First Nations doesn't match the ideals, so we sweep the issue under the rug. Tolerance as a goal made sense twenty or thirty years ago, but today we need something closer to equality." Shad also thinks that aspects of our self-image are delusional. "We're proud of being polite and not offending you, but we're guarded. When I go to Texas, the people there are way more friendly, more outgoing, more generous."

So how would Shad describe the country we live in today, I ask him. There is a long pause, then he grins: "Still an exciting experiment." Along with many immigrants from less settled countries, he still believes the promise that in Canada, the best is yet to come.

꘎

In the last century and a half, Canada has grown into its nationhood. Yet Canadian nationalism rarely erupts, and many of us resist overt displays of national pride. Canada Day is a big deal on Ottawa's Parliament Hill, where an all-Canadian music show draws the crowds and the cameras, but elsewhere? Not so much. Recently attendance at Remembrance Day ceremonies in the capital and other communities has grown more dramatically, but perhaps this is related to the rising number of Canadian soldiers killed in ongoing conflicts in Afghanistan and elsewhere. We were an undemonstrative people even before the population became so diverse and polyglot.

These days, glued to our smartphones, we connect digitally if we connect at all. National organizations and charismatic leaders are less important than the invisible bonds of the Internet and social media. And from time to time, the celebrated Canadian reticence can look like apathy.

Shortly after his election, Prime Minister Justin Trudeau made a virtue of this diffidence in an interview with the *New York Times*. He suggested that Canada is "the first postnational state" and offered a catalogue of shared values: "openness, respect, compassion, willingness to work hard, to be there for each other, to search for equality and justice." He insisted, "There is no core identity, no mainstream in Canada."[11]

There is a downside to the fluidity of this idea, one identified by those who, in the past, have felt intense surges of attachment to place and people, and who regret the loss of such community spirit among today's youth.

Emotional links can bond fellow citizens. Within this country's multi-ethnic sprawl, such links are most evident at a sub-national level through a shared loyalty to region, for example, or common ancestry. The most dramatic example while I've lived here has been Quebec's sovereignty movement. During various national unity crises, I've been stirred by the

In 2015 Prime Minister Justin Trudeau told the *New York Times*, "There is no mainstream in Canada."

fervour of demonstrations held on Saint-Jean-Baptiste Day, Quebec's Fête Nationale, celebrated each June 24. Lise Bissonnette, the distinguished Montreal journalist and author, was one of the most articulate advocates for the *indépendantiste* movement in these years. At *Le Devoir*, the small but prestigious Montreal-based newspaper, she spent much of her career in the middle of debates on the future of both Quebec and Canada.

Bissonnette's columns and editorials were always cool and logical, but they fed the passion for independence that galvanized Quebecers. Her pen, commented Graham Fraser, at the time a *Globe and Mail* reporter, "could peel a peach at a stroke."[12] Quebec's nationalists read her with enthusiasm. She stirred their blood. Her argument was straightforward—and a total contradiction of George-Étienne Cartier's position in 1867. Only independence from the rest of Canada, she maintained, could protect Quebec's homogeneity and unique culture and allow it to achieve its full potential. It was ridiculous for the province to remain a linguistic minority, subject to an English-speaking majority. As the newspaper's editor-in-chief in 1992, in response to the Charlottetown Accord, she had published a one-syllable editorial: "NON."

In 1995 Quebec's demand for far more control of its future triggered a

Journalist Lise Bissonnette distrusts talk of "Canadian values."

rare example of Canadians on both sides of the debate at fever pitch: the reticence, apathy, diffidence—call it what you will—was temporarily shattered. A separatist government in Quebec City launched a second referendum on the issue of independence. *Le Devoir* was the only newspaper in Canada to openly urge the citizens of the province to vote for independence in the forthcoming referendum. As Canada appeared to be on the brink of breaking up, the passion of the *indépendantistes*—and the prospect of a separatist victory—triggered an unprecedented reaction in the rest of the country. At Montreal's Place du Canada, a hundred thousand Canadians from within and outside Quebec rallied to celebrate a united Canada and to plead with Quebecers to vote no in the referendum. It was the biggest political demonstration ever held in Canada, and the most emotional. Three days later, in the referendum vote, the separatists were defeated by less than 1 percent. While independence supporters within the province wept at their loss, the narrowness of the margin shocked Canadians elsewhere who were used to taking their country for granted.

Today the passion of that fight has dissipated. Although the 1982 Constitution Act still lacks Quebec's signature, the majority of Quebecers show little interest in issues of sovereignty. Cartier's vision prevails. In Bissonnette's view, the Canadian federal system "will never be renovated. We are condemned to the status quo."

Looking back on her years as a crusading journalist, Bissonnette, now aged seventy, explains: "I was never hostile to Canada itself, or Canadians. But I never felt a sense of belonging: I was indifferent." From journalism, Bissonnette moved on to a significant cultural initiative to preserve her province's distinct cultural history: the creation of the Bibliothèque et Archives Nationales du Québec, an institution that collects and promotes Quebec's archival and literary heritage and makes it accessible to everyone. She retired from the position of chief executive in 2009 but has continued to be involved with cultural and artistic organizations within and outside Quebec. As chair of the board of the Université du Québec à Montréal, known as UQAM, she observes the current generation of Quebec students.

Today's students belong to the Facebook generation, and according to

Bissonnette, there are different preoccupations: feminism, Indigenous rights, the environment. "These are the fashionable issues right now. Nobody is interested in questions of Canadian identity." She still doesn't sense much cohesion to Canada: UQAM students, she notices, are more likely to choose American universities for graduate studies rather than schools in the rest of Canada. The kind of claim that Justin Trudeau makes, about particular values binding together today's Canadians, elicits exasperation. "I'm allergic to talk of 'values,' and there is no agreement on anything beyond democracy and human rights—the values of every developed country. I'm not a romantic about the past. I just live here."[13] The absence of sentimental bonds among Canadians is just a fact of national life.

⌁

Perhaps the laxity of community bonds is irrelevant in the twenty-first century. But it is not just the unity of our country that, after 150 years, we have learned to take for granted. From dirt-poor beginnings, this country has coasted toward an enviable prosperity. Yet we are starting to wonder whether we can maintain our standard of living in the years ahead.

Of the various people I've written about here, only Harold Innis, Tommy Douglas, and Preston Manning thought or wrote much about the Canadian economy. From fur to logs, from rocks to oil and gas, our country's wealth of primary resources provided the backbone of prosperity through most of the twentieth century. Railways, shipping lines, manufacturing, and agricultural machinery provided employment and growth in the early years of the Dominion, and as education levels rose, more sophisticated industries took off. With the grim exception of the 1930s Depression, the twentieth century was not unkind to Canada as it developed its economy under the umbrella first of its British links and then of its proximity to American markets. Perhaps it was the Scottish traditions of caution and financial rectitude that led Canadian banks and insurance companies to be particularly successful.

But the country has never vibrated with entrepreneurial energy. Since 1867 Canadian business people have relied heavily on government to invest in industrial enterprises and (until recently) protect our markets. With some striking exceptions, such as Quebec's Bombardier, this country has produced few entrepreneurs and innovators. Those who yearned for the adrenalin rush of daring deal-making often gravitated to London, New York, or Hong Kong.

Until recently, Canadian politicians boasted that we had one of the most successful economies in the world. But as the value of resources (particularly oil) has tumbled and new economic giants such as China and India have emerged on the other side of the globe, the yo-yoing Canadian dollar underlines the unpredictability of the future. Roger Martin, former dean of the Rotman School of Management at the University of Toronto, observes, "In 1904, Sir Wilfred Laurier predicted that the twentieth century would belong to Canada. He was wrong. It turned out that the twentieth century belonged to very large, highly homogeneous countries that had big internal markets: the United States, Japan, and Germany." Canada, a small market in an expanding global economy, looks increasingly vulnerable in the maelstrom of social, fiscal, environmental, and democratic challenges ahead.

The danger, suggests the business leader Annette Verschuren, is complacency. Verschuren is the kind of risk-taking go-getter, working with developing technologies, whom the rest of us will depend on to secure Canada's future economic health. Her story is another typical New World parable: the daughter of Dutch immigrants who arrived here in 1951 and began farming on Cape Breton's rocky landscape, she has grasped Canada's potential with both hands. The fifty-nine-year-old graduate of St. Francis Xavier University in Nova Scotia started her career in that province's mining industry, but ambition and hard work have propelled her far beyond coal. During fifteen years at the helm of the Canadian subsidiary of Home Depot, the multinational home improvement giant based in Atlanta, Verschuren grew the company tenfold, from 19 stores and $600 million in revenues to 179 stores and $6 billion in revenues. Today she could be running an American-based multinational company, had she chosen that path. However, instead of ascending to a top job in American retail, Verschuren opted to remain in Ontario and secure financing for a

Business innovator Annette Verschuren
thinks "we've got to work harder."

risky start-up in a new tech field. Her company, NRStor, is developing
innovative ways to store energy, particularly from renewable sources like
solar and wind.

Verschuren remained in Canada, she says, because "I just feel this is my
country." She appreciates the social justice for which Bertha Wilson fought
and the health care system that Tommy Douglas championed; she is uncomfortable with America's gun culture, acrimonious politics, and deep
inequities. But her compatriots' Canadian restraint irks her. "The world is
very competitive, and if you think you're going to get it on a platter, wake
up. In most of my career, I've never just got a job—I've had to find it."[14] Like
Shad, she sees the gap between Canadian self-satisfaction and the reality
around us. "We're not competitive. We have to work with our Indigenous
peoples and truly listen to them and let them lead in their success. We need
to ensure our health care system is sustainable and climate change is seriously addressed. . . . We're losing ground. We've got to do more. We've got
to work harder."

Roger Martin remains sanguine about Canada's potential in the years
to come, as long as productivity rates improve. "Thanks to open trade and

relative peace, a small country with a highly educated population and an ethnically and culturally diverse workforce is better positioned to prosper."

It will be up to people like Verschuren to secure that prosperity.

♦⌒♦

Looking ahead, there are so many uncertainties . . . Can Canadians continue to absorb people from so many different cultures? Can the country's economy continue the shift from primary resources to the knowledge economy? Will we be able to improve our productivity and maintain the social safety net? Each generation reimagines the country in different ways and adds a layer of identity, but there is no guarantee that this country is sufficiently robust to surmount the challenges ahead.

For example, the 2015 election demonstrated that racial prejudices once openly expressed still lie close to the surface. The Conservatives had campaigned on national security, insisting that jihadism was a dangerous threat to Canada. They introduced legislation that allowed Ottawa to revoke the citizenship of Canadians with dual nationality who are convicted of terrorist offences—which made Canadians born elsewhere into second-class citizens. Cabinet members argued that Muslim women should not be allowed to wear a niqab during citizenship ceremonies or as employees in the federal public service. These statements ignited a ferocious debate on the limits of religious tolerance, and several incidents of anti-Muslim hostility. If the terrorist attacks in Paris or San Bernardino, California, had erupted immediately before voting day instead of a few weeks later, the election result might have been very different. In the age of terrorism, pluralism may have brittle bones.

But there are now articulate champions for the inclusiveness that has become a Canadian ideal. One person who spoke out against politicizing religious differences was Calgary mayor Naheed Nenshi. "This is disgusting," he told journalists. "It is playing with fire." Nenshi, a Harvard-educated Ismaili Muslim whose parents had fled to Canada from Tanzania, appealed to Canadians to defend pluralism "from voices that seek to divide us."

Nenshi, like Shad, is a product of public institutions that welcomed him

Calgary mayor Naheed Nenshi champions Canadian pluralism.

into the mainstream. "I was nurtured by a community that cared about me," Nenshi explains. As a youngster in Marlborough, a blue-collar immigrant neighbourhood in northeast Calgary, he watched his immigrant parents struggle to raise their family on very limited means. Nevertheless, thanks to publicly funded schools, libraries, and health care, not to mention civic amenities such as public swimming pools and public transport, Nenshi flourished. His teachers recognized the potential of this gregarious, quick-witted boy and sent him to the city's school for gifted students: the prestigious Queen Elizabeth High School. From there he would go on to study at the University of Calgary. Without public investment in his success, he might never have achieved this trajectory.

In the late 1990s Naheed Nenshi attended Harvard's prestigious John F. Kennedy School of Government. Most of the Canadians who studied alongside him at Harvard never returned to Canada. Instead, they disappeared into well-paid jobs elsewhere; Nenshi himself was courted by the Disney company. But he walked away from the sunlit patio in Los Angeles where he had met the Disney executives, knowing he wouldn't take a job there. "I know this sounds incredibly cheesy," he remarks. "But I couldn't do it. I have it so deeply in my bones that I'm a Canadian that I feel obliged to work for this country. Canada has given me so much."

Since then, Nenshi has been elected twice to run Canada's fourth-largest city. His administration is characterized by his own commitment to the collectivist model for society that drove Tommy Douglas's campaign for a health care program. Volunteerism is a priority, in order to foster neighbourliness.

His public message is always that Canadians' belief in community welfare cannot be taken for granted, and Canadian social programs will continue only as long as the economy can support them. He doesn't hesitate to acknowledge the less savoury episodes in our past: "We are the nation of Japanese internment camps, residential schools, Chinese head taxes." But our future will be secured by our commitment to the common good. "This country is not about carbon atoms in the ground or the maple sap in the trees. Its core strength is that we have figured out that our neighbour's

Private sponsors, non-governmental organizations, churches, and governments joined together to welcome Syrian refugees, fleeing the violent turmoil back home. By March 1, 2016, 25,000 refugees had arrived.

strength is our strength—that the success of any one of us is the success of every one of us. When Canada works, it works better than anywhere."

✢

Being an immigrant makes a difference. An immigrant, as Bertha Wilson observed, is always strung between two worlds—the one she left, and the one she now lives in. For every immigrant, "home" continues for years to denote the land left behind. When I came to live in Ottawa, I knew embarrassingly little about this country, so I had to start from scratch. One old friend particularly enjoys reminding me that, while writing an article for a British magazine on a 1980 political rally in the Montreal Forum, I phoned him to ask what game was played there.

I began my immersion in Canada through writing about its federal politics: this was the only Ottawa subject in which Toronto editors had much interest. I wrote articles about government policies, cabinet ministers, scandals, and the capital's social life. In the 1980s and 1990s there was lots of action: elections, constitutional crises, furious rows about resources and power. But the more I wrote, the more I realized how little I understood about the country I was describing. When writing profiles of senior officials and ministers, I was often more absorbed by family backstories than by the newest proposals for developing oil fields or modernizing health care. My notebooks filled with details about the extraordinary range of people in Canada's public life: the Mennonite whose parents had fled Russian pogroms in the 1920s and settled on the prairies; the daughter of Canadian missionaries who had lived in China until she was sent back to Canada to attend high school; the Quebecer from a large rural family who became the first in his family to attend university or speak English. Had I remained in England, I would never have encountered such diversity.

After fifteen years of political reporting, I switched to history so I might better understand how this untidy, sprawling country had unobtrusively evolved its political and cultural identity. I discovered that Canadian history is littered with visionaries and eccentrics, dynamos and dreamers. There were so many questions—usually questions that nobody raised here would bother to ask. Some were trivial, such as "Why so many doughnut shops?" (Doughnuts are a great Canadian tradition that predates Tim Hortons. All the essential ingredients, including lard, flour, and maple sugar, could be produced on a pioneer farm.) Other questions were more disturbing. Why had previous generations callously mistreated Indigenous peoples while allowing newcomers to reinvent themselves? (The nineteenth-century pseudoscience of racism had played into the colonists' land grab.)

Sometimes particular artifacts drilled down through the layers of history, creating a personal link for me with this country. There was the little box I noticed in Library and Archives Canada in which lay a lock of hair, a few auburn strands glinting in the thick white curl. It was a relic of Susanna Moodie, the young English writer who arrived here in 1832 and developed skills and a resilience she would never have acquired in England. In the Museum of Vancouver a few years later, I admired the buckskin outfit constructed by the performance artist Pauline Johnson (who also called herself by her Mohawk name, Tekahionwake) in the late nineteenth century. She wore this costume for her coast-to-coast performances of fierce ballads and lyric verse. The sweat marks on the sleeves hinted at how hard she had worked to transmit to skeptical audiences her own love of nature and respect for her Indigenous forebears.

Other times it was physical surroundings that impressed upon me this country's sturdy continuity during a century and a half of dramatic growth and change. When I was writing about a sensational court case heard in Toronto in 1915, I meandered through the streets of today's affluent metropolis. In the shadows of the glittering high-rises I found solid brick homes and public buildings that participants in my book *The Massey Murder* would have recognized. Back in Ottawa, I bicycled over to the house (now a museum) where Prime Minister Mackenzie King lived for twenty-seven years. While telling the story of his strange relationship with his mother, Isabel Mackenzie King, I could visit the room in which he conducted his séances. The tug of history is very strong when you find yourself within the setting.

Almost unconsciously, I developed a sense of belonging to this country. My British identity shrank as my Canadian connections grew. I started to understand how for 150 years our leaders have worked around the country's contradictions and limitations: intense regionalisms across a cold and underpopulated landscape; the cultural influence of first the British Empire, then the United States; tension between the fiction of a linear national narrative and the bilingual, multicultural reality. Cartier, Steele, Carr, Innis, Douglas, Atwood, Wilson, Harper, Manning, and so many others—they knitted the country together despite the obstacles and ensured that this country kept abreast of a changing world.

Canada may not have the global swagger of larger, older countries, but we have what many envy: a society that is progressive and confident, tolerant and open to the world. There are cracks in this picture: a dollop of smugness, a tendency to complacency, a denial of endemic racism. Nevertheless, Canada is unique. Those I met who are shaping tomorrow's Canada exhibit the same optimism, adaptability, and pragmatism that shaped the Canada we know today.

Canadians remain low-key people who when asked "How are things?" are likely to respond, "Not too bad, all things considered." Understatement is our forte. Opportunities for Canadians to do that very un-Canadian thing and flaunt our patriotism remain few. Sport is one—particularly hockey, which has been almost a religion in this country for over a century. Although Lise Bissonnette professes no attachment herself to Canadian symbols, she was interested to observe the behaviour of young Quebecers at the 2006 Winter Olympic Games in Turin. "That's where I met young Quebecers who wore the maple leaf on their sleeves, and who *felt* they were Canadians." Similarly, as I mentioned at the start of this book, the response to Shane Koyczan's poem at the 2010 Olympics proved that the multilingual population of one of the world's coldest countries can roar with one voice on occasion.

Today's Canada cultivates images and customs unrelated to stalwart Mounties, maple syrup, or snow-capped mountains. I've participated in a few bizarre rituals myself and relished the combination of alcohol, tradition, and yuck factor they involve. In 1982, in Trapper John's bar in St. John's, I swigged a shot of the local rum, stuttered out the obligatory Newfoundland refrain "Long may yer big jib draw!" and kissed a cod. This was my "screech ceremony," which celebrates four centuries of dependence on cod stocks (sadly depleted since then) while allowing me to claim honorary Newfoundlander status. Twenty-six years later, at the other end of the country in the Downtown Hotel in Dawson City, Yukon, I underwent another bonding ritual with past and place. I downed a sourtoe cocktail—the famous whisky cocktail that includes a preserved toe that the drinker must touch with her lips. Local lore suggests that the toe was found preserved in ice and may have dated back to the 1890s Klondike Gold Rush. (Bolder drinkers than me have actually swallowed the toe, but a backup always seems to be available.)

Nobody can undergo such rites, deep-rooted in our collective past, and cling to time-worn stereotypes about our lack of humour or history. But there are other traditions that speak to the future and illustrate Canada's endless ability to adapt to changing realities. Take Mount Royal Park in downtown Montreal on a summer Sunday. This is where hundreds of people from across Canada and beyond—Haitians, Americans, Indonesians, Australians, Chinese, Jamaicans—mingle together for the Tam-Tams weekly festival. Dressed in everything from denim to dashikis, the good-natured crowd drums, picnics, and plays Frisbee, within the province that has guarded its language and autonomy so fiercely.

There is a marvellous aspect to this scene. In the middle of the crowd stands an impressive stone monument, one hundred feet tall and topped by an angel holding a laurel wreath. Few Tam-Tams participants spare a glance at the monument or look at the frock-coated bronze figure standing below the angel. Fewer still would recognize the man's name if they were told it. Yet it is Sir George-Étienne Cartier waiting to be crowned with the laurel wreath—Cartier, the Father of Confederation who ensured that different peoples could live alongside each other in this country. There he is, presiding over a montage of urban Canada in the twenty-first century. Sometimes the secret handshake is with our own history.

TIMELINE

1814: **George-Étienne Cartier** is born in Lower Canada.

1848: **Samuel Benfield Steele** is born in Upper Canada.

1864: Cartier plays a pivotal role at first in the Charlottetown Conference, then in the Quebec Conference, at which the deal that leads to Confederation is hammered out.

1866: Battle of Ridgeway: Irish-American radicals (the Fenians) are defeated on Canadian soil.

1867: The British North America Act is passed in London, and the **Dominion of Canada** is established. Sir John A. Macdonald is sworn in as prime minister.

1869: Canada purchases all the Hudson's Bay Company territory; the Métis, led by Louis Riel, begin the Red River Rebellion.

1870: Métis rights are recognized and Manitoba becomes a province, but Riel is forced to flee.

1871: **Emily Carr** is born in British Columbia, which joins Confederation this year.

1873: Sam Steele joins the newly formed North West Mounted Police, created to keep order in the West.

Prince Edward Island joins Confederation.

George-Étienne Cartier dies in England.

1875: The Supreme Court of Canada is established in Ottawa.

1876: The Toronto Women's Literary Club is founded to advance women's education and is soon campaigning for votes for women.

1877: Ottawa takes over the last big section of prairie land when the local Indigenous people sign Treaty 7.

1879: McGill University students play the first organized hockey game with a flat puck.

1880: Britain transfers the Arctic, which it claims to own, to Canada.

The Canadian Pacific Railway recruits thousands of underpaid Chinese labourers.

1884: International Standard Time, advocated by Sir Sandford Fleming, is adopted.

1885: The Northwest Rebellion ends with the Battle of Batoche. Louis Riel is hanged in Regina.

The CPR is completed when the Last Spike is driven at Craigellachie, British Columbia.

1891:   Sir John A. Macdonald dies in Ottawa.

1893:   Governor General Lord Stanley donates the Stanley Cup as a hockey trophy.

1894:   **Harold Innis** is born in Ontario.

1896:   The Klondike Gold Rush begins when gold is discovered in the Yukon.
        Wilfrid Laurier becomes Canada's first French-Canadian prime minister.

1899:   The first contingent of Canadian volunteers set off to fight alongside the British in the Boer War, Canada's first foreign war. Nearly nine thousand Canadians would see combat in South Africa.

1902:   The first symphony orchestra in Canada is established in Quebec City.

1904:   Early-maturing Marquis wheat, developed by Charles Saunders, turns the prairies into "the breadbasket of the empire."
        Tommy Douglas is born in Scotland.

1905:   Saskatchewan and Alberta join Confederation; sponsored by Ottawa, European immigrants flood west to farm the prairies.

1906:   Roald Amundsen reaches Alaska, after sailing the entire Northwest Passage.

1907:   Tom Longboat from the Six Nations Reserve wins the Boston Marathon.

1908:   Lucy Maud Montgomery publishes *Anne of Green Gables*.

1909:   First manned flight in the British Empire takes place at Baddeck, Nova Scotia, thanks to Alexander Graham Bell.

1910:   The Royal Canadian Navy is formed.

1914:   In Vancouver Harbour, the *Komagata Maru* is refused permission to disembark almost all its 376 East Indian passengers.
        Canada is automatically drawn into conflict with Germany when Britain declares war.

1915:   Battle of Ypres: Canadian forces face a gas attack.
        John McCrae writes "In Flanders Fields."

1916:   Women win the vote in Manitoba, Saskatchewan, and Alberta.
        The National Research Council is established to promote scientific and industrial research.

1917:   Five demonstrators are killed during anti-conscription riots in Quebec City.
        At the Battle of Vimy Ridge, more than ten thousand Canadians are killed or wounded.
        Ottawa introduces income tax as a "temporary" measure.
        The National Hockey League is founded in Montreal.
        Canadians are victorious at the Battle of Passchendaele, but there are more than fifteen thousand casualties.
        The Halifax Explosion kills sixteen hundred people, injures nine thousand, and devastates the city.

1918:   Women win the right to vote in federal elections.
        An armistice to end the First World War goes into effect on November 11.

1919:   **Samuel Benfield Steele** dies in England.
        Winnipeg is brought to a standstill by a general strike.

1920: The Group of Seven holds its first art show in Toronto.

Canada joins the new League of Nations.

1921: Agnes Macphail becomes the first woman to sit in the House of Commons.

1923: Banting, Best, Macleod, and Collip share the Nobel Prize for the discovery of insulin.

Foster Hewitt makes the first hockey broadcast.

Bertha Wrenham Wilson is born in Scotland.

1926: Armand Bombardier of Quebec develops the snowmobile.

1927: The first coast-to-coast radio broadcast celebrates Canada's sixtieth birthday.

An old-age pension of twenty dollars a month is granted to a limited number of Canadians seventy years or older.

Emily Carr's paintings are included in the National Gallery of Canada exhibition of West Coast art.

1929: The British Judicial Committee of the Privy Council declares that women are legally "persons" and therefore eligible to sit in the Senate.

The Great Depression begins.

1930: Harold Innis publishes *The Fur Trade in Canada*.

1931: The Statute of Westminster grants Canada full legislative authority in both domestic and foreign affairs.

1934: The birth of the Dionne quintuplets attracts international attention.

The Bank of Canada is established.

1935: A thousand unemployed men begin the On-to-Ottawa Trek to protest conditions.

1936: The Canadian Broadcasting Corporation is established.

1939: Canada declares war on Germany, one week after Britain does so.

Margaret Atwood is born in Ontario.

1940: Women in Quebec finally win the vote in provincial elections.

1941: The first national unemployment insurance program is established.

After the Japanese capture of Hong Kong, more than five hundred Canadians die in battle or prisoner-of-war camps.

1942: Twenty-two thousand Japanese Canadians are rounded up and interned as security risks in British Columbia.

In the disastrous Dieppe Raid on the coast of France, 907 Canadians are killed and 1,946 captured by German forces.

The Royal Canadian Mounted Police ship *St. Roch* reaches Halifax after the first voyage west to east through the Northwest Passage.

Preston Manning is born in Alberta.

1943: Canadian forces capture Ortona, Italy, a stronghold on the Adriatic coast held by the Germans.

1944: In Saskatchewan, Tommy Douglas's Co-operative Commonwealth Federation forms the first socialist government in North America.

1945: The Second World War ends.

The Family Allowance Act grants all families a monthly sum or "baby bonus" for each child under sixteen.

Canada is a founding member of the United Nations.

Emily Carr dies in British Columbia.

Lise Bissonnette is born in Quebec.

1947: Alberta's oil boom begins with the strike in Leduc.

1948: Figure skater Barbara Ann Scott wins an Olympic gold medal.

1949: Newfoundland (later named Newfoundland and Labrador) joins Canada as the tenth province.

1950–53: During the Korean War, 516 Canadian military personnel are killed and more than 1,200 injured, making it Canada's third-bloodiest overseas conflict.

1951: Ottawa passes the Old Age Security Act, which gives all Canadians aged seventy and over a pension of forty dollars a month.

1952: **Harold Innis** dies in Ontario.

1953: The Stratford Shakespearean Festival opens in Ontario.

1955: Montrealers riot when Maurice "Rocket" Richard, top scorer with the Montreal Canadiens, is suspended.

1957: The Canada Council for the Arts is established to foster Canadian culture.

Lester B. Pearson is awarded the Nobel Peace Prize for his role in resolving the Suez Crisis.

Annette Verschuren is born in Nova Scotia.

1959: The St. Lawrence Seaway, a joint Canada–United States project, opens.

1960: *Refus global* initiates Quebec's Quiet Revolution.

The vote is finally granted to Indigenous peoples.

1961: **Douglas Coupland** is born in Germany.

1962: The new health insurance program in Saskatchewan provokes a doctors' strike.

1965: Canada gets its new Maple Leaf flag.

1966: The federal Medical Care Act provides universal public health care across Canada.

1967: Expo 67 in Montreal celebrates Canada's 100th birthday and attracts more than fifty-five million visitors.

1970: Crisis in Quebec: political kidnappings prompt Ottawa to invoke the War Measures Act and suspend civil rights.

1972: Paul Henderson scores the winning goal for Canada against the Soviet Union in the first Summit Series between the two countries.

Margaret Atwood publishes *Survival: A Thematic Guide to Canadian Literature.*

Naheed Nenshi is born in Ontario.

1976: The pro-independence Parti Québécois, led by René Lévesque, forms the government in Quebec.

1978–80: Canada welcomes over fifty thousand refugees from Vietnam.

1980: Quebecers defeat "sovereignty-association" in a referendum, in favour of a renewal of Confederation.

Prompted by rising oil prices, Ottawa introduces the controversial National Energy Program.

"O Canada" is officially declared the national anthem.

1981: Forced to retire from his cross-Canada Marathon of Hope the previous year, Terry Fox dies of cancer.

1982: The Canadian Constitution comes home, with a new Charter of Rights and Freedoms.

Bertha Wilson is appointed to the Supreme Court.

Shadrach Kabango is born in Kenya.

1984: Marc Garneau becomes the first Canadian in space, aboard the U.S. space shuttle *Challenger*.

1986: **Tommy Douglas** dies in Ontario.

1987: The Meech Lake Accord begins the process of federal and provincial approval.

In Winnipeg, Preston Manning establishes the Reform Party.

1989: Marc Lépine kills fourteen women and injures ten women and four men in a shooting rampage at the École Polytechnique in Montreal.

1990: In Manitoba, Elijah Harper secures defeat of the Meech Lake Accord.

1992: The Charlottetown Accord is rejected in a national referendum.

Roberta Bondar becomes the first Canadian woman in space, aboard the U.S. space shuttle *Discovery*.

1994: The North American Free Trade Agreement links Canada, the United States, and Mexico.

1995: The second Quebec referendum on sovereignty is narrowly defeated.

1999: The new Arctic territory of Nunavut is created; it is the least populous and the largest in area of all provinces and territories. Nunavut means "our land" in Inuktitut, the Inuit language.

2000: Research in Motion, based in Waterloo, Ontario, launches its first BlackBerry smartphone.

2005: Same-sex marriage is legalized throughout Canada.

2007: **Bertha Wilson** dies in Ontario.

2008: In the global economic crisis, Canada's "Big Five" banks remain stable.

2010: Canada sets a record for gold medals at the Vancouver Winter Olympic Games.

The Truth and Reconciliation Commission begins hearings on residential school abuse.

2012: Idle No More marchers protest against mineral exploitation on First Nations land.

2013: **Elijah Harper** dies in Ontario.

Alice Munro wins the Nobel Prize for literature.

2015: The Report of the Truth and Reconciliation Commission is published.

2017: Canada celebrates its 150th birthday.

ACKNOWLEDGEMENTS

This book was an ambitious undertaking, and I am grateful to experts (academic and non-academic) who generously offered advice, read and commented on particular chapters, corrected my facts, argued with my point of view, and suggested additional sources. Many thanks to Dr. Frances Abele, Justice Rosalie Abella, Ellen Anderson, Sara Angel, the Hon. Monique Bégin, Mary Innis Cates, the Right Hon. Joe Clark, PC, Pauline Comeau, Anne Innis Dagg, the Hon. Judy Erola, Dr. Tom Flanagan, Graham Fraser, Dr. Norman Hillmer, Dr. Michael Hogue, André Juneau, Justice Claire L'Heureux-Dubé, Justice James MacPherson, Dr. Roger Martin, Dr. Marc Meyer, Sarah Milroy, Andrea Nemtin, Anita Olsen Harper, Michael Ostroff, Professor Jim Phillips, Peter Raymont, Robin Sears, Jeffrey Simpson, David R. Smith, Dr. David Staines, Justice David Stratas, George Thomson, Aritha van Herk, Christopher Wernham, and Dr. Brian Young.

Some good friends went way beyond the call of duty and read the whole manuscript in various stages of its development: I can never give sufficient thanks to Dr. Sandy Campbell, Dr. Tim Cook, Dr. Rod Macleod, and Dr. Duncan McDowall. Their feedback immeasurably improved the final draft: the mistakes that remain are entirely my own.

I particularly want to thank those who agreed to appear in the book and be interviewed: Margaret Atwood, Preston Manning, Shadrach Kabango, Lise Bissonnette, Annette Verschuren, the Right Honourable Michaëlle Jean, and Mayor Naheed Nenshi. It was great to talk to the smart young staffers at Historica Canada, and to hear who they thought had helped shape Canada. Thank you, President and CEO Anthony Wilson-Smith, for giving me this opportunity.

My friends were sympathetic to my discoveries, frustrations, and confusions, which they heard (too much) about at every get-together. I am grateful to Wendy Bryans, Maureen Boyd, Judith Moses, Cathy Beehan, Patricia Potts, Sheila Williams, and Barbara Uteck.

My husband, George Anderson, is always a source of steady support and good advice, and I am deeply grateful to him for his help. His clear analysis and sharp opinions helped me find my own way. He could not have made my transition from an English emigrant to a Canadian immigrant easier—even if, four decades ago, he never came clean about the depths to which mercury sinks in an Ottawa winter. He has been endlessly supportive during expeditions to Quebec City, the Richelieu River valley, Montreal, Newfoundland, and other research-driven destinations. Alex, Nick, and Oliver Anderson and Frances Middleton provided me with questions, answers, and ideas about my adopted country—often without realizing they were doing so.

I was thrilled to work once again with Phyllis Bruce, the most rigorous and tactful editor any writer could hope to have. (How many editors read manuscripts within hours of the author pressing send?) The Simon & Schuster team was extraordinary, from company president Kevin Hanson to Brendan May (associate editor), Adria Iwasutiak (director of publicity), Ceileigh Mangalam (editorial assistant), Sarah St. Pierre (assistant managing editor), and the superb design team led by Paul Barker. Barbara Czarnecki was the freelance copy editor, dealing patiently with my punctuation and other failings, and Barbara Kamienski was the freelance photo researcher. My agent Hilary McMahon, from WCA, was helpful and encouraging at every stage of the process. I would like to thank Brian Pirie for looking after my website, www.charlottegray.ca.

Finally, I am grateful to the City of Ottawa for financial support. The City's continued support of its writing community demonstrates its commitment to both writers and readers, and to the importance of literature within the nation's capital.

A Note on Terminology

As I've been writing this book, the language around Canada's Indigenous peoples has shifted. Terminology is important: certain words may be loaded with negative implications while others can be empowering. At the same time, Indigenous individuals may describe themselves in ways that it is inappropriate for non-Indigenous people to use. For example, some use the words "native" or "Indian," although those terms have been replaced by "Indigenous" in much government usage. In November 2015, on the advice of senior Indigenous leaders, the federal government renamed Aboriginal Affairs and Northern Development Canada: it is now Indigenous and Northern Affairs Canada. A helpful guide to terminology can be found at http://indigenousfoundations .arts.ubc.ca/home/identity/terminology.html.

NOTES

1. A TAPESTRY OF PEOPLES

1. Alastair Sweeny, "Confederation's True Father? George-Étienne Cartier," *Globe and Mail*, January 3, 2014.
2. John J. Bigsby, *The Shoe and Canoe* (London: Chapman and Hall, 1850), 206–7. Quoted in Alastair Sweeny, *George-Étienne Cartier: A Biography* (Toronto: McClelland & Stewart, 1976), 40.
3. Ibid., 48.
4. J.-C. Bonenfant, "Cartier, Sir George-Étienne," in *Dictionary of Canadian Biography* vol. 10 (Toronto: University of Toronto/Université Laval, 2003–), accessed March 31, 2016, http://www.biographi.ca/en/bio/cartier_george_etienne_10E.html.
5. Christopher Moore, *Three Weeks in Quebec City: The Meeting That Made Canada* (Toronto: Allen Lane, 2015), 31.
6. *Globe*, June 18, 1853, quoted in Sweeny, *George-Étienne Cartier*, 88.
7. Ibid., 104.
8. Ibid., 58.
9. Ibid., 131.
10. Moore, *Three Weeks in Quebec City*, 33.
11. Bonenfant, "Cartier," *Dictionary of Canadian Biography*.
12. Quoted in Brian Young, *George-Étienne Cartier, Montreal Bourgeois* (Kingston and Montreal: McGill-Queen's University Press, 1981), 81.
13. Quoted in Ibid., 30.
14. P. B. Waite, *Macdonald: His Life and World* (Toronto: McGraw-Hill Ryerson, 1975), 51.
15. Young, *George-Étienne Cartier*, 34.
16. *Times* (London), October 24, 1864, quoted in Sweeny, *George-Étienne Cartier*, 151.
17. Ibid., 149.
18. The Quebec Conference is covered in fascinating detail in Moore, *Three Weeks in Quebec City*.
19. J. K. Johnson and P. B. Waite, "Macdonald, Sir John Alexander," in *Dictionary of Canadian Biography*, vol. 12 (Toronto: University of Toronto/Université Laval, 2003–),

accessed March 31, 2016, http://www.biographi.ca/en/bio/macdonald_john
_alexander_12E.html.

20. Sweeny, *George-Étienne Cartier*, 151.
21. *Parliamentary Debates on Confederation of the British North American Provinces* (Quebec: Hunter, Rose & Co., 1865), 60.
22. Richard Gwyn, *John A.: The Man Who Made Us* (Toronto: Random House, 2007), 326.
23. Blair Fraser, *The Search for Identity* (Toronto: Doubleday, 1967), 2.
24. Quoted in Waite, *Macdonald*, 39.
25. Quoted in Richard Gwyn, *Nation Maker: Sir John A. Macdonald: His Life, Our Times* (Toronto: Random House, 2011), 3.
26. W. L. Morton, ed., *Manitoba: The Birth of a Province* (Winnipeg: Manitoba Record Society, 1965), 95, quoted in Sweeny, *George-Étienne Cartier*, 212.
27. Lena Newman, *The John A. Macdonald Album* (Montreal: Tundra Books, 1974), 89.
28. Sweeny, *George-Étienne Cartier*, 225.
29. Bonenfant, "Cartier," *Dictionary of Canadian Biography*.
30. Ibid.
31. Sweeny, *George-Étienne Cartier*, 172.
32. Ibid., 320.

2. MOUNTIE MYTHOLOGY

1. Estimates of the Indigenous population are sheer guesswork. Census numbers for non-Indigenous populations are available online from *Statistics Canada* under "Censuses of Canada 1665 to 1871," http://www.statcan.gc.ca/pub/98-187-x/4151287 -eng.htm.
2. Richard Gwyn, *John A.*, 400–404.
3. Wallace Stegner, *Wolf Willow: A History, a Story, and a Memory of the Last Plains Frontier* (New York: Viking, 1955), 100–110.
4. R. C. Macleod, *Samuel Benfield Steele* (Edmonton: University of Alberta Press, forthcoming), chap. 2, p. 8.
5. Ibid., chap. 3, p. 1.
6. Quoted in Robert Stewart, *Sam Steele, Lion of the Frontier*, 2nd ed. (Regina: Centax Books, PrintWest Group, 1999), 40.
7. Samuel Benfield Steele, *Forty Years in Canada* (1915; repr., Toronto: Prospero Books, 2000), 41.
8. Macleod, *Samuel Benfield Steele*, chap. 3, p. 2.
9. Stewart, *Sam Steele*, 41.
10. Steele, *Forty Years in Canada*, 67.
11. Quoted in Macleod, *Samuel Benfield Steele*, chap. 3, p. 4.
12. See E. C. Morgan, "The North West Mounted Police: Internal Problems and Public Criticism, 1874–1883," *Saskatchewan History* 26 (Winter 1974): 41–62.
13. Stewart, *Sam Steele*, 171.

14. Ibid., 196.

15. Stewart, *Sam Steele*, 199.

16. Benedict R. O'G. Anderson, *Imagined Communities: Reflections on the Origin and Spread of Nationalism*, 3rd ed. (London: Verso, 2006), 6.

17. Quoted in R. C. Macleod, *The North West Mounted Police and Law Enforcement 1873–1905* (Toronto: University of Toronto Press, 1976), 164–65.

18. Ibid., 167.

19. Stewart, *Sam Steele*, 200.

20. Ibid., 200–201.

21. Ibid., 216.

22. Roderick Charles Macleod, "Steele, Sir Samuel Benfield," in *Dictionary of Canadian Biography*, vol. 14 (Toronto: University of Toronto/Université Laval, 2003–), accessed April 25, 2014, http://www.biographi.ca/en/bio/steele_samuel_benfield_14E.html.

23. Steele Collection, University of Edmonton, Box 25, SS to MS, September 9, 1898.

24. Ibid., Box 23, SS to MS, September 14, 1898.

25. Ibid., Box 24, SS to MS, February 16, 1899.

26. Ibid., Box 23, SS to MS, May 6, 1898.

27. Ibid., SS to MS, Box 23, January 1, 1899.

28. *McClure's Magazine*, May–October 1899, 225–35.

29. Christopher Reed, "Colonel Sam Steele in the Yukon," *Scarlet and Gold* 3 (1921): 23.

30. Michael Dawson, *The Mountie: From Dime Novel to Disney* (Toronto: Between the Lines, 1998), 35–53.

31. Chicago: Reilly & Britton, 1906. Baum published this book under the pen name Captain Hugh Fitzgerald. He later changed the title to *The Boy Fortune Hunters in Alaska* and republished it under the pen name Floyd Akers.

32. Pierre Berton, *Hollywood's Canada: The Americanization of Our National Image* (Toronto: McClelland & Stewart, 1975), 111.

33. A. L. Haydon, *The Riders of the Plains* (London: Andrew Melrose, 1910) vii, 2.

34. New York and London: Century Co., 1927.

35. Steele Collection, University of Edmonton, Steele Personnel File, T. Morris Longstreth to Harwood Steele, December 11, 1927.

36. Library and Archives Canada (LAC), North West Mounted Police Personnel Records, S. B. Steele file. Harwood also complained to the RCMP commissioner and copies of all the correspondence with Longstreth ended up in their records. Harwood Steele to Commissioner Cortlandt Starnes, October 28, 1927.

37. R. C. Macleod, "An Old Soldier Fades Away: Major-General Sir Sam Steele in the First World War," in Adriana A. Davies and Jeff Keshen, eds., *The Frontier of Patriotism: Alberta and the First World War* (Calgary: University of Calgary Press, 2016), in press.

38. Dawson, *The Mountie*, 18.

3. Looking Inward, Looking Outward

1. J. M. Bumsted, *A History of the Canadian Peoples* (Toronto: Oxford University Press, 2003), 274.
2. Eric Newton, "Canadian Art through English Eyes," *Canadian Forum* 18 (February 1939): 344–55.
3. Michael Ostroff, *Winds of Heaven: Emily Carr, Carvers & The Spirits of the Forest* (Toronto: White Pine Pictures, 2011).
4. Emily Carr, "Beginnings," *The Book of Small* (1942; Project Gutenberg, 2004), http://gutenberg.net.au/ebooks04/0400201.txt.
5. Ian Dejardin, "A Life of Emily Carr," in *From the Forest to the Sea: Emily Carr in British Columbia* (Fredericton: Goose Lane Editions, 2014), 23.
6. Carr, "Silence and Pioneers," *The Book of Small.*
7. Ibid., "Schools."
8. Paula Blanchard, *The Life of Emily Carr* (Vancouver: Douglas & McIntyre, 1987), 48.
9. Emily Carr, *Growing Pains: The Autobiography of Emily Carr* (Toronto: Clarke, Irwin, Toronto, 1966), 15.
10. Blanchard, *The Life of Emily Carr*, 12.
11. Quoted from *Growing Pains* ms., quoted in Blanchard, 81.
12. Carr, *Growing Pains*, 176.
13. Ibid., 139.
14. Maria Tippett, *Emily Carr: A Biography* (Toronto: Oxford Unviersity Press, 1979), 14.
15. Arnold Watson, "In the Haunts of a Picture Maker," *Week* (Victoria), February 18, 1905.
16. Blanchard, *The Life of Emily Carr*, 103.
17. Carr, *Growing Pains*, 211.
18. *Province* (Vancouver), June 26, 1909.
19. Carr, *Growing Pains*, 215.
20. Doris Shadbolt, *Emily Carr* (Vancouver: Douglas & McIntyre, 1990), 37.
21. Carr, *Growing Pains*, 216.
22. Shadbolt, *Emily Carr*, 35.
23. Lawren Harris, "The Group of Seven in Canadian History," *The Canadian Historical Association: Report of the Annual General Meeting Held at Victoria and Vancouver, June 16–19, 1948* (Toronto: University of Toronto Press, 1948), 31, quoted in Ross Howard, *Defiant Spirits: The Modernist Revolution of the Group of Seven* (Vancouver: Douglas & McIntyre, 2010), 26.
24. Lawren Harris, "The Story of the Group of Seven," in *The Best of the Group of Seven*, ed. Joan Murray (Edmonton: Hurtig Publishers, 1984), 27.
25. *Toronto Daily Star*, April 12, 1913.
26. *Toronto Daily Star*, December 12, 1913, quoted in Howard, *Defiant Spirits*, 107.
27. Ibid., 108.
28. Ibid., 332.

29. Harold Town and David Silcox, *Tom Thomson: The Silence and the Storm* (Toronto: McClelland & Stewart, 1977), 21.

30. Daniel Francis, *National Dreams: Myth, Memory, and Canadian History* (Vancouver: Arsenal Pulp Press, 1997), 141.

31. Emily Carr lecture notes, quoted in Doris Shadbolt, *The Art of Emily Carr* (Vancouver: Douglas & McIntyre, 1979), 38.

32. Carr, *Growing Pains*, 227.

33. Shadbolt, *The Art of Emily Carr*, 42.

34. *Growing Pains* ms., quoted in Blanchard, 142.

35. *Growing Pains* ms., quoted in Blanchard, 178.

36. Shadbolt, *The Art of Emily Carr*, 42.

37. Ibid., 137.

38. Harris to Carr, undated (probably late 1929), quoted in Shadbolt, *Emily Carr*, 135.

39. Emily Carr, *Hundreds and Thousands: The Journals of Emily Carr* (Vancouver: Douglas & McIntyre, 2006), 185.

40. Ibid., 126.

41. Newton, "Canadian Art through English Eyes," 345.

42. Quoted in Tippett, *Emily Carr*, 240.

43. Shadbolt, *The Life of Emily Carr*, 216.

44. Carr, *Hundreds and Thousands*, 101.

45. Marcia Crosby, "Construction of the Imaginary Indian," *Vancouver Anthology: The Institutional Politics of Art*, ed. Stan Douglas (Vancouver: Talonbooks, 1991), quoted in *Beyond Wilderness: The Group of Seven, Canadian Identity, and Contemporary Art*, eds. John O'Brian and Peter White (Montreal and Kingston: McGill-Queen's University Press, 2007), 220–22.

46. See Gerta Moray, "Emily Carr and the Traffic in Native Images," *Anti-modernism and the Traffic in Native Images*, ed. Lynda Jessup (Toronto: University of Toronto Press, 2001).

47. Laura Cummings, *Observer*, November 2, 2014.

4. BEAVER TALES

1. Quoted in Margaret MacMillan, *The War That Ended Peace* (Toronto: Allen Lane, 2013), 124.

2. Quoted in J. M. Bumsted, *A History of the Canadian Peoples*, 283.

3. Ibid., 280.

4. Ibid., 281.

5. Robert Borden, *Robert Laird Borden: His Memoirs* (Montreal and Kingston: McGill-Queen's University Press, 1969), 216.

6. Innis papers, University of Toronto Archives, B1972.0003 Series 17/003 (003).

7. Lithograph NAC C-147822, Library and Archives Canada.

8. Anne Innis Dagg, "Memoir of Harold Adams Innis," *Canadian Journal of Communication* 29.2 (2004), http://www.cjc-online.ca/index.php/journal/article/view/1472/1591.

9. Donald Creighton, *Harold Adams Innis: Portrait of a Scholar* (Toronto: University of Toronto Press, 1957), 19.

10. Innis papers, University of Toronto Archives, B1972.0003 Series 17/004 (03).

11. Quoted in Alexander John Watson, *Marginal Man: The Dark Vision of Harold Innis* (Toronto: University of Toronto Press, 2006), 79.

12. Creighton, *Harold Adams Innis*, 31.

13. Dagg, "Memoir of Harold Adams Innis."

14. Quoted in Sandra Gwyn, *Tapestry of War* (Toronto: HarperCollins Publishers, 1992), 374.

15. Dagg, "Memoir of Harold Adams Innis."

16. Creighton, *Harold Adams Innis*, 43.

17. Ibid., 48.

18. Ibid., 56.

19. Harold Innis, "A Trip through the Mackenzie River Basin," *University of Toronto Quarterly* (January 1925): 151.

20. See Jim Mochoruk, "Harold Adams Innis and Northern Manitoba," in *Harold Innis and the North*, ed. William J. Buxton (Montreal and Kingston: McGill-Queen's University Press, 2013), 149–64.

21. Dagg, "Memoir of Harold Adams Innis."

22. Matthew Evenden, "The Northern Vision of Harold Innis," in *Harold Innis and the North*, 78.

23. Creighton, *Harold Adams Innis*, 62.

24. Evenden, "The Northern Vision," 78.

25. Mary Quayle Innis, Personal Diary, April 12, 1924, UTA-IFR, B1991-0029/057 (02).

26. Personal communication, Mary Innis Cates, July 25, 2015.

27. Creighton, *Harold Adams Innis*, 63.

28. Evenden, "The Northern Vision," 77.

29. Ibid., 83.

30. Ibid., 85.

31. Harold Innis, *The Fur Trade in Canada* (Yale University Press, 1930; repr., Toronto: University of Toronto, 1970), 391.

32. Ibid., 42.

33. Ibid., 388.

34. Ibid., 392.

35. Ibid., 393.

36. Ibid., 401.

37. Quoted in John Bonnett, *Emergence and Empire: Innis, Complexity, and the Trajectory of History* (Montreal and Kingston: McGill-Queen's University Press, 2013), 3.

38. "Diamond Jubilee Broadcast Links Canadians," *CBC Digital Archives*, http://www.cbc.ca/archives/entry/1927-diamond-jubilee-broadcast-links-canadians.

39. *Times Literary Supplement* (London) July 17, 1930.

40. *New York Times*, September 28, 1930.

41. *Boston Globe*, June 14, 1930.

42. Frank H. Underhill, writing in the *Canadian Forum*, October 1930.
43. Carl Berger, *The Writing of Canadian History* (Toronto: Oxford University Press, 1976), 97.
44. Creighton, *Harold Adams Innis*, 82–83.
45. Ibid., 74.
46. Evenden, "The Northern Vision," 91–92.
47. Sandra Campbell, *Both Hands: A Life of Lorne Pierce of Ryerson Press* (Montreal and Kingston: McGill-Queen's University Press, 2013), 329– 35.
48. Creighton, *Harold Adams Innis*, 77.
49. Ibid., 101.
50. Ibid., 110.
51. Harold Innis, "Some English-Canadian University Problems," *Queen's Quarterly* (Spring 1943): 35–36.
52. Quoted in Bonnett, *Emergence and Empire*, 3.
53. Watson, *Marginal Man*, 282.

5. CARING FOR EACH OTHER

1. Joseph Roberts Smallwood, *I Chose Canada* (Toronto: Macmillan, 1973), 256.
2. Jeffrey Simpson, *Chronic Condition: Why Canada's Health-Care System Needs to Be Dragged into the 21st Century* (Toronto: Allen Lane, 2012), 1.
3. Ibid., 60.
4. Margaret Conrad and Alvin Finkel, *Canada: A National History* (Toronto: Longmans, 2003), 380.
5. "Farming: Praire Drought and Recovery," in *The Canadian Atlas Online*, http://www .canadiangeographic.ca/atlas/themes.aspx?id=farming&sub=farming_20thcentury _drought&lang=En.
6. Charlotte Gray, *Canada: A Portrait in Letters, 1800–2000* (Toronto: Doubleday, 2003), 357–58.
7. Don Haldane, *Drylanders* (National Film Board, 1962), https://www.nfb.ca/film/ drylanders/.
8. Quoted in Walter Stewart, *The Life and Times of Tommy Douglas* (Toronto: McArthur & Co., 2003), 321.
9. Lewis H. Thomas, *The Making of a Socialist: The Recollections of T. C. Douglas* (Edmonton: University of Alberta Press, 1982), 30.
10. Conrad and Finkel, *Canada: A National History*, 372.
11. Stewart, *Life and Times of Tommy Douglas*, 31–32.
12. Thomas, *Making of a Socialist*, 60–61.
13. Stewart, *Life and Times of Tommy Douglas*, 71.
14. Thomas, *Making of a Socialist*, 64–67.
15. Vincent Lam, *Extraordinary Canadians: Tommy Douglas* (Toronto: Penguin, 2011), 219–21.
16. Thomas, *Making of a Socialist*, 350.

17. Ibid., 348.
18. "Regina Manifesto" (Ottawa: Mutual Press Limited, 1933), in the Bruce Peel Special Collection, http://peel.library.ualberta.ca/bibliography/5674/reader.html#9.
19. Bill Waiser, *Saskatchewan: A New History* (Calgary: Fifth House, 2005), 315.
20. Quoted in Dave Margoshes, *Tommy Douglas: Building the New Society* (Montreal: XYZ Publishing, 1999), 82.
21. Thomas, *Making of a Socialist*, 104–5.
22. Waiser, *Saskatchewan*, 342.
23. Ibid., 342.
24. Stewart, *Life and Times of Tommy Douglas*, 159.
25. Lam, *Extraordinary Canadians*, 148.
26. Stewart, *Life and Times of Tommy Douglas*, 165.
27. *Time*, "Canada: Prairie Socialism," May 16, 1960.
28. Waiser, *Saskatchewan*, 195.
29. Quoted in Edwin A. Tollefson, "The Medicare Dispute," *Politics in Saskatchewan*, eds. Norman Ward and Duff Spafford (Toronto: Longmans, 1968), 245, 272, n. 67, cited in Waiser, *Saskatchewan*, 384.
30. Quoted in Stewart, *Life and Times of Tommy Douglas*, 229.
31. Waiser, *Saskatchewan*, 387.
32. Quoted in Lam, *Extraordinary Canadians*, 180.
33. L. D. Lovick, *Tommy Douglas Speaks* (Vancouver: Douglas & McIntyre, 1979), 220.
34. Quoted in Margoshes, *Tommy Douglas*, 149.
35. Lam, *Extraordinary Canadians*, 171.

6. Landscaping a Literature

1. Marshall McLuhan BrainyQuote.com, no date, retrieved August 13, 2015, http://www.brainyquote.com/quotes/quotes/m/marshallmc385321.html.
2. Roy MacSkimming, *The Perilous Trade: Publishing Canada's Writers* (Toronto: McClelland & Stewart, 2003), 186.
3. George Woodcock, review in *Vancouver Sun*, 1972.
4. Pamela Ingleton, "Margaret Atwood, Dennis Lee and the Survival of Canadian Literature," in *Historical Perspectives on Canadian Publishing*, 2010, http://hpcanpub.mcmaster.ca/case-study/margaret-atwood-dennis-lee-and-survival-canadian-literature.
5. Quoted in Rosemary Sullivan, *The Red Shoes: Margaret Atwood Starting Out* (Toronto: Harper Flamingo, 1998), 75.
6. Quoted in Charlotte Gray, *Sisters in the Wilderness* (Toronto: Penguin, 1999), 89.
7. See Campbell, *Both Hands*.
8. Ibid., 268.
9. Ibid., 271.
10. Ibid., 268.
11. Quoted in ibid., 317.
12. MacSkimming, *Perilous Trade*, 24.

13. Hugh MacLennan, *Thirty and Three* (Toronto: Macmillan, 1954), 53.

14. Graeme Gibson, *Eleven Canadian Novelists* (Toronto: Anansi, 1973), 281.

15. J. D. M. Stewart and Helmut Kallmann, "Massey Commission," in *Canadian Encyclopedia*, February 7, 2006, last edited March 4, 2015, http://www.thecanadianencyclopedia.ca/en/article/massey-commission-emc/.

16. Margaret Atwood, *Moving Targets: Writing with Intent 1982–2004* (Toronto: Anansi, 2004), 41.

17. Ibid., 34.

18. Margaret Atwood and Charles Pachter, *The Illustrated Journals of Susanna Moodie* (Toronto: Cormorant Books, 2014), 75.

19. Sullivan, *Red Shoes*, 201.

20. Constance Rooke, *Writing Home: A PEN Anthology* (Toronto: McClelland & Stewart, 1997), 6.

21. Sullivan, *Red Shoes*, 33.

22. Ibid., 49.

23. Michael Rubbo, *Margaret Atwood: Once in August* (National Film Board, 1984), https://www.nfb.ca/film/margaret_atwood_once_in_august.

24. Margaret Atwood, *Stone Mattress* (Toronto: McClelland & Stewart, 2014), 20.

25. Sullivan, *Red Shoes*, 111.

26. Douglas Fetherling, *Travels by Night: A Memoir of the Sixties* (Toronto: Lester Publishing, 1994), 238.

27. Quoted in Sullivan, *Red Shoes*, 126.

28. Kildare Dobbs, *Toronto Star*, September 12, 1972.

29. Quoted in Sullivan, *Red Shoes*, 289.

30. Margaret Atwood, "Great Unexpectations," *Ms*, July/August 1987, 196.

31. Sullivan, *Red Shoes*, 309.

32. "The Margaret Atwood Society," http://themargaretatwoodsociety.wordpress.com.

33. Carl Spadoni, "Publishers' Catalogues and a Chariot on Yonge Street: Marketing Canadian Books," in *Historical Perspectives on Canadian Publishing*, http://hpcanpub.mcmaster.ca/case-study/publishers-catalogues-and-chariot-yonge-street-marketing-canadian-books.

34. Judy Donnelly, "Jack McClelland and McClelland & Stewart," in *Historical Perspectives on Canadian Publishing*, http://hpcanpub.mcmaster.ca/case-study/jack-mcclelland-and-mcclelland-amp-stewart.

35. Margaret Atwood, *Survival* (Toronto: House of Anansi, 1972), 265–66.

36. Sullivan, *Red Shoes*, 303.

37. MacSkimming, *Perilous Trade*, 393.

38. Quoted in Sullivan, *Red Shoes*, 310.

7. Establishing Our Rights

1. Christopher Moore, *Founding the Writers' Union of Canada: An Oral History* (Toronto: The Writers' Union of Canada, 2015), 43.

2. Jane O'Hara, et al., "Trudeau 30 Years Later," in *Canadian Encyclopedia*, March 17, 2003, last edited August 1, 2014, http://thecanadianencyclopedia.com/en/article/trudeau-30-years-later/.

3. Pierre Elliott Trudeau, *Memoirs* (Toronto: McClelland & Stewart, 1993), 322–23.

4. John Ibbitson, "The Charter Proves to Be Canada's Gift to the World," *Globe and Mail*, April 15, 2012, last updated September 6, 2012.

5. Interview, January 27, 2015.

6. Bertha Wilson, "Speech to Women's Canadian Club, Ottawa, September 23, 1982," in *Speeches Delivered by the Honourable Bertha Wilson, 1976–1991* (Ottawa: Supreme Court of Canada, 1992), 21.

7. Ibid., 23.

8. "A hundred years of immigration to Canada 1900–1999," in *Canadian Council for Refugees*, May 2000, http://ccrweb.ca/en/hundred-years-immigration-canada-1900-1999.

9. *Herald-Chronicle*, September 10, 1949.

10. Wilson, *Speeches*, 130.

11. Bertha Wilson, "Reminiscences of My Years at Dalhousie Law School," *Ansul Magazine*, January 1977.

12. Sandra Gwyn, "Sense & Sensibility," *Saturday Night*, July 1985, 13.

13. Wilson, *Speeches*, 25, quoted in Wilson, "Reminiscences of My Years."

14. Phyllis R. Blakeley, "Henry, William Alexander," in *Dictionary of Canadian Biography* (Toronto: University of Toronto/Université Laval, 2003–), vol. 11, accessed April 1, 2016, http://www.biographi.ca/en/bio/henry_william_alexander_11E.html.

15. Paul Weiler, *In the Last Resort: A Critical Study of the Supreme Court of Canada* (Toronto: Carswell/Methuen, 1974), 4.

16. The only diamond in this bucket of gravel was Justice Ivan Rand in the 1950s, who showed a more enlightened approach to the law in Roncarelli v. Duplessis.

17. Interview, January 22, 2015.

18. Philip Slayton, *Mighty Judgement: How the Supreme Court of Canada Runs Your Life* (Toronto: Penguin, 2011), 34–35.

19. Gwyn, "Sense & Sensibility," 17.

20. Angela Fernandez and Beatrice Tice, "Bertha Wilson's Practice Years (1958–75)," *Justice Bertha Wilson: One Woman's Difference*, ed. Kim Brooks (Vancouver: University of British Columbia Press, 2009), 19.

21. Bertha Wilson, "Mount Saint Vincent University Convocation Address, 1984," in *Speeches*.

22. Gwyn, "Sense & Sensibility," 17.

23. Ellen Anderson, *Judging Bertha Wilson: Law as Large as Life* (Toronto: Osgoode Society for Canadian Legal History, University of Toronto Press, 2002), 88.

24. Tracey Tyler, "Bertha Wilson, 83: First Female Supreme Court Justice," *Toronto Star*, May 1, 2007.

25. The cases are Pettkus v. Becker (1978), Ontario Human Rights Commission v. Ontario Rural Softball Association (1979) and Bhadauria v. Board of Governors of Seneca College of Applied Arts and Technology (1981). Much of the information about these cases comes from the Gwyn article.

26. Interview, January 20, 2015.

27. Bertha Wilson, "Will Women Judges Really Make a Difference?" Barbara Betcherman Memorial Lecture, Osgoode Hall Law School, February 8, 1990, *Speeches*.

28. Bertha Wilson, "Aspects of Equality-Rendering Justice," unpublished speech given in Hull, Quebec, on November 19, 1995, quoted in Anderson, *Judging Bertha Wilson*, 30.

29. Shell Oil Co. v. Commissioner of Patents, [1982] 2 SCR 536, 1982 CanLII 207 (SCC), http://canlii.ca/t/1z1d3, retrieved on March 1, 2016.

30. "Voices on the Charter's 30th Anniversary," *CBC News*, April 17, 2012, last updated April 18, 2012, http://www.cbc.ca/news/politics/voices-on-the-charter-s-30th -anniversary-1.1132863.

31. Wilson, *Speeches*, 506.

32. Ibid., 523, quoted in Anderson, *Judging Bertha Wilson*, 419.

33. Interview, February 13, 2015.

34. Jeffrey Simpson, *Faultlines: Struggling for a Canadian Vision* (Toronto: HarperCollins, 1993), 96–97.

35. F. Morton, Peter Russell, and Michael Withey, "The Supreme Court's First One Hundred Charter of Rights Decisions: A Statistical Analysis," *Osgoode Hall Law Journal* 30 (1992): 44.

36. Anderson, *Judging Bertha Wilson*, 228.

37. R v. Morgentaler, January 28, 1988.

38. Anderson, *Judging Bertha Wilson*, 219.

39. Personal communication, February 2015.

40. Benjamin Shingler, "Charter of Rights, Universal Health Care Top Canadian Unity Poll," *Canadian* Press, June 30, 2014.

41. R. E. Hawkins and R. Martin, "Democracy, Judging and Bertha Wilson," *McGill Law Journal* 41, no. 1 (1995): 13.

42. *The Lawyers Weekly*, April 13, 2012.

43. Personal communication.

44. Personal communication.

45. Mark Tushnet, "The *Charter's* Influence around the World," *Osgoode Hall Law Journal* 50 (2013): 527–46.

46. Wilson, *Speeches*, 715.

8. Silent No More

1. Quoted in Pauline Comeau, *Elijah: No Ordinary Hero* (Vancouver: Douglas & McIntyre, 1993), 175.
2. Interview, Anita Olsen Harper, March 27, 2015.
3. Quoted in Comeau, *Elijah*, 162.
4. "Aboriginal Peoples in Canada: First Nations People, Métis and Inuit," *Statistics Canada*, last modified December 23, 2015, http://www12.statcan.gc.ca/nhs-enm/2011/as-sa/99-011-x/99-011-x2011001-eng.cfm.
5. James Daschuk, *Clearing the Plains: Disaster, Politics of Starvation, and the Loss of Aboriginal Life* (Regina: University of Regina Press, 2013), 118.
6. Ibid., 127.
7. Comeau, *Elijah*, 47.
8. Ibid.
9. Ibid., 48.
10. Ibid., 66.
11. Ibid., 88.
12. Ibid., 111.
13. Andrew Cohen, *A Deal Undone: The Making and Breaking of the Meech Lake Accord* (Vancouver: Douglas & McIntyre, 1990), 175.
14. Comeau, *Elijah*, 138.
15. "Elijah Harper: The Man with a Feather Who Changed the Course of History," *Working Effectively with Indigenous Peoples*, May 21, 2013, http://www.ictinc.ca/blog/elijah-harper-the-man-with-a-feather-who-changed-the-course-of-history.
16. Cohen, *A Deal Undone*, 268.
17. Comeau, *Elijah*, 202.
18. J. R. Miller, *Skyscrapers Hide the Heavens: A History of Indian-White Relations in Canada*, 3rd ed. (Toronto: University of Toronto Press, 2011), 403.
19. Shawn McCarthy, "First Nations Leader Phil Fontaine," *Globe and Mail*, May 16, 2014.
20. Arthur J. Ray, *Telling It to the Judge: Taking Native History to Court* (Montreal and Kingston: McGill-Queen's University Press, 2011), xix.
21. Phil Fontaine interview, March 16, 2015.
22. David Neel, "Just Say No [Elijah Harper]," Library and Archives Canada, David Neel Collection, 1991.

9. What Does the West Want?

1. Aritha van Herk, *Mavericks: An Incorrigible History of Alberta* (Toronto: Viking, 2011), 3.
2. Ibid., 1.
3. See Richard Connors and John M. Law, *Forging Alberta's Constitutional Framework* (Edmonton: University of Alberta Press, 2005), chap. 11.

4. Preston Manning, *Think Big: My Adventures in Life and Democracy* (Toronto: McClelland & Stewart, 2003), 3.
5. Interview, May 14, 2015.
6. Preston Manning, *The New Canada* (Toronto: Macmillan, 1992), 8–9.
7. W. O. Mitchell, *Who Has Seen the Wind* (Toronto: Macmillan, 1947; repr., Toronto: McClelland & Stewart, 1991), 192.
8. Preston Manning, "Federal Provincial Tensions and the Evolution of a Province," in Connors and Law, *Forging Alberta's Constitutional Framework*, 315–341.
9. Bradford J. Rennie, *Alberta Premiers of the Twentieth Century* (Regina: Canadian Plains Research Center, University of Regina, 2004), 172.
10. Premier Manning's 1951 New Year's Address, quoted in Doug Owram, "1951, Oil's Magic Wand," *Alberta Formed, Alberta Transformed*, ed. Michael Payne, Donald Wetherell, and Catherine Cavanaugh (Calgary: University of Alberta Press, 2005), vol. 2, 570.
11. Ibid.
12. Quoted in Frances Swyripa, "1955: Celebrating Together, Celebrating Apart," *Alberta Formed, Alberta Transformed*, 589–611.
13. Quoted in Rennie, *Alberta Premiers*, 196.
14. Aritha van Herk, *Audacious and Adamant: The Story of Maverick Alberta* (Toronto: Key Porter, 2007), 63.
15. Manning, *Think Big*, 21.
16. Interview, May 14, 2015.
17. Manning, *The New Canada*, 7.
18. Interview, May 14, 2015.
19. Quoted in Tammy Nemeth, "1980, Duel of the Decade," *Alberta Formed, Alberta Transformed*, 677–702.
20. Manning, *Think Big*, 25.
21. Interview, May 14, 2015.
22. Interview, May 14, 2015.
23. Ian Pearson, "The West Wants In," *Saturday Night* (December 1990): 34–43, 74–75.
24. Interview, June 25, 2015.
25. Manning, *Think Big*, 66.
26. Ibid., 94.
27. Jean Chrétien, *My Years as Prime Minister* (Toronto: Knopf, 2007), 132.
28. Manning, *The New Canada*, 310.
29. Interview, November 4, 2015.
30. Conrad Black, "Conrad Black: Stephen Harper Did Many Great Things for This Country, but He Hung On to Power a Little Too Long," *National Post*, October 17, 2015, last updated October 19, 2015.
31. Interview, June 25, 2015.
32. Margaret Atwood, "Preston Manning, Man of the Future," *National Post*, August 28, 2015.

10. Secret Handshake

1. Hans Ulrich Obrist, "In Conversation with Douglas Coupland," *Douglas Coupland, everywhere is anywhere is anything is everything,* ed. Daina Augaitis (London: Vancouver Art Gallery, Black Dog Publishing, 2014), 42.

2. Shadrach Kabango, "Fam Jam (Fe Sum Immigrins) Lyrics," *Genius,* http:// genius .com/Shad-fam-jam-fe-sum-immigrins-lyrics.

3. "Projections of the Diversity of the Canadian Population," *Statistics Canada,* March 8, 2010, http://www23.statcan.gc.ca/imdb/p2SV.pl?Function=getSurvey&SDDS= 5126&lang=en&db=imdb&adm=8&dis=2.

4. Andrea Nemtin, CEO Inspirit, interview November 9, 2015.

5. Douglas Coupland, "Growing up Utopian," in Augaitis, *Douglas Coupland,* 107.

6. Daina Augaitis, "Everywhere is Anywhere is Anything is Everything: Locating Douglas Coupland's Visual Art Practice," in Augaitis, *Douglas Coupland,* 28.

7. Obrist, "In Conversation with Douglas Coupland," in Augaitis, *Douglas Coupland,* 40.

8. Ibid., 43.

9. Kabango, "Fam Jam."

10. "Who Is Shad? 4 Things to Know about the New Face of Q ," *Thestar.com,* March 11, 2015, http://www.thestar.com/entertainment/2015/03/11/who-is-shad-4-things -to-know-about-the-new-face-of-q.html.

11. Guy Lawson, "Trudeau's Canada, Again," *New York Times Magazine,* December 8, 2015.

12. Graham Fraser, *René Lévesque and the Parti Québécois in Power* (Montreal and Kingston: McGill-Queens University Press, 1984), 222.

13. Telephone interview, October 29, 2015.

14. Ibid.

Sources

I list here the major sources for *The Promise of Canada*. More detailed information can be found in the Notes.

There were several reference works that I relied on heavily as I travelled through more than 150 years of Canadian history. The online *Dictionary of Canadian Biography* (www.biographi.ca/en) was crucial, as was the online *Canadian Encyclopedia* (http://www.thecanadianencyclopedia.ca/en/). Several surveys of Canadian history are now well-thumbed, including *The Illustrated History of Canada*, edited by Craig Brown (Toronto: Key Porter, 1997); J. M. Bumsted's *A History of the Canadian Peoples* (Toronto: Oxford University Press, 2003); and *Canada: A National History*, by Margaret Conrad and Alvin Finkel (Toronto: Pearson Education Canada, 2003).

Preface

The long search for Canadian identity has been charted in many books: those I read include *The Search for Identity*, by Blair Fraser (New York: Doubleday, 1967); *On Being Canadian*, by Vincent Massey (London: J. M. Dent & Sons, 1948); *Lament for a Nation: The Defeat of Canadian Nationalism*, by George Grant (1965; repr., Montreal and Kingston: McGill-Queen's University Press, 2005); *What Is a Canadian?*, edited by Irvin Studin (Toronto: McClelland & Stewart, 2006); *The Canadians*, by Andrew Malcolm (Markham: Fitzhenry & Whiteside, 1985); *The Unfinished Canadian*, by Andrew Cohen (Toronto: McClelland & Stewart, 2007); and *Nationalism without Walls: The Unbearable Lightness of Being Canadian*, by Richard Gwyn (Toronto: McClelland & Stewart, 1995).

1. A Tapestry of Peoples

There are two biographies of George-Étienne Cartier on which I relied for this chapter: *George-Étienne Cartier*, by Alastair Sweeny (Toronto: McClelland & Stewart, 1976); and *George-Étienne Cartier: Montreal Bourgeois*, by Brian Young (Montreal and Kingston: McGill-Queen's University Press, 1981).

I also drew on Richard Gwyn's magisterial two-volume biography of John A. Macdonald (*John A: The Man Who Made Us*, published in 2007, and *Nation Maker: Sir John A.*

Macdonald: His Life, Our Times, published in 2011, by Random House in Toronto). An-other important source on our first prime minister was P. B. Waite's *Macdonald: His Life and World* (Toronto: McGraw-Hill Ryerson Ltd., 1975).

Christopher Moore has written two excellent books on negotiations leading up to Confederation: *1867: How the Fathers Made a Deal* (Toronto: McClelland & Stewart, 1997) and *Three Weeks in Quebec City: The Meeting That Made Canada* (Toronto: Allen Lane, 2015).

2. MOUNTIE MYTHOLOGY

The papers of Samuel Benfield Steele can be found in the Bruce Peel Special Collections Library at the University of Alberta, where archivists are currently cataloguing them and making much of the material available online: https://bpsc.library.ualberta.ca/collec tions/sir-samuel-benfield-steele-family-archive.

Dr. Rod Macleod at the University of Alberta is currently completing a new biography of Sam Steele, to be published by the University of Alberta Press, and he generously shared his drafts. Macleod is also author of the useful *The North-West Mounted Police and Law Enforcement, 1873–1904* (Toronto: University of Toronto Press, 1976). I also drew on *Sam Steele: Lion of the Frontier*, 2nd ed. (Regina: Centax Books, PrintWest Group, 1999), by Robert Stewart, and Steele's own memoir, *Forty Years in Canada* (1915; repr. Toronto: Prospero Books, 2000). Three lively books deal with the mythicization of the Mounties: Pierre Berton's *Hollywood's Canada: The Americanization of Our National Image* (Toronto: McClelland & Stewart, 1975); Daniel Francis's *National Dreams: Myth, Memory, and Canadian History* (Vancouver: Arsenal Pulp Press, 1997); and Michael Dawson's *The Mountie: From Dime Novel to Disney* (Toronto: Between the Lines, 1998).

3. LOOKING INWARD, LOOKING OUTWARD

Emily Carr's own writings are the source of great insights into this complicated artist: I particularly enjoyed *Klee Wyck*, first published in 1941, and *Hundreds and Thousands: The Journals of Emily Carr* (Vancouver: Douglas & McIntyre, 2006). Many of her books are available online at Project Gutenberg (gutenberg.org).

There are many wonderful biographies of Emily Carr, and explorations of her work and influence. Those I consulted included *Emily Carr*, by Doris Shadbolt (Vancouver: Douglas & McIntyre, 1990); *The Life of Emily Carr*, by Paula Blanchard (Vancouver: Douglas & McIntyre, 1987); *Emily Carr: A Biography*, by Maria Tippett (1979; repr. Toronto: Stoddart, 1994); *Emily Carr: New Perspectives on a Canadian Icon*, edited by Charles C. Hill, Johanne Lamoureux, and Ian M. Thom (Vancouver: Douglas & McIntyre, 2006); and *Unsettling Encounters: First Nations Imagery in the Art of Emily Carr*, by Gerta Moray (Vancouver: University of British Columbia Press, 2006).

Accompanying the magnificent 2014–15 show at London's Dulwich Gallery and the Art Gallery of Ontario, *From the Forest to the Sea: Emily Carr in British Columbia*, was a catalogue with the same title, curated (like the show) by Sarah Milroy and Ian Dejardin (Fredericton: Goose Lane Editions, 2015).

My main source of information on the Group of Seven was Ross King's *Defiant Spirits: The Modernist Revolution of the Group of Seven* (Vancouver: Douglas & McIntyre, 2010). Another useful source was *Beyond Wilderness: The Group of Seven, Canadian Identity, and Contemporary Art*, edited by John O'Brian and Peter White (Montreal and Kingston: McGill-Queen's University Press, 2007).

4. Beaver Tales

The University of Toronto's Thomas Fisher Library has a significant collection of Innis papers. Harold Innis's best-known and most accessible work, and the most relevant to this chapter, is *The Fur Trade in Canada: An Introduction to Canadian Economic History* (New Haven: Yale University Press, 1930). The most recent biography of Harold Innis is Alexander John Watson's *Marginal Man: The Dark Vision of Harold Innis* (Toronto: University of Toronto Press, 2006). Other recent discussions of particular aspects of Innis's work include John Bonnett's *Emergence and Empire: Innis, Complexity and the Trajectory of History* (Montreal and Kingston: McGill-Queen's University Press, 2013) and *Harold Innis and the North: Appraisals and Contestations*, edited by William J. Buxton (Montreal and Kingston: McGill-Queen's University Press, 2013). The chapter by Matthew Evenden in the latter is particularly informative. The fullest portrait of the man emerges in the short biography by his contemporary Donald Creighton: *Harold Adams Innis: Portrait of a Scholar* (Toronto: Toronto University Press, 1957). David Staines's chapter "Forms of Non-fiction: Innis, McLuhan, Frye, and Grant" in the *Cambridge History of Canadian Literature*, edited by Coral Ann Howells and Eva-Marie Kröller (Cambridge: Cambridge University Press, 2009), usefully situates Innis within the larger context of Canadian culture in the early to mid-twentieth century.

For beaver enthusiasts, a delightful read is Frances Backhouse's *Once They Were Hats: In Search of the Mighty Beaver* (Toronto: ECW Press, 2015).

5. Caring for Each Other

Jeffrey Simpson's *Chronic Condition: Why Canada's Health-Care System Needs to Be Dragged into the 21st Century* (Toronto: Allen Lane, 2012) is the best analysis of medicare today. I drew on several biographies of Tommy Douglas, including Dave Margoshes's *Tommy Douglas: Building the New Society* (Montreal: XYZ Publishing, 1999); Walter Stewart's *The Life and Times of Tommy Douglas* (Toronto: McArthur & Co., 2003); and Vincent Lam's *Extraordinary Canadians: Tommy Douglas* (Toronto: Penguin, 2011). Lewis H. Thomas's *The Making of a Socialist: The Recollections of T. C. Douglas* (Edmonton: University of Alberta Press, 1982) has Tommy's colourful memories of his early life.

An absorbing account of Douglas's role in Saskatchewan's development emerges in Bill Waiser's *Saskatchewan: A New History* (Calgary: Fifth House, 2005).

6. LANDSCAPING A LITERATURE

I cannot claim to have read, let alone reread, Margaret Atwood's considerable body of work, but in preparation for this chapter I looked again at *The Edible Woman* (Toronto: McClelland & Stewart, 1969), *Surfacing* (Toronto: McClelland & Stewart, 1972), *Survival: A Thematic Guide to Canadian Literature* (Toronto: Anansi, 1972), *The Journals of Susanna Moodie* (Toronto: Oxford University Press, 1970), *Alias Grace* (Toronto: McClelland & Stewart, 1996), and *Moving Targets: Writing with Intent, 1982–2004* (Toronto: Anansi, 2004).

Running parallel to Margaret Atwood's extraordinary output of novels, poetry, non-fiction, criticism, newspaper articles, and lectures is an Atwood industry of literary commentary.

Background to this chapter on Canada's literary culture came from Sandra Campbell's *Both Hands: A Life of Lorne Pierce of Ryerson Press* (Montreal and Kingston: McGill-Queen's University Press, 2013) and Roy MacSkimming's *The Perilous Trade: Publishing Canada's Writers* (Toronto: McClelland & Stewart, 2003). For early biographical details I turned to Rosemary Sullivan's *The Red Shoes: Margaret Atwood Starting Out* (Toronto: Harper Flamingo Canada, 1998). Douglas Fetherling's *Travels by Night: A Memoir of the Sixties* (Toronto: Lester Publishing, 1994) illuminated the cultural ferment in Toronto in this period.

7. ESTABLISHING OUR RIGHTS

The remarks in which Bertha Wilson famously raised the question "Will Women Judges Really Make a Difference?" are printed in the *Osgoode Hall Law Journal* 28, no. 3 (1990): 507–22.

My main source of information about Justice Wilson's life and career, other than comments in interviews by Wilson's colleagues and by Wilson herself, was Ellen Anderson's thorough and respectful biography *Judging Bertha Wilson: Law as Large as Life* (Toronto: The Osgoode Society for Canadian Legal History, University of Toronto Press, 2002). An additional brief but invaluable source was the article that Sandra Gwyn published in *Saturday Night*, July 1985.

Justice Bertha Wilson: One Woman's Difference, edited by Kim Brooks (Vancouver: University of British Columbia Press, 2010), includes several reassessments of Wilson and is available online: http://www.ubcpress.ca/books/pdf/chapters/2009/JusticeBertha Wilson.pdf.

8. SILENT NO MORE

Details about Elijah Harper's life are taken from *Elijah: No Ordinary Hero* (Vancouver: Douglas & McIntyre, 1993), by Pauline Comeau, who conducted several long interviews with Harper and also watched the 1990 events in Manitoba.

Other important source materials for this chapter included James Daschuk's *Clearing the Plains: Disease, Politics of Starvation, and the Loss of Aboriginal Life* (Regina: University of Regina Press, 2013); Andrew Cohen, *A Deal Undone: The Making and Breaking of the Meech Lake Accord* (Vancouver: Douglas & McIntyre, 1990); and Arthur J. Ray, *Telling It to the Judge: Taking Native History to Court* (Montreal and Kingston: McGill-Queen's University Press, 2011).

Thomas King's multi-award-winning *The Inconvenient Indian: A Curious Account of Native People in North America* (Toronto: Doubleday, 2012) puts the issues presented in this chapter in a wider North American context.

9. WHAT DOES THE WEST WANT?

Examining Canadian history from an Alberta perspective proved more difficult than I imagined because there are few provincial histories. The liveliest is Aritha van Herk's *Mavericks: An Incorrigible History of Alberta* (Toronto: Viking, 2001). I also drew on Bradford J. Rennie (ed.), *Alberta Premiers of the Twentieth Century* (Regina: Canadian Plains Research Center, University of Regina, 2004), and the two-volume *Alberta Formed, Alberta Transformed*, edited by Michael Payne, Donald G. Wetherell, and Catherine Cavanaugh, published to celebrate Alberta's centennial in 2005 (Edmonton and Calgary: University of Alberta Press, University of Calgary Press, 2006). In addition to my interviews with Preston Manning, I drew on his two books: *The New Canada* (Toronto: Macmillan, 1992) and *Think Big: My Adventures in Life and Democracy* (Toronto: McClelland & Stewart, 2003). For background, I read Murray Dobbin's *Preston Manning and the Reform Party* (Toronto: James Lorimer & Co. Ltd., 1991); Tom Flanagan's *Waiting for the Wave: The Reform Party and Preston Manning* (Toronto: Stoddart, 1995); and Craig Oliver's *Oliver's Twist: The Life and Times of an Unapologetic Newshound* (Toronto: Viking, 2011).

10. SECRET HANDSHAKE

Most of the information in this chapter is drawn from interviews with those mentioned in it. For the artist Douglas Coupland, I drew on essays in *Douglas Coupland: everywhere is anywhere is anything is everything*, edited by Daina Augaitis (London: Vancouver Art Gallery, Black Dog Publishing, 2014).

ILLUSTRATION CREDITS

Endpapers: Frank Grant / Library and Archives Canada / PA-185522.

page iv Governor General Michaëlle Jean. THE CANADIAN PRESS / Fred Chartrand.

page viii Demonstrators at flag debate, 1964. Ted Grant / National Gallery of Canada / AC 64-3988.

page x "A Girl from Canada." T. A. Chandler / Library and Archives Canada / C-063256.

page xx The Dominion's splendid Parliament Buildings, under construction in 1864. H. Spencer / Library and Archives Canada / C-000606.

page 3 The Fathers of Confederation outside Government House, Prince Edward Island, after the 1864 Charlottetown Conference. John A. Macdonald, seated in the middle, and George-Étienne Cartier, on his left. George P. Roberts / Library and Archives Canada / C-000733.

page 5 George-Étienne Cartier standing by podium. Notman / Library and Archives Canada / PA-74102.

page 8 Cartier's house in Saint-Antoine-sur-Richelieu. McCord Museum II-230554.0.2.

page 16 Sir John A. Macdonald. William Notman & Son / Library and Archives Canada / C-003811.

page 21 Miss Cuvillier, Montreal, Quebec, 1865. McCord Museum I-16253.1.

page 32 Portrait of Louis Riel. Library and Archives Canada / PA-139073.

page 34 Chinese work camp. Glenbow Archives NA-1234-5.

page 39 North West Mounted Police Town Station on 4th Avenue in Dawson City, Yukon, 1898. Stuart Taylor Wood / Library and Archives Canada / C-022074.

page 46 Samuel Steele, portrait as young man. Bruce Peel Special Collections Library, University of Alberta (2008.1.2.1.6.1.1).

page 53 Indigenous women mending a birchbark canoe. Library and Archives Canada / PA-074670.

page 63   Sam Steele and wife. Bruce Peel Special Collections Library, University of Alberta (2008.1.1.5.1.1).

page 71   Skidegate Indian Village of the Haida tribe in the Queen Charlotte Islands. George M. Dawson / Library and Archives Canada / PA-037756.

page 84   Emily Carr illustration. "11" from *Sister and I in Alaska* (Figure 1 Publishing, 2013) reproduced with permission from the Estate of Ruth Daly.

page 89   Group of Seven artists at Toronto Arts and Letters Club luncheon. Archives of Ontario. I0010313 F-1066. William Colgate Collection.

page 95   Empress Hotel. Albertype Company / Library and Archives Canada / PA-031859.

page 96   Emily Carr with pets. Library and Archives Canada / C-020368.

page 103   Freight canoe, Hudson's Bay Company post, Lake Temagami. G. M. Kelley / Library and Archives Canada / PA-123355.

page 108   Harold Adams Innis, military portrait. University of Toronto Archives, B1972-0003 / 034 (07), 2001-77-120MS.

page 111   Vimy Ridge Memorial. National Film Board / Library and Archives Canada / C-007492.

page 115   Innis canoeing on the Peace River. University of Toronto Archives, B1972-0003 / 034 (01), 2003-21-2MS.

page 120   "Modifications of the Beaver Hat." Horace T. Martin's *Castorologia, or The History and Traditions of the Canadian Beaver* (London, E. Stanford, Ltd., 1892).

page 125   Jubilee celebrations on Parliament Hill. Diamond Jubilee / Library and Archives Canada / PA-027624.

page 128   Commercial fishing catch of cod. U.S. Library of Congress / Prints and Photographs Division / ppmsc.01626.

page 132   Members of Parliament with new Canadian flag, 1964. Duncan Cameron / Library and Archives Canada / PA-142624.

page 135   Prairie farmer in field during drought. Provincial Archives of Alberta, A3742.

page 142   Tommy Douglas, portrait as a young man. Arthur Roy / Library and Archives Canada / PA-046989.

page 145   NWMP in Winnipeg strike. Royal Canadian Mounted Police / Library and Archives Canada / e004666108.

page 150   Single Men's Unemployed Association. *Toronto Star* / Library and Archives Canada / C-029397.

page 157   Mackenzie King with soldiers. Laurie A. Audrain / Canada. Dept. of National Defence / Library and Archives Canada / PA-152440.

page 163   Anti-medicare rally in Regina, 1962. Saskatchewan Archives Board, R-A12109-4.

page 165 Douglas giving speech at founding convention of NDP. Duncan Cameron / Library and Archives Canada / C-036222.

page 168 Joey Smallwood. Duncan Cameron / Library and Archives Canada / PA-113486.

page 169 Expo 67 Collage. Library and Archives Canada / e000756917.

page 174 Margaret Atwood. Ron Bull / Getty / 515083601.

page 181 *The Journals of Susanna Moodie*, by Atwood, 1st ed. cover. Copyright © Margaret Atwood, 1970. Used with permission from the author.

page 186 Line-up for The Riverboat. Albert Lee / *Toronto Star* / Getty / 538553606.

page 189 Joni Mitchell. York University Libraries, Clara Thomas Archives & Special Collections, *Toronto Telegram* fonds, ASC01162.

page 194 Celia Franca. Ken Bell / Library and Archives Canada / e008439031.

page 198 Scotiabank Giller Prize 2013. Tom Sandler.

page 203 Charter of Rights and Freedoms in Arabic. Image courtesy of the Department of Canadian Heritage. © All rights reserved. Reproduced with permission of the Minister of Canadian Heritage, 2016.

page 207 Dalhousie University graduation photo. Image courtesy of Chris Wernham.

page 209 Young family portrait. Image courtesy of Chris Wernham.

page 215 Supreme Court under construction. Public Works Dept. / Library and Archives Canada / PA-053120.

page 216 Queen Elizabeth II signing the Constitution Act with Trudeau. Robert Cooper / Library and Archives Canada / PA-141503.

page 226 Abortion demonstration. York University Libraries, Clara Thomas Archives & Special Collections, *Toronto Telegram* fonds, ASC04612.

page 234 Man waves flag on Saint-Jean-Baptiste Day, 1980. Boris Spremo / Getty Images / 502804453.

page 237 Idle No More border blockade. Jenna Pope.

page 239 Vietnamese immigrants arriving in Canada. Bob Olsen / Getty / 499293253.

page 240 Harper holding eagle feather. Wayne Glowacki / THE CANADIAN PRESS.

page 251 Schoolroom. Special thanks to Wendy Knechtel and Christopher James at Concordia University Libraries.

page 260 Oka, Quebec standoff. Shaney Komulainen / THE CANADIAN PRESS.

page 267 Joseph Boyden. Chris Putnam, University of Saskatchewan.

page 268 Tanya Tagaq. Six Shooter Records Inc.

page 269 Electric Fields Festival poster. Ross Proulx.

page 271 Imperial Oil's Leduc No. 1 burning. THE CANADIAN PRESS.

page 277   Preston Manning and Stephen Harper in House of Commons, 1993. University of Calgary Archives, SPC 2001.066_ph1.15-6.

page 281   *Who Has Seen the Wind.* Image courtesy of Allan King Films Ltd.

page 294   Cartoon poking fun at Manning reform. Adrian Raeside / *Victoria Times Colonist.*

page 295   Celebrant during Saint-Jean-Baptiste Day. Gabor Szilasi.

page 301   Manning in front of Canadian flags. Adrian Wyld / THE CANADIAN PRESS.

page 303   Parliament as seen across the Ottawa River. Image courtesy of Ottawa Tourism.

page 306   Douglas Coupland. Keith Beaty / Getty / 169961654.

page 309   Shadrach Kabango. CBC Still Photo Collection / Pascal Chiarello.

page 313   Prime Minister Justin Trudeau with cabinet. Justin Tang / THE CANADIAN PRESS.

page 314   Lise Bissonnette. Image courtesy of Université du Québec à Montréal.

page 318   Annette Verschuren. Image courtesy of Anthony Sarmago.

page 320   Calgary mayor Naheed Nenshi. Todd Korol / Getty / 509013864.

page 321   Syrian refugees. Thomson Reuters.

page 326   Relatives awaiting the arrival of Canadian soldiers from overseas aboard the S.S. *Ile de France*, Halifax, Nova Scotia, Canada, June 1945. Lieut. Richard Graham Arless / Canada. Dept. of National Defence / Library and Archives Canada / PA-192969.

Insert 1: ARTISTIC VISIONS OF CANADA

page 1   George A. Reid, *Logging,* 1888, oil on canvas, 107.4 x 194 x 2.3 cm, National Gallery of Canada, Ottawa, Transfer from Foreign Affairs and International Trade Canada, 2011, gift of the Brig. Gen. W. F. Sweny, C.M.G, DSO, in memory of his father, Col. George A. Sweny, 1938, photo © NGC.

page 2   Homer Watson, *The Flood Gate,* c. 1900–1901, oil on canvas, mounted on plywood, 86.9 x 121.8 cm, National Gallery of Canada, Ottawa, photo © NGC.

page 3   Emily Carr, Canadian, 1871–1945, *Indian Church,* 1929, oil on canvas, 108.6 x 68.9 cm (42 ¾ x 27 ⅛ in.), Art Gallery of Ontario, Bequest of Charles S. Band, Toronto, 1970, 69/118, © Art Gallery of Ontario, Toronto.

page 4   (*left*) Emily Carr, *Scorned as Timber, Beloved of the Sky,* 1935, oil on canvas, 112.0 x 68.9 cm, collection of the Vancouver Art Gallery, Emily Carr Trust, photo: Trevor Mills, Vancouver Art Gallery.

   (*right*) Douglas Coupland, *Carr no. 3* (*Scorned as Timber, Beloved of the Sky*), 2011.

page 5   Tom Thomson, Canadian, 1877–1917, *The West Wind*, Winter 1916–1917, oil on canvas, 120.7 x 137.9 cm (47 ½ x 54 $^5/_{16}$ in.), Art Gallery of Ontario, gift of the Canadian Club of Toronto, 1926, 784, © 2016 Art Gallery of Ontario.

page 6   Frederick Varley, *For What?*, 1918, CWM 19710261-0770, Beaverbrook Collection of War Art, Canadian War Museum.

page 7   Pegi Nicol MacLeod, *Untitled*, 1944, CWM 19710261-5820, Beaverbrook Collection of War Art, Canadian War Museum.

page 8   Paul-Émile Borduas, *Leeward of the Island (1.47)*, 1947, oil on canvas, 114.7 x 147.7 cm, National Gallery of Canada, photo © NGC.

page 9   Jean Paul Lemieux, *Charlottetown Revisited*, 1964, oil on linen, 197.2 x 380.4 cm, collection of Confederation Centre Art Gallery, commissioned with funds from Samuel and Saidye Bronfman, Montreal, © Gestion A.S.L. Inc., copyright holder of the artwork of Jean Paul Lemieux.

page 10   David Blackwood, Canadian, born 1941, *Hauling Job Sturge's House*, 1979, etching and aquatint on wove paper, 32.9 x 81.3 cm (12 $^{15}/_{16}$ x 31 ¾ in.), 43.9 x 88 cm (17 $^5/_{16}$ x 34 ⅝ in.), Art Gallery of Ontario, gift of David and Anita Blackwood, Port Hope, Ontario, 1999, 99/948, © 2016 David Blackwood.

page 11   Joyce Wieland, Canadian, 1931–1998, *Reason Over Passion*, 1968, quilted cotton, 256.5 x 302.3 x 8 cm, National Gallery of Canada, Ottawa, photo © NGC.

page 12   Kenojuak Ashevak, Canadian, 1927–2013, *Luminous Char*, 2008, stonecut and stencil, 52 x 63.8 cm, Gallery Phillip.

page 13   Christopher Pratt, *Four White Boats: Canadian Gothic*, 2002, oil on board, 36 ¼ x 80 ½ in., private collection.

page 14   Kent Monkman, *The Academy*, 2008, acrylic on canvas, 72 x 108 in., collection of the Art Gallery of Ontario, image courtesy of the artist.

page 16   Sarah Anne Johnson, *Explosions*, 2011, courtesy of Stephen Bulger Gallery, Toronto, and Julie Saul Gallery, New York, © Sarah Anne Johnson.

Insert 2: ADVERTISING IN CANADA

page 1   *Enlist!*, 1914–1918, Library and Archives Canada, Acc. No. 1983-28-826.

page 2   *Help Canada Secure Business in Foreign Markets*, 1914–1918, Library and Archives Canada, Acc. No. 1983-28-566.

page 3   *Canada's Egg Opportunity*, 1918, Library and Archives Canada, Acc. No. 1983-28-686.

page 4   *Canadian National Exhibition Toronto*, 1919, Library and Archives Canada, Acc. No. 1983-29-111.

page 5   (*top*) Advertisement, 1892, Library and Archives Canada, nlc-16306.

           (*bottom*) *Canada West: Canada—the New Homeland*, 1925, Library and
           Archives Canada, C-030619.

page 6   *Britishers!*, Canadian Pacific Steamships, 1929, Exporail, the Canadian Railway
           Museum, Canadian Pacific Railway Collection.

page 7   (*top*) *Canadian Pacific: Holidays in Canada*, 1925, Library and Archives
           Canada, Acc. No. 1990-106-7, image courtesy of Canadian Pacific Archives.

           (*bottom*) *Canadian Pacific Airlines: Straight to the Point*, 1955–1960, Library
           and Archives Canada, R1300-1151, image courtesy of Canadian Pacific
           Archives.

page 8   *Votez Libéral*, 1930, Library and Archives Canada, Acc. No. 1996-76-13.

page 9   *Nugget Shoe Polish: the Very Best!*, 1930–1939, Library and Archives Canada,
           R1300-1161.

page 10   *Get Your Teeth into the Job*, 1941, CWM 19790385-109, Canadian War
           Museum.

page 11   *Newfoundland—Canada's Newest Province*, 1949, Roger Couillard, Library and
           Archives Canada, Acc. No. R1409-21.

page 12   *The 1967 World Exhibition—Show of the Century*, 1967, Library and Archives
           Canada, Acc. No. 1994-272-1.

page 13   *Captain Canuck*, image courtesy of Chapterhouse Comics and Captain Canuck
           Inc.

page 14   *Artists—Athletes 1976 Olympics*, 1976, Library and Archives Canada, Acc.

page 15   *St. James Park*, 2011, Occupy Toronto.

page 16   Franke James, *No Keystone XL*, from her *Oh No Canada!* art show in
           Washington, DC, in 2013.

INDEX

Italicized page numbers refer to picture captions.